Forschungsgruppe Konsum und Verhalten

Die Forschungsgruppe „Konsum und Verhalten", die von Professor Dr. Werner Kroeber-Riel begründet wurde, veröffentlicht ausgewählte Ergebnisse ihrer Arbeiten seit 1997 in dieser Reihe. Im Mittelpunkt steht das Entscheidungsverhalten von Abnehmern materieller und immaterieller Güter bzw. Dienstleistungen.

Ziel dieser Schriftenreihe ist es, Entwicklungen in Theorie und Praxis aufzuzeigen und im internationalen Wettbewerb zur Diskussion zu stellen. Das Marketing wird damit zu einer Schnittstelle interdisziplinärer Forschung.

Isabell Koinig

Pharmaceutical Advertising as a Source of Consumer Self-Empowerment

Evidence from Four Countries

Foreword by Prof. Dr. Sandra Diehl

Springer Gabler

Isabell Koinig
Klagenfurt, Austria

Dissertation Alpen-Adria-Universität Klagenfurt, Austria, 2015

Veröffentlichung mit Unterstützung des Forschungsrats der Alpen-Adria-Universität Klagenfurt aus den Fördermitteln der Privatstiftung Kärntner Sparkasse und des Instituts für Medien- und Kommunikationswissenschaften

OnlinePlus material to this book can be available on
http://www.springer-gabler.de/978-3-658-13134-0

Forschungsgruppe Konsum und Verhalten
ISBN 978-3-658-13133-3 ISBN 978-3-658-13134-0 (eBook)
DOI 10.1007/978-3-658-13134-0

Library of Congress Control Number: 2016933236

Springer Gabler

Printed on acid-free paper

This Springer Gabler imprint is published by Springer Nature
The registered company is Springer Fachmedien Wiesbaden GmbH

Foreword

The topic of health communication has taken center stage in the 21st century, which has been labeled the "health communication renaissance". Health communication is a broad research field and can take a variety of forms.

The primary focus of Dr. Isabell Koinig' s dissertation is on pharmaceutical advertising as one form of health communication, and in particular she deals with the question of whether pharmaceutical advertising can serve as a source of consumer empowerment. The thesis can, therefore, be classified as belonging to a research agenda, which has been growing in significance in recent years. Pharmaceutical advertising encompasses all promotion activities related to medications, as well as medical products and services, with the goal of informing and influencing the target group. Due to current trends, such as an aging population, switches in the status of drugs from prescription to non-prescription drugs (OTC – Over the Counter drugs), and the predicted shortage of physicians, the OTC drug sector is steadily gaining in importance. Compared to the effects of prescription drug advertising, the effects of OTC advertising have received significantly less attention. Dr. Isabell Koinig narrows her focus to non-prescription pharmaceuticals (OTC drugs) and to the role pharmaceutical advertising plays in self-medication and consumer self-empowerment. Her dissertation makes a highly valuable contribution to this research discipline.

Dr. Isabell Koinig develops a theoretically sound model that explains the effects of pharmaceutical advertising in relationship to the construct of self-empowerment. She analyzes her model in four countries and on three continents, utilizing four standardized ads with different appeal types. She was able to confirm her model in large part. With regard to the quantitative study, it should be emphasized that the investigation was based on a large non-student sample (967 subjects). In addition to important OTC markets such as the US, Germany and Austria, the emerging Brazilian pharmaceutical market, which is expected to become an increasingly important market in the future, was included as well. With this dissertation, the author contributes to the empirical intercultural advertising research field and also to the long-standing debate on standardization vs. differentiation of advertising. The study results show that a mixed advertising appeal is the most promising approach for a standardized international advertising campaign promoting non-prescription pharmaceuticals. Dr. Isabell Koinig introduces the concept of self-empowerment, a well-established concept in cultural studies and media education, to the field of international marketing communication. Due to the extensive availability of pharmaceuticals and health-related products, patients are increasingly becoming "prosumers." No longer passive and dependent, their role has been redefined. They are becoming active consumers, who demand a stronger say and wish to be integrated in their health-related decisions. In this context, ads play a critical role, as they have the potential to strengthen consumers' competencies and to help them make better-qualified decisions. The empowerment gained via advertising is influenced by the appeal incorporated in an ad, and mixed appeals were found to be particularly suitable for reinforcing consumer empowerment.

In summary, Dr. Isabell Koinig's dissertation addresses a very relevant topic and contributes to research development in the fields of pharmaceutical advertising, self-empowerment and health communication. The implications of the current thesis are highly relevant for researchers as well as for practitioners interested in the areas of pharmaceutical advertising, self-empowerment and health communication.

ao. Univ.-Prof. Dr. Sandra Diehl

Department of Media and Communications
Alpen-Adria-Universität Klagenfurt, Austria

Preface

According to the IMS Institute for Health, the global pharmaceutical market is currently worth almost USD 1 trillion a year – a figure that is expected to increase to USD 1.2 trillion by 2017. North America is responsible for the largest portion, generating more than 40 % of these revenues. The world's ten largest drug companies control over one third of this market, six of which are based in the United States, while the other four are located in Europe. The pharmaceutical industry is, hence, of immense importance as a global sector. Currently, pharmaceutical companies spend one third of their total sales revenues on marketing their drugs; by comparison, they spend only half of that sum on research and development. With regard to their promotional efforts, academic research has so far focused on direct-to-consumer prescription drug advertising, which is solely permitted in the U.S. and New Zealand. Significantly less research has been conducted in the area of non-prescription drug advertising – also known as over-the-counter (OTC) advertising. While these pharmaceutical ads are clearly persuasive in nature, such advertisements can also provide useful information that empowers consumers to arrive at qualified decisions regarding their health and well-being. Apart from a very small number of investigations, neither consumer evaluations of OTC drug ads, nor the topic of consumer empowerment gained from such messages, have been explored. The primary goal of the investigation at hand is to shed light on the contribution of pharmaceutical promotions to individual self-empowerment and to understand whether manifestations of cultural dimensions affect the evaluation of such commercial messages. This study examines how standardized promotional messages for a fictitious OTC pain medication are perceived by consumers in four countries (Austria, Germany, the U.S. and Brazil), and the degree to which advertisements incorporating varying appeal types (informative, emotional, mixed and corporate social responsibility) contribute to consumers' sense of self-empowerment. The relations amongst the different variables are conceptualized as a model, which will be put to the test. Study limitations are addressed and implications for further research are provided.

Numerous people have been part of this journey and I would take the opportunity to express my gratitude to them. First and foremost, I would like to thank my supervisor

Sandra Diehl, who did not only encourage me to pursue a PhD in the first place, but also provided me with advice, guidance and constructive criticism along the way. Already during my Master's degree, Sandra kindled my interest in pharmaceutical advertising and her mentoring encouraged me to take my research to the next level. To her, I owe being introduced to Barbara Mueller, who I would like to mention at this point as well: I am grateful to her for supporting my research (especially in the United States) and her kind, encouraging words. I would also like to mention Ralf Terlutter at this point, who patiently answered my statistical questions.

A special thank you goes out to Matthias Karmasin, who continuously expressed his trust in my competencies and made me try even harder. Moreover, I am deeply grateful to my colleagues and friends (you know who you are!) for their help and words of comfort. The largest thank you is reserved for my family and Jonathan, without whom I would have been lost on the way. If it were not for them, I would not have taken much-needed breaks, experienced reassurance and found some distraction.

I highly appreciate the confidence and trust everyone has put in me. Your continuous reassurance, love, and endless support were what made me strive for more and helped me get to the place I wanted to be. Now the journey is over, I have conquered the mountain called PhD. It is time to start looking again, to find the next peak to climb. I cannot wait for whatever is out there.

Isabell Koinig

Table of Contents

1 Introduction 1
1.1 General Introduction 1
1.2 Fundamentals of the Present Investigation 6
2 Conceptual Foundations 9
2.1 Health | Disease | Illness 9
2.2 Health Communication 10
2.3 Advertising 11
2.4 Pharmaceutical Advertising 12
2.5 Culture 14
2.6 Standardization vs. Localization 15
2.7 Health-Conscious Consumers | Empowerment 16
3 Perceptions of Health and Illness and Their Bodily Relevance 18
3.1 The Relevance of Health to Individuals' Self-Identity 18
3.2 Healthy Bodies As 'Social' Bodies 20
3.2.1 Bodies and Social Capital: Expectations of Conformity 20
3.2.2 Foucault: Enforcing Bodily Politics Through the Gaze 22
3.3 Medicine and Its Regulatory Power 24
3.4 Empowerment: From Passivity to Active Involvement 26
3.4.1 The Emergence of the (Active) Health-Conscious Consumer 27
3.4.2 Health(-Conscious) Consumers and the Enterprise of the Self 28
4 Effects of Health Communication and Pharmaceutical Advertising 32
4.1 Health Communication in the 21st Century 33
4.1.1 Communicating about Health 34
4.1.2 Approaches to Health: Focus on Health or Disease? 35
4.1.3 Goal-Directed Health Campaigns: Pushing Information to the Public 37
4.2 Health Communication's Contribution to Health Literacy 40
4.2.1 Health Promotion and Pharmaceutical Advertising as Sources of Information and Empowerment 43
4.2.2 Deconstructing Pharmaceutical Advertisements: What Can They Achieve? 45

4.3 Taking Matters Global: The (Im)Possibilities of Cross-Cultural Advertising 50
4.3.1 Negotiating Meaning: Communication's Cultural Determinism 50
4.3.2 Dimensions of Cultural Difference 53
4.3.3 Advertising across (National) Boundaries: Cross-Cultural Challenges 59
4.3.4 Standardization vs. Differentiation 61
4.3.5 Standardized or Localized Ad Campaigns: What Pays Off? 61
4.3.6 Ad Appeals and Promotional Considerations 63
5 Theoretical Background and Model Development 66
5.1 Social Cognitive Theory 66
5.2 Advertising Evaluation Models 68
5.2.1 The Elaboration Likelihood Model 69
5.2.2 The Message Interpretation Process 72
5.3 Models and Theories of Health (Communication) 74
5.3.1 The Health Belief Model (HBM) 75
5.3.2 The Health Action Process Approach 78
5.4 Conceptual Framework: Core Variables 80
5.4.1 Locus of Control 81
5.4.2 (Advertising) Message Evaluation 84
5.4.3 Cues to Action 88
5.4.4 Attention | Comprehension | Advertising Effectiveness 89
5.4.5 Health Status 91
5.4.6 Involvement 91
5.4.7 Responses: Cognitive vs. Emotional Effects 96
5.4.8 Credibility 105
5.4.9 Past Experiences 107
5.4.10 Health Literacy | Health Education 107
5.4.11 Social Support 109
5.4.12 Product Evaluation 111
5.4.13 Purchase Intention 112
5.4.14 Motivation | Behavioral Intention 113
5.4.15 Behavioral Change | Behavior 115
5.4.16 Consumer Self-Empowerment: Increasing Consumer Control and Choice 117

5.4.17 Modelling Consumer Self-Empowerment 129
6 Project Description and Design 135
6.1 Research Design and Methodology 135
6.1.1 Questionnaire and Variable Operationalization 137
6.1.2 Study Design and Ad Development 153
6.1.3 Introductory Remarks 166
6.2 Study Results and Test of Hypotheses 186
6.2.1 Study Population 188
6.2.2 Individual Opinions of and Attitudes Towards Health 188
6.2.3 Self-Medication Practices and Abilities 190
6.2.4 Opinions Towards Different Drug Types 193
6.2.5 Sources of Health Information 196
6.2.6 Self-Medication and Advertising 200
6.2.7 Consumer Responses to Different Advertising Styles 203
6.2.8 Advertising's Contribution to Consumer Self-Empowerment: The case of OTC drugs 216
6.2.9 Testing for Interactive Effects: Model-Deduced Hypotheses 223
7 Conclusion: Discussion of Results, Implications, Limitations, and Recommendations 231
7.1 Discussion of Results 231
7.2 Implications and Recommendations 245
7.3 Limitations and Directions for Future Research 246
8 Bibliography 253
9 Appendix 329
Appendix A: Advertisements 329
Appendix B: Questionnaire 333
Appendix C: Mean values 339
Appendix D: T-Tests/Contrast Tests 351
Appendix E: Discriminant Validity and Path Estimates 370

List of Figures

Figure 1: Paradigms of Medicine 24
Figure 2: Health Communication Influences 33
Figure 3: OTC Drug Information - Sources and Trust Levels 42
Figure 4: The Hofstede Model of Cross-Cultural Advertising 59
Figure 5: Social Cognitive Theory 67
Figure 6: The Elaboration Likelihood Model 70
Figure 7: The Message Interpretation Process 72
Figure 8: The Health Belief Model 76
Figure 9: The Health Action Process Approach 78
Figure 10: Conceptual Framework to Measure the Reception of OTC Drug Promotions in a Cross-Cultural Context 80
Figure 11: Global Locus of Control Manifestations 82
Figure 12: Preferred Global Communication Styles 86
Figure 13: Global Acceptance of Communication Styles 87
Figure 14: Global Caring Tendencies 120
Figure 15: Interdependence of Literacy, Empowerment and Patient Behavior 124
Figure 16: A Model Measuring Consumer Self-Empowerment Derived from Advertising . 129
Figure 17: Study Design 153
Figure 18: Actions Taken After Print-Ad Exposure in Magazines 156
Figure 19: Aspirin Promotions by Bayer 157
Figure 20: CSR Promotions by Pampers and UNICEF 160
Figure 21: Individual Health Perceptions 190
Figure 22: Self-Medication Evaluations 193
Figure 23: Acceptance of Different Drug Types 194
Figure 24: Sources of Health Information – Interpersonal Sources 197
Figure 25: Sources of Health Information – Media Sources (Advertising) 199
Figure 26: Sources of Health Information – Media Sources (Editorials) 200
Figure 27: Attitudes and Skepticism towards Advertising and Pharmaceutical Advertising 202
Figure 28: Attitude towards the Ad (single Question) 205
Figure 29: Attitude towards the Ad (Factorized Questions) 207
Figure 30: Cognitive Involvement I (Credibility) Scores 208
Figure 31: Involvement II (Comprehensibility) Scores 209

Figure 32: Product Evaluation Scores 211
Figure 33: Purchase Intention Scores 214
Figure 34: Message Empowerment Scores 218
Figure 35: Self-Medication Confidence Scores 219
Figure 36: Self-Medication Interest Scores 220
Figure 37: Health Empowerment Scores 222
Figure 38: Conceptual Framework incl. all Hypotheses 224
Figure 39: Conceptual Framework incl. Confirmed Hypotheses 230
Figure 40: Factors Influencing Health Behaviors 243
Figure 41: The Wired Patient 250

All figures can be accessed on www.springer.com under the author's name and the book title.

List of Tables

Table 1: GLOBE Study (Cultural Practices) 57
Table 2: GLOBE Study (Cultural Values) 57
Table 3: Operationalization of Health Consciousness 138
Table 4: Operationalization of Health Information Orientation 138
Table 5: Operationalization of Health Information Seeking and Sources of Health Information 140
Table 6: Operationalization of Health Self-Efficacy 141
Table 7: Operationalization of Attitude and Skepticism towards (Pharmaceutical) Advertising 142
Table 8: Operationalization of OTC Background Information 144
Table 9: Operationalization of Evaluation of Pharmaceutical Product Types 145
Table 10: Operationalization of (OTC) Drug Usage 145
Table 11: Operationalization of Product (Category) Involvement 146
Table 12: Operationalization of Overall Ad Evaluation 146
Table 13: Operationalization of Message Involvement, Information Processing and Affect. 147
Table 14: Operationalization of Perceived Susceptibility and Message Relevance 148
Table 15: Operationalization of Consumer Self-Empowerment 149
Table 16: Operationalization of Attitude towards the Product 150
Table 17: Operationalization of Purchase Intention 151
Table 18: Operationalization of CSR Relevance 152
Table 19: Operationalization of Demographic Information 153
Table 20: Evaluations of Product and Company Names 161
Table 21: Pre-Test 1 Questionnaire (Excerpt) 163
Table 22: Pre-Test 2 Questionnaire (Excerpt) 164
Table 23: Pre-Test 3 Questionnaire 165
Table 24: Model Fit - Group Scores 176
Table 25: Model Fit - Cluster and Country Scores 177
Table 26: Composite Reliability and Average Variance Extracted for Cultural Clusters 178
Table 27: Composite Reliability and Average Variance Extracted for Individual Countries . 178
Table 28: Discriminant Validity (Established by Chi^2-Tests) 179
Table 29: Discriminant Validity (Established by Fornell-Larcker-Criterion) 180
Table 30: Measurement Invariance – Cluster and Country Scores 185

Table 31: Overview of Hypotheses 188
Table 32: Path Coefficients and Critical Ratios (H 8a, H 8b, H 8c) 225
Table 33: Path Coefficients and Critical Ratios (H 9a, H 9b) 227
Table 34: Path Coefficients and Critical Ratios (H 10a, H10b) 228
Table 35: Path Coefficients and Critical Ratios (H 11) 229
Table 36: Path Coefficients and Critical Ratios (H 12) 230
Table 37: Research Questions and Theory-Deduced Hypothesis - Overview of Results 240
Table 38: Model-Deduced Hypothesis - Overview of Results 242

1 Introduction

In the 21st century, the human body has emerged as an object of study in the area of marketing, where it has been linked to both the consumption of goods and the reception of advertising messages (Falk, 1994). In the process, health has been turned into a commodity (Aggleton, 1990) and an awareness of bodily relevance has degenerated into an obsession with (bodily) appearance, which is accompanied by a constant pursuit of vitality, youthfulness and aesthetics. Achieving this goal is aided by a consumer culture that provides adequate products and services to meet individual (health and beauty) needs (Bunton and Burrows, 1995; Featherstone, 1991; Glassner, 1992; Glassner, 1995; Lupton, 1995): "In the health sphere the growth in 'health-related' goods and services is influenced by a market logic which produces both new products and new, more discerning, health-conscious consumers" (Bunton, 1997: 235). To create demand for said products, consumers need to be familiarized with product offerings and services – a task taken up by (pharmaceutical) advertising.

1.1 General Introduction

With communication having become more market-oriented, consumers are exposed to more information on health and health care alike, which should motivate them to get more involved in their well-being and strengthen them in their sovereignty (Bunton and Petersen, 1997). As 'sovereign consumers' they use products to add value to their bodies, extending their self-worth and health by boosting their self-esteem and quality of life respectively (du Gay, 1996; Sabel, 1990; Rose, 1990). Consumption enables them to express their individualism (de Certeau, 1984; du Gay, 1996; Willis, 1990), whereby the availability of numerous products and services has contributed to the commercialization of the health (care) domain (Nettleton, 1997). Consequently, consumers have grasped the possibility of making future investments in themselves, acquiring health products advertised in the media and taking care of as well as shaping their bodies (Nettleton, 1997): "The health consumer of advanced liberalism is positioned not as a passive, cultural dope but as an active, enterprising and self-caring subject capable of selectively consuming health products and selectively reading his or her own health messages" (Bunton and Petersen, 1997: 10).

However, false (health) consumer needs are created repeatedly, proclaimed and disseminated by the mass media (Goldthorpe et al. 1969). But how come health products and services are increasingly demanded throughout the world? The explanation to this question states the obvious: Health and health-related topics have been repeatedly addressed communicatively, having experienced a revival in the 21st century (Krisberg, 2004). This era has, thus, become known as a "health communication renaissance" (Bernhardt, 2004: 2051), whereby health communication refers to "any type of human communication whose content is concerned with health" (Rogers, 1996: 15). Generally, it is directed at individuals as well as organizations with the goal of preventing illness and fostering health (Thompson et al., 2011). By use of information, messages want to not only involve but also motivate consumers to take care of their bodies, allowing them to actively manage their own health. The potential is innate to all kinds of health messages, may they be commercial or public (solely educational) in nature. Hence, media has the ability to raise "the profile of health issues on the public agenda" (Green and Tones, 2010: 362), with communication serving as "a means to assist patients in understanding the intended treatments and decisions that may be taken" (Brown et al., 2007: 24).

The investigation at hand is particularly concerned with one specific form of health communication, namely pharmaceutical advertising, which can function as a source of consumer self-empowerment and depends upon the mass media as a communication vehicle. It covers all "attempts to create consumer demand for medications by constructing advertising messages in the popular media that promote the attractiveness of the product to the public along with messages encouraging people to ask their doctor [or pharmacist] about the drug" (Wright et al., 2008: 192; Bradley and Zito, 1997; Hollon, 1999). Reports from 2015 reveal that pharmaceutical manufacturers dedicate the largest proportion of their budget towards this marketing form, with nine out of ten companies spending significantly more money on advertising than on researching new drugs (VOX, 2015). At times, the allocated budget is even twice as large as the firm's designated research fund (BBC, 2015). This recent trend conveys a troubling image of the pharmaceutical industry as being "market-driven" (Science Daily, 2008), pushing advertising messages in an attempt to boost sales and inform a broad, dispersed public about treatment options. Nonetheless, medicinal promotions are useful too, meant to "provide timely, accurate and trustworthy [as well as concrete and comprehensible] information to safeguard [and restore] people's health and well-being" (Zarcadoolas, 2005: 197).

In all countries to be investigated herein (Austria, Germany, the United States and Brazil), OTC drug sales are on the rise, whereby increases in turnover are predominantly attributed to so-called drug switches, meaning that after patent expirations former prescription drugs (Rx) are increasingly made available as over-the-counter (OTC) preparations in an attempt to guarantee reduced health-care costs. These switches generally affect medications holding a low potential for abuse and whose benefits outweigh potential risks (DeLorme et al., 2010). From the 1970s onwards, more than 100 active ingredients as well as 700 products have been approved for switch processes in the United States (CHPA, 2010b; CHPA, 2014), leading consumers to save up to almost USD 102 bn. annually (CHPA, 2013). For instance, as of 2014, consumers were able to save up to USD 2 bn. on switched nicotine medications and USD 750 m. on heartburn preparations respectively (CHPA, 2014). This trend is expected to continue throughout the years to come as numerous patents are about to expire.

The relevance of non-prescription drugs has also been pointed out by recent surveys: Classified as a mainstream medicine (Segen's Medical Dictionary, 2012), OTC medications have become a permanent feature in every (U.S.) household, where they are used by nine out of ten respondents on a regular basis (Accenture, 2014). As self-medication preparations and home remedies (Robinson and Zhang, 2011), they have started to pervade consumers' lives, having reportedly offered relief to 60 m. people who would not have sought treatment otherwise (CHPA, 2013). This is the case as 89 % of Americans regard those preparations as part of their household inventory that can be utilized for treating minor medical conditions (CHPA, 2010) and as first response to initial symptoms (81 %; CHPA, 2010), including flu-like symptoms (e.g., cough, cold; 84 %), pain (82 %), digestive problems (77 %), and allergies (75 %; CHPA, 2013).

These findings build upon results brought about by the Consumer Healthcare Products Association's study of the previous year, in which respondents claimed to specifically rely on non-prescription drugs by virtue of their efficacy (50 %) and convenience (39°%), which were succeeded by cost savings (19 %) and safety of use (2 %). As such, OTC drugs present a means of empowering consumers, reducing health expenses and allowing consumers to share responsibility with experts in today's health care marketplace (CHPA, 2013). At the same time, the utilization of OTC drugs also lifts some weight off experts' shoulders, reducing the public's over-reliance on expert advice, since approximately 10 % of all consultations could have been self-diagnosed and self-treated (CHPA, 2013). Hence, OTC drugs are a valuable cost-saving initiative, reducing annual health-care spending considerably (CHPA, 2013). This increase in savings is also due to the continuously broadening range of non-prescription products, vastly expanding the medical market place that is, more and more, characterized by an abundance of choice (CHPA, 2013; CHPA, 2014).

Given drugs' known relevance to individuals' health and well-being, together with manufacturers' heavy advertising activities throughout the world – particularly in the United States and New Zealand, where even prescription drugs are admitted for public promotion – it appears that only little research has been done in the area of non-prescription drug advertising. Apart from a few contributions (e.g., Diehl et al., 2008; DeLorme et al., 2010; Main et al., 2004), neither consumer opinions on OTC medications nor evaluations of non-prescription drug ads have been intensively studied; furthermore, until now, no prospective model testing responses to this product category has been proposed. Yet, since a better and more thorough understanding of advertising appeals' effectiveness can benefit both academics and practitioners – also in an international context – the present investigation will attempt to reduce this clear research gap.

Another purpose of this investigation is to add to the body of knowledge regarding culture's influence on consumer responses to OTC drug advertising messages. Its major goal lies in determining whether respondents from the four chosen cultures, which are renowned to be quite different (individualistic: Austria, Germany and the United States; collectivistic: Brazil), evaluate distinct yet (standardized) print advertisements for a non-prescription (OTC) drug distinctively or in a similar manner, examining if differences and/or similarities can indeed be traced back to cultural particularities. In addition, the difference in adverts' amount of information is expected to lead to varying degrees of consumer self-empowerment derived from said advertising messages.

The last aspect – consumer self-empowerment – is of specific interest for, nowadays, health has become "the enterprise of oneself" (Greco, 1993: 357) in the course of which "patients have become strong advocates of their own healthcare" (Blackett and Harrison, 2001: 48). As a consequence, the term patient empowerment has become commonly used and has risen in its importance to present-day medical practice, establishing itself as "one of the central pillars of health communication strategies" (Schiavo, 2007: 58). Empowerment should serve as a guarantor of positive health (Green and Tones, 2010), with individuals reclaiming their long-lost power and becoming active agents in their health care once more (WHO, 2001). Individuals are specifically empowered by better access to education and an increasing number of information sources – both traditional, digital and interactive; at the same time, they have an increasing income at their disposal, which allows them to have a greater say in their own medical treatment (David, 2001).

In the advent of health commercialization, health has been turned into a commodity that can be acquired through financial means. For this reason, the term patient – referring to individuals as passive dopes in the hands of medical experts – has been substituted by the more pro-active concept of the health (care) consumer (Porter, 1985), who is actively involved in their health-care and does not hesitate to question dominant opinions (Nettleton, 1997). Moreover, technological advances have led consumers to become empowered, taking a hands-on approach by looking for and demanding information conducive to their well-being and health respectively (Auton, 2004; Royne and Myers, 2008; Lyles, 2002). Pharmaceutical advertisements present one such source of information and will be consulted in the thesis at hand, which sets out to provide answers to the following two research questions:

RQ 1: How is a standardized OTC drug ad (utilizing either an informative, emotional, mixed or CSR appeal) evaluated in different cultural contexts (Germany, Austria, the United States and Brazil)?

RQ 2: Out of the four advertising appeals, which appeal leads to the highest degree of consumer self-empowerment?

1.2 Fundamentals of the Present Investigation

Individuals have to be healthy and fit in order to enjoy and live life to its fullest. In the present-day health and beauty marketplace, they can purchase products and services that are intended to assist them in achieving this objective. At times, however, they lack guidance as to which products are available in the market and are left clueless about their intended purposes and effects. To familiarize people with (new or improved) product offerings and educate them on their potentials, (pharmaceutical) advertising messages present a suitable tool to reach this goal.

With health being a multi-faceted and abstract construct (Earle, 2007), the present thesis sets out to analyze which factors influence individuals' health-related decisions, especially when asked to choose from an array of pharmaceutical products advertised for a broad range of medical conditions. For this exact reason, numerous models from two very distinct academic backgrounds will be carefully assessed and combined into a comprehensible conceptual framework that is meant to explain how individuals' decisions in the health realm are influenced by personal factors. The model developed herein attempts to overcome some of the more isolated assumptions of health – as proclaimed by the (bio-)medical model (Blaxter, 2004) or the social model (Earle, 2007) – in favor of an integrated approach, which pays tribute to personal, economic as well as social factors impacting decisions with regard to individual health and well-being. Those will be paired up with an advertising elaboration model in order to determine to which extent the evaluation of pharmaceutical advertisements depends upon personal factors as well as message features.

After a short introduction into the investigation's overall conceptualization **(chapter 1)**, **chapter 2** will start out by defining the most central terms to the present investigation, including concepts like health, illness/disease, and health communication, which will be proceeded by pharmaceutical advertising, standardization/differentiation as well as culture. Afterwards, these concepts will be put in relation to the overall topic of cross-cultural health communication and pharmaceutical advertising. Moreover, the relevance of health communication – defined as a specific communicative activity that "links the domains of communication and health" (U.S. Department of Health and Human Services, 2005: 11ff.) – will be pointed out. In this context, the area of pharmaceutical advertising is ascribed increasing relevance as one of the reasons why drug switches from prescription to non-prescription (Rx-to-OTC) status are on the rise (Diehl et al., 2008; DeLorme et al., 2010). In academia, the self-medication industry is not only characterized by an immense research gap (Main et al., 2004), but is also rising in its relevance to health-conscious consumers who long to be involved and are willing to assume liability for their bodies and well-being respectively.

Subsequently, **chapter 3** will scrutinize the area of health, carving out its relevance to individual identity plus the role it occupies in legitimizing social acceptance. It is crucial to redefine the notion of the body, which has received its value on the grounds of its productive capacities alone for the longest time (du Gay, 1996; Mayo, 1933; Braverman, 1974). Nonetheless, the body's usefulness should not be limited to its productive nature but needs to be captured as a whole – as a means of elevating human happiness and quality of life (Rod and Saunders, 2004; Green and Tones, 2010; Buchanan, 2000). Just as bodies are prerequisites for human existence, so is health; the body and individual identity cannot be regarded as separate entities but are interconnected, for the body is "home" to the inner self. As the human body runs the risk of attracting illness and disease, if not maintained or looked after carefully (Lupton, 1995; Petersen and Lupton, 1997), health becomes a project of the self (Pond et al., 2010), with individuals taking preventive action (e.g., through the use of OTC drugs) to avoid or cure disease symptoms, which are to be seen as an expression of individuals' failure to take appropriate care of their bodies (Lupton, 2012).

When looking for information on how to become actively involved in their health, individuals can turn to different sources of health communication; amongst them is pharmaceutical advertising, which presents the focus of **chapter 4**. It covers all mass-mediated messages through which policy makers and advertisers alike want to create appealing images of (and ultimately desire for) their services or pharmaceutical product offerings (Wright et al., 2008; Bradley and Zito, 1997; Hollon, 1999). Advertising messages by pharmaceutical marketers in particular intend to provide consumers with information on drugs as well as diverse treatment options and, thus, present a means that empowers them, allowing them to arrive at qualified health decisions (Assael, 2004).

The study's theoretical foundation will be explained in **chapter 5**, where a framework suited to test consumer responses to health messages in a cross-cultural setting will be conceptualized. As the topic at hand – pharmaceutical advertising – presents a merger between two rather distinct areas of analysis, theories applied to the field of commercial health promotion alone are insufficient but have to integrate aspects of both existing advertising evaluation models and health theories. A framework incorporating selected yet highly-relevant factors will be developed and tested, borrowing components from the Elaboration Likelihood Model of Persuasion (ELM; Petty and Cacioppo 1981a; Petty and Cacioppo, 1981b), the Health Belief Model (HBM; Hochbaum, 1958; Turner, 2004) and the Health Action Process Approach (HAPA; Schwarzer, 1992), amongst others.

Chapter 6 presents the investigation's empirical part and is meant to provide in-depth insights into how respondents from four different cultural backgrounds evaluate standardized OTC drug promotions utilizing four different advertising appeals. While pharmaceutical marketers have relied on informative messages for the longest time (Koinig, 2012; Main et al., 2004), the present study intends to test the extent to which other ad appeals might foster consumer education as well as empowerment. Borrowing from direct-to-consumer advertising research, where emotional appeals have proven to be successful (Wolfe, 2002), this study will extend previous research by employing two more approaches, namely mixed and CSR appeals. Thereby, the investigation's ultimate goal involves pointing out to which degree these promotional strategies work and lead to consumer empowerment.

The empirical part will be succeeded by a detailed discussion of results in **chapter 7**; in conclusion, implications and limitations for both academic research and international marketing practice – with a special focus on the pharmaceutical industry – will be presented.

2 Conceptual Foundations

In accordance with the investigation's predefined focus and the previously introduced research questions, several terms will be used throughout the paper. To guarantee they are grasped as intended by the author, they will be narrowed down and defined beforehand.

2.1 Health | Disease | Illness

Health, often referred to as a fundamental human right (WHO, 2013), is an intangible and abstract concept that is quite hard to define (Earle, 2007). Following the WHO (1946, 2006), health refers to "a state of complete physical, mental and social well-being" and implies the lack of disease (Balog, 1978; Boruchovitch and Mednick, 2002). Another definition stresses the fact that health lays the foundation for individual achievement and success (Seedhouse, 2001), may it be personal or professional, regarding it as the "state of optimum capacity of an individual for the effective performance of the roles and tasks for which s/he has been socialized" (Parsons, 1951). Those two definitions vary widely in their focus, as without a doubt, the WHO's view on health is very positive and idealistic: It presupposes the absence of infirmity (WHO, 2006) by taking a very utopian, if not even unattainable stance (Lucas and Lloyd, 2005). Moreover, it is very limited, disregarding dimensions of culture and environmental influences (Ewles and Simnett, 2003). Hence, the latter definition (Parsons, 1951), which is more to the point and conceives health as being dependent upon numerous factors, is deemed appropriate and will be consulted in the present paper.

Notions of and beliefs about health vary widely, covering assumptions of "health as a functional capacity" (Blaxter, 1982), "health as a social requirement" (Blaxter, 2010), "health as emotional well-being" (MacInnes and Milburn, 1995) as well as "the [healthy] body as a physical ideology" (Bourdieu, 1977). All these views emphasize health's contribution to a smoothly functioning society, and pursuing health for both a society's and an individual's sake is seen as a noble and highly virtuous mission (Crossley, 2003). Hence, it presents a central component of the 'good citizenship' ideal, according to which individual fitness and health are linked to the functioning of society as a whole (Warwick-Booth, 2012), constituting "a resource of life [and] not the object of living" (WHO, 1986). This suggests that health guarantees a good quality of life if maintained properly (Rod and Saunders, 2004; Green and Tones, 2010; Buchanan, 2000) and, consequently, renders it a core component of human happiness, "equivalent to the set of conditions that enable a person to work to fulfill her realistic chosen and biological potentials" (Seedhouse, 1986: 61).

Health is often seen as one end of the continuum; the other end is reserved for disease or illness. While synonyms for health involve terms like vigor and well-being, disease is often referred to as affliction and sickness (Aghadiuno and Dowrick, 2010). In the case of illness, the (healthy) body transgresses from the social norm (Aghadiuno and Dowrick, 2010) and individuals are prevented from fulfilling their designated social roles; consequently, disease becomes an "unmotivated deviance" that cannot be tolerated but needs to be attended to (Health Knowledge, 2007a). In case of illness, a body malfunctioning occurs (Porter, 1992) that can be ascribed to numerous social factors, such as stress, unhealthy lifestyles but also bad working and poor living conditions (Cockerham, 2013). Although illness and disease are used simultaneously most of the time, these two constructs are fundamentally different from one another: while illness alludes to a social and lived-through experience (with individuals suffering from physical symptoms), it is limited to humans; disease, on the other hand, applies to both human and non-human beings, where it refers to the absence of human (life) qualities (Turner, 1996). This means that the term illness is used to account for a person's subjective experience of disease (Aghadiuno and Dowrick, 2010) and is a purely social phenomenon, descriptive of the "meaning social actors employ to make sense of observed or experienced events" (Locker, 1981). Health, on the other hand, is regarded as bodily fitness and is linked to individual welfare, both on a mental and physical level.

2.2 Health Communication

On a very basic level, health communication is concerned with the practice of communicating and disseminating information on health topics to a widely dispersed mass audience (U.S. Department of Health and Human Services, 2014). It is predominantly utilized for educational respectively commercial purposes and captures a vast array of activities, e.g., public health campaigns, health education materials as well as doctor-patient interactions (Schiavo, 2007). The provision of (mass-mediated) information happens with one goal in mind; that is to foster individual health literacy and influence personal decisions with regard to health and well-being (U.S. Department of Health and Human Services, 2014). In the process, the mass media has the ability to influence and even alter people's health behaviors dramatically and sustainably (Wright et al., 2008), functioning as a leveler by placing lay persons on an almost equal footing with health experts and professionals (Parrott, 2003).

Communication is, without question, a valuable asset to the health domain: "Health communication, like health education, is an approach which attempts to change a set of behaviors in a large-scale target audience regarding a specific problem in a pre-defined period of time" (Clift and Freimuth, 1995: 68). Regardless of it being applied by (commercial) manufacturers or (non-commercial) public service providers, health messages have "come to be understood as public [and commercial] health action which is directed towards improving people's control over all modifiable determinants of health" (Nutbeam, 2000: 261). As such, communication activities draw individuals' attention to environmental influences that impact health, also addressing individuals' skills and abilities (Green and Tones, 2010). In this process of raising awareness and creating familiarity with medical conditions, the mass media assists people in reducing their uncertainties about health issues, providing them with useful and enabling information that should ease their at times intense health situations (Wright et al., 2008). Even though individuals might fear receiving biased, false or incomplete information they cannot make sense of (due to its complexity), mass mediated health messages are, nevertheless, useful points of reference: they can stimulate respondents to reflect about their disease symptoms and make them seek information from a wide array of commercial and non-commercial sources, that explicitly address and are conducive to individual health and well-being.

2.3 Advertising

Being the most widely researched area of the marketing mix (Okazaki and Taylor, 2006), advertising can be one relevant source of information. It refers to "the nonpersonal communication of information, usually paid for and usually persuasive in nature about products, services or ideas by identified sponsors though the various [mass] media" (Bovee, 1992: 7). Through their promotional messages, marketers do not only want to push relevant product information to an anonymous crowd but also intend to disseminate messages that invoke positive feelings and create desire for their offerings (Richard and Curran, 2002). Given that advertising pursues varying motivations, going beyond what consumers request, this promotional form can be considered to be a text genre that is motivated by clear sales intentions on the parts of the marketers and producers alike (Behrens, 2001; Forceville, 1996). Marketers rely on this communication form to create affective responses in recipients and wish to "create awareness, understanding, interest, and willingness to accept and to try the firm's offerings (products and services)" (Wind, 1994: 321). Advertising is meant to satisfy existing consumer needs while, at the same time, it wants to create new wants for products (Woodside and Taylor, 1978), alluding to its capability to stimulate mental changes in consumers right away or in the (near) future (Weilbacher, 2001; Richard and Curran, 2002; Rossiter and Percy, 1997).

2.4 Pharmaceutical Advertising

Pharmaceutical advertising is one specific form of advertising that covers all promotional endeavors by marketers of medical services and medicinal products, encompassing all "messages created by marketers of pharmaceutical products that attempt to inform, persuade and even entertain members of the target audience with the goal of influencing recipients' attitudes – and ultimately behavior – in a favorable manner" (Diehl et al., 2008: 100). Generally, it is concerned with the promotion of either prescription or non-prescription drugs (Wind, 1994). Prescription drugs are medications intended to cure severe diseases and require a doctor's prescription, since significant adverse effects and risks are attributed to their use (Diehl et al., 2008). By contrast, non-prescription drugs are meant to treat more insignificant medical conditions and do not depend on a practitioner's approval (DeLorme et al., 2010). Increasingly, they are referred to as home remedies or self-medication substances (Robinson and Zhang, 2011) and present a prototypical way of engaging (health) consumers, strengthening them in their self-medication abilities.

In American households alone, OTC medicines are used as a primary self-treatment response to minor illnesses in 70 to 90 % of all cases (CHPA, 2014). Eight out of ten consumers put their trust in OTC drugs – a trust that is shared by practitioners and pharmacists alike (CHPA, 2013). On average, non-prescription drugs are acquired 26 times per year via one of over 50,000 pharmacies or in more than 750,000 retail stores (CHPA, 2014), making those medications account for 8 % of the total pharmaceutical sales in the United States alone (CHPA, 2014). They form an affordable alternative to prescription drugs and almost 90 % of Americans are convinced that OTC drugs can drastically reduce their health-care expenses (CHPA, 2014). Non-prescription drugs are, additionally, easy to use thanks to easy, comprehensible product labels that have to comply with predefined FDA regulatory statutes (CHPA, 2014).

It appears as if U.S. Americans hold few reservations to using OTC drugs: they are very open to trying non-prescription medication for a variety of conditions on the grounds of their numerous upsides. In a more current research project, consumers put trust in this product class' effectiveness (9.1 points out of 10), few adverse reactions (8.3 points), and safe ingredients (7.6 points; CHPA, 2013). The convenience of self-medication substances is exploited, which does not require individuals to consult with a professional before purchasing the product (80 %; CHPA, 2013). In terms of category, pain medications are used on a more occasional basis (53 %), whilst allergy preparations are utilized slightly more frequently (57 %; CHPA, 2013). In total, 80 % of consumers remark on having claimed a more (pro-)active position in their healthcare due to the availability of OTC drugs (CHPA, 2014).

Pharmaceutical adverts for OTC drugs, which will serve as stimulus material in the present investigation, are subject to extended and tight regulation processes throughout the world due to their specific promotional character. Governments intervene by monitoring (and ultimately approving) pharmaceutical messages with regard to their credibility (Ryan and Vaithianathan, 2009), reviewing "any descriptive printed matter issued or caused to be issued by the manufacturer, packer, or distributor with respect to the drug" (Kracov and Davar, 2010: 321). With the publication of deceptive or misleading content being prohibited, pharmaceutical advertising can be of value to patients, promoting self-medication practices and enabling recipients to become an active agent in their health-care (Diehl et al., 2008).

Despite their numerous benefits, pharmaceutical adverts have been heavily criticized as well, often accused of solely emphasizing drugs' benefits over their prospective by-effects (Diehl et al, 2007). In addition, with big pharma allocating the greater part of their funding to advertising (VOX, 2015; BBC, 2015), smaller brands are doomed to lose the battle for public recognition (Diehl et al., 2007). Notwithstanding those two trends painting a rather dubious picture of pharmaceutical marketers, suggesting them to be rather profit-driven (BBC, 2015), public promotions are capable of educating consumers (Morse, 1993) and reinforcing them in their self-medication abilities.

2.5 Culture

On a very basic level, culture presents a lens through which the world is perceived by a particular group of people (McCracken, 1986). The GLOBE study (House et al., 2004), which will act as a vital source of reference for this thesis, adopts Redfield's (1948) definition and perceives culture as "shared understandings made manifest in act and artifact" (cf. Triandis, 2004: xv). This means that human behavior has become ingrained in people's minds through socialization processes and can neither be altered quickly nor completely (Hofstede and Minkov, 2010). Culture models human life experiences and, as such, presents "the collective programming of the mind that distinguishes the members of one group or category of people from other [cultures and/or nations]" (Hofstede, 1984: 51).

Cultural values are at the heart of each and every society (Markus and Kitayama, 1991) and are essential to the individual self-concept (McCracken, 1986), shaping people's very actions (Masuda et al., 2012). Usually, cultural codes (later to be renamed as cultural dimensions; House et al., 2004) not only shape different cultural practices but also affect communication. In order for advertising to trigger positive responses and create lasting impacts, cultural parameters have to be taken into consideration, for messages are decoded by use of a uniform and shared coding system that is particular to a given culture and ideology (Frith and Mueller, 2004). Cultural codes constitute individuals' "mental programmings" (Hofstede and Minkov, 2010: 4), meaning that individual socialization takes place through social institutions (and the media); consequently, their personality is shaped according to culturally-accepted values that have not only been adopted early on in life, but have also been internalized and manifested over time (Markus and Kitayama, 1991). Only if advertising utilizes those cultural conventions efficiently and effectively, is it able to reach its ultimate goals, attention and liking (Scott, 1994). Hence, promotions are never sales messages alone, but also "social and cultural texts" (Frith, 1998: 1).

2.6 Standardization vs. Localization

In a globalized and converging world (Diehl and Karmasin, 2013), advertising executives are challenged when deciding whether to deploy a standardized or localized promotional strategy. Dmoch (1999) describes standardized or globalized advertising as any kind of promotional message that is executed in an identical manner in different countries, the only exception being the translation of its textual elements. Localized or differentiated/adapted advertising, in contrast, emphasizes the cultural peculiarities of each country setting it is utilized in. A standardized (or global) advertising strategy, hence, presupposes consumer homogeneity (Levitt, 1983; Okazaki et al., 2006) over consumer heterogeneity (Hofstede et al., 1999) and facilitates the creation of a consistent (brand) image across cultures (Backhaus and van Doorn, 2007).

Following research, not all product categories as well as local environments are equally suited for standardized advertising (Doherty and Ennew, 1995; Okazaki et al., 2013), which might explain global marketers' reluctance to take such an approach (Kanso, 1992). Localized approaches might further serve as an expression of advertising's low uniformization potential by virtue of its heavy reliance on cultural parameters (Boddewyn et al., 1986; Hite and Fraser, 1990). Another reason hampering ad unification might stem from an uncertainty as to when an advertisement "ceases to be a standardized advertisement and becomes localized instead" (Onkvisit and Shaw, 1999: 19). Agreement, however, is reached that the prevalence of a common theme across cultures – with minor adaptations being permitted – labels a promotion as being standardized (Onkvisit and Shaw, 1999).

In the advent of a growing globalized market, standardized advertising practice receives more recognition than ever (Agarwal, 1995), where it is applied as part of an enterprise's global marketing strategy (GMS; Zou and Cavusgil, 2002). By focusing on cultural similarities, it blends out potential differences amongst its target audience and presupposes consumer homogeneity with regard to their psychological needs (Onkvisit and Shaw, 1990; Link, 1988). Hence, if consumer communalities dominate, marketers are advised to pursue a standardized advertising approach.

2.7 Health-Conscious Consumers | Empowerment

Being characterized by dynamic alterations over the past decades, the concept of the patient has experienced a redefinition recently, particularly through the commodification of both health-care services and products (Aggleton, 1990; Nettleton, 1997). The power of diagnosing the body and informing the patient about its symptoms was originally inherent to doctors, acclaimed experts in their fields, whose role involved observing, if not even correcting the human body in order to achieve perfect health – the norm (Rabinow, 1984; Rouse, 2003). This role distribution, however, does not prevail any longer – at least not solely. Lately, the term patient – connoting passivity and subjectivity to doctors' recommendations and expertise (Jewson, 1976) – has been replaced by the concept of the "health(-conscious) consumer" (Porter, 1985: 3). This new type of consumer has emerged through lay people assuming expert status in health matters; they are involved with their bodies and personal health records, eager to actively acquire health knowledge and take away power from practitioners and their God-like status (Lupton, 1997). Self-care and self-medicalization can, thus, be seen as forms of empowerment, as an extension of medical expertise to the general population (Kickbusch, 1989).

The consumerism movement has heightened and increased consumer involvement in their healthcare. Hereby, the term consumerism refers to "a social movement seeking to augment the rights and powers of buyers in relation to sellers" (Kotler, 1972: 49). In the new millennium, patients emerge as empowered consumers, who are equipped with the skills that allow them to manage their health conditions and achieve a certain, desirable (health) outcome (Rappaport, 1987). They are encouraged "to 'take back' control over their health by engaging in preventive health activities, challenging the decisions and knowledge of doctors in the medical encounter, joining patient advocacy groups and eschewing medicine by seeking the attentions of alternative practitioners" (Lupton, 1997: 97) as well as coming to rely on self-management and self-medication practices. Beliefs in individuals' abilities gear them towards the realization of their own skills, allowing them to have an increased say in their health-care (e.g., by practicing self-medication). Yet, individuals depend upon information that can educate them and turn them into 'mature' health (care) consumers.

Before discussing the investigation's theoretical background, the relevance of health to both the human body and individual identity needs to be established.

3 Perceptions of Health and Illness and Their Bodily Relevance

From the beginning, humans have been judged with regard to their performances (Dubin, 1962; Goldthorpe et al., 1969) and their productive capacities (du Gay, 1996; Mayo, 1933; Braverman, 1974), on the grounds of which they received their person- and livelihood (Bottomore and Rubel, 1963). In a time of fierce competition, human essence is not derived from creative labor alone anymore (Burawoy, 1979), but subjects are evaluated along a variety of dimensions (Harding, 1997), which need to be perceived in relation to their biggest individual value, namely their health. Governmental interventions have elevated the role of medicine respectively its restoring function to guarantee social functioning, and individuals have subconsciously agreed to it by bowing down to established rules and what constitutes the norm – the "imperative of health" (Hurd Clarke et al., 2008).

3.1 The Relevance of Health to Individuals' Self-Identity

Ralph W. Emerson has quite rightly claimed that "man's first wealth is health" (Washington Post, 2008). A similar stance is taken by the World Health Organization, which describes it – almost in line with Emerson – as "a resource of life [and] not the object of living" (WHO, 1986) as well as a means of accomplishing "a socially and economically productive life" (WHO, 1978). Health guarantees that a good quality of life is maintained (Rod and Saunders, 2004; Green and Tones, 2010; Buchanan, 2000) and constitutes a core component of human happiness, as without health individuals are deemed to feel miserable and become stigmatized as outsiders: "Health is the essential foundation that supports and nurtures growth, learning, personal well-being, social fulfillment, enrichment of others, economic production, and constructive citizenship" (Jenkins, 2003: 4).

As citizens, people are never solely private but publically exposed (entities), "located within the field of visibility, subject to mechanism of objectification, and thereby to the exercise of power" (Smart, 1985: 87). For this reason, identity's postmodern nature as layered (Faulkner and Hecht, 2007) and processual (Hecht et al., 2004) has to be borne in mind. Lock (1987) breaks down the body into three distinct layers that, albeit separate, overlap to the largest extent and produce the 'social body': (1) the individual body (an individual's distinct self-experience), (2) the social body (the visible, socially constructed entity), and (3) the bio-political body (the controlled, regulated individual; Lock, 1987).

Individual health (or the absence thereof) can be put in relation to these three body categories as well: the individual body incurs disease through a variety of physical symptoms, with individuals taking action to eliminate these, e.g. by use of medication. Disease, however, also manifests itself through visible symptoms on the social body, where individual experiences become labeled as 'normal' and 'abnormal' and invoke people to act in accordance with social norms (e.g., take preventive action and/or see a health expert). Finally, signs of illness concern the bio-political body, as the government provides means and services to restore the individual body as a functioning organism (e.g., through hospitals and clinics, health-care plans, etc.).

All these notions reveal one criteria of identity that must not be left out of sight: the fact that subjectivity, the awareness of oneself, involves an interaction with other members of society, suggesting that identity is always constructed in relation to the overall social norm (Berger and Luckmann, 1971; Burr, 2003; Clarke, 2008; Garfinkel, 1967; Gergen, 2000). As such, identity is not solely a personal matter but a public process at the same time: "The self comes into being through taking on the attitudes of others towards it within communicative interaction. Language is the most significant element in this process because it is only through language that people 'internalize' the attitudes of the social group and thus constitute themselves as subjects" (du Gay, 1996: 36; see also Aggleton, 1990).

Through medicine and its health-restoring function, the physical body is restored while – due to its conformity – the social body does not experience exclusion (Risse, 1992; Smith, 1985). Medicine enables individuals to maintain and restore their health and, thus, aids them in avoiding stigmatization or even punishment. Therefore, medications and other treatment options are highly relevant to the individual self-concept, leading health (care) and diligence to pay off by granting individuals both success and profit – together with social acceptance (Galvin, 2002; Lupton, 1995).

3.2 Healthy Bodies As 'Social' Bodies

In today's political and extravagant economy, self-indulgence and an excessive lifestyle devoid of any self-discipline come at a price: health (Daneski et al., 2010; Monaghan and Hardey, 2009), a core asset. Good health provides individuals with "access to and control over the basic material and nonmaterial resources that sustain and promote life at a high level of satisfaction" (Baer et al., 1986: 5). Thereby, people's activities serve as expressions of their agency, as only healthy and fit bodies enable them to function (and succeed) in a competitive world (Petersen, 1997). This goes hand in hand with what the medical sociologist Greco (1993) has coined as 'Healthism' – the conceptualization of delegating the responsibility for a healthy body to the individual; failure to take care of it can be attributed to inappropriate lifestyles or the absence of health-enhancing behaviors (Greco, 1993). It is through Healthism that individuals concern themselves with appearance and increasingly engage in accompanying trends, such as fitness, exercise and diets, but also self-medication practices (Dutton, 1995).

All those attempts are meant to counteract potential harm to the physical body, which runs the risk of attracting illness and disease if not maintained and looked after carefully (Lupton, 1995; Petersen and Lupton, 1997). Being sick constitutes both a biological phenomenon as well as a physical experience (Parsons, 1951); this being the case, disease is closely linked to individual identity (Barry and Yuill, 2012). In case of disease, a body malfunctioning occurs (Porter, 1992) that can be attributed to numerous social factors, such as stress, unhealthy lifestyles, but also bad working and poor living conditions (Cockerham, 2013). Hence, it presents a deviance, serving as an expression of individuals' failure to look after and manage their bodies properly (Lupton, 2012). At the same time, disease poses an economic as well as a political problem for society and is in need of regulation (Lupton, 2012; Armstrong, 1983). Subjects are called upon to take the necessary steps to uphold their social identities, for avoiding disease becomes a prerequisite for social acceptance (Rowe and Kahn, 1998).

3.2.1 Bodies and Social Capital: Expectations of Conformity

At the core of each action, consistent with social expectations, lies the thinking or knowing subject (Pusey, 1987) who is aware of its social role and the specific tasks that have to be fulfilled in order not to sacrifice the status attributed to this role (Barry and Yuill, 2012). Knowledge about what is acceptable as well as appropriate is always cultural, mediated through the process of socialization (Pusey, 1987) – a process that takes place in a lifeworld, the "background consensus of everyday life", the horizon against which all experiences are formed and evaluated (Honneth et al., 1981). Socialization, therefore, also refers to the "adaptation of [an individual's] 'inner nature' to society" (Habermas, 1975: 13).

According to Identity Theory (Cooley, 1902; Goffman, 1967), individual identity is postulated to be based on social role ascriptions nurtured by social performances in general and communication in particular (Banton, 1965; Goffman, 1967). It posits that "individuals internalize social interactions, relationships, and a sense of self into identities through communication. In turn, identity is expressed or enacted through communication" (Hecht and Choi, 2012: 139). Inasmuch identity develops out of individuals' social experiences of themselves as well as through communicative interactions with other members of society (Mead, 1934; Blumer, 1969), identity and communication are reciprocally linked (Hecht et al., 2003). Yet, such an inclusion into society requires justification and only remains reserved for individuals with healthy bodies (Turner, 2004).

One area of research analyzing the motivations and roots of individual behavior(al intentions) is sociology. Sociology looks at interactions and behavioral patterns on the society level (Giddens, 2009) and is also interested in individual identity construction processes. Dependent upon which specific area of research is deconstructed in detail, a specific focus will be adjunct. In the context of health and medicine, medical sociology will be consulted, alluding to the study of how social causes impact individual health in general and health behavior in particular (Cockerham, 2013). Moreover, it defines "the science which investigates the laws regulating the relations between the medical profession and human society as a whole [and] everything related to the subject" (McIntire, 1849: 425).

One concept that is of relevance to the medical sociology realm is that of social capital, describing all "investments" people make in society, implicating memberships in different social institutions (Bourdieu, 1986). It is expressive of a "capital of social connections, honourability, and respectability" (Bourdieu, 1984: 122), that is capable of enhancing both individuals' cultural and economic worth, granting them support in form of support on behalf of other members and experiencing feelings of belonging (Cockerham, 2013). As social capital, (healthy) people present the pillars upon which a functioning society is built, rendering health and citizenship interrelated concepts. For this reason, society has given in to the urge to embark on social initiatives in response to both treating and preventing disease (Rabinow, 1984). Thereby, health is not regarded as an absolute (unchanging) state but as relative (changeable), as determined by governmental interventions and power (Bunton and Petersen, 1997).

Power fulfills a disciplining function in that it tries to ensure that one point of view or ideology is maintained and not questioned (Barry and Yuill, 2012). Health is contested and subject to power relations as well, rendering it both a political and socio-economic experience, which is enforced through public surveillance (Gastaldo, 1997). The physical body presents the locus of disciplinary power, which Foucault conceives "not as natural or neutral but as reproduced in specific sets of practices and discourses" (Bunton and Petersen, 1997: 5). The (modern) self only emerges through the utilization of disciplinary tactics and practices, such as hierarchical observation and normalizing judgment (Foucault, 1991; Rabinow, 1984). Individual bodies are permanently monitored as "[s]urveillance of the self plays a central role in domination strategies" (Spitzack, 1987: 362), ensuring that order is not threatened.

3.2.2 Foucault: Enforcing Bodily Politics Through the Gaze

> *"Foucault [...] offers a theory of the body in social relations as the site of both negative and constitutive power and provides the most comprehensive account of the role of language in constructing illness and the body, both of which he conceives as cultural rather than natural entities" (Eckermann, 1997: 167).*

Foucault was interested in how human bodies are produced, regulated and represented, with these processes being dependent upon disciplinary surveillance (Turner, 1984). The primary mechanism through which surveillance and power are exercised is the 'gaze', which gathers information that creates and nurtures discourses on particular subject matters (Foucault, 1976; Foucault, 1979; Foucault, 1980). The 'gaze' allows for an in-depth examination and understanding of the body with regard to its operation and social functioning in general (Foucault, 1973), and with regard to its social construction in particular. It is always associated with power and authority (Copjec, 1994), located "in the field of the Other" (Lacan, 1981: 84), transforming individuals into self-conscious beings by making them aware of their visibility and, simultaneously, their public exposure (Krips, 2010). The gaze is vital to maintaining order, inducing "a state of conscious and permanent visibility that assures the automatic functioning of power" (Foucault, 1977: 201). This permanent analysis of the body leads to the distinction between what becomes labeled as normal ('healthy') or abnormal ('sick', 'ill'; Barry and Yuill, 2008). Individuals are haunted by the idea of constant surveillance, which fools them into believing that they do not have any other choice but to conform to the norm (Clarke, 2008).

In the area of medical sociology, the gaze is turned into the medical gaze. The downside to this public surveillance is subjugation, whereby the medical gaze is extended to the population, which judges individuals solely along the norm and criticizes derivations (Gastaldo, 1997). Since identification is crucial to individual identity, the community becomes a powerful point of reference and "exercises control over the conduct of its individual members" (Mead, 1934: 155), constituting the 'gaze' as a collective yet anonymous construct at the same time (Foucault, 1996). The gaze is "interiorized" by the subject "to the point he is his own observer, each individual thus exercising [...] surveillance over and against himself" (Foucault, 1980: 155). Inasmuch as it holds the potential of "ordering" social lives (Foucault, 1977), it is often accompanied by anxiety (Krips, 2010) that renders visibility "a trap" (Clarke, 2008: 515).

The need to obey the dominant ideology becomes engrained in people's minds (Copjec, 1994; Krips, 2010); subjects are literally forced to conform, condemned to perish if they do not: so the only option they have, the only freedom they can exercise, lies in choosing from a range of predetermined options (Krips, 2010). "[T]he subject who is constituted as a subject – who is 'subjected' – is he who obeys" (Foucault, 1990: 85). Only if people accept a consensus – meaning they are willing to give in to established ideological standards – can they avoid exclusion from society (Lupton, 2012). Individuals can (and will) be held accountable for their failure to conform to established norms and standards (Petersen, 1997) and, in order to classify as normal, they have to model themselves according to standards they have subconsciously agreed to (Finkelstein, 1990).

In response to public surveillance and control, individuals turn to rituals to discipline their bodies (Lupton, 2012). The practices they enact are "a form of social relations and in giving these relations visible expression they enable people to know their own society. The rituals work upon the body politic through the symbolic medium of the physical body" (Douglas, 1980: 128). An important role is assumed by medicine in the process, which is affiliated or even inscribed with power (Rabinow, 1984).

3.3 Medicine and Its Regulatory Power

Bedside medicine	Clinical medicine	Laboratory medicine
• Disease as a total 'psychosomatic' experience • Lay and 'medical' practitioners • Place of treatment: home	• Specific aetiology of diseases • Specialist practitioners in possession of specialist knowledge about the body • Place of treatment: hospital	• Disease as a 'biochemical disturbance' • Specialist practitioners, knowledge of cellular construction of the body • Place of treatment: laboratory

Figure 1: Paradigms of Medicine (Barry and Yuill, 2008: 25)

Enlightenment has resulted in the notion that human bodies and their functioning should (and can) be explained through scientific reasoning (Barry and Yuill, 2008). Knowledge about health and illness as well as medicine and its curative function are the product of social discourses (Health Knowledge, 2007b), leading to the development of the medical discourse, in which medicine is utilized as a specific kind of knowledge intended to care for the human body (Barry and Yuill, 2012). Medical knowledge is conceptualized in different paradigms; relative to their severity, the following three paradigms of medicine can be distinguished: bedside medicine, clinical medicine, and laboratory medicine (see Figure **1**); the first form is of particular relevance to the present project, as OTC drugs are generally used at home by 'lay' people to treat minor medical conditions.

No matter which paradigm is being chosen, at the core of each lies the human body, the shell of human identity (Lupton, 2012). In western societies, the body has increasingly become medicalized, for people's "capacity to experience the body directly, or theorize it indirectly, is inextricably medicalized" (Frank, 1990: 136). Medicalization, first introduced in the 1970s, has turned rather mainstream, as certain (problematic) aspects of life have become attributed to the medical realm, suggesting that these 'new' lifestyle issues can be treated by the use of drugs (Zola, 1972; Conrad, 1975; Illich, 1975). The concept proposes that "non-medical problems become defined and treated as medical problems, usually in terms of illness or disorders" (Conrad, 1992: 209) and it is often accused of fostering an increase in medical treatment (Abraham, 2010). A 'medicalization' of society is said to have occurred (House of Commons Health Committee, 2005) due to the increasing availability of pharmaceutical products that can be acquired either with or without prescription and are inscribed with the capacity to alleviate human suffering and restore health (Williams et al., 2008). Medicalization, often used synonymously with Pharmaceuticalization, is thought to refer to "the transformation of human conditions, capacities or capabilities into pharmaceutical matters of treatment or enhancement" (Williams, 2008: 851) or even "the process by which social, behavioral or bodily conditions are treated or deemed to be in need of treatment with medical drugs by doctors or patients" (Abraham, 2010: 604).

Pharmaceuticalization' is slightly distinct from Medicalization, though, and alludes to pharmaceutical products playing an ever-increasing role in individuals' personhood and self-perceptions (Abraham, 2010; Fox and Ward, 2008; Marshall, 2009; Martin, 2006). Increases in public pharmaceuticalization levels originate especially out of increased advertising activities (Abraham, 2010), which promote individuals' active roles in health matters by emphasizing "the capacity of individuals to control their risk of becoming sick" (Iriart et al., 2011: 6). The booming drug market has, however, resulted in an over-medicalization of society, with "more medication and less therapy" (Young, 2003: 37).

This argument builds on Foucault (1975), who saw medicine as an "institution" labeling bodies as normal/abnormal, hygienic/unhygienic, and appropriate/inappropriate (Lupton, 2012). The author conceives the medicalization of the body as "a process of social control" (Bilton et al., 1996), in the course of which medicine is meant to re-establish health and restore the body as a functioning organism (Risse, 1992; Smith, 1985), which then, benefits society as a whole. Due to its restoring capacity, medicine belongs to one of the public organs that Foucault labels 'institutions of normative coercion' (Turner, 1992). They are paramount in that they implement specific forms of surveillance, restricting transgressive actions while fostering adjuvant ones (Turner,

1997). Medicine, thereby, presents the one means developed to make for a healthy population, serving the goal "to perpetuate social inequalities, the divide between the privileged [healthy] and underprivileged [unhealthy]" (Lupton, 2012: 6).

Especially in western societies, medicine has grown into a strong agent, allegedly imputing massive influence and power (Lupton, 1997). This is particularly the case with biomedicine, conceptualized as "a branch of medical science concerned [...] with the capacity of human beings to survive and function in abnormally stressful environments and with the protective modification of such environments [through medicine]" (Merriam Webster, 2014). Biomedicine postulates that illness and medical suffering can only be cured by the use of medical preparations or through surgical procedures (Cockerham, 2013). As a result, a "medicalization of life" is said to have taken place (Illich, 1976), meaning that individuals trust medical preparations and drugs to work their "magic" by taking control of their afflictions (Dubos, 1959). Consequently, biomedicine is regarded as a weapon capable of winning the fight over disease (Lupton, 2012): "For almost all diseases something can be done; some can be prevented or fully cured" (Porter, 1997: 595).

Yet, the use of medicine to treat literally "every ill" has not been without criticism (Ericson, 2014), as almost all areas of human life have become medicalized (Lupton, 1997). New and formerly untreated diseases, that are usually related to people's lifestyles (e.g., baldness, infertility, etc.), are discovered on a regular basis and become medicalized as well, with the pharmaceutical industry researching cures for these new "diseases" (Zola, 1972; Freidson, 1970). "Medicine is a dominant institution that in Western societies has come to play an increasingly important role in everyday life, shaping the ways we think about and live our bodies" (Lupton, 1997: 106). Once again, this stresses the role medicine has taken on in the health discourse: it has been established as a normalization mechanism (Rose, 1994).

3.4 Empowerment: From Passivity to Active Involvement

Despite keeping numerous social issues obscured, medicine has the potential of both engaging and empowering people (Lupton, 1997). Thereby, the prominent health paradigm has started to experience a redefinition: The power of diagnosing the body and informing as well as educating the patient was originally inherent to doctors, acclaimed experts in their fields, whose role concerned observing, examining, if not even correcting the human body in order to achieve perfect health – the norm (Rabinow, 1984; Rouse, 2003). This self-conception, has been substituted by the "health(-conscious) consumer" (Porter, 1985: 3) – a person who is actively involved in his/her own health care and even dares to question expert opinions.

3.4.1 *The Emergence of the (Active) Health-Conscious Consumer*

Consumers' changing roles are facilitated by various movements in the medical sector, such as the self-care movement (Ferguson, 1980), the consumer movement (Gordon, 1980) as well as the wellness movement (Bloch, 1984). The consumerism movement, the most relevant to the investigation at hand, is often equated with consumer protection or consumer activism. However, it is not only concerned with heightened consumer involvement by use of extensive and detailed information alone, but also wants to offer them a chance of "voicing [their] discontent and the furtherance of corrective actions" (Maynes, 1990: 6). Consumerism has led to the availability of goods in abundance and has contributed to the commercialization of the health domain (Nettleton, 1997). In the process, patients' roles have also been changed lastingly: "If the subject of contemporary consumer culture is defined as a self-regulating individual actor seeking to maximize the worth of his or her existence to him-/herself through personalized acts of choice in a market-based universe, then the producing subject must be seen now, first and foremost, as a consumer" (du Gay, 1996: 80). People who claim this elevated role, brought about by lay people assuming expert status in health matters, are commonly referred to as "health(-conscious) consumers" (Porter, 1985; Bunton and Peterson, 1997; Nettleton, 1997) or "health-care consumers" (Gould, 1988).

Being part of the media culture (Veblen, 1899), the media plays an important part in proclaiming consumerist messages and involving recipients, which can be perceived as an advantage to the health domain as well. Conditioned by those developments, "the health care consumer is faced with a bewildering set of choices among competing therapeutic modalities [...] and with an equally bewildering barrage of information and health news, both good and bad" (Gould, 1988: 97). Bodily appearance is constantly emphasized by media messages, where it seemingly presents a topic that has been made a permanent item on the public agenda. On the pages of glossy magazines and on TV, attractive bodies are exclusively healthy bodies; messages then stress that both states – attractiveness and health – can solely be reached and retained by appropriating consumer goods (Nettleton and Watson, 1998; Barry and Yuill, 2012). The body is, thus, turned into a commodity that can be enhanced and modified at liberty through consumption practices (McCracken, 1988: 83).

By providing individuals with tools to constitute themselves as sovereign consumers, consumption is a means that enables individuals to express their individuality (de Certeau, 1984; du Gay, 1996; Willis, 1990). They are sovereign in that they add value to their bodies, extending their self-worth and boosting their self-esteem and quality of life respectively through consumption practices (du Gay, 1996; Sabel, 1990; Rose, 1990). Especially the material form of products permits for an extension of lifestyle attributes, fostering the creation of a specific social identity (Giddens, 1991; Mirowsky and Ross, 2003). Through the 'sovereign consumer', the productive subject and its identity conceptualization experience a redefinition (Clutterbuck and Crainer, 1988): "People make a project of themselves and […] develop a style of living that will maximize the worth of their existence to themselves" (du Gay, 1996: 78). The relevance of goods in their lifestyle-enhancing function has drastically increased over the past years: In response to the "lifestyles […] suggested by glossy magazines and advertising images" (Giddens, 1991: 81), consumption goods provide individuals with directions as to who they want to or should be. At the same time, these goods are also inscribed with power relations, offered with the intention of upholding social order and disciplining autonomous, health-conscious consumers.

3.4.2 Health(-Conscious) Consumers and the Enterprise of the Self

A neo-liberal regime provides individuals with new possibilities of self-governance, calling upon them to take care of their selves (Petersen, 1997), summoned to actively prevent risk and protect themselves from harmful (outside) influences (Scott and Williams, 1991). As autonomous selves, people can reconfigure their self-hood, leaving their passivity and docility behind in favor of active responsibility and self-control (Arney and Bergen, 1984; Greco, 1993; Nettleton, 1989; Ogden, 1995): "[T]he presupposition of the autonomous, choosing, free self as the value, ideal and objective underpinning and legitimating political activity imbues the political mentalities of the modern West" (Rose, 1992: 142). Healthy, autonomous citizens are empowered and actively involved in the pursuit of their health, engaging in processes of constant self-evaluation. They obey a "regime of self" (Rose, 2001), deploying practices that permit them to create their individual identities; practices of the self rely on the interdependent relationship between subjects and the discourses through which they have come into existence, with individuals being inscribed with the power of autonomously controlling their lives (McNay, 1992).

Drawing from a humanistic research paradigm, health requires individuals to deal with and adapt to changing circumstances in order to achieve a heightened degree of well-being, self-esteem and self-fulfillment (Warwick-Booth, 2012), accompanied by empowerment. The latter "is based on the idea that giving [individuals] skills, resources, authority, opportunity, motivation, as well holding them responsible and accountable for outcomes of their actions, will contribute to their competence and satisfaction" in the long run (Business Dictionary, 2014). Empowerment thus evolves around the inclusion of lay perspectives – perspectives by non-expert or ordinary people (Bury, 2005; Earle, 2007; Martin, 2008). According to Blaxter (2007: 26), "lay understanding can be better defined as commonsense understandings and personal expertise, imbued with professional rationalizations". In spite of lay knowledge often having been stigmatized as unprofessional humbug, it is informed by expert (medical) knowledge (Blaxter, 2007; Shaw, 2002) and even extends it by emphasizing the role of subjective experience to the health context (Lawton, 2003). In the present-day health communication context, the inclusion of non-expert opinions proves to be vital, for illness experiences are far from being homogenous, but are instead heterogeneous or 'multi-factorial' (Popay et al., 2003).

In the process of empowerment, the body becomes a site of struggle upon which the individual wants to mold its self-image (Lupton, 1995; Petersen and Lupton, 1997). Subjects claim ownership over their bodies, which they manage themselves and shape in a socially acceptable way (du Gay, 1996; MacIntyre, 1985), literally becoming entrepreneurs (of their selves) by turning their bodies into enterprises of the self. Certain qualities and characteristics are said to be characteristic of enterprising subjects: they are said to possess personal responsibility, autonomy, initiative (Rose, 1990), boldness, self-reliance, risk-affinity (du Gay, 1996) as well as productivity (Gordon, 1987). The enterprising self constantly weighs its options, "calculat[ing] about itself, and [...] works upon itself in order to better itself" (Rose, 1989: 7f.).

The notion of life as an enterprise is grounded in the assumption that "one remains always continuously employed in (at least) that one enterprise, and that it is part of the continuous business of living to make adequate provision for the preservation, reproduction, and reconstruction of one's own human capital" (Gordon, 1991: 44). As a self-reliant enterprise, individuals are in charge of taking "care of the self" (Gordon, 1991: 44), whereby the entrepreneurial subject utilizes technologies of the self to positively influence their health and well-being either by themselves or by involving others; the ultimate goal of this engagement then concerns achieving an improved state of well-being coupled with happiness and content (Foucault, 1998a).

Technologies of the self (Foucault, 1994) encompass four distinct components, of which the first two forms – the technologies of production and sign systems – are primarily concerned with linguistic and scientific matters. The third type – the technology of power – deals with how individuals' subjective status is influenced by power relations, which are closely linked to the fourth and final technology – referred to as the technology of the self. It examines "the ways in which we relate ourselves [and] contribute to the forms in which our subjectivity is constituted and experienced" (Davidson, 2005: 127). Taken together, these technologies then allow individuals to be reminiscent and "to become someone else [they] were not at the beginning" (Sawicki, 1994: 288).

As part of counteracting disease and attaining empowerment, the above-mentioned technologies of the self can be deployed. Disease, perceived as a form of social deviance (Holton and Turner, 1986), can be thwarted by conscious individual actions (Martin et al., 1988). For instance, individuals who readily accept doctors' advice and obey their orders (e.g., by taking a prescribed medication or starting a diet) are not regarded as passive (dopes) but as engaging in self-forming practices, which they perceive as supportive of their health and well-being (Lupton, 1997). They might seem to be prototypical consumers at first sight; yet, upon further examination, their decisions are expressions of their own, individual choices. The same holds true for those patients who deliberately chose not to utilize any recommended practice and product, consciously rejecting the dominant ideology and the status quo embodied by their doctor (aka medical expert) (Lupton, 1997). Instead, they may opt to consult with similar-minded people in an Internet chatroom or acquire a self-medication substance out of their own effort. Independent of their agreement or disagreement, "in each case, the individual has a personal, emotional investment in presenting her- or himself in a certain manner, as a certain 'type of person' engaged in 'rational' and 'civilized' behavior consonant with his or her social or embodied position at the time" (Lupton, 1997: 105).

No matter which technologies are deployed, it is necessary to point out that "the mastery of the self is […] a prerequisite for health" (Greco, 1993: 361). Yet, how do individuals figure out which technologies are best applied? How are they made aware of the availability of options and alternatives that should allow them to claim a more active stance in their own health? One potential way of fostering and achieving engagement is through health communication, which is concerned with empowering consumers, granting them permission to take control over their bodies.

4 Effects of Health Communication and Pharmaceutical Advertising

Health is essential to human existence as it "provides a person the potential to have the opportunity and ability to move toward the life he or she wants" (Becker et al., 2010: 26). In the western world health has become a prerequisite, at times even classifying as an "expectation or entitlement" (Becker et al., 2010: 26). Yet, health environments have been considerably altered over the past decades and, as a result, researchers have been urged to start broadening their (theoretical) horizons, with "the avant-garde suggesting and integrating new theoretical approaches and practices" in the area of health communication (Drum Beat, 2005).

On a very basic level, health communication wants to inform individuals, motivate them to take action and achieve some kind of behavioral change. Through information, not only individuals' understandings of the health condition should be fostered, enabled respectively improved, but also health-related knowledge should be increased, ultimately engaging and empowering people (Kreps, 2012; Campbell and Scott, 2012; Hornik, 2008; CDC, 2011; Muturi, 2005). Therefore, health communication objectives can be either of behavioral, social and/or organizational nature (Schiavo, 2014). Through communicative means, several health goals should be obtained: messages intend to raise awareness for medical conditions and their symptoms respectively, increase consumer knowledge on treatment options, change recipients' health-related attitudes (from health-compromising to health-enhancing behaviors), facilitate communicative exchanges between different parties (e.g., patients, experts, policy-makers, and like-minded individuals), and enhance people's literacy rates as well as (health) skills (Schiavo, 2014).

Numerous factors influence people's health and well-being, such as physical, social and generic conditions, plus the availability of medical services and treatment options (Jonas et al., 2007; Parker et al., 2008: 4). New developments in the health domain, such as an increasing longevity and declining birth rates, have induced people to attribute a higher degree of importance to their health (Kotlikoff and Burns, 2005); this trend is accompanied by people's heightened willingness to step up and (re)claim responsibility over their bodies. The advancement of both technical and technological devices allows for a more intense and thorough treatment of health issues (Gully,

2008), leading medical knowledge amongst consumers to increase (Parker and Thorson, 2008). Through health communication, they are made aware that "health and well-being are affected by interaction among multiple determinants including biology, behavior, and the environment. Interaction unfolds over the life course of individuals, families, and communities, and evidence is emerging that societal-level factors are critical to understanding and improving the health of the public" (Gebbie et al., 2003: 32).

4.1 Health Communication in the 21st Century

Figure 2: Health Communication Influences (Schiavo, 2014: 35; own illustration)

A boost in public attention has not only been triggered by the abovementioned alterations, but also by increasing health communication activities that present "a multifaceted and multidisciplinary approach to reach different audiences and share health-related information with the goal of influencing, engaging and supporting individuals, communities, health professionals, special groups, policy makers and the public to champion, introduce, adopt, or sustain a behavior, practice or policy that will ultimately improve health outcomes" (Schiavo, 2007): Through health communication efforts, both policy makers and pharmaceutical marketers plan to offer support to individuals as well as mobilize communities with regard to their health-decisions, summoning them to adapt, sustain and maintain health-enhancing behaviors (Schiavo, 2007). As such, health communication combines influences from different theoretical backgrounds and disciplines, "such as health education, marketing, mass communication, social sciences, anthropology, psychology, as well as sociology" (Bernhardt, 2004; World Health Organization, 2003; Institute of Medicine, 2003; see Figure **2**).

Relating to health, communication has to be perceived as "a necessary and irreplaceable part of the process of attaining essential medical knowledge" (Brown et al., 2007: 24; Widder, 2004). Its task is to provide patients and consumers with information on both the nature and probable progression of their medical conditions, while not neglecting to provide guidance regarding potential treatment options at the same time (Gafni et al. 1998). Hence, communication fulfills the function of vehemently assuring recipients of the availability of therapeutic and diagnostic measures that can provide a relief to symptoms in the long run (Brown et al., 2007).

4.1.1 Communicating about Health

In academia, health communication research "focuses on the relationships between communication and health, health attitudes and beliefs, and health behavior" (Welch Cline, 2003: 285). From a practitioner's perspective, health communication refers to "the study and use of communication strategies to inform and influence individual and community decisions that enhance health" (Center for Disease Control and Prevention; CDC, 2001; U.S. Department of Health and Human Services, 2005). As such, it provides audience members with valuable pieces of information, invoking them to take preventive action for health issues of (public and personal) relevance (U.S. Department of Health and Human Services, 2005). These approaches have one common denominator: in both cases, health communication's ultimate goal is to substantially influence people and motivate them to unlearn health-compromising behaviors in favor of health-enhancing behaviors (Bernhardt, 2004; U.S. Department of Health and Human Services, 2005; Schiavo, 2007). Research predominantly focuses "on people's attitudes, beliefs, values, and feelings about health-related concepts and messages"

(Wright et al., 2008: 6), which are addressed in communicative interventions. The purpose of communication is to not just deliver a message alone but to affect a change in recipients with respect to their knowledge, attitudes or, eventually, behaviors (Fletcher, 1973). Health communication wants to achieve "disease prevention through behavior modification" (Freimuth et al., 2000: 337); as such, it is crucial to the individual perception of health and well-being (Berry, 2006; Wright et al., 2008: 115; Welch Cline, 2003; Lupton, 1994). If rated as beneficial and educational, health communication can literally 'empower' individuals, offering them insights into and an understanding of health problems and treatment options respectively (Muturi, 2005; Widder, 2004).

In total, health communication comprises a variety of activities, such as educational events, professional-patient interactions, self-help groups, health hotlines and mailing lists as well as mass media campaigns (Health Communication Unit, 2006). Regardless of the channel they are utilized in, health communication messages set out to trigger involvement on various levels and require the cooperation of different parties in diverse settings – a process that is facilitated by both the provision of information and communicative interventions: "Communication can play an important role in supporting behavioral intentions and increasing the likelihood that they would become actual behaviors. This requires the development of adequate tools that would facilitate and make it easy for people to try, adopt, and integrate new health behaviors in their lifestyles" (Schiavo, 2007: 41).

In order to become effective, communication must be accompanied by a learning process, which can bring about a durable change in recipients (Green and Tones, 2010). As part of health messages, it is not enough to define a recommended behavior as "healthy" or "life-saving"; rather, all statements need to be backed up by evidence (Chiu et al., 1998) and translated into tools that allow for their practical application (Schiavo, 2007). The tools individuals have at their disposal also depend upon the argumentative strand taken, which can either focus on either health or disease.

4.1.2 Approaches to Health: Focus on Health or Disease?

When analyzing and dissecting health, different theoretical approaches have to be distinguished: the medical model and the social model. Moreover, within recent years, a holistic understanding of both the body and health care has developed, which warrants inclusion as well.

The Medical Model of Health: The (bio)medical model of health turns to scientific reasoning for input, leading it to be labeled the mainstream 'Western scientific model' (Blaxter, 2004). In terms of understanding, it is renowned to be mechanical and individualistic; since it also puts an emphasis on disease, it is predominantly concerned with diagnosing and treating afflictions and, as such, the medical model is part of the pathological research agenda (Warwick-Booth, 2012). In the medical notion, the physical body is seen in isolation, independent of social and environmental factors (Lyons and Chamberlain, 2006). Disease is only traced back to biological and psychological origins and it does not take other sources into account (Warwick-Booth, 2012). Moreover, treatment and diagnosis of the human body are reserved for medical experts.

The Social Model of Health: While the 'negative' medical model refrains from putting individuals in charge of their own health and well-being, the social model of health does involve and empower them. In addition to delegating responsibility to individuals and including lay perspectives of health, it takes different factors into consideration, which might fuel health-related behaviors and outcomes, such as economic, social as well as environmental components (Earle, 2007). In the social model, sources of individuals' mal-being are located outside of the physical body (Warwick-Booth, 2012), whereby each person is called upon to take up health-enhancing behaviors, reducing expert involvement.

The Holistic Model of Health: The third model integrates aspects of the two theories, proposing the combination of two conflicting views, which proclaim the separation of mind and body (Lappé, 1979). As such, it also turns to non-conventional treatment methods in an attempt to restore the mal-functioning body, postulating open-mindedness and self-competence (BHMA, 2014): "Holistic health encourages a transition away from the patient dependency fostered by traditional medical practices towards self-reliance and responsibility – and where appropriate, self-care" (Lappé, 1979: 477). The holistic model presumes health to have and interact with multiple determinants – both internal and external (Earle, 2007) – while perceiving the person in its completeness, consisting of a mind, body and soul (Patterson, 1997). What distinguishes this model from the remaining ones is that it almost entirely focuses on individuals and their capabilities in managing their health, which need to be activated and strengthened (Cronin de Chavez et al., 2005; Earle, 2007). Hence, it is vital for how individuals approach OTC medications, which presuppose the existence of adequate skills that allow individuals to manage their health themselves.

In line with these approaches, two major strands of research have developed within the field of health communication: a disease-oriented branch (pathogenesis) and a health-oriented branch (salutogenesis; Williamson and Pearse, 1966; Antonovsky, 1996). The former takes patients' medical conditions as a starting point, looking at how individuals attempt to avoid, manage or cure their infirmities. The pathogenetic approach classifies human beings as either healthy or unhealthy, whereby each disease has known, detectable causes and can be treated and/or eased by appropriate interventions and remedies. Disease involves "naming and defining its cause" (Thompson, 2000: 3), whereby medicine functions as a social institution in charge of regulating illness (Engel, 1979). The latter – salutogenesis – is concerned with health together with the methods and ways in which it can be maintained and fostered (Antonovsky, 1985). Salutogenesis presumes illness and disease to occur naturally since humans are subject to outside harm (Williamson and Pearse, 1966). It then sets out to detect the causes and prerequisites for health, addressing humans' capabilities and resources that need to be mobilized and strengthened to reduce risks and health-compromising behaviors (Lindström and Eriksson, 2005); the pathogenesis approach, however, solely deals with prevention and risk management in order to avoid disease (Antonovsky, 1985).

Even though a more positive approach is definitely worthwhile, the present investigation will take a pathogenetic path due to its focus on humans, their subjective health evaluations as well as their health-enhancing skills and competencies that enable them use OTC drugs (Faltermeier, 2005). These preventive measures and skills are also increasingly put at the center of health campaign messages in general and advertising messages in particular.

4.1.3 Goal-Directed Health Campaigns: Pushing Information to the Public

Health campaigns present a special area of academic research and can be ascribed to the fields of public health, health communication, as well as advertising studies. Due to their broad focus, they "are an essential part of health promotion, or efforts to enhance health and prevent disease on a large scale. Health campaigns can be defined as a systematic effort to change health behaviors [...] within a target population of people who are at risk for a health problem" (Wright et al., 2008: 233; Bennett and Murphy, 1997; Salmon and Atkin, 2003). These communicative activities are goal-oriented attempts, mostly directed at a relatively large, well-defined audience (Rogers and Storey, 1988; Snyder, 2001) and consist of a series of coordinated activities over a given period of time, deployed on a community, interpersonal as well as (mass) media level (Wakefield et al., 2010).

Up until now, campaign research has predominantly focused on major social issues, such as HIV (Niebel and Davidson, 2012), smoking or drug abuse and selected prevention programs like cancer screening (Jones and Owen, 2006). A vast number of individual evaluation studies of specific (topical) campaigns has produced proof of health campaigns being effective indeed (Whittingham et al., 2008; Hornik, 2002; Bunton et al., 1991; Irwin, 1989; Petersen, 1994), e.g., by increasing immunization rates (Porter et al., 2000; Paunio et al., 1991), elevating knowledge on vaccines (McDivitt et al., 1997), motivating individuals to go through cancer screenings (Ramirez et al., 1999), and enhancing people's disease coping abilities as well as their adherence with either nutrition or fitness regimes (PEW Internet and American Life Project, 2007). Two recent meta-analyses on health campaigns also support this assumption (Derzon and Lipsey, 2002; Snyder and Hamilton, 2002). However, little attention has been dedicated towards emergent topics and current trends, such as an aging population, a shortage in practitioners and medical personnel, cultural diversity, new approaches to health care, funding, insurance and managed care, the impact of new technologies on healthcare (Neuhauser and Kreps, 2003) as well as drug switches from prescription to non-prescription status (Rx-to-OTC; Diehl et al., 2008; DeLorme et al., 2010).

Health campaigns "utilize three basic communication processes to move the target audience toward the desired response: awareness, instruction, and persuasion" (Salmon and Atkin, 2003: 455). Awareness messages educate people about what to do and who should adopt a defined behavior, offering cues on the time and place of engagement. Instruction messages then present recipients with the 'how to do it' information (Salmon and Atkin, 2003) until, finally, persuasive elements list reasons for why audience members should take up an advocated action (Salmon and Atkin, 2003). This path is eased once useful information is provided: "[A]n important objective of health campaigns is getting audiences to seek information, for this indicates that they found campaign content personally relevant enough to take active steps to obtain additional information" (Parrott, 2003: 446). In the case of pharmaceutical promotions, then, information should guide individuals' (OTC) purchasing intentions, strengthening them in their self-medication practices at the same time.

Health communication fulfills the purpose of assisting a public audience in understanding health related issues; unless it uses a language that reflects and corresponds with the capabilities as well as preferences of a pre-defined target segment, it cannot achieve this goal (Schiavo, 2007). It builds upon a heightened consciousness for consumers' personal profiles since ad comprehension is often hampered by the complexity of ad content, e.g., missing definitions, extensive use of medical jargon and statistical data (Steyr, 1999; Paasche-Orlow and Wolf, 2007; Zarcadoolas et al., 2005; Berry, 2007). Before designing a single advertisement or a whole promotional campaign, advertising executives should "gain an in-depth understanding of the health issue: its medical and situational causes, risk factors, severity, and statistical significance among different audiences and groups" (Schiavo, 2007: 240f.). These insights then have to be molded into concise yet clear pieces of information, at best evidence-based (Schiavo, 2007) as well as new and newsworthy (Snyder and Hamilton, 2002). In order to achieve higher levels of comprehensibility, marketers are advised to develop "appropriate written materials and [reach an] improvement in skills of those people with limited literacy" (U.S. Department of Health and Human Services, 2005: 11–15), making it "simple and easy to understand" (American Medical Association, 2005b) and reducing confusion or misunderstandings to a minimum (Manoff, 1985).

Communication in the health realm has utilized a variety of message appeals (Rogers, 1975; Rogers, 1983; Witte and Allen, 2000), such as fear appeals, action step appeals, reward appeals, threat appeals, efficacy appeals as well as hope appeals, which have been successful in reaching pre-defined health goals (Schiavo, 2014). The use of negative or fear appeals, nonetheless, has been criticized due to the approach's tendency to literally "backfire" (Witte and Allen, 2000). However, results have not been exclusively negative, as some success stories can also be reported (e.g. 'Brain on drugs' campaign [Mayfield, 2006] or 'Suffering every Minute' [NYC Department of Health and Mental Hygiene, 2012]). On the other hand, positive (fear-avoiding) appeals – addressing respondents' self-esteem – have been adopted by UNICEF in support of their disability awareness efforts (UNICEF, 2013).

The examples included above indicate that health communication strategies need to be modeled in accordance with the campaign's pre-defined health goals, insinuating that once health communication goals have been set, they have to be strategically implemented. Thereby, health communication strategies describe all approaches taken to accomplish the previously defined goals (Schiavo, 2014). Usually, they comprise the definition of a target audience to which the product endorser should be modeled. In addition, a network – facilitating (follow-up) research, purchase and exchange – needs to be created (e.g., by including calls to action; Wells et al., 2006). A suitable health message should then center on the most relevant (product) aspects to varying degrees, depending on which ad appeal is deployed (see section 5.4.2.). For instance, informative appeals could sell the (pharmaceutical) product as not only meeting consumers' health needs but also point out the offering's contribution to their individual health goals (Kotler and Roberto, 1989; Lefebre, 2013). In the case of emotional approaches, a lifestyle is sold instead.

4.2 Health Communication's Contribution to Health Literacy

The role and relevance of mass media to the health communication realm can be summarized very briefly: media's core duty consists of "acting as a specter of influence" (Parrott, 2003: 445), addressing relevant health issues and putting them on the public agenda in accordance with its agenda-setting function (Green and Tones, 2010). Related to health, the media literally pushes selected health-topics, elevating their public relevance; in addition, messages assist individuals in developing coping mechanisms and schemes by circulating information and presenting scientific facts in a comprehensible manner (Scheufele, 1999; Viswanath et al., 2008; Nelkin, 2001). Mass media messages are spread to the end that recipients' uncertainties about health problems are reduced by offering them relevant information that should permit them to make better choices with regard to their health and well-being respectively (Wright et al., 2008).

Hence, effective health communication can be seen as a source of empowerment, raising individual health literacy and health education rates.

Health literacy presents one of the most important assets to be achieved through health communication (Zagaria, 2004; Schiavo, 2007). It alludes to "the degree to which individuals have the capacity to obtain, process, and understand basic health information and services needed to make appropriate health decisions" (U.S. Department of Health and Human Services, 2005: 15-20; Selden et al., 2000). Nonetheless, it is a relatively new concept and has not managed to gain a foothold in the health communication discourse yet (Nutbeam, 2000), where the term is commonly used to refer to routine practices and activities which individuals participate in as part of their illness control mechanisms (Marks et al., 2005; Lorig and Holman, 2003; Bodenheimer et al., 2002).

More precisely, health literacy comprises "the ability to read, understand, and act appropriately on health information" (Behringer et al., 2004), describing the sum of all "personal, cognitive and social skills which determine the ability of individuals to gain access to, understand, and use information to promote and maintain good health" (Nutbeam, 1998/2000: 263). Nutbeam (1998 and 2000) distinguishes three layers of health literacy that are touched upon so that recipients can make qualified health decisions: functional health literacy, interactive health literacy, and critical health literacy (Nutbeam, 2000). Basic or functional (health) literacy regards fundamental reading and writing skills as prerequisites for health-related decisions and message comprehension (Nutbeam, 2000). Communicative or interactive (health) literacy requires more advanced cognitive skills on the part of patients that enable them to (socially) participate in disease prevention activities, also fueling (informed) communicative exchanges with professionals and other peer group members (Nutbeam, 2000). Critical (health) literacy, the most advanced form, is concerned with thoroughly analyzing and reflecting upon medical information and (OTC) advertising content, qualifying (empowered) patients to exercise an increased degree of control over their lives and well-being (Nutbeam, 1998; Nutbeam, 2000). Health literacy is, therefore, crucial in strengthening patients' attitudes towards their own self-medication competencies and self-care practices, which in turn affect respondents' attitudes towards OTC drug ads (Nutbeam, 2000; Paasche-Orlow and Wolf, 2007).

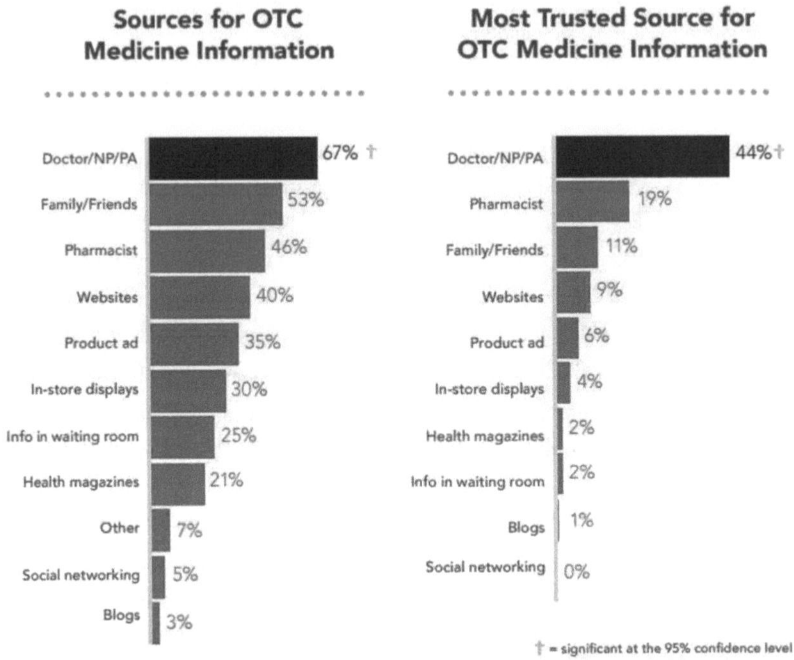

Figure 3: OTC Drug Information - Sources and Trust Levels (Accent Health, 2014: 8)

Health literacy presents an individual asset, which is essential in enabling patients to become actively engaged in all health-related decisions (Nutbeam, 1998; Nutbeam, 2008). For the purpose of information search and interpretation, different media channels can be utilized, which foster varying degrees of responsiveness and elaboration on behalf of individuals; nevertheless, these are not met with equal trust levels (see Figure 3). Following a recent survey, doctors continue to be consulted most often for guidance and advice (67 %) and also enjoy high degrees of trust (44 %; Accent Health, 2014). Even though family and friends rank second as consultants (53 %) right before pharmacists (46 %), the latter's opinion is given higher credibility (19 %; family and friends: 11 %; Accent Health, 2014). Websites come in fourth place regarding both relevance (40 %) and trust (9 %), with the fifth rank already being awarded to product ads independent of the channel featured (relevance: 35 %; trust: 6 %; Accent Health, 2014).

Given that the Internet has begun to conquer the domain of health communication within the last decades, health-related content, such as advertisements or promotions, has been unaffected by this recent trend. Instead, the health industry still heavily relies on traditional marketing channels, such as print media. "Although newspapers, magazines, radio and television are often criticized for inaccurate and biased reporting, in industrialized countries they remain the most influential sources for everyday information on risks to health [and remedies]" (WHO, 2002: 42). Belonging to the area of self-paced media, promotional messages in newspapers and/or magazines hold some advantages: they can be controlled by the audience, studied at their own pace and reflected upon (Chaiken and Eagly, 1976). As a result, public agencies and privately owned enterprises should employ these channels when attempting to reach prospective consumers and patients alike. On the grounds of this reasoning, the study at hand will turn to print ads when testing consumer responses to health promotion messages in a cross-cultural setting.

4.2.1 Health Promotion and Pharmaceutical Advertising as Sources of Information and Empowerment

Health promotion has to be regarded as "any combination of health education and related organizational, economic, and environmental supports for behavior of individuals, groups, or communities conducive to health" (Green and Kreuter, 1991; Green and Tones, 2010). In this way, health promotion "recognizes the fundamental importance of environmental influences on health and the complex interplay between these factors and health-related behavior" (Green and Tones, 2010: 1). Information uttered for promotional or educational purposes, thus, takes on the role of 'social support' and can help people in times of need (Ford et al., 1996): it sets out to assist people in "chang[ing] their lifestyle toward a state of optimum health. [...] Lifestyle changes can be facilitated by a combination of efforts to enhance awareness, change behavior, and create environments that support good health practices" (O'Donnell, 1989). Through health promotion, individuals learn how to activate their personal skills in order to increase their well-being and might even be motivated to seek advice from their peers after being exposed to (useful) information (McLaurin, 1995).

In order to transform health-compromising behaviors into health-fostering or health-enhancing efforts, a variety of sources – interpersonal and medial – need to be taken into account. All communicative efforts are – or ought to be – outcome-oriented (Parrott, 2004) and achieving an ideal physical state requires "a commitment to dealing with the challenges of reducing inequities, extending the scope of prevention, and helping people to cope with their circumstances [by] creat[ing] environments conducive to health, in which people are better able to take care of themselves" (Epp, 1986). In this process, the mass media occupies a significant position and opts to decrease individual uncertainties about health problems and disease symptoms, offering solutions for temporary improvement as well as permanent cure (Wright et al., 2008).

Stemming from its remaining and unquestioned relevance to the medical field, pharmaceutical advertising will be put at the center of the present investigation. It constitutes a specific health communication form that endorses pharmaceutical products as well as medicinal services and is directed at either professionals or consumers. It captures all promotional "messages created by marketers of pharmaceutical products that attempt to inform, persuade and even entertain members of the target audience with the goal of influencing recipients' attitudes – and ultimately behaviour – in a favourable manner" (Diehl et al., 2008: 100). The present investigation will focus its attention exclusively on promotions for non-prescription drugs, as this field is characterized by an immense research gap (Main et al., 2004) together with rather outdated and fragmented research results (DeLorme et al., 2010). In their 2010 article, the authors provided a comprehensive overview on research activities in the pharmaceutical realm, pointing out that – in spite of being solely permitted in two countries globally – direct-to-consumer advertising has been and still is extensively surveyed (approximately 150 studies over the past 10 years). By comparison, OTC drug advertising, which is allowed in every country and subject to far less legal regulation, has received very limited attention to date, as only approximately 50 studies and academic texts have taken up this issue over the past 50 years (DeLorme et al., 2010). Yet, this segment is rapidly growing in relevance throughout the world due to patent expirations (DeRuiter and Holston, 2012) and drug switches from prescription to over-the-counter status (Rx-to-OTC; CHPA, 2014). The present project, hence, is meant to help reduce this significant research gap by proposing (and testing) a model measuring consumer responses to

OTC drug promotions in diverse cultural settings and the self-empowerment derived therefrom.

Drug promotions want to induce consumers to seek or purchase a medical product (Norris et al., 2004), whereby promotional activities can be utilized for two forms of preparations, namely prescription or non-prescription drugs (Wind, 1994). Prescription drugs are medications intended to cure severe diseases and presuppose a doctor's prescription, since significant adverse effects and risks are attributed to their use (Diehl et al., 2008). By contrast, non-prescription drugs are meant to treat more insignificant medical conditions and do not require a practitioner's approval (DeLorme et al., 2010). Increasingly, they are referred to as home remedies or self-medication substances (Robinson and Zhang, 2011) that are available for purchase in grocery and wholesale stores throughout the world (Doktoruz, 2007).

Through pharmaceutical ads and health messages placed in a vast range of media channels, consumers have been literally flooded with information on pharmaceutical products; predominantly, they provide information on familiar health concerns, identifiable without the help of a practitioner (Frith and Mueller, 2004) and are, therefore, not without controversy, accused of fostering the medicalization of society by prescribing "A Pill for every Ill" (Ericson, 2014). As a consequence, consumer responses regarding the acceptance of pharmaceutical ads have been inconclusive: while promotional messages for drugs are believed to help individuals to get more involved in their health care (74 %), educating them about both risks and benefits attributed to a drug's use (67 %), these ads also cause confusion (61 %; Steyer, 1999). So, one important question needs to be posed: How can a heightened degree of comprehensibility and, thus, compliance, engagement or even empowerment be achieved? A potential explanation needs to start by looking at how advertising messages are placed and designed, as well as consumed.

4.2.2 Deconstructing Pharmaceutical Advertisements: What Can They Achieve?

In the process of acquiring information on pharmaceutical products and drugs alike, several media vehicles can be utilized. To date, television is still the most frequently used medium, particularly in the area of direct-to-consumer advertising (DTCA; Reid, 1999). With the advent of the Internet, however, advertisers are increasingly moving their promotional activities online, where online-pharmacies and virtual chat rooms are booming, clustered with drug recommendations and information on alternative medications (Frith and Mueller, 2004). This strategic move alludes to marketers' increasing concern for cost-effective and more precisely targeted communications (Reid, 1999). But they have to be cautious, since the Internet is not equally suitable for promoting all drug forms and does not yet constitute the most relevant source of information for (non-)prescription drugs. In spite of the World Wide Web gaining dominance, one traditional media channel still remains unchallenged as a source of information for OTC drugs, namely magazines (DeLorme et al., 2010; Magazines Canada, 2010), which will be put at the center of the investigation at hand.

On a ***global*** level, the pharmaceutical industry achieved a market value of USD 808.1 bn. in 2013, presenting a 5 % increase when compared against 2012 (MarketLine, 2014). Regionally, the Americas (comprising both North America and South America) represented the leading drug market (43.8 %), far ahead of the Asia-Pacific region (28.7 %) and Europe (26.6 %; MarketLine, 2014). Accounting for 80.5 % of the Americas' pharmaceutical market, the **United States**' industry volume arrived at USD 284.6 bn. in 2013 (+ 4.2 %; MarketLine, 2014). In terms of accumulated profits, the **European pharmaceutical market** was able to reach a market value of USD 211.4 bn., constituting an increase of 0.1 % when compared to 2013 (MarketLine, 2014). **Germany** represented the largest European single market for pharmaceuticals (16.8 %), which was able to accrue a growth of 0.4 % in 2013, amounting to USD 35.6 bn. in profits (MarketLine, 2014). On the other side of the globe, more precisely in **Brazil**, the pharmaceutical industry was able to score significantly higher wins in market share than in other countries (+ 9.8 %), landing a market value of USD 18.2 bn. (MarketLine, 2014). In spite of it only accounting for 5.1 % of the market value in the Americas, it had managed to grow considerably from 2009 to 2013. When compared to other nations, the Brazilian drug market is quite specific, as approximately half of the total profits can be assigned to the generic sector. Reasons for the segment's importance are numerous, including increased import tariffs to push domestic pharmaceutical production, price caps, control of pharmaceutical products and a reference pricing system amongst others (MarketLine, 2014).

In the following, **the OTC drugs**' segments' particularities will be discussed in detail, since they present the investigation's overall focus. **Globally**, OTC drug revenues were marked by a light increase in sales (+ 3.8 %) in 2012, reaching a turnover of USD 132,178 bn. that year (MarketLine, 2013). In terms of region, the **United States** occupied the third place (21.8 %) after the Asia-Pacific region (35.8 %) and Europe (31.3 %; MarketLine, 2013). Following a recent growth of 2.1 %, the U.S.-American OTC drug market was able to score a turnover of USD 28,784.9 m. in 2012. OTC drug sales in **Europe** accounted for approximately one third of global sales (MarketLine, 2013), reaching a market value of USD 41,354.8 m. after a 3.1 % increase in 2012. Thereby, the largest part of OTC drug sales in Europe was generated by **Germany**, which accounted for 17.7 % of the continent's total market value. In spite of being the industry leader, Germany had to face marginal decreases in sales (-0.1 %); nonetheless, it was able to obtain a market value of USD 7,335.8 m. in 2012 (MarketLine, 2013). With regard to market size, **Brazil** made up 13.8 % of the Americas non-prescription drug market value, while the United States accounted for 68.8 % (MarketLine, 2013). When comparing developments of different regional markets, the Brazilian OTC drug industry was able to report significantly higher growth rates (+ 12.4 %) than, for instance, the U.S. or Germany, reaching a total of USD 5,771.9 m. in sales in 2012 (MarketLine, 2013). After passing through a period of steady growth between 2008 and 2013, market performance is even predicted to accelerate slightly more by 2017 (+ 4.1 %), when the OTC drug segment is expected to realize sales of USD 161,260.2 bn. globally (MarketLine, 2013). Traditional OTC drugs presented the market's largest segment (19.7 %), followed by cough and cold preparations (17.9 %) and analgesics (13.1 %; MarketLine, 2013), which will be put at the focus of the project at hand.

In all countries to be examined herein, both general interest and special interest magazines are listed amongst the most crucial and relevant sources of information for over-the-counter preparations (DeLorme et al., 2010; Verbraucheranalyse, 2008). Pharmaceutical advertisers are well aware of this trend, assigning most of their advertising budget towards these media vehicles (IGEPHA, 2011). They also cater to advertisers' causes: As all advertisements are layered, consisting of both visual and textual elements, they assume consumers to have a sufficient amount of time at their disposal to examine messages in detail. Print media, categorized as an internally paced communication form, is especially beneficial then, leaving it up to consumers to decide how much time and/or attention they are willing to invest in examining a given promotion and its content respectively (Pieters et al., 1999).

Making sense of advertising content is not straightforward but requires ad literacy. Malmelin (2010) recommends consumers to examine promotions along a variety of dimensions, with each dissected level corresponding to different dimensions of (ad) literacy: informational literacy (information evaluation), aesthetic literacy (comprehension of aesthetic and visual codes and meanings), rhetorical literacy (message evaluation and reflection thereon) and promotional literacy (reflection on the promotion's overall purpose; Malmelin, 2010). What he implies is that breaking down an advert into little pieces of information (either visual and/or textual) can assist consumers in understanding how advertising operates, as well as which objectives it pursues; furthermore, ad literacy wants to scrutinize how consumers are convinced by use of rather subtle means and ad (design) techniques, e.g., attractive product endorsers, pleasant settings and appealing or persuading advertising messages, which are often modeled in accordance with recipients' lifestyles.

The present-day advertising landscape is characterized by overstimulation (95-98 %; Kroeber-Riel et al., 2009; Esch, 2008) and, as a consequence, only approximately 2 % of all (print) advertisements are apprehended by recipients (Bauer et al., 2012). In order for marketers to stand out from the clutter, promotions have to be designed in an innovative and appealing way to create a pleasing reading experience. In the present, fast-paced world, visuals have become well-featured elements in all kinds of advertisements, where their potential of transmitting a message rapidly and convincingly has been grasped (Patti and Freizer, 1988). Additionally, their capacity to transport more meaning at once (Kroeber-Riel, 1986; Mandel et al., 2006) and their story-telling ability, which aids recall, are of advantage to marketers (Lord, 1980; Swann and Miller, 1982). Illustrations are recommended to complement and/or build upon the headline, establishing the relevance of the intended advertising message amongst the respondents (Wells et al., 2003).

Before marketers start designing a single advertisement or a whole promotional campaign, it is essential for them to gain a thorough understanding of the issue. In the health context, this comprises "its medical and situational causes, risk factors, severity, and statistical significance among different audiences and groups" (Schiavo, 2007: 240f.). Most consumers, who are health-conscious and engaged in their well-being, welcome information on drugs and treatment options and are especially responsive to evidence-based information and facts (Schiavo, 2007), as long as they are "simple and easy to understand" (American Medical Association, 2005b; Beltramini, 2006; Schaeffer and Volpe, 1999). According to Hoeck and Gendall (2002), only the use of simplified and less complex information can aid consumers in grasping the gist of advertisers' intended messages, positively influencing product recall. In addition, messages providing two-sided information (on drug risks and benefits) are perceived as being more believable, credible and informative than one-sided (framed) messages (Etgar and Goodwin, 1982; Kamins et al., 1989; Pechmann, 1992). Yet, even though the use of two-sided arguments is recommended (Jansson-Boyd, 2010), one-sided messages still prevail and were chosen for the present project, modelled after findings from an earlier content analysis that confirmed the common use of positive (result-based) messages in OTC drug advertising (95 %; Koinig, 2012).

Message design components are incorporated for strategic purposes, e.g., to increase identification and liking amongst (prospective) consumers belonging to a pre-defined audience segment. Identification is usually achieved by means of specific lifestyle attributes, whereby lifestyle is perceived as "a general way of living based on the interplay between living conditions in the wide sense and individual patterns of behavior as determined by sociocultural factors and personal characteristics" (WHO, 1986). Those specifics heavily depend upon another component, which is health literacy (see sections 4.2. and 5.4.10.).

Lifestyle and health literacy are also presumed to moderate both responses towards (pharmaceutical) advertising in particular (Vakratsas and Ambler, 1999) and health in general (Fuchs, 1986; McGinnis and Foege, 1993; Nutbeam, 2000; Diehl et al., 2011; WHO, 2007; Zaracadoolas et al., 2005; Contoyannis et al., 2004). Health literacy is a necessary prerequisite for the autonomous and self-caring individual (Wilson and McLemore, 1997), who can only be empowered through the provision of information. In the case of advertising, messages should invoke a core desire in individuals to strengthen and build up both motivation and central competencies, which allow them to manage disease hardships and eventually overcome them (Schiavo, 2007). Health literacy is, thereby, perceived as an asset that enables patients to become actively engaged advocates in their health care and all related decisions (Nutbeam, 1998; Nutbeam, 2008: 2074). Having the potential of transforming future patient-provider exchanges in a positive and lasting manner, both health promotion and health literacy are vital variables in shaping individuals' attitudes towards their own self-medication competencies, which in turn shape their evaluations of OTC drug ads (Nutbeam, 2000) in both a local or global setting.

4.3 Taking Matters Global: The (Im)Possibilities of Cross-Cultural Advertising

At the heart of cross-cultural studies lies the perception of culture. Culture presents a lens through which the world is perceived by a particular social group (McCracken, 1986), shaping their ways of communication – including advertising; as a communicative form it is determined by culture, described as "a complex whole, which includes knowledge, beliefs, art, morals, law, custom, and any other capabilities and habits acquired by individuals as members of society" (Taylor, 1871: 1). The term culture refers to a group's shared values, beliefs, and practices, also including its native language(s) that are used to establish the social norms and rules guiding individual behaviors and actions (O'Hair et al., 2002). Being geographically bound "to the local contexts within which [...] meanings are constituted and negotiated" (Dutta, 2008), culture permeates every aspect of life, also influencing individual perceptions and experiences (Wright et al., 2008; Adler and Elmhorst, 2008).

4.3.1 Negotiating Meaning: Communication's Cultural Determinism

Each human interaction is based on shared symbols and codes that are culturally shaped and have been internalized by individuals at an early stage in life. According to Samovar and Porter (1991), the following six characteristics are particulates of every culture:

(1) culture is not innate but learned (DeVito, 2003), meaning that it is not inscribed or coded in people's genes but only becomes ritualized through socialization processes;

(2) culture is transmissible and can be passed on within generations, to individuals as well as groups respectively;

(3) culture is subject to change and, therefore, dynamic in nature. As time progresses, so does culture, whereby cultural values are modified and adopted to altering social circumstances and living conditions;

(4) culture is selective as well, with societies attributing varying degrees of importance to specific characteristics, e.g., time or customs;

(5) cultural facets must not be regarded in isolation but are interrelated, meaning that cultural aspects usually affect more than one area of life;

(6) lastly, culture exhibits ethnocentric tendencies by lifting one society's own norms and values above those of other cultures (Samovar and Porter, 1991).

Culture is a participatory process (Dutta-Bergmann, 2004a; Dutta-Bergmann, 2004b; Dutta-Bergmann, 2005) and subject to a constant re-definition through communication (Dutta, 2008; Ford and Yep, 2003), to which it is closely linked: "The art and manner in which one understands the world is determined to a large extent by language; but language, at the same time, is an expression of a specific group-experience of the world, and therefore may itself be shaped by the Weltanschauung as well as the wishes, expectations, and motivations of the group using it" (Maletzke, 1976: 74). As culture steers human interaction, advertising, which is composed and encoded according to specific (cultural) norms and values, is expressive of a given culture (Frith, 1998). Advertisements depict norms and values; since they are designed keeping a given culture in mind, they are reminiscent of social customs and practices.

Leaving culture behind or overcoming it is virtually impossible since it "has penetrated to the roots of [their] nervous system and determines how [individuals] perceive the world. [...] People cannot act or interact in any meaningful way except through the medium of culture" (Hall, 1966). This is also true for the health context: As culture affects human attitudes, values and belief structures, it has an impact on individuals' health behaviors and outcome expectations (Davis and Resnicow, 2012). For this reason, individuals from different cultural backgrounds might experience as well interpret bodily symptoms in a different manner; conditioned by their cultural background, they might attribute varying degrees of importance to disease constituents, acceptable treatment options and medical interventions respectively (Rosal and Bodenlos, 2009; Betancourt, 2006; Waite, 2006; Ward, 2007).

Culture becomes further visible in form of knowledge about diseases, acquired through communication with other peer group members, who usually belong to the same cultural group, rendering these health-related notions culture-specific as well (Galanti, 1991; Lupton, 1994; Wright et al., 2008): "The language for engaging in the discourses of health and the meanings of health that become possible are constituted in the domain of culture. It is through the culturally situated symbols that individuals communicate with each other, interact with the social structures, and come to organize collectively to address the structures" (Dutta, 2008: 8). As a consequence, health presents "a cultural construct [that] must be rooted in the cultural codes and meanings, inherently tied to values" (Dutta, 2008: 19).

When it comes to determining culture's relevance to deconstructing promotional (health) messages, four distinct layers of expression need to be consulted: (1) symbols, (2) heroes, (3) rituals and (4) values (Hofstede, 1990). For the present project, the last category is of particular relevance as cultural values are located at the heart of each society, where they serve as indicators of individual behavior and conduct (Markus and Kitayama, 1991). A value describes "an enduring belief that a specific mode of conduct or end state of existence is personally and socially preferable to an opposite or converse mode of conduct or end state of existence" (Rokeach, 1973: 27). Broadly defined as general tendencies towards subject matters, they traditionally come in pairs of opposites (de Mooij, 1994) and are more deeply embedded than behaviors or attitudes, directly influencing people's desires and choices (Mueller, 2011). Values are also commonly consulted in the advertising design process, where they are enunciated and built upon to guide recipients' evaluations of and responses towards advertisements.

In the marketing context, values can be regarded as almost universal and "represent a learned organization of rules for making choices and resolving conflicts" (Steward, 1972: 74; Schwartz, 1992; Rokeach, 1968). They "determine, at a basic level, people's choices and desires [and, as such] may be one of the most powerful explanations of, and influences on, consumer behavior" (Okazaki and Mueller, 2007: 504). Advertisements that incorporate (culture-specific) values have been reported to trigger affective responses in recipients (Kahle, 1983); as a consequence, these have proven to be more effective and influential than value-free ads (Kahle, 1983). This is the case as values (re)present "goals or desirable end-states" (Howard and Woodside, 1977), with product purchases accomplishing the purpose of meeting consumers' objectives (Gutman, 1983).

Nevertheless, values are not the only parameters that have to be borne in mind when composing advertising messages; rather, cultural distinctions are powerful determinants, claimed to "have important implications for advertising content, persuasiveness of appeals, consumer motivation, consumer judgment processes and consumer response style" (Shavitt et al., 2008: 1103). In the following, the main types of cultural differences will be discussed in detail, pointing out their applicability to the project at hand.

4.3.2 Dimensions of Cultural Difference

Besides artefacts and signs, culture also comprises more abstract systems, such as place, time and language (Triandis, 1995), which are based on (culturally created) symbols and governed by abstract (culturally established) conventions and rules (Gudykunst et al., 1989). These concepts do not only reflect culture per se but are also expressive of cultural values (Giles and Franklyn-Stokes, 1989; Kashima and Kashima, 1998). While language helps to define a cultural group (Mueller, 2011), it is by no means universal but follows either a high-context or low-context orientation. Thereby, context refers to "the information that surrounds an event and is inextricably bound up with the meaning of that event. The elements that combine to produce a given meaning – event and context – are in different proportions depending on culture" (Hall and Hall, 1987: 7). This differentiation can be traced back to Hall's classification of high- and low-context cultures (Hall, 1976), which offers the most comprehensible account of culture-specific preferences in communication styles (de Mooij, 2011). Whereas individualistic or low-context cultures stress the importance of words and direct communication, collectivistic or high-context cultures deem contextual (nonverbal) cues and abstractness more important than the overall message (Hall, 1976). This further suggests that high-context messages are only marginally coded and very explicit, whereas in low-context communication meaning is less accessible, as most elements are implicitly coded and disguised (Hall, 1976).

Describing and comparing cultures presupposes the definition of cultural dimensions or characteristics as exemplified by Harris and Moran (1987), who discuss a culture's particularities along a variety of criteria, such as communication, self-hood, values and norms, etc. Following Hall, Geert Hofstede was the first to recognize culture's influence on communication patterns, leading him to develop a classification system of differences, which he later used to group countries (Hofstede, 1980). He initially came up with four dimensions: Power Distance, Individualism/Collectivism, Masculinity/Femininity, and Uncertainty Avoidance (Hofstede, 1980). Only a few years later, another dimension – Long-Term/Short-Term Orientation – was added as a relevant cultural determinant (Hofstede and Bond, 1988). Until today, these dimensions have served as the basis for many extensions and will be introduced very briefly in the following paragraphs, also pointing out their relevance to the area of (cross-cultural) advertising studies.

(1) Power Distance (PD) is concerned with the extent of (in-)equality amongst people and the acceptance thereof in given societies, whereby countries exhibiting high degrees of Power Distance favor hierarchies over loose structures (Carl et al., 2004). In the field of advertising, high scoring cultures tend to readily believe testimonial statements by celebrities and/or experts, who constitute credible sources; the same holds true for typical product users (Zandpour and Campos, 1994). In terms of message appeals, advertisements basing their arguments on reason and logic are highly valued and well-received in countries, where low power distance is the norm and equality and opportunity are emphasized (Mueller, 2011); high Power Distance cultures, by contrast, favor visual recounts and emotional stimuli instead.

(2) Individualism/Collectivism (I/C) pertains to whether a society regards the individual or the group as more important. Highly individualistic countries (e.g., the U.S.) vehemently fight for individual rights and self-fulfillment (Gelfand et al., 2004) and believe in upholding democracy, liberty and freedom by all means necessary; in collectivistic cultures, in contrast, individual wishes and desires are secondary to group interests (Mueller, 2011). Advertisements targeting members of highly individualistic societies should therefore depict only one single person

(Frith and Sengupta, 1991), whereas recipients in collectivistic countries would like to be exposed to more than one product endorser (Diehl et al., 2003).

(3) Masculinity/Femininity (M/F) refers to one characteristic according to which countries stress either masculine traits (e.g., independence, success, assertiveness) or feminine traits (e.g., modesty, harmony, relatedness; Mueller, 2011; Emrich et al., 2004). Consumers in countries ranking high on the Masculinity scale are most responsive to promotions stressing achievement and status, also deploying direct product comparisons at times (Milner and Collins, 2000). Feminine countries, however, are more receptive of qualities such as harmony and group belongingness (Frith and Mueller, 2004; Mueller, 2011).

(4) Uncertainty Avoidance (UA) addresses the degree to which a society feels confident with ambiguity and takes necessary steps towards preventing uncertainties. Nations with low extents of Uncertainty Avoidance reject rules and formality in favor of loose structures, which are characteristic of higher scoring cultures (de Mooij, 1998). Advertisements utilized in high Uncertainty Avoidance countries will attract more attention if they stress product safety, also providing detailed information and reasons for product purchase (Zandpour and Campos, 1994); emotional appeals, with their atmospheric stimuli and implied messages, tend to be preferred in low Uncertainty Avoidance contexts (de Luque and Javidan, 2004).

(5) Long-Term vs. Short-Term Orientation (LT/STO) alludes to whether a country appreciates long-term commitment and tradition (LTO) or discards the past as being irrelevant to present and future developments (STO; Mueller, 2011).

One recent project both modifying and extending previous cross-cultural research is the GLOBE study, the term being an acronym for Global Leadership and Organizational Behavior Effectiveness Research Program (House et al., 2004). Conducted in 2004, this study adapted some previously identified dimensions to changing (social) circumstances and came up with four new classifications, which are meant to contribute to the completeness of any international examination. Robert House and his fellow researchers, thereby, introduced the following (revised as well as extended) cultural classification categories:

(2) (a) The Individualism/Collectivism dimension was split into two distinct categories, namely Collectivism I or Institutional Collectivism (IC) and Collectivism II or In-Group Collectivism (IGC; Gelfand et al., 2004). While the former looks at how institutions manage and reward collective actions and resources, the latter is located on an individual level, scrutinizing how members of society express their personal identities (House et al., 2004).

(3) (a) Gender Egalitarianism (GE) was introduced instead of the Masculinity/Femininity distinction, examining society's role in reducing gender inequalities and promoting the equal treatment of the sexes (House et al., 2004; Emrich et al., 2004).

(6) Assertiveness (A) describes individuals' proneness to tolerate violence and conflict in order to achieve their personal goals (House et al., 2004; Den Hartog, 2004).

(7) Future Orientation (FO) presents a substitute for the Long-Term/Short-Term Orientation, referring to the degree according to which individual members of society are forward-looking in their conduct, exhibiting behaviors such as planning ahead and saving up (House et al., 2004; Ashkanasy et al., 2004).

(8) Performance Orientation (PO) is concerned with all practices a society passes forward in an attempt to foster as well as reward achievement and excellence (House et al., 2004; Javidan, 2004).

(9) Humane Orientation (HO) looks at the extent to which a society values (and rewards) fairness, generosity and care for others (House et al., 2004; Kabasakal and Bodur, 2004).

The usefulness of the GLOBE study to the area of advertising research has been pointed out through the above-listed examples and has also been repeatedly recognized by renowned researchers (e.g., Terlutter et al., 2006; Okazaki and Mueller, 2007; House et al., 2010; Diehl et al., 2014; Mueller et al., 2015), especially against the background of its distinctive features: it is based on an extensive data resource, features 62 countries worldwide and does not only present a rather recent but also solid foundation, extending previous studies by explicitly differentiating between cultural practices ('as is') and cultural values ('as should be'; see Tables **1** and **2** for scores of the countries scrutinized; House et al., 2004; de Mooij, 2005).

	Austria	Germany East	Germany West	Germany Mean	United States	Brazil
Assertiveness	4.59 Band A	4.77 Band A	4.66 Band A	4.72 Band A	4.50 Band A	4.25 Band A
Institutional Collectivism	4.34 Band B	3.67 Band C	3.97 Band C	3.82 Band C	4.21 Band B	3.94 Band C
In-Group Collectivism	4.89 Band B	4.59 Band B	4.16 Band C	4.38 Band B/C	4.22 Band C	5.16 Band B
Future Orientation	4.47 Band A	4.04 Band B	4.41 Band B	4.23 Band B	4.13 Band B	3.90 Band B
Gender Egalitarianism	3.18 Band B	3.17 Band B	3.25 Band B	3.21 Band B	3.36 Band B	3.44 Band B
Humane Orientation	3.77 Band C	3.45 Band D	3.30 Band D	3.38 Band D	4.18 Band C	3.76 Band C
Performance Orientation	4.47 Band A	4.16 Band B	4.42 Band B	4.29 Band B	4.45 Band A	4.11 Band B
Power Distance	5.00 Band B	5.70 Band A	5.48 Band B	5.59 Band A/B	4.92 Band B	5.24 Band A
Uncertainty Avoidance	5.10 Band A	5.19 Band A	5.35 Band A	5.27 Band A	4.15 Band B	3.74 Band C

Table 1: GLOBE Study (Cultural Practices; House et al., 2004)

	Austria	Germany East	Germany West	Germany Mean	United States	Brazil
Assertiveness	2.85 Band C	3.24 Band B	3.21 Band C	3.23 Band B/C	4.36 Band B	3.06 Band C
Institutional Collectivism	4.78 Band B	4.86 Band B	5.07 Band B	4.97 Band B	4.20 Band C	5.57 Band A
In-Group Collectivism	5.32 Band C	5.38 Band C	5.46 Band C	5.42 Band C	5.79 Band B	5.17 Band C
Future Orientation	5.15 Band C	5.36 Band B	5.06 Band C	5.21 Band B/C	5.34 Band B	5.60 Band A
Gender Egalitarianism	4.83 Band A	4.97 Band A	5.06 Band A	5.02 Band A	5.03 Band A	4.91 Band A
Humane Orientation	5.68 Band A	5.56 Band B	5.63 Band B	5.60 Band B	5.51 Band B	5.52 Band B
Performance Orientation	6.12 Band B	6.24 Band B	6.27 Band B	6.26 Band B	6.14 Band B	5.98 Band B
Power Distance	2.52 Band D	2.74 Band C	2.66 Band C	2.70 Band C	2.88 Band C	2.59 Band D
Uncertainty Avoidance	3.65 Band D	4.02 Band C	3.38 Band D	3.70 Band C/D	3.99 Band C	5.00 Band B

Table 2: GLOBE Study (Cultural Values; House et al., 2004)

In addition to reporting scores for both practices and values, House et al. (2004) developed a classification system, grouping countries with similar value manifestations into so-called bands (see Table **1** and **2**). Societies of one band are assumed to share important characteristics and might even be allocated to the same cultural cluster (on the grounds of their geographic location or shared history; House et al., 2004); the closer societies are, the higher the ad standardization potential; the further apart they are in terms of scores, the more diverse are said nations, reducing the likelihood of promotional unification. The values of the countries selected for the present study suggest a high similarity and are confirmed by GLOBE's band allocation; for this reason, a high standardization potential of advertising content is assumed.

Inasmuch as individual socialization takes place through social institutions, cultural values have not only been adopted early on by individuals but have also been internalized over time (Markus and Kitayama, 1991), taking the form of practices (House et al., 2004). They serve as crucial points of reference for cross-cultural advertising studies, as adverts are said to incorporate established social values and practices (Diehl et al., 2014). For the present study, four dimensions are of specific interest, namely *Uncertainty Avoidance* (UA), *Power Distance* (PD), *Individualism/Collectivism* (I/C) and *Gender Egalitarianism* (GE). Looking at a society's comfort with both ambiguity and doubtfulness (de Luque and Javidan, 2004; Hofstede, 1980), ***Uncertainty Avoidance*** can be consulted in the present study for various purposes. On the one hand, it explains variations in responses to information: while countries with high Uncertainty Avoidance scores prefer expert statements and product specifics, nations with low Uncertainty Avoidance peculiarities are more drawn to results (de Mooij, 2011). On the other hand, communication styles come into play as well, with low context and weak UA cultures being more accepting of exacting communication styles, in which only the information required to form a decision is provided (de Mooij, 2011). In the health context, attitudes and behaviors are intertwined with the cultural dimension of Uncertainty Avoidance as well. For instance, countries expressing high UA levels express high nutritional preferences, while countries at the other end of the continuum (low UA) are keen on exercise (de Mooij, 2011). Additionally, Uncertainty Avoidance scores moderate sustainable consumption patterns: in high scoring countries, individuals state that environmental problems impact their lives but do little about it; yet, people from low Uncertainty Avoidance countries are eager to get involved and are willing to change their consumption habits for the environment's sake (Eurobarometer, 2008).

4.3.3 Advertising across (National) Boundaries: Cross-Cultural Challenges

> *"Cross cultural differences in advertising [are] a growing and important area of research, primarily because an understanding of these differences is needed in order to take on the creative challenge of communicating to people of diverse cultural backgrounds" (Biswas et al., 1992: 73).*

As indicated beforehand, individuals are always socialized in a particular cultural context, where they are exposed to and have absorbed particular values, norms and beliefs that are expressive of said culture, shaping their responses to promotional messages. One theory designed to answer the question of how advertising messages are received in diverse cultural settings is the Hofstede Model of Cross-Cultural Advertising (de Mooij and Hofstede, 2010; see Figure 4). Although Hofstede's framework is not the most recent theory of cross-cultural communication, it is still widely used due to the simplicity attributed to his dimensions (Magnusson et al., 2008) as well as its rather big data corpus (76 countries; Hofstede, 2001; Hofstede and Hofstede, 2005). The concept has been frequently cited and is consulted to explain how individuals' notions of themselves respectively their identities affect individual responses to advertising messages and marketing strategies (de Mooij and Hofstede, 2010).

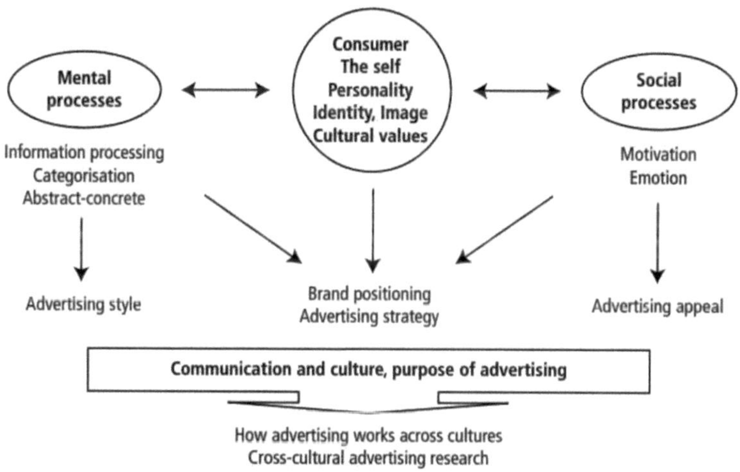

Figure 4: The Hofstede Model of Cross-Cultural Advertising (De Mooij and Hofstede, 2010: 86)

Central to Hofstede's theory is the concept of the self with all its personal traits and attributes, which is embedded in a dynamic environment and is affected by both mental and social processes (de Mooij and Hofstede, 2010: 86): "Mental processes are mostly internal processes, how people think, learn, perceive, categorise and process information. Social processes are about how [consumers] relate to other people, including motivation and emotions". Both these processes are subject to interpersonal and mass-communication effects, moderating the acceptance of ad appeals and messages respectively (de Mooij and Hofstede, 2010).

When studying cultural differences in advertising, two methodological approaches prevail: the descriptive content analysis, and empirical studies testing advertising effectiveness. To date, cross-cultural research is nurtured by content analyses, which are numerous (for an overview, see Okazaki and Mueller, 2007) yet not without criticism, accused of "providing description without prescription" (Samiee and Jeong, 1994). This allegation sounds a bit exaggerated though and has to be weakened at this point, for content analysis is vital in providing a starting point for future research, observing and documenting advertising practice's effectiveness at a certain point in time (McQuarrie and Phillips, 2008).

This is also what the present project builds upon. Based on an earlier content analysis (Koinig, 2012), this investigation proposes a conceptual model that will set out to explain how evaluations of several standardized non-prescription drug ads designed pertinent to the findings of said analysis are influenced by both health variables and message components. It will further try to determine the impact selected cultural dimensions exercise on the perception and evaluation of those advertisements. The basic concept behind the model presented in this project is that a standardized advertising stimulus is likely to be perceived and evaluated distinctively in selected cultures, dependent upon the pronunciation of cultural values and practices in those countries. Since the GLOBE framework of cultural dimensions (House et al., 2004) as well as Hofstede's cultural criteria (Hofstede, 2010) have been applied in numerous studies (for an overview, see Diehl et al., 2014), they will be also deployed in the present project. In developing a culturally based theoretical framework that is meant to explain varying responses to advertising material, the project at hand wants to contribute to the development of a more general and applicable theory incorporating culture's relevance to advertising reception, which has repeatedly been stressed as a core area for future research in a global(ized) advertising landscape (Taylor 2005; Taylor, 2007; Taylor, 2010). By including the United States, Germany, Austria and Brazil for analysis, cross-cultural differences are expected.

4.3.4 *Standardization vs. Differentiation*

Increasingly, consumers' purchasing decisions and product evaluations do not take place on a local level anymore but are globalized. Research suggests that – through the process of globalization – consumers become more alike and are driven by similar values throughout the world (Keillor et al., 2001; van Ittersum and Wong, 2010). One theory that attempts to explain the changes the consumer segment is facing in the present-day marketplace is consumer-culture theory (CCT; Holt et al., 2004), which addresses "how consumers actively rework and transform symbolic meanings encoded in advertisements, brands, retail settings, or material goods to manifest their particular personal and social circumstances and further their identity and lifestyle goals" (Arnould and Thompson, 2005: 871).

Consumer Culture Theory posits that individual identity is expressed through consumption (Holt, 2002) which has become globally-oriented (Ritzer, 2007; Steenkamp and DeJong, 2010), characterized by unified consumption-related values, patterns and symbols (Holt et al., 2004). Given the utterance of said unified consumption motives and patterns, products nowadays aid consumers in their 'global' self-expressions (Waters, 1995), resulting in an "increasing interconnectedness of varied local cultures as well as [...] the development of cultures without a clear anchorage in any one territory" (Hannerz, 1990: 237). Building on this assumption, companies have started to position their brands in a similar manner around the globe, utilizing shared symbols in their marketing communication efforts (Quelch, 2003). This argumentation can be read in favor of a standardized ad execution strategy.

4.3.5 *Standardized or Localized Ad Campaigns: What Pays Off?*

> *"The world is becoming a common marketplace in which people – no matter where they live – desire the same products and life-styles. Global companies must forget idiosyncratic differences between countries and cultures and instead concentrate on satisfying universal drives" (Lynch, 1984: 49).*

Established corporations no longer operate only locally, but increasingly also globally. Regardless of their international business relations, most advertisers have relied on localized messages until now (Kanso, 1992), corresponding with (national) cultural standards and expectations. Enterprises have, however, started to express vivid interest in a globalized message approach and seem to be willing to standardize their international advertising campaigns. In practice, standardization refers to the unification of the overall advertising strategy (including visuals, slogans and other textual elements; Brown, 1923; cf. Agarwal, 1995), while only translating textual information (Taylor and Johnson, 2002; Onkvisit and Shaw, 2003), but not implementing any other changes in terms of executional strategy (Backhaus et al., 2001).

Standardization originated out of experts' continuous claims in support of an emerging global culture with unified values (Melewar and Vemmervik, 2004). Over the years, advertising standardization has become one of the most commonly researched yet controversial topics in the marketing field (Okazaki et al., 2006). In focusing on countries' similarities, potential cultural differences are disregarded in the process (Melewar and Vemmervik, 2004). Standardization usually implies that marketers do not completely replicate the same ad in diverse cultural settings, but suggests that promotions are characterized by a large degree of uniformity (Ozomer et al., 1991). Slight adaptions, such as translations into the local language, do not violate the standardization concept (Onkvisit and Shaw, 2003), awarding it a certain degree of flexibility in terms of market conditions and executional circumstances (Harris and Attour, 2003).

Yet, the existence of homogenous markets is readily contested. Amongst another group of researchers, the notion of unification across cultures is rejected by virtue of advertising's unsuitability for standardization, which it owes to its reliance on cultural values and lifestyle attributes (Cavusgil et al., 1993; Boddewyn et al., 1986; Hite and Fraser, 1990). These scholars claim that standardization is often impeded by local customs, which are – and will remain – culture-specific (Howard and Ryans, 1989); likewise, they hold a deep conviction that consumers are not becoming more homogenous; on the contrary, some proclaim that consumer preferences are diverging, developing into different directions, which forces advertisers to deal with heterogeneous tendencies and preferences (Onkvisit and Shaw, 1999).

So are those experts arguing in favor of standardization indeed correct? Does a unified promotional strategy offer the biggest benefit to marketers? Standardized advertising messages do have some clear advantages, such as their cost-efficiency and their potential to create a universal corporate image (Okazaki et al., 2006), facilitating a successful global marketing strategy (Doherty and Ennew, 1995). Even though sales might be higher in the case of local (adapted) advertising campaigns, standardization might result in lower production (editorial) costs (Quelch and Hoff, 1986). A unified approach is, furthermore, likely to generate a competitive advantage (Levitt, 1983); nonetheless, only a handful of studies have produced proof of these campaigns' effectiveness and success (Banerjee, 1994; Zinkhan, 1994; Taylor, 2005).

The motivation, in which the present project is grounded, follows a clearly defined objective: While companies initially only opt for marketing and selling their products domestically, they eventually decide to enter new markets and start to cultivate countries with similar (cultural) practices. Later on, they even choose to access culturally more distinct nations. For this reason, marketing executives are expected to value practical information on advertising strategies that could ease their entrance into rather diverse markets, receiving a clear benefit from data on the perception and evaluation of their standardized promotions in various (foreign) markets. Insights into current practices would then allow them to develop some guidelines as to how to adapt their advertising campaigns to specific markets in general and their (cultural) characteristics in particular. As research on the perception and evaluation of standardized advertising messages in different cultures is quite limited (Hudson et al., 2002; Callow and Schiffman, 2004), the present project will try to add to the body of research in this area, putting a special focus on non-prescription drugs.

4.3.6 Ad Appeals and Promotional Considerations

The distinguishing mark that separates successful from unsuccessful promotional strategies is the so-called ad appeal, which is used to literally 'woo' recipients: "The life giving spark of an advertisement is the promise of the special significant benefit the product will provide – a promise the product must be able to fulfill. The special significant benefit [then] becomes the appeal of the advertisement" (Kleppner, 1979). It alludes to any kind of promotional message that has the goal of motivating consumers to seek (and purchase) the product or service mentioned therein (Mueller, 1987). Ad appeals describe the way in which advertisers want to trigger attention in recipients, influencing and shaping their interests and feelings towards a particular product and/or brand in a favorable manner (Belch and Belch, 1993). Ad appeals are part of the promotional message's overall execution, referring to the cues utilized in promotional messages to attract both consumer interest and attention, further steering their feelings towards the advertised service or product (Kinnear et al., 1995). Promotional appeals are usually transported through both the ad's headline and the visual (including a product illustration), with the body copy backing up as well as building upon those two components (Mueller, 1987). Hereby, two main forms can be distinguished: informative appeals that make explicit mention of the product's functionality and its distinctive features, and emotional appeals that rely on visual stimuli to tell (subjectively) appealing stories (Okazaki et al., 2010; Leonidou and Leonidou, 2009).

Relying on 'hard' and tangible product facts as well as quality and performance aspects, informative appeals are often referred to as hard-sell appeals (Mueller, 1987; Okazaki et al., 2010) and, thus, induce rational thinking processes in recipients (Churchill and Peter, 1998). They are very direct and want to sell the actual product quickly by utilizing reason and explicit message features (Okazaki et al., 2010). Emotional appeals, by contrast, are also labeled soft-sell appeals that pursue a rather subtle sales proposition, convincing recipients by use of "a beautiful scene or the development of an emotional story" (Mueller, 1987: 53). They also stimulate a heightened level of arousal, which is highly likely to lead individuals to engage in certain (consumption-related) actions (Hawkins et al., 2003; Okazaki et al., 2010), triggered by feelings elicited through the ad (Leonidou and Leonidou, 2009). Rarely, they make "any explicit mention of the quality of the product" (Homer, 2008). These two theoretical concepts, nonetheless, blur at times, creating mixed advertising appeals characterized by both product specifics together with emotional statements (Kroeber-Riel and Esch, 2011). As part of companies' ethical and moral commitments (Wells et al., 2006), one more type of promotional appeal is starting to get used more frequently, namely CSR appeals, with marketers integrating references to their social and/or environmental projects in hopes of generating (more) favorable public responses (Diehl et al., 2014).

Having discussed the benefits of each message strategy, the question of which ad appeal should be utilized in OTC drug advertising arises. Affecting people's well-being and health, pharmaceuticals can be said to be rather high-involvement products (Diehl et al., 2007): they do not only constitute a highly sensitive topic but are also acquired rather sporadically; nonetheless, consumers prefer to gather information from numerous sources and engage in lengthy review processes before coming to a decision (Diehl et al., 2007). In terms of advertising, non-prescription drugs require extensive and detailed information to aid consumers in their evaluations that allow them to arrive at qualified purchasing decisions (Diehl et al., 2007). For this reason, informative ad appeals might be recommended, with the trend swaying towards mixed approaches (Koinig, 2012). Drawing upon insights from Direct-To-Consumer Advertising practices of prescription drugs, which generates considerable returns on investment in both the United States and New Zealand, emotional messages have also proven to be successful (Wolfe, 2002). This assumption will be put to the test in the present project, also including two rather new advertising approaches (mixed and CSR appeals) in addition to the two classical message strategies. Ads utilizing these four distinct appeals will be developed and tested in a cross-cultural setting in an attempt to answer the following question: "If the same appeal is homogeneously and favorably perceived in different markets, [why] should such an appeal [not] be a good candidate for use as part of a GCC [promotion] strategy?" (Okazaki et al., 2010: 20).

5 Theoretical Background and Model Development

The topic at hand presents a merger between two rather distinct areas of analysis; a theory applied to the field of pharmaceutical advertising, thus, warrants the integration of both existing advertising evaluation models and health models. Studies have shown that when elaborating on messages, recipients are far from being neutral; rather, some important variables influence their personal judgments and evaluations of advertisements (Vakratsas and Ambler, 1999). In the present investigation, a model incorporating those factors together with health-related variables will be developed and tested. After discussing selected models taken from both fields of research, suitable theories from both areas will be selected, borrowing components from the Elaboration Likelihood Model of Persuasion (ELM; Petty and Cacioppo 1981a; Petty and Cacioppo, 1981b), the Message Interpretation Process (MIP; Austin and Johnson, 1997), the Health Belief Model (HBM; Hochbaum, 1958; Turner et al., 2004) and the Health Action Process Approach (HAPA; Schwarzer, 1992). As such, the framework conceptualized herein is meant to overcome a separate examination of the health advertising domain by taking an interdisciplinary approach that can prove to be beneficial to both academics and practitioners alike.

The two core model types chosen for this project – the (advertising) message elaboration model as well as health models – are concerned with bringing about some kind of behavioral (intention) change. For this reason, the present thesis should not neglect to look at Social Cognitive Theory (SCT; Bandura, 1976) first, which is commonly used to predict behavioral modification or change in diverse contexts.

5.1 Social Cognitive Theory

Social Cognitive Theory (SCT) is devoted to scrutinizing how individuals turn to either media or social sources – in form of observations – in an attempt to acquire socially relevant knowledge on behavioral patterns and conducts (Bandura, 1976). (Non-)media-related sources offer guidance as to which behavior is socially accepted and how it is properly implemented. Thus, SCT has also become "known as social learning theory" (Schiavo, 2007: 39), emphasizing a reciprocal determinism between people and their environments (Glanz et al., 2008: 170).

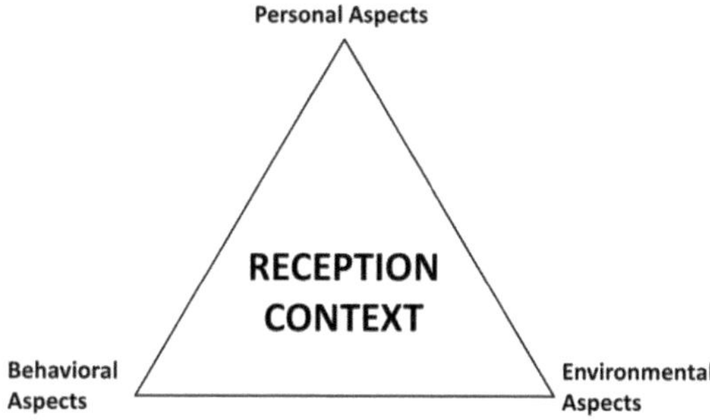

Figure 5: Social Cognitive Theory (Bandura, 1977/1986; own illustration)

SCT is a frequently consulted model to examine the degree of influence media messages and portrayals exert on individual thought processes, behavior(al intentions) and actions respectively (Bandura, 1997; Bandura, 2001). It presupposes an agentic approach (Bandura, 1986; Bandura, 2001b) by positing that every behavioral disposition is subject to personal aspects, environmental aspects and behavioral aspects, which constitute a "triadic, dynamic, and reciprocal interaction" (Rosal and Bodenlos, 2009: 49; see Figure **5**). Through observations, individuals develop an understanding of how they should behave (Bandura, 2001), drawing input and feeling (un)motivated to behave in a similar manner. In addition, individuals are given the chance to consult with peer members, who present valuable points of reference (Pelz, 1983) and function as a safety net offering guidance and support along the change process (Bandura, 1997; Bandura, 2001a). They can also act as role models who – through observational learning – allow individuals to draw inferences on how to activate their personal skills and engage in problem-solving activities and behaviors (Bandura, 1986; Bandura, 1997; Meichenbaum, 1984).

The thought and reflexive processes activated in the observation process affect human cognition; therefore, SCT classifies as a cognitive-motivational model. Applied to the health-care sector, it takes a variety of cognitive processes into consideration, e.g. "expectations, self-efficacy, attitudes, beliefs, and values, [which] influence various health-related behaviors" (Wright et al., 2008: 235) and facilitate adherence to treatment regimens (Dunbar-Jacob et al., 2009). Cognitive processes can take two forms, focusing on either threat appraisal or coping appraisal (Rogers, 1983; Pechmann et al.,

2003). This suggests that people's "behaviors are guided by two sets of expectations: (1) the expectation that an action will lead to a particular outcome and (2) the expectation a person has about his or her ability to perform this action [aka motivation]" (Wright et al., 2008: 236).

SCT owes its inclusion in the present project to one of its core variables, which is Self-Efficacy, which is closely linked to the empowerment concept. Assuming a person's very own expectations in their capabilities to drive the overall result, their level of perceived control is assumed to lead to more positive outcome expectancies (Wright et al., 2008; Bandura, 1977). Self-Efficacy thus impinges on the empowerment construct, alluding to "the situation-specific confidence that people have when they can cope with high-risk situations without relapsing to their unhealthy or high-risk habits" (Prochaska et al., 2009: 63). It is regarded as one of the most vital predictors of behavioral change in the health context (Rimal and Adkins, 2010; Ajzen and Fishbein, 1980), also determining behavioral implementation and maintenance (Schwarzer and Fuchs, 1996; Rimal and Adkins, 2010). Self-Efficacy may be activated and strengthened through the provision of information, which can be either of educational or commercial character, linking it to the advertising domain.

5.2 Advertising Evaluation Models

When it comes to determining how consumers are influenced respectively affected by advertising messages, different effectiveness or active path models try to offer comprehensible answers. Numerous theoretical approaches have set out to demonstrate how advertising works, ultimately convincing consumers to buy products or services they do (not necessarily) need (Vakratsas and Ambler, 1999). Those concepts, nonetheless, vary widely in focus: While some theories center on intermediate effects, other models pay more attention to behavioral effects. Whereas the former refer to consumer attitudes and beliefs, the latter portend to factors relating to buying behavior, for instance brand choice (Vakratsas and Ambler, 1999).

Research has dealt quite extensively with Advertising Evaluation Models, pointing out different hierarchies and paths that can be pursued. These range from market response and cognitive information models, over pure affect and persuasive hierarchy or low involvement hierarchy models to integrative and hierarchy-free models (for an overview, see Vakratsas and Ambler, 1999). However, as discussing all of these theories in detail would clearly exceed the scope of this thesis, only one category will be elaborated on in depth, namely Persuasive Hierarchy Models. This approach is deemed suitable for one central reason: In the case of non-prescription as well as prescription drugs, the classical hierarchy-of-effects sequence is assumed to apply, identified as "an order in which things happen, with the implication that the earlier effects, being necessary preconditions, are more important" (Vakratsas and Ambler, 1999: 32). Thereby, a stage of awareness is followed by the generation of knowledge which precedes liking, preference and conviction before a purchase intention is formed, ideally followed by an actual purchase (Vaughn, 1986).

Progressing through those stages suggests advertising effects to be subject to a particular linear order. Overall, a model belonging to this category claims that adverts offer (useful) information in the first place, which is then translated into persuasion in a second step (Vakratsas and Ambler, 1999). In this context, the most important factors determining both effects – information and persuasion – are personal involvement together with attitude towards the ad, which have both been comprehensively researched (Batra and Ray, 1985; Burke and Edell, 1989; Cacioppo and Petty, 1985; Homer, 1990; MacKenzie and Lutz, 1989; MacKenzie et al., 1986; Petty et al., 1983; Sawyer and Howard, 1991) and will also be incorporated in the framework conceptualized herein. Of the numerous models belonging to this category, the Elaboration Likelihood Model (ELM; Petty and Cacioppo, 1981b; Petty and Cacioppo, 1981b; Petty and Cacioppo, 1986) has been chosen as a point of reference, for it best meets the present study's requirements.

5.2.1 The Elaboration Likelihood Model

In 1981, Petty and Cacioppo came up with a very comprehensive persuasive model that has not lost its validity until today: the Elaboration Likelihood Model (ELM) of persuasion (Petty and Cacioppo, 1981a and 1981b). The model originated out of the authors' attempts "to integrate the many seemingly conflicting research findings and theoretical orientations under one conceptual umbrella" (Petty and Cacioppo, 1986: 125). Generally, the authors perceive elaboration as "the extent to which a person thinks about the issue relevant arguments contained in a message" (Petty and Cacioppo, 1986: 128), whereby elaboration is thought of as a continuum (Berry, 2007: 36). Moreover, it is seen, first and foremost, as a cognitive trait that follows certain, predefined stages. Hence, the ELM qualifies as a path model, with persuasion taking place through one of two prospective routes, a central route or a peripheral route, to be precise (see Figure **6**).

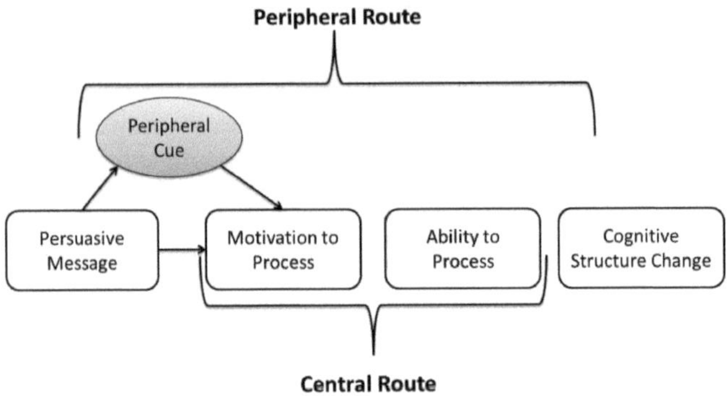

Figure 6: The Elaboration Likelihood Model (following Cacioppo and Petty, 1984; own illustration)

The central route regards information as crucial to individuals' opinion formation processes and considers advertisements as useful means to gain facts and knowledge about products and their features alike (Bettman, 1979; Hovland et al., 1953; McGuire, 1976). The peripheral route, by contrast, reaches an altered attitude not by means of information, but through personal reflection that is based upon (positive and/or negative) cues, which could, for instance, involve knowledgeable sources (also referred to as endorsers; Kelman, 1961; Mitchell and Olson, 1981; Mowen, 1980) and their expert statements (referred to as interferences; Petty et al., 1983). The inclusion of these cues makes a thorough and detailed (ad content) evaluation obsolete, as the source's credibility is not subject to questioning (Petty et al, 1983).

These two ELM routes correspond with two varying forms of information assessment, namely elaborate and non-elaborate evaluation. While the former refers to the rating of ad attributes and product features incorporated in the message, the latter judges attributes on a more subjective basis, such as product endorsers and implied stories (Vakratsas and Ambler, 1999; Berry, 2007). If an advertisement aims at triggering thought processes in consumers by utilizing extensive information, a central route is pursued. In this case, details on product features are included in the promotion, intending to convince consumers by use of tangible attributes and specifics (Petty, 1977; Petty and Cacioppo, 1978). A peripheral route applies more subtle mechanisms to catch buyers' attention, often generating approval by depicting attractive endorsers and appealing settings that are emotionally loaded, not giving any indication of product benefits or risks alike; messages then appeal to individual preferences instead.

As to attitude change's permanence, it has to be noted that in the case of a central path, change is considered to be lasting and permanent, whereas in peripheral pursuits, alterations are predicted to be only temporary and rather unstable (Cialdini et al., 1981; Petty and Cacioppo, 1980; Cook and Flay, 1978; Petty, 1977). Both high degrees of motivation and consumers' abilities to process issue-related information serve as preconditions for a central route; for peripheral paths, those two variables do not have to be necessarily high, as it is up to cues (to action) to determine attitude (Petty and Cacioppo, 1986): "The route taken is influenced by both motivational and ability factors. The former includes the relevance of the message and compatibility with previously held beliefs and attitudes. The latter includes the ability to process information logically and have the time to do so" (Green and Tones, 2010: 369). The ELM assumes messages to change individual attitudes by inducing a person to reflect upon the points made by the message (in the case of a central route) or manages to achieve conviction by use of compelling stimuli (in the case of a peripheral route; Berry, 2007).

An availability of numerous alternatives to the ELM cannot be denied (Batra and Ray, 1985; Bagozzi et al., 1979; Bagozzi and Burnkrant, 1979; Bagozzi, 1981; Fishbein and Ajzen, 1975; Lutz, 1975; Lutz, 1991), which proclaim consumer attitudes to predominantly be of utilitarian nature, deeming the route approach redundant. Opponents of the ELM further reject the notion of factual information being a necessary precondition for forming opinions towards products, but rather assume hedonic effects to take place: advertisements are said to generate a positive attitude toward a product without any form of evaluation taking place beforehand (Hirschman and Holbrook, 1982; Holbrook and Batra, 1987). This assumption is, however, seen to not apply to pharmaceuticals, which constitute high involvement products that depend on facts and rational arguments to 'sell' consumers (Diehl et al., 2008).

Nevertheless, the model will not be deployed on its own but will be paired up with elements derived from a theory concerned with message interpretation and meaning formation.

5.2.2 The Message Interpretation Process

Message interpretation is a relevant component in individuals' opinion forming and decision making processes (Fischhoff and Quadrel, 1991), which require "the consideration of options, possible consequences, and obstacles, ideally in a thoughtful and logical way" (Austin et al., 2002: 158). A theoretical model dealing with the interpretation and processing of those components is the Message Interpretation Process (MIP; Austin and Johnson, 1997), which was developed with the intention of providing a useful framework to trace consumers' cognitive involvement with messages of varying kinds.

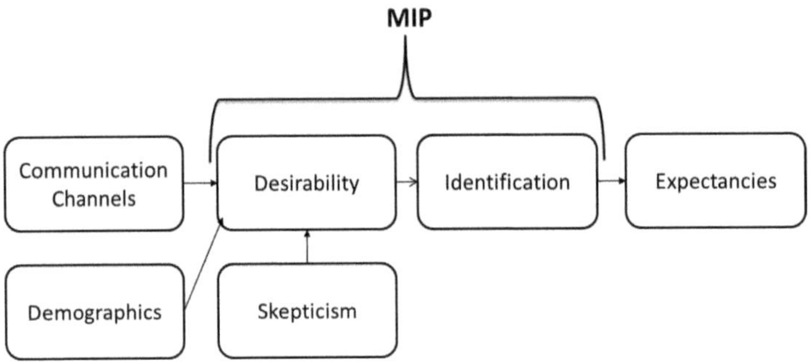

Figure 7: The Message Interpretation Process (Austin et al., 2006; own illustration)

Drawing from Social Cognitive Theory (Bandura, 1986), Expectancy Theory (Goldman et al., 1987) together with Persuasion Theory (Chen and Chaiken, 1999), this model sets out to describe how (advertising) messages are internalized by means of diverse processing strategies, which are either logically or emotionally loaded (Austin et al., 2002: 156). As depicted in Figure 7, the MIP identifies 'zones of relevance' (Austin and Johnson, 1997; Adoni and Mane, 1984) that trigger identification in recipients; once identification is achieved, a second process is initiated and beliefs of perceived similarity set in when content is measured against personal experiences or norms (Austin and Meili, 1994).

Since messages are interpreted in terms of their real-life resemblance (Austin and Meili, 1994; Austin et al., 1990; Gitlin, 1990), perceptions of similarity evoke positive feelings in consumers, leading them to conform (Austin et al., 1999; Austin et al., 2000; Austin and Knaus, 2000; Austin and Meili, 1994). For this reason, the MIP "theorizes that decisions that influence expectancy development, such as determinations of desirability, and identification, eventually will lead to decisions about actual behavior once opportunity and desire converge" (Austin and Knaus, 2000). In simplified terms, this means that "desirability should predict identification, which should predict expectancies, which should predict behavior" (Austin and Knaus, 2000).

In order to trigger those feelings and desires, messages have to gain consumers' attention first, which constitutes a central variable in the area of behavioral and cognitive psychology (Anderson, 2004): If attention is generated, recipients dedicate processing resources towards an object or event, also rendering this a well-researched concept in the marketing realm in general and in consumer psychology in particular (Johnson and Proctor, 2004). There, it is predominantly consulted to offer some indication of how attention can lead to behavior(al intention) as well as cognitive processing (Johnson and Proctor, 2004). The degree of attention elicited in consumers depends on various factors, of which some are visually dependent (e.g., color, intensity, conventional vs. unconventional design, endorsers, etc.) while others are textual (e.g., comprehension and understanding and/or message length, etc.).

An aspect missing from the two advertising evaluation models is the ultimate advertising goal, namely purchase intention. A model paying tribute to this exact aspect is the AIDA formula (Lewis, 1903). Being an acronym for the concept's step-by-step approach – consisting in consumers' **a**ttention to promotional activities (see section 5.4.4.), **i**nterest in product offering, **d**esire for product offering, and finally, **a**ction or actual product purchase – it perceives an advert's mission as follows: "The mission of an advertisement is to attract a reader, so that he will look at the advertisement and start to read it; then to interest him, so that he will continue to read it; then to convince him, so that when he has read it he will believe it. If an advertisement contains these three qualities of success, it is a successful advertisement" (Lewis, 1903). Once these three criteria have been fulfilled, the likelihood of purchase is not hampered.

Albeit the AIDA formula does not rely on information alone, it is regarded as a cognitive information model emphasizing the relevance of information and tangible product attributes (Vakratsas and Ambler, 1999) and utilizing consumer responses as well as communicative effects as a starting point by examining how they directly influence ad evaluations (Vakratsas and Ambler, 1999; Olsen et al., 1978). This model category is based on the assumption that the textual elements contained in advertisements influence consumer beliefs, attitudes, and ultimately actions (Mitchell and Olsen, 1977). It presupposes consumers to acquire information from texts, which is then either integrated into existing cognitive structures or dismissed, if regarded as being of little use (Mitchell and Olsen, 1977). By reducing search time and costs respectively, advertisements are expected to aid consumers in their purchase decisions (Bharadwaj et al., 1993; Nelson, 1970; Nelson, 1974). In this context, product category also comes into play: in the case of high-experience or high-involvement products, information on the product offering can guide purchasing decisions while decreasing price sensitivity (Davis et al., 1991; Lambin, 1976). As to message appeals, informative ads increase the likelihood of immediate purchase whereas in the case of emotional promotions, the likelihood of purchase is postponed (Rossiter and Percy, 1985).

Consulting solely two advertising models turns out to be insufficient for the present project. As a consequence, those approaches will be paired with two of the most central theories taken from the realm of health and health communication.

5.3 Models and Theories of Health (Communication)

Many different models have analyzed some health hazards in detail as well as addressing related preventive behaviors and measures. Amongst them, the most prominent ones are the Health Belief Model (HBM; Becker, 1974; Janz and Becker, 1984; Kirscht, 1988), Protection Motivation Theory (PMT; Maddux and Rogers, 1973; Prentice-Dunn and Rogers, 1986; Rogers, 1983), Subjective Expected Utility Theory (SEU; Edwards, 1954; Ronis, 1992; Sutton, 1982), the Theory of Reasoned Action (TRA; Ajzen and Fishbein, 1980; Fishbein and Ajzen, 1975), the Theory of Planned Behavior (TPB; Abrahman and Sheeran, 2000; Armitage and Conner, 2000; Conner and Sparks, 2005; Sutton, 2005; Weinstein, 2007), the Health Action Process Approach (HAPA; Schwarzer, 1992) and the Health Action Model (HAM; Tones, 1979; Tones,

1981; Tones, 1987). However, not all of the abovementioned theoretical approaches will be elaborated on in the present investigation in order to not exceed its scope. Only the two most valuable contributions will be discussed, whose core variables will then be integrated into an advertising elaboration model suited to examine evaluations of and responses to health promotions and medicinal advertisements in a cross-cultural context. These are the HBM and the HAPA.

5.3.1 The Health Belief Model (HBM)

The Health Belief Model (HBM) "is one of the first theories developed to explain the process of change in relation to health behavior" (Schiavo, 2007: 37). It was initially designed to predict patients' non-conformities with disease prevention measures or treatment adherence (National Cancer Institute and National Institutes of Health, 2002) and in response to "the widespread failure of people to accept disease preventives or screening tests for the early detection of asymptomatic disease" (Rosenstock, 1974: 328). Only later on was it applied to other medical conditions (Kirscht, 1974; Becker, 1974), leading the HBM to become the most commonly applied concept to explain both health behavior and promotion (Glanz et al., 2002; Sheeran and Abraham, 1996).

Since the 1950s, the HBM has managed to establish itself as one of the most widely used models in the health behavior research domain, where it has also risen in interest to health behavioral interventions (Glanz et al., 2008; Bond et al., 1992; French et al., 1992; Gillam, 1991; Witte et al., 1993). Being applied to other health contexts, it looked at people's responses to symptoms (Kirscht, 1974), their reactions to diagnosed illnesses, and especially their adherence to medical regimens (Becker, 1974; Glanz et al., 2008). Together with another long-standing health behavior theory (the Self-Regulation Model; Leventhal et al., 1980), the HBM is the only model to explicitly include symptoms as "central to patients' experiences of disease" (Glanz et al., 2008: 152) and proves to be useful by theorizing "that medical symptoms are cues to action that prompt behavior" (Glanz et al., 2008: 152).

Generally, the HBM is understood as a "risk learning model because the goal is to teach new information about health risks and the behaviors that minimize those risks" (Pechmann, 2001: 189). It focuses on how individuals perceive health-related threats as well as how they respond to these threats in terms of behavioral intentions and actions (Becker, 1974). This theory is, thus, one of the few approaches to consider the influence of personal opinions and their impact on health-related issues (Hochbaum, 1958), arguing "that decision making depends on individuals believing that a particular course of action will result in the likelihood of a valued outcome being achieved" (Green and Tones, 2010: 119).

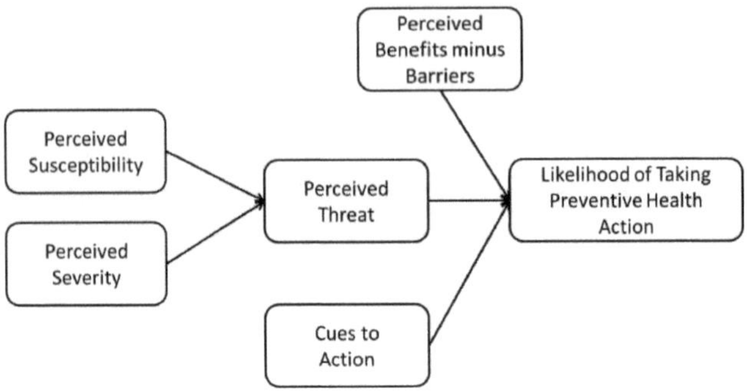

Figure 8: The Health Belief Model (Rosenstock, 1966; Rosenblatt et al., 1986; own illustration)

Originally, the HBM consisted of the following five components (see Figure **8**): (1) Perceived severity refers to the seriousness of an illness experience as felt by the individuals (Turner et al., 2004) and is often grounded in their medicinal knowledge (McCormick-Brown, 1999). (2) Perceived susceptibility alludes to how much risk is attributed to a particular medical condition, driving individuals in their preventive behaviors and measures (de Wit et al., 2005; Belcher et al., 2005). (3) Perceived threat defines the extent to which an individual regards itself as being at risk of attracting an illness (Rosenstock et al., 1988). (4) Perceived benefits judge the usefulness and value of a specific treatment option with regard to its risk-reducing potential, making it the major force that drives the adaption of preventive measures and precautions (Frank et al., 2004). (5) Perceived barriers relate to all hazards and obstacles that need to be overcome by an individual to arrive at a change in habits and behavior and, consequently, result in a heightened sense of well-being (Janz and Becker, 1984). Thereby, personal attitude towards transformation and evolution (and its success respectively) determines the ultimate (health) outcome (Center for Disease Control and Prevention, 2004).

The HBM was expanded over time in response to changing complexities and the following two core elements were added: (6) Cues to action involve numerous and diverse sources, such as people or events that might be capable of moving patients towards (adopting) a particular behavior (Graham, 2002). In the field of health care, service providers as well as public (advertising) campaigns or product labels are the most relevant means (Ali, 2002). (7) Finally, Self-Efficacy looks at how individuals' belief in themselves plays into the evaluation of their (own) abilities to achieve a specific goal (e.g., to find a cure for their disease or illness; Bandura, 1977). Building up this competence is of uppermost importance, as it highlights its relevance to the person affected. Health messages can, for instance, benefit respondents by reducing their levels of perceived threat, providing useful guidance on how to reduce said threat, simultaneously raising their perceived Self-Efficacy levels (Meyerowitz and Chaiken, 1987).

The HBM presumes that individuals are only willing to engage in any health-enhancing behavior if they are made aware of (1) the risks brought about by non-compliance or acts of omission and (2) the benefits associated with their actions (Becker et al., 1977; Janz and Becker, 1984; Stretcher and Rosenstock, 1997): "When confronted with information about a disease or illness, people generally assess their perceived susceptibility to the threat and attempt to gauge the severity of the threat were it to affect them" (Wright et al., 2008: 238). In order to adapt health-enhancing behavioral patterns, benefits of adherence or action must be conceived to outweigh potential barriers (Schiavo, 2007). These are then evaluated in relation to the incurred costs, which control both threat management and avoidance mechanisms (Wright et al., 2008). Hereby, the HBM heavily relies on the previously introduced "cues to action, or message features that prompt individuals to pay attention to the content of messages" (Wright et al., 2008: 239; Murray-Johnson and Witte, 2003). Distinguishing between internal and external cues to action, the former are initiated by the individual itself, as is the case with people who decide to start exercising or dieting out of their own accord; in the second instance, cues can be external, lying outside of the individual. External cues usually involve a third party member (e.g., family or peer group representative), who e.g. voices their concern or exerts pressure on behavioral change. They can also be media-mediated with, for instance, celebrities serving as role models or idols that trigger health-related behavioral change (Wright et al., 2008). If marketers want to ensure consumer engagement, they have to establish these cues as fixed components in their promotional messages (Murray-Johnson and Witte, 2003), recognizing them as useful features, which prompt recipients to pay special attention to message content (Wright et al., 2008; Murray-Johnson and Witte, 2003). At the same time, cues to action need to impinge on people's motivation to act, calling upon individuals to evaluate the resources they have at their disposal (Wright et al., 2008; Murray-Johnson and Witte, 2003).

5.3.2 The Health Action Process Approach

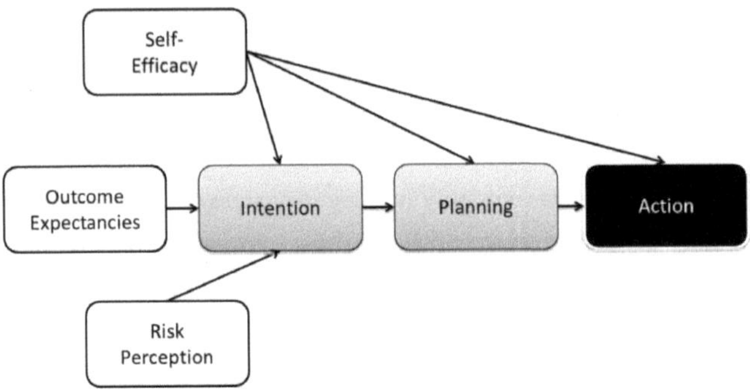

Figure 9: The Health Action Process Approach (Schwarzer, 1992; own illustration)

Just like the HBM, the Health Action Process Approach (HAPA; Schwarzer, 1992) presents a theory of health behavioral change due to its concern for the motives driving individual preventive action. Basing its assumptions on psychological theories, the HAPA "suggests that the adoption, initiation and maintenance of health behaviors must be explicitly conceived as a process that consists of at least a motivation phase and a volition phase" (Schwarzer, 2011). It assumes the change process individuals undergo to consist of at least two distinct stages (a motivational and a volitional stage), making this theory classify as a continuum or stage model (Schwarzer, 2008; Schwarzer and Luszczynska, 2008). Thereby, the following two phases need to be distinguished: (1) a pre-intentional (motivational) phase and (2) a post-intentional (volitional) phase (Schwarzer and Luszczynska, 2008). Whereas the first stage is said to directly bring about an intention to act, during the latter stage the actual intention is put into practice and (ideally) maintained in the long run (Schwarzer and Luszczynska, 2008; Heckhausen and Gollowitzer, 1987). Thus, the HAPA is predominantly used to "predict, explain and change health-related behaviors" (Sutton, 2008: 66; see Figure **9**).

Borrowing from the Theory of Planned Behavior (TPB; Ajzen, 2002), intention both precedes and directly determines actual behavior (Sutton, 2008; Schwarzer et al., 2007). During the initial phase, an individual arrives at the intention to act due to a perceived risk or threat. The moment a potential danger is detected, thoughts about prospective competencies, consequences and outcomes arise, leading directly into the volitional phase. These factors are considered to be crucial to self-treatment practices and moderate (health) outcomes; e.g. high perceived Self-Efficacy leads to positive expectations and, thus, benefits outcome results (Heckhausen and Gollowitzer, 1987; Schwarzer and Luszczynska, 2008).

In order to fully grasp the volitional process, the two components constituting this phase need to be examined in detail: Self-Efficacy and planning (Schwarzer and Luszczynska, 2008). Derived from SCT (Bandura, 1976), Self-Efficacy covers all cognitive beliefs in individuals' abilities to control both their immediate environments and influence their behaviors (Bandura, 1997). This means that Self-Efficacy "is concerned with judgments of how well one can execute courses of action required to deal with prospective situations" (Bandura, 1982: 122), also having an effect on the energy and effort individuals direct towards planning and implementing behavioral change (Schwarzer and Luszczynska, 2008).

Besides perceived Self-Efficacy, risk perceptions and outcome expectancies serve as predictors of intentions and behaviors respectively (Schwarzer, 2011), whereby the last determinant is regarded as the planning process' strongest driving force. In order for intentions to be translated into actual actions, they need to be 'originated' and planned with care – appointing a specific time, place and modality to the action – which then facilitates a change in individual behavior (Gollowitzer and Sheeran, 2007). Therefore, action "planning is specified as a mediator of the intention-behavior relationship" (Sutton, 2008: 67f.).

Both the Health Belief Model and the Health Action Process Approach classify as "theories that focus on beliefs and actions of individuals [and] were among the first theories of health behavior to be developed and remain the most widely used today" (Glanz et al., 2008: 150). They have not been subject to any significant changes within the past 15 years (Weinstein and Rothman, 2005), indicating their uncontested validity. What those theories have in common with regard to their approaches is that each of them (1) aims to avoid negative health conditions (2) by use of medications and/or (3) through self-protective means (Weinstein, 1993); one minor difference exists, though: they use different terms and labels in their conceptualizations (Weinstein, 1993). In order not to break with an established tradition, but also due to the fact that they have been proven to be suitable for application in different contexts, these theoretical elements will serve as a base for the model development in the present investigation.

5.4 Conceptual Framework: Core Variables

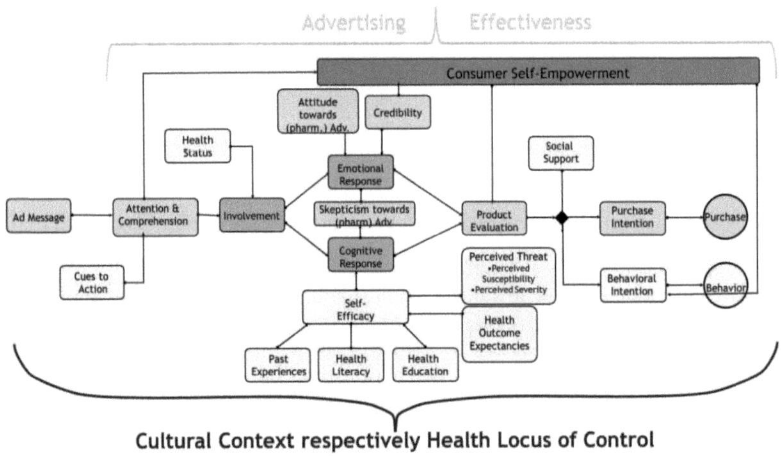

Figure 10: Conceptual Framework to Measure the Reception of OTC Drug Promotions in a Cross-Cultural Context (own representation)

In the following, a conceptual framework incorporating some core variables of the above-discussed theories will be developed. It will follow Fishbein's assumption, who contends that the most important variables influencing behavioral change include Self-Efficacy, intention, attitude as well as risk and outcome expectancies amongst others (Fishbein, 2008). The aim of this project is to develop and test a conceptual model which is meant to offer some insights into how a standardized stimulus ad (for a fictitious OTC medication) – corresponding in terms of design with results won from an earlier content analysis (Koinig, 2012; Koinig and Diehl, 2013) – is evaluated in different cultural settings. Variations in ad effectiveness are expected on the grounds of both individuals' health involvement and advertising involvement respectively, which might be culturally shaped; moreover, these might moderate degrees of consumer self-empowerment received from said stimulus ad (see Figure **10**).

The text fields are colored in accordance with their original theoretical background: blue variables are derived from advertising evaluation models whilst yellow boxes are taken from health communication theories; as some elements are featured in both disciplines, green boxes have been integrated as well. Consumer self-empowerment has been assigned to a red box as it has not been featured in research before and presents one focus of the project at hand (see RQ 2). Likewise, cultural context and Health Locus of Control (LoC) have been highlighted in red and are not only considered to influence all other variables, but are also assumed to moderate overall responses to pharmaceutical promotions (see RQ 1 and RQ 2).

In this upcoming section, relevant hypotheses will be developed in line with the most important theoretical concepts chosen for this project. A focus will be put explicitly on cultural factors that might moderate varying results across the diverse cultural dimensions (Uncertainty Avoidance, Power Distance, and Gender Egalitarianism) in general and Individual/Collectivism in particular, which will be incorporated into the discussion when required. Before discussing each variable individually, a cultural characteristic that is not part of the GLOBE project yet crucial to the present investigation needs to be introduced, namely the individual's Locus of Control (Rotter, 1966).

5.4.1 Locus of Control

One construct that is vital to the health context and likely to explain variations in both health involvement as well as self-medication practices is the Locus of Control dimension (LoC; Rotter, 1966). Despite not being explicitly listed as a variable of its own, it is relevant to the empowerment concept overall: "Locus of control refers to the extent to which cultural members perceive themselves to be in control of their health behaviors and health outcomes" (Dutta, 2008: 72f.). In general, it is either internally or externally located: if it is internal to the person, individuals are convinced that their very own behaviors can help them to achieve a desired outcome (individual responsibility);

in the case of an external locus of control, power and authority over the outcome are delegated to others (outer responsibility) and/or results are left to fate (Rotter, 1990).

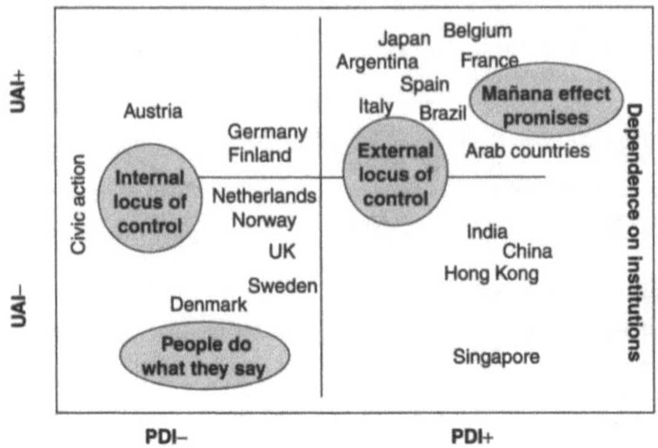

Figure 11: Global Locus of Control Manifestations (de Mooij, 2011: 242)

Figure **11** demonstrates that Locus of Control is dependent upon manifestations of two other cultural dimensions, namely Power Distance and Uncertainty Avoidance. Depending upon their cultural heritage, the countries can be assigned to either an internal Locus of Control (Germanic Europe) or an external Locus of Control culture (e.g., Latin America; House et al., 2004). Countries like Germany and Austria (low PD and high UA) are characterized by an internal locus of control, meaning that citizens are likely to take civic action and become actively involved, believing in their own capabilities to achieve (health-related) change. Brazil, on the other hand, is a nation exhibiting high degrees of Power Distance and Uncertainty Avoidance, where individuals seem to be more externally oriented and are likely to delegate responsibility to external sources or authorities instead of getting personally involved (de Mooij, 2011). The U.S., whose LoC manifestation is missing from Figure 10, is assumed to be quite similar to Austria and Germany by virtue of its GLOBE scores (House et al., 2004), insinuating that individualistic countries tend to possess an internal LoC (Smith et al., 1995).

The Locus of Control concept has also been transferred to the health domain, where it has received a considerable amount of academic attention (e.g., Wallston and Wallston, 1981; Helmer et al., 2012). While countries with a rather internal locus of control are assumed to impose responsibility for health-related matters onto individuals, who are invoked to consider and weigh options as well as tend to control the outcome themselves (de Mooij, 2011), externally oriented cultures place responsibility in the hands of acclaimed experts, reducing individual engagement to a minimum (Dutta, 2008; Pérez-Stable et al., 1992). For this reason, the following propositions can be derived:

P 1a: Externally-oriented individuals (e.g., Brazilians) are less interested in self-medication practices than internally-oriented nations (e.g., Austria, Germany, and the U.S.).

P 1b: Externally-oriented individuals (e.g., Brazilians) delegate responsibility for health-related matters to experts, which is less common in internally-oriented countries (e.g., Austria, Germany, and the U.S.).

An individual's health locus of control is a multidimensional construct consisting of three distinct theoretical components that moderate outcome perceptions: first, it is dependent upon people's evaluations of their capabilities respectively their willingness to take preventive action (internal locus); second, it is also subject to the actions taken by people in one's immediate environment (powerful-others locus) and, third, it considers intangible factors, such as fate or luck (chance locus; Anderson and Dedrick, 1990). The first dimension is of particular relevance to the area of self-medication: with health having been delegated to the individual and having been turned into a "personal responsibility" (Rose, 1990; Arney and Bergen, 1984), an internal orientation is presumed to prevail (Stewart et al., 1985), especially in individualistic countries, where autonomy and sovereignty are emphasized. In addition, an internal locus of control enables individuals e.g., to take their diet and exercise into their own hands and should also correspond with high self-medication practices, as it is expected to strengthen people's beliefs in their own skills: "Many people will feel especially positive about medications they took the initiative to obtain" (Findlay, 2001: 115). Based on these arguments, the following proposition can be derived:

P 1c: Internally-oriented individuals (e.g., respondents from Austria, Germany, and the U.S.) hold a more positive attitude towards self-medication practices than their externally-oriented counterparts (e.g., respondents from Brazil).

Research has come up with evidence that countries scoring low on the Masculinity (and high on the Gender Egalitarianism) index emphasize the value and quality of life.

In those countries, products are not utilized as status symbols but for their usefulness (de Mooij, 2011). It can be assumed that people from feminine countries are more responsive to OTC drug promotions as they consider these products beneficial to their health and well-being respectively. Yet, similar results are anticipated for masculine cultures, where people are advised to obey established norms, which advise them to fit in instead of sticking out.

5.4.2 (Advertising) Message Evaluation

Advertising messages are of uttermost relevance to commercial enterprises who want to sell their products to end users. By use of a unique design and message composition, desire for the offering is meant to be created. Thereby, the message comprises all elements – both visual and textual – through which consumers should be convinced and called to action (Rossiter and Bellman, 2005). Only if messages are regarded as appealing and/or of relevance, correspond with user demands and elicit favorable feelings, the ad's inherent sales intention is fruitful. Illustrations are frequently deployed to quickly familiarize the target audience with the marketer's sales proposition (Leonidou and Leonidou, 2009; Okazaki et al., 2010) – a function that cannot be taken up by written text blocks, which are, nonetheless, regarded as being more formal and credible (Piller, 2001).

Advertisements vary depending on the degree of product information they incorporate. In the health context, advertising executives have been advised to only use fear-evoking devices selectively (Piller, 2001), keep their ads' textual components rather short by focusing on the most relevant product information as well as stressing their offerings' unique features (USP; Piller, 2001). Textual and visual elements should be geared to each other (Batra et al., 1996), while textual elements alone have to be indicative of a common thread as well (headline, slogan and body text; Piller, 2001).

In theory, different advertising appeals can be distinguished: three traditional ad appeals (informative, emotional, and mixed appeals) and one progressive (CSR) appeal.

5.4.2.1 Traditional Ad Appeals

(1) Informative appeals are rather explicit and direct in their nature, basing their arguments on tangible information and proof (Okazaki et al., 2010a). They focus on prod-

uct-related aspects, such as their functionalities as well as utilities (Okazaki et al., 2010b), which can be evaluated independently and in all objectivity (Leonidou and Leonidou, 2009; Edell and Staelin, 1983). (2) Emotional approaches are characterized by a clear visual dominance and convey rather general associations and/or emotional messages with regard to a promoted brand (Okazaki et al., 2010a). These image-centered and subtle marketing approaches come in two forms: positive and negative emotional appeals (Main et al., 2004), with the former deploying humor and fantasy, while the latter intends to invoke fear or anger; the product is, hereby, praised as being the solution to a perceived problem (e.g., disease; Main et al., 2004). Positive emotional ads can contain, e.g. humor, nostalgia, fantasy or even sex. Negative emotional promotions, by contrast, normally center on negative emotions, such as fear, guilt, shame or anger. Thereby, the advertised product or service is presented as a solution or cure to a current medical condition (Main et al., 2004). (3) These concepts, nonetheless, rarely occur in their pure form in reality but blur at times, taking mixed forms. Thereby, mixed appeals are characterized by both product information and facts coupled with emotional recounts or personal statements (Kroeber-Riel and Esch, 2011).

5.4.2.2 The Progressive (CSR) Appeal

(4) Recently, discourses and standards on sustainability have been gaining in importance, with companies being pressured to publicly address (corporate) social and environmental practices. For this reason, CSR aspects are more frequently put at the center of companies' business and advertising communications, aiding firms in strengthening their positions by attributing a heightened relevance to sustainable, green or CSR claims (Esteban, 2008). Corporate Social Responsibility (CSR) builds on the assumption that today's "new consumers", who are more skeptical and demanding (Traulsen and Noerreslet, 2004), will reward enterprises for their sustainable and future-oriented programs by preferably buying their products (Levy, 1999), while punishing those who fail to do so (Sen and Bhattacharya, 2001; Simmons and Becker-Olsen, 2004; Koco, 2000).

Borrowing from social marketing, CSR messages often resemble the sick-baby-well-baby appeal, where a social topic ('sick baby') receives support or a cure that results in a transformation ('well baby'), serving as a firm's contribution to solving the social topic (Obermiller, 1995; Pomering, 2011). In the case of CSR appeals, messages are combined with elements borrowed from corporate image advertising strategy, which promotes the company itself rather than an actual product (Pomering, 2011). Hence, CSR appeals present hybrid promotional approaches (Rossiter and Percy, 1997) expressive of a holistic communication disposition that permits consumers to form "company images on the basis of [their] total experience of the company" (Kennedy, 1977: 121); credibility of CSR message appeals can be enhanced through endorsements by third-party organizations (Pomering, 2011).

This also holds true for the pharmaceutical industry, which has to face the public's decreasing trust in its products and services (Fontanarosa et al., 2004). Manufacturers are called upon to shape and control the release of information to various parties (Abraham, 2010; Collier and Iheanacho, 2002), whereby transparency especially concerns the disclosure of information on producers' responsible practices and efforts (O'Reilly, 2010; Sillup and Porth, 2008). For pharmaceutical companies, being (both ethically and socially) responsible means, first and foremost, providing affordable drugs to the public (Nussbaum, 2009). "[P]harmaceutical corporations have a moral obligation to society to provide the people, especially the poor, with affordable medication. Presently, pharmaceutical giants have disregarded this responsibility and therefore have ignored their Corporate Social Responsibility" (Lefebvre and Miller, 2006).

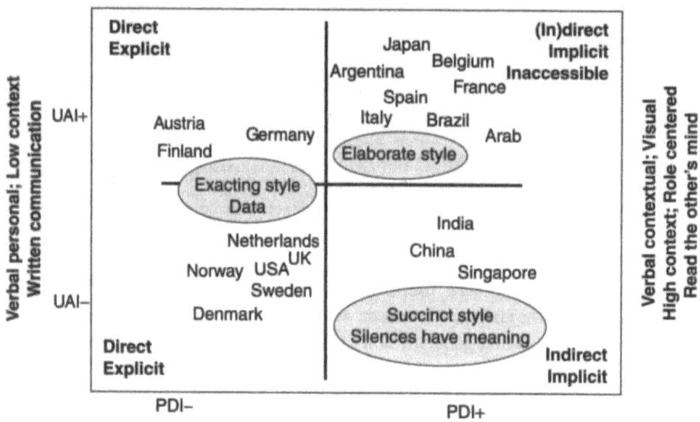

Figure 12: Preferred Global Communication Styles (de Mooij, 2011: 269)

In general, advertising messages have to be molded in accordance with recipients' preferred communication styles, which are influenced by both a nation's degrees of Power

Distance and Uncertainty Avoidance (House et al., 2004). These can be either direct, fact-centered (informative appeal) or indirect and image-centered (emotional appeal; see Figure **12**). Taking the U.S. American advertising style as an example, promotions are likely to stress values such independence, autonomy, assertiveness, competitiveness as well as explicit communication (Varnun et al., 2010) – a characteristic of individualistic cultures. Likewise, Austria and Germany (high UA and low IND/COL) are countries renowned to be linear-thinking and organized, consequently expressing the highest rates of acceptance for structured promotional messages. The United States (low UA and low PD), nonetheless, are said to be less serious, preferring humor and puns when contrasted with factual information (de Mooij, 2011). Consulting Spanish/Portuguese advertising styles, a less direct approach is taken, with messages being visually oriented, corresponding with the nation's more feminine orientation (de Mooij, 1998). Furthermore, collective relationships are stressed, leading marketers to depict people as part of their kin, underlining core values such as belongingness and individual's place in society.

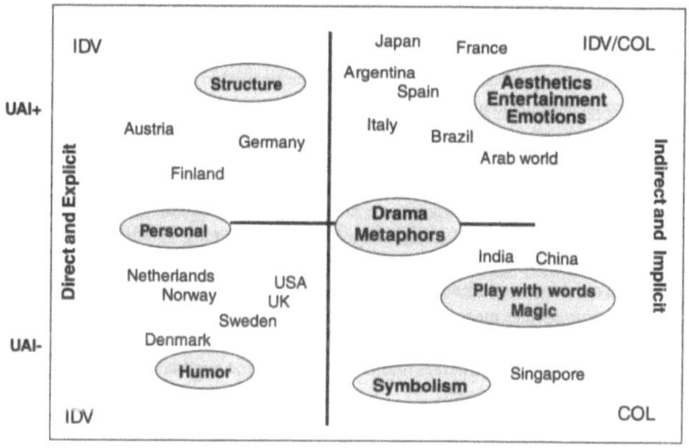

Figure 13: Global Acceptance of Communication Styles (de Mooij, 2011: 277)

An individualistic stance is reinforced by the use of personalized taglines that directly address and involve recipients. Product-merit appeals are utilized at the same time and are paired up with both direct and indirect comparisons, indicating the superiority of the product to be acquired (de Mooij, 1998). In the United States (low PD and low UA), print advertisements utilizing direct and explicit messages perform best, which could also be deployed in Austria and Germany (low PD and high UA); however, promotions should be very factual and structured, as the German promotional style tends to avoid words suggesting uncertainty (e.g., might, maybe). This does not necessarily have to be the case in the U.S. (Koinig, 2012; de Mooij, 1998; see Figure **13**).

Clear similarities exist between the three individualistic countries: Americans as well as Europeans tend to be rather analytic, focusing on clues that allow recipients to establish links and draw interferences linearly (Peng and Nisbett, 1999; Monga and John, 2007); likewise, analytic (reason-why) thinking is common as each issue is meant to be understood at its core (Walker et al., 2002). The fourth market to be examined in this study is Brazil, which is located at the other end of the continuum (high PD and high UA): There, promotions incorporating indirect, implicit as well as intangible information are said to be evaluated most favorably (de Mooij, 2011).

In spite of emotional messages being said to be received more favorable in a cross-cultural setting and especially suited for standardization (see section 4.3.4), choice of ad appeal is also influenced by product class: non-prescription drugs, which have been classified as rather high-involvement products (see section 4.3.6. in this chapter) warrant extensive review processes before an actual purchase is initiated and, thus, benefit from factual data (Diehl et al., 2007; Leonidou and Leonidou, 2009; Okazaki et al., 2010a). Hence, promotions for this product category are expected to appease and satisfy consumers' needs for information and are recommended to be based on tangible product attributes and features. Hence, the following hypothesis can be derived:

H 1: Informative ads for pharmaceuticals yield better results with regard to ad evaluation than (a) mixed or (b) CSR ads, which yield even better results than (c) emotional ads in all countries.

5.4.3 Cues to Action

Originally conceptualized as an essential component of the Health Belief Model (Rosenstock, 1974a; Rosenstock, 1974b), cues to action have become crucial elements of numerous well-designed health campaign messages (Murray-Johnson and Witte, 2003). "In order to effectively motivate target audience members to change health behaviors, campaign designers need to incorporate cues to action within campaign messages" (Wright et al., 2008: 239; Murray-Johnson and Witte, 2003). Cues to action involve numerous and diverse sources, such as people or events that might be capable of moving patients towards (adopting) a particular (health-enhancing or health-restoring) behavior (Graham, 2002; Dutta, 2008; Janz and Becker, 1984; Mattson, 1999). In the field of health care, service providers, public (advertising) campaigns or product labels are the most relevant means (Ali, 2002) and are consulted on a regular basis.

As message features prompting individuals to pay attention to health messages' content (Wright et al., 2008: 239; Murray-Johnson and Witte, 2003), cues to action are responsible for motivating individuals to appraise their available resources respectively skills to act upon a message by taking up a proposed action (Murray-Johnson and Witte, 2003). They are innate to the message itself and can – in the case of OTC drug advertising – cover references as to where further information can be found (e.g., on social networks and/or the manufacturer website), as well as include direct calls to action, e.g., coupons. No matter which call form is utilized, each of them prompts and stirs individual attention towards selected message elements (Murray-Johnson and Witte, 2003), ultimately reaching consumer engagement and empowerment once additional information is claimed.

5.4.4 Attention | Comprehension | Advertising Effectiveness

Research has uncovered that "the greater the number of ads, the less people pay attention to them" (Pappas, 2000). In an over-stimulated environment, people are literally flooded with advertising messages, leading to an overexposure respectively advertising clutter. Marketers are well aware of this dilemma and the frustration of targeting individuals who "are so dazed and cynical about ads that they automatically ignore them or turn off" (Voight, 2000). When questioned about how they feel in the process of encountering adverts, the most commonly cited words are "frustration, distrust and hostility" (Voight, 2000), with recipients perceiving messages as intrusive and unwelcome (Frith and Mueller, 2004).

In order to be recognized, promotional messages need to catch recipients' attention. Attention is only generated if content is of personal relevance to consumers and if they express motivation to process it (Klinger, 1975). As such, it is also contingent upon message characteristics (see section 5.2.). While visual information is more striking, images alone will not do but require information, the structure and clarity of which are key elements in consumers' information processing patterns (Menon et al., 2003; Menon et al., 2004) and factor into ad comprehensibility. Whereas too much information is said to lead to an information overload, too little information may result in trade-offs (Menon et al., 2004; Morris et al., 1989). In combination, both elements are assumed to foster understanding, defined as the comprehension of message content (Bereiter, 2002). Accomplishing comprehension together with understanding is vital, evoking desire in consumers to become more engaged in the decision-making and decision-finding process, especially in the pharmaceutical industry: "Stimulating consumers to seek more information about an advertised drug is an important behavioral outcome related to ad effectiveness" (Menon et al., 2004: 101).

Taken together, message attention and the resulting comprehension are some desired outcomes of advertising effectiveness, "defined as the degree to which a company's advertising induces the consumer to like the brand, improve its image, and/or purchase the brand" (Okazaki et al., 2006: 21; see section 5.2.). Ad effectiveness is concerned with whether or not a message has 'worked' and is commonly used to signal the degree according to which marketers' pre-defined promotional objectives have been achieved (Tones and Tilford, 2001). Just like ad persuasiveness – the potential of a message to influence recipients – effectiveness is conditioned by audience demographics, psychographics, health-related factors as well as consumer involvement (Menon et al., 2004).

Advertising effectiveness is also heavily dependent upon product category. Consumers are willing to readily believe claims promoting low-involvement goods (e.g. products used on a daily basis, such as toiletries) but statements in support of high-involvement products (like luxury goods) are less readily believed. As they impact people's health and wellbeing, pharmaceutical products are considered to be rather high-involvement products (see section 4.3.6.), which benefit from repetitive rational arguments and factual information stressing product benefits and distinctive features (Leonidou and Leonidou, 2009; Okazaki et al., 2010a). Consequently, when promoting OTC drugs and similar high-involvement products, informative appeals are considered the ideal promotional strategy. On the grounds of OTC drugs' product allocation, advertisers' claims are subject to heavy questioning and skepticism (Mueller, 2006; Obermiller et al., 2005). For this exact reason, effective "messages [need to] create the motivation to respond to a health threat and also cause the audience members to believe they have the appropriate resources to take action" (Murray-Johnson and Witte, 2010: 488), unfolding their empowerment potential.

5.4.5 Health Status

People's levels of health consciousness and their very own (subjective) health status need to be evaluated as a variable in its own right, whereby a lot of factors factor into this category (Gould, 1988), including (public and individual) health care and prevention measures. Health (problem) status refers to an individual's actual bodily state in terms of health and well-being (Bolton et al., 2006), which is affected by personal as well as behavioral aspects and further serves as an expression of a person's lifestyle (Nutbeam, 2000). An individual's subjective health experience is closely linked to human identity and self-perception (Petrie et al., 2007) and, as such, health status and its related constructs are not only constituents of recovery, but also of treatment adherence (Leventhal et al., 1997; Weinman and Petrie, 1997).

Bringing illness perception to patients' minds is highly relevant, not only facilitating their recovery but also their self-medication practices and, thus, enabling people to take personal control in treatment and preventive processes (Leventhal et al., 1980). A useful and uncomplicated tool to assess people's health states together with their individual illness perceptions is the Illness Perception Questionnaire (IPQ; Weinman et al., 1996), which allows both practitioners and patients to make sense of an illness as well as its symptoms, risks and problems (Weinman et al., 1996). To the area of OTC drug advertising, its last aspect – control– is of significance, which is closely linked to the empowerment construct by focusing on people's potential disease control mechanisms.

5.4.6 Involvement

A useful measure to judge the effectiveness of and consumers' responsiveness to advertising messages is the involvement construct. Definitions of involvement are as diverse as the areas it has been applied to, ranging from "personal relevance" (Zaichkowsky, 1985), over the "amount of arousal, interest, or drive evoked by a particular stimulus" (Mittal, 1982) to "a person's activation level" (Cohen, 1982). It is goal-directed in its very nature (Park and Mittal, 1985) and, according to Krugman (1965 and 1975), involvement needs to be perceived as the amount of linkages established between the promoted product and consumers' lifestyles at the moment of ad exposure. This initial perception was also taken up by Rothschild (1984: 127), who described the term as "an unobservable state of motivation, arousal or interest [...] evoked by a particular stimulus or situation [that] has drive properties. Its consequences are types of searching, information-seeking and decision-making". Involvement is, thus, a multidimensional construct deployed to predict consumer behavior (Thomsen et al., 1995; Jensen et al., 1989), assisting researchers in explaining how promotions work as well as how brand attitudes are formed (Andrews et al., 1990; Park and Young, 1986; Petty et al., 1983). In Kroeber-Riel and Esch's view (2011), involvement constitutes one of the most central concepts in advertising and consumer research, where it serves as a descriptor of a "person's perceived relevance of the object based on inherent needs, values, and interests" (Zaichkowsky, 1985; 342), impinging on both individual motivation to engage in an information search as well as information processing itself (Trommsdorf and Teichert, 2011).

"Involvement is a trait specific to the individual and not a function of a message or product" (Menon et al., 2004: 95f.), suggesting that it cannot be directly measured but qualifies as a hypothetical variable (Kapferer and Laurent, 1985) that can be ascertained by use of one of the following two instruments: the Consumer Involvement Profile (CIP; Laurent and Kapferer, 1985) or consumers' Personal Involvement Inventory (PII; Zaichkowsky, 1985; Rodgers and Schneider, 1993). The CIP looks at the antecedents of consumer involvement (Laurent and Kapferer, 1985), while the PPI primarily attributes involvement to a product's, ad's or situation's personal relevance (Zaichkowsky, 1985), turning involvement into an individual variable of difference (Laurent and Kapferer, 1985).

Regarding involvement as being solely dependent upon personal motivation is far too limiting; rather, it is a complex construct that is subject to numerous influences, such as personality variables, product variables, brand variables, situational variables, combined with both media and advertising variables (Zaichkowsky, 1985; Laurent and Kapferer, 1985; Muehling et al., 1993). Hence, besides (1) situational involvement, (2) personal involvement, (3) product or brand involvement, (4) media respectively advertising involvement, and (5) purchasing involvement also need to be distinguished (Esch, 2011).

Situational involvement functions as a filter (Kroeber-Riel and Esch, 2011), conditioning the intensity and relevance of product perception. Personal involvement is characterized by individual values and norms respectively, shaping the attributions products create in recipients. Product/Brand involvement is concerned with how perceptions of price, relevance and risk influence individual evaluations, also moderating personal gain. Media involvement factors in information processing and the amount of attention dedicated towards product examination (Zaichkowsky, 1985; Laurent and Kapferer, 1985; Muehling et al., 1993; Kroeber-Riel and Esch, 2011). Ultimately, purchasing involvement is subject to message factors and demographic information, which come into bearing in consumer behavior research (Slama and Tashchian, 1985; Lakshmi, 2011).

People's responses towards advertising and media messages are contingent upon people's actual states of **situational involvement**. As the name already suggests, specific – usually personally relevant – situations result in consumers being highly involved with a personal matter, product and/or event. Highly involved consumers, on the grounds of the offering's perceived usefulness and relevance, engage in lengthy and extensive decision processes, particularly paying attention to information concerning the product or similar offerings in the same product class (Robertson, 1976; Assael, 1981). Thinking back to the Elaboration Likelihood Model (ELM; Petty et al., 1983; for a detailed discussion, see section 5.2.1. in this chapter), very involved individuals are predicted to value information – they might even actively search for additional details and arrive at attitudes based on their cognitive evaluations. Thus, their reasoning is formed on the basis of the ELM's central route. Under low involvement conditions, factual information is not considered; instead, recipients solely pay attention to cues of action (see section 5.4.3.) and conviction occurs subtly through visual stimuli. Consequently, the ELM's peripheral route is pursued in low-involvement conditions (Petty et al., 1983). These elaborations reveal that situational involvement impacts ads as well as product relevance (Zaichokwsky, 1985; Celsi and Olson, 1988) and might only be temporary, differing from enduring involvement, which is more permanent (Havitz and Mannell, 2005).

Second, products can be classified in terms of their **personal involvement**. While low-involvement products are used on a regular basis and require little cognitive resources during their purchase, high-involvement products are bought irregularly and, at times, present a significant financial and/or cognitive investment; hence, they are attributed a higher risk than low-involvement products (Bloch, 1981; Antil, 1984; Laurent and Kapferer, 1985). Affecting people's wellbeing and health, pharmaceuticals classify as rather high-involvement products, which can be best marketed when including rational arguments and concrete product attributes (Diehl et al., 2007).

Advertisements are characterized by different goals, one of them being the creation of desire for a product and, ultimately, initiating a product purchase. According to Laurent and Kapferer (1985), there are four noteworthy antecedents to **product and brand involvement**: (1) product importance and perceived risk (imporisk); (2) the likelihood of a mispurchase (risk probability); (3) the product's symbolic value (sign or utilitarian value); and (4) the product's emotional value (hedonic value). Suggesting a product to be always judged with regard to its benefits and risks, the negative effects associated with mispurchases must be reduced; moreover, product usability (utilitarian dimension) as well as its pleasantness need to be established (hedonic dimension; Batra and Ahtola, 1990). Thereby, "the hedonic determinant of overall evaluations is presumed to be based on the consumer's assessment of how much pleasure he gets; his utilitarian determinant is based on his assessment about the instrumental value of the brand's [or product's] functional attributes" (Batra and Ahtola, 1990). Consumption experiences are, nonetheless, not limited to either form but rather present a mix between utilitarian and hedonic components; the latter are present in every consumption situation to a greater or lesser extent (Havlena and Holbrook, 1986). For non-prescription drugs, product relevance is high once first signs of illness are noticed; as soon as individuals start looking for remedies to ease their conditions, OTC drug risks are evaluated as being far lower than those of other (prescription) substances. Consequently, they might be acquired by merit of their health-restoring function and efficacy. Unless recipients are not reminded of the promotional campaign or encounter an attractive poster at the drug's point of sale, hedonic values and emotional experiences do not have a bearing at this stage.

Involvement with a given product is central to promotional success and said to lead to **media** and/or **(advertising) message involvement** in turn (Laczniak et al., 1999), with the intrinsic sources of the former being directly related to the latter (Celsi and Olson, 1988), plotting product involvement as an immediate determinant of advertising message involvement: "Consumers' involvement in products is believed to moderate considerably their reactions to marketing and advertising stimuli" (Kapferer and Laurent, 1985: 48). Advertising message involvement is then conceptualized as an individual's motivational state, which is likely to trigger message processing (Laczniak et al., 1989). Studies have produced evidence of product involvement affecting numerous other measures, amongst which brand attitude, ad attitude and brand name recall are the most important ones (Phelps and Thorson, 1991; McGrath and Mahood, 2004; Gardner et al., 1985). For instance, media messages are particularly appealing to individuals who have been struck my disease and have started to pay special attention to adverts promoting a remedy for their conditions. So, if they feel the need to acquire a medical product, their involvement with respective media messages is assumed to be positive.

Finally, **purchasing involvement** comes into play, which can be both cognitive and affective, elicited by corresponding advertising styles (Park and Young, 1984): "Cognitive involvement stresses the individual's informational processing activities and the achievement of idealization states" (Zaichkowsky, 1994: 60). By contrast, affective involvement is driven by emotional states, underlining the individual achievement associated with product purchase and, ultimately, use (McGuire, 1974; Zaichkowsky, 1994). When processing non-prescription drug promotions, both states can be activated, depending on the advertising appeals utilized: if informative messages are encountered, consumers might be cognitively involved due to the promotion's focus on rational arguments and tangible product features. Unless combined with flattering visual stimuli, as it is the case with mixed appeals, no affective states are triggered; however, they dominate, if emotional promotions are utilized and want to convince consumers by, e.g. portraying desirable end results (see section 5.4.2).

From the start, involvement has been regarded as a psychological construct (Slama and Tashchian, 1985) that is closely related to the individual in general and its ego specifically (Sherif and Cantrill, 1947). As such, it is connected to behaviors and attitudes, which it directly influences (Slama and Tashchian, 1985). Involvement is driven by positive effects, beliefs in people's own capabilities and outcome expectations (Chaffee and McLeod, 1973), which will be discussed in the next section amongst other cognitive and emotional variables.

5.4.7 Responses: Cognitive vs. Emotional Effects

In the area of advertising (effectiveness) research, two streams of argumentation have developed, proclaiming that responses to promotional messages are either cognitive (Greenwald, 1968) or emotional (Holbrook and Hirschman, 1982; Holbrook, 1984) and, thus, mutually exclusive. But is this really the case – or can responses instead of being either cognitive or emotional be both cognitive and emotional?

Cognitive reactions to message stimuli occur as a result of persuasive communication attempts (Petty et al., 1981) and are conditioned by the ways recipients cope with the information they are presented with (Greenwald, 1968), resulting in attitude changes and behavioral modifications. Attitudes are best conceptualized as "global and relatively enduring evaluations of objects, issues, or persons" (Petty et al., 1991: 242) that act as predictors of individual behavior (Webb et al., 2000). Following a cognitive structural approach (Lutz and Swasy, 1977; Olson and Mitchell, 1975), beliefs are the core components of (ad) effectiveness, moderating attitudes, behavioral intentions and actual behavior (Fishbein and Ajzen, 1975). Established trends in consumer psychology proclaim (pre-)established knowledge to be linked to recipients' expectations about a particular product (category), further fueling their motivations to process and consider advertising stimuli as relevant (Sujan, 1985). New information always builds on established knowledge-structures, so-called schemata (Goodstein, 1993), whereby the information contained in an advertisement activates cognitive structures and is integrated into existing cognitive patterns; previous and current beliefs are combined, impinging on the modification of both attitude and behavior (Fishbein and Ajzen, 1975).

Responses to communication are always personal and affective, too (Kelman, 1953; Festinger and Maceoby, 1964; Wright, 1974), warranting the inclusion of emotional parameters. Reactions originate out of the assumption that attitudes towards the ad consist of two dimensions, namely a cognitive and an emotional one (Shimp, 1981). While consumers' cognitive responses are fostered by both the ad's overall execution and source characteristics, credibility as well as product attributes, emotional aspects pay tribute to the general feelings induced by the ad, such as joy, love, fear, etc. (Hill and Mazis, 1986). Moreover, responses are said to differ, depending on the advertising appeal used (Golden and Johnson, 1983), which justifies the utilization of bi-polar scales when measuring advertising effectiveness (Mitchell and Olson, 1981). In order to nourish both trains of thought, relevant cognitive as well as emotional variables will be discussed in the following.

5.4.7.1 Self-Efficacy (Cognitive Variable)

Individual responses towards media content may vary and are subject to the context of reception together with personal skills, among which a person's perceived Self-Efficacy is the most relevant factor of influence (Nutbeam, 2008). Being one of the most reliable predictors of behavioral change (Rimal and Adkins, 2010), Self-Efficacy looks at how individuals' beliefs in themselves play into the evaluations of their (own) abilities to achieve a pre-defined goal (e.g., to find a cure, treatment or remedy for their disease or illness; Bandura, 1977). It is understood as "the power to produce an effect" (Wurtele and Maddux, 1987), which sets up Self-Efficacy as an essential aspect in all stages of behavioral change in the health domain (Bandura, 1997). Generally, (pre-)action Self-Efficacy, coping Self-Efficacy as well as recovery Self-Efficacy need to be differentiated (Marlatt at al., 1995). (Pre-)Action or task Self-Efficacy, as the term suggests, precedes action and alludes to the moment an intention to act originates. Coping or maintenance Self-Efficacy refers to individuals' own optimisms towards their capabilities, enabling them to improve (and, in the long run, preserve) their positive health states. Recovery Self-Efficacy addresses all potential negative action outcomes, which force an individual to reflect upon their doings and start anew by regaining faith in their competencies (Marlatt, 2002). Promotional messages can also appeal to an individual's Self-Efficacy: as soon as people start showing first signs of illness symptoms, they might feel invoked to take some action (pre-action Self-Efficacy); if they conceive of themselves as being capable of treating themselves, they are likely to purchase a self-medication preparation (coping Self-Efficacy). Ideally, the cycle ends here; in case the remedy does not work, however, respondents have to look for alternatives (e.g., new or different treatment options; recovery Self-Efficacy).

Self-Efficacy is, furthermore, closely linked to two forms of expectancy: efficacy expectancy or individuals' beliefs in their own capabilities (e.g., to exercise and/or adopt a particular behavior) and outcome expectancy or the likelihood of the (behavioral) action resulting in a desired outcome (Dunbar-Jacob et al., 2009; Bandura, 1977). Self Efficacy Theory (Bandura, 1977) proclaims individuals to only take up (and later, maintain) a behavior, if their beliefs in their own skills dominate (efficacy expectancy) and if they are convinced that their behavior can produce a desired effect (outcome expectancy; Dunbar-Jacob et al., 2009). As relapses are possible at any time of the process, some general characteristics surface: (1) Self-Efficacy is both reciprocal and dynamic, conditioned by a person's immediate environment and its interplay with the individual affected (Frankish et al., 1999). (2) It is context-specific, depending upon a person's ability to perform a given or intended action (Bandura, 1977). (3) Previous relapses or failures are likely to negatively affect a person's degree of perceived Self-Efficacy (Murray-Johnson and Witte, 2010).

In the theoretical context, Self-Efficacy is only addressed in Protection Motivation Theory (PMT; Maddux and Rogers, 1973; Prentice-Dunn and Rogers, 1986; Rogers, 1983; Bandura, 1977), where it considers all problems that might be encountered while working towards overcoming a particular threat or disease (Bandura, 1977). Yet, it is of essence to include this variable into a present-day health-related model, since it "is an important influencing agent in motivational, cognitive and affective processes" (Bandura, 1992), impinging on the degree of effort and preservation individuals direct towards the task being executed (Schwarzer, 2011).

Based on this argumentation, Self-Efficacy becomes a core determinant in the health care domain (Hendershot et al., 2009), where it wields some power in the areas of health behavior change (Bagozzi and Warshaw, 1990; Schwarzer, 1994), health maintenance (Wright et al., 2008) as well as health-information seeking practices (Rimal, 2001). Individuals' degrees of Self-Efficacy control for the likelihood of behavior initiation and/or modification, with volitional control impacting behavioral change in the first place (Ajzen and Fishbein, 1980), as well as maintenance in the second place (Schwarzer and Fuchs, 1996; Rimal and Adkins, 2010). Individuals displaying heightened degrees of Self-Efficacy are renowned for initiating health-enhancing behaviors more frequently, put more effort into maintaining their current health status, and also do not recoil from setbacks, but decide to start all over again (Bandura, 1977; Bandura, 1986; Maibach and Murphy, 1995; Rimal and Adkins, 2010). As such, "Self-Efficacy influences the choices individuals make, their aspirations, how much effort they mobilize in a given endeavor, how long they persevere in the face of difficulties and setbacks, whether their thought patterns are self-hindering or self-aiding, the amount of stress they experience in coping with taxing environmental demands, and the vulnerability of depression" (Dutta, 2008: 30; Bandura, 1986: 257). If Self-Efficacy is highly distinct, individuals might be more inclined to favorably rate their (self-medication) capabilities than people with weaker manifestations; promotions appealing to and reinforcing those skills should, thus, be met with more positive responses by the former group, while leaving the latter rather unaffected.

Self-Efficacy is both situation and context specific (Prochaska et al., 2009; Bandura, 1997) and inasmuch as individual abilities are subject to constant reassessment, perceived degrees of Self-Efficacy allow people to organize and execute a specific course of action to attain a specific goal (Dutta, 2008: 30; Bandura, 1986). But individual capabilities alone are insufficient to measure Self-Efficacy and need to be paired up with resources drawn from individuals' immediate environments, which together award consumers the opportunity to seize control over a given risk situation, counteracting any potential harm through the utilization of health-enhancing behaviors (Bandura, 1977; Wright et al., 2008).

The implementation of Self-Efficacy, nevertheless, often falls victim to barriers, which "act as obstacles to the performance of a recommended response" (Murray-Johnson and Witte, 2010: 483; Witte, 1995). Perceived barriers are numerous and diverse in nature, covering health expenses, bodily discomfort, environmental constraints plus social shortcomings (Murray-Johnson and Witte, 2010). A lack of specific knowledge might be perceived as a barrier, too, that prevents Self-Efficacy from originating (Parrott et al., 1998). Barriers can be either internal (discomfort, ache) or external (health expenses, social stigmatization; Allison et al., 1999; Murray-Johnson and Witte, 2010), reducing individuals' likelihood to perform a recommended behavior or response (Witte, 1995). In order to circumvent the creation of barriers, health messages must be tailored to audience needs and wishes, specifically stressing the benefit of achieving desired health outcomes through the mobilization of self-efficient actions and measures (Murray-Johnson and Witte, 2010).

5.4.7.2 Health Outcome Expectancies (Cognitive Variable)

Following Bandura (1987), individual behavior is highly influenced by the desired outcome of a given action, which is guided by people's expectations (Scheier et al., 1984) and perceived Self-Efficacy (Hendershot et al., 2009). Outcome expectancies are conceptualized as all "anticipated outcomes of a given behavior or experience" (Hendershot et al., 2009: 138) that are nourished by individual beliefs of an initiated performance resulting in specific outcomes, may they be positive or negative; these expectations then either trigger or suppress said actions (Murray-Johnson and Witte, 2010; Rosenstock and Kirscht, 1988). Nutbeam (2000) distinguishes between three different forms of health outcomes, namely (1) health and social outcomes, (2) intermediate health outcomes and (3) health promotion outcomes. The last category is of uttermost important to the project at hand, alluding to "those personal, social and structural factors that can be modified in order to change the determinants of health" (i.e. intermediate health outcomes) by use of communicative means (Nutbeam, 2000: 261). Promotions can, for example, invoke respondents to slightly change their behaviors or take up recommended actions to improve their current health situations (e.g., through the usage of an appropriate self-medication substance, signs of pain can be relieved temporarily whilst improving bodily functionality).

(Health) outcome expectations cover both perceived benefits and risks (barriers). Perceived benefits judge the usefulness and value of a specific treatment option, with the goal of reducing any potential risk, driving patients in the adoption of preventive measures and precautions (Frank et al., 2004). All hazards and obstacles that need to be overcome by an individual to achieve a change in habits and behaviors are encompassed by perceived risks (Paasche-Orlow and Wolf, 2007); an awareness for their existence as well as ways respectively means of overcoming them should result in a heightened sense of personal well-being (Janz and Becker, 1984). Thereby, individuals' attitudes towards both bodily transformation and evolution (and its success) determine the ultimate (health) outcome, steering consumer expectations at the same time (Center for Disease Control and Prevention, 2004).

"[E]xpectations are consumer-defined probabilities of the occurrence of positive and negative events if the consumer engages in some behavior" (Oliver, 1981: 33). When estimating expectations of both illness risks and disease outcomes, different factors (of social, economic and environmental nature) come into play (Townsend et al., 1988; Harris et al., 1999). Differences in response are usually conditioned by consumers' varying encoding strategies, values, goals as well as self-regulation practices (Mischel et al., 1996). The last component, self-regulation, signifies a process in the course of which people initiate, adapt, or abandon actions that help them to promote the attainment of their individual goals, plans, or objectives (Carver and Scheier, 1998). It is closely related to outcome expectancies, which drive individual decisions vehemently (Nenkov et al., 2007), specifically if information is provided. The availability of information on a health matter can be useful as "[s]uch information leads to better self-regulation and more appropriate behavior modification" (Nenkov et al., 2007: 127); it is usually also accompanied by a reduced amount of uncertainty towards the disease respectively potential treatment options (Czaja et al., 2003).

5.4.7.3 Perceived Severity and Perceived Susceptibility (Cognitive Variables)

Two cognitive variables assumed to involve consumers in health(-related) matters are perceived severity and perceived susceptibility (borrowed from the Health Belief Model [Becker, 1974; Rosenstock, 1974] and the Protection Motivation Theory [Rogers, 1975; Rogers, 1983]). Perceived severity describes the seriousness of illness experience as felt by the individual (Turner et al., 2004) and is often grounded in a person's medicinal knowledge (McCormick-Brown, 1999). It "relates to the magnitude of harm believed to be a likely consequence of the [health] threat" (Murray-Johnson and Witte, 2010: 478), whereby the greater the perceived severity, the higher are both attention towards message content and motivation to take up self-protective measures to combat the perceived threat (Murray-Johnson and Witte, 2010).

Perceived susceptibility, in contrast, is understood as the amount of vulnerability or risk individuals assign to a particular medical condition, driving their preventive and health-fostering behaviors (de Wit et al., 2005; Belcher et al., 2005). Thereby, individuals judge their potential of contracting a disease; if addressed as part of a health message, the likelihood of developing an illness might be counteracted (Ronis, 1992). So, while the latter variable deals with individuals' very own assessments of their own capabilities to overcome their unhealthy states, the former pays attention to the expected outcome in case a preventive behavior is taken up (Dutta, 2008; Mattson, 1999; Rosenstock, 1966). In combination, those two variables (perceived susceptibility and perceived severity) constitute the perceived threat that is innate to a disease (Witte, 1992). In the worst case scenario (e.g., when a disease gets evaluated as highly serious or even contagious), a state of threat is entered (Stretcher and Rosenstock, 1997), meaning "the likelihood that individuals will experience the negative consequences associated with a threat" (Murray-Johnson and Witte, 2010: 480; Witte, 1992a; Witte, 1992b). This new variable has an impact on how individuals receive and respond to health information, channeling their strife to engage in health enhancing behaviors (Sturges and Rogers, 1996; Witte, 1992).

In case message designers set out to create perceptions of susceptibility, they have to utilize personalized references instead of neutral or general statements to increase individuals' motivation to act (Murray-Johnson and Witte, 2010; Witte, 1993). Marketers can achieve a heightened state of threat experience by depicting an endorser recipients identify with or someone who is similar to them (Murray-Johnson and Witte, 2010): "Messages showing individuals of the same age, ethnic orientation, socioeconomic status, and education level tend to increase perceived susceptibility" (Murray-Johnson and Witte, 2010: 480; Gonzales et al., 1990).

Apart from the abovementioned components, two additional variables need to be added to this complex yet flexible health model: attitude towards (pharmaceutical) advertising and skepticism towards (pharmaceutical) advertising.

5.4.7.4 Attitude and Skepticism Towards Advertising and/or the (Print) Ad (Emotional and/or Cognitive Variables)

Attitudes are defined as "general evaluations people hold in regard to themselves, other people, objects, and issues" (Petty and Cacioppo, 1986: 127). These assessments bear on experiences, which can be cognitive, affective or behavioral in their nature and guide future actions (Petty and Cacioppo, 1986). Attitudes are central components in social psychology (Green and Tones, 2010), where they represent "a person's general feeling of favorableness or unfavorableness towards some stimulus object" (Fishbein and Ajzen, 1985) as well as a function of their attribute evaluations (Fishbein and Ajzen, 1985).

Attitude towards advertising is understood as an evaluation of message content in affective and cognitive terms (Diehl et al., 2008; Lutz et al., 1983; Edell and Burke, 1987): "The cognitive element consists of subjects' judgments of the ad's characteristics (i.e., descriptions of the ad itself, such as 'humorous, informative...') whereas the affective element is based on feelings subjects experience during ad exposure (e.g., amused, fed up, moved)" (Burke and Edell, 1989: 70). Attitude is said to be an important variable consulted to both determine and measure consumers' reactions towards the promotions encountered, rendering it a valuable predicator of purchasing behavior (Diehl et al., 2008). According to Biel (1990), positive attitudes towards the ad are also closely connected to individual awareness, behavior or preference (Franzen, 1994).

Over the years, attitude has become one of the most intensively researched aspects of ad effectiveness (Brown and Stayman, 1992), with attention towards and liking of an ad being said to correlate with positive brand attitudes (Holbrook, 1978). As such, attitudes are seen in relation to the values and beliefs held by individuals about product and brand attributes (McQuarrie and Langmeyer, 1985). Inasmuch as brand cognitions constitute important links connecting a brand with ad attitudes (Homer, 1990), these statements can be read in support of the claim that "attitudes clearly have become the central focus of consumer behavior" (Kassarjian and Kassarjian, 1979: 3).

Skepticism has to be distinguished from attitude and defines individuals' tendencies to meet advertising claims with disbelief (Obermiller and Spangenberg, 1998). The construct was first introduced by Friestad and Wright (1994) as part of their persuasion knowledge model, which posits that skepticism is not only socially learned but also prone to alteration over time on the grounds of continuous persuasion processes (Obermiller and Spanberg, 1998; Obermiller et al., 2005). It refers to a cognitive state of mind over the course of which thoughtful processing, information evaluation data gathering occur (Austin et al., 2002; Austin and Knaus, 2000; Blosser and Roberts, 1985). Skepticism is concerned with an individual's degree of willingness to believe (consider) or disbelieve (dismiss) advertising claims (Obermiller and Spanberg, 1998; Obermiller et al., 2005); relating to promotional information, messages' truthfulness and relevance as well as advertisers' motivations are repeatedly subject to scrutiny (Obermiller and Spanberg, 1998).

Skepticism towards promotional messages is moderated by both individual and social factors, since consumers are socialized to doubt the information they are presented with (Darby and Karni, 1973; Ford et al., 1988; Nelson, 1970). Doubt (aka skepticism) can originate in response to various ad elements, such as message claims, motives held by the promotional party, congruence between promoted and individual values, audience specifics, and/or product category (DeLorme et al., 2009). Since a multitude of factors impinge on skepticism, it is closely linked to other marketing concepts, such as attitude towards advertising or a particular ad, ad believability, ad truthfulness and ad trust (Obermiller et al., 2005: 10; DeLorme et al., 2009). This being the case, skepticism is believed to influence or even alter recipients' immediate responses to advertisements (Obermiller et al., 2005)

While scrutinizing both constructs in isolation is unavoidable, they are, nevertheless, closely related to one another (Diehl et al., 2008). Studies have shown that people displaying negative attitudes and/or high levels of disbelief towards a promotion are also more likely to distrust and be skeptical of its content, dismissing promotional messages as irrelevant far more quickly than their more optimistic counterparts (Pollay and Mittal, 1993). Numerous studies have produced proof of widespread skepticism and distrust amongst consumers in general (Boush et al., 1994; Calfee and Ringold, 1994); here, the area of pharmaceutical advertising does not present an exception (Diehl et al., 2007; Diehl et al., 2008), where studies have further proven skepticism to be negatively associated with drug involvement, comprehensibility of ad content as well as advertising as a source of health information in general (Diehl et al., 2007; Huh et al., 2012).

While similar results might be anticipated for attitude towards drug advertising, results in the pharmaceutical realm are somewhat contradictory: although consumers tend to regard pharmaceutical promotions as having low levels of likeability , they are not very skeptical of them (Diehl et al., 2008): two cross-cultural studies reported that ads promoting OTC drugs were perceived more favorably by the public than those messages advertising prescription (DTC) drugs (Diehl et al., 2008). In terms of skepticism towards medical advertising, levels were less established than scores measuring skepticism towards advertising in general, independent of drug category (prescription vs. non-prescription medications; Diehl et al., 2007). Yet, intercultural differences could be detected, with U.S. American consumers displaying a lesser degree of skepticism towards advertising in general and towards non-prescription drug promotions in particular, when compared against German recipients (Diehl et al., 2008).

Both consumers' negative attitudes and skepticism levels towards (pharmaceutical) ads might be grounded in messages' complex structures (e.g., the excessive use of medical jargon; Steyr, 1999) as well as advertisers' communication practices, who often have a habit of apparently 'whitewashing' potential risks and side effects (Levitt, 1996). Thus, consumers might be tempted to disregard any promotional information as irrelevant, ignoring leaflets or other printed content altogether (Herzenstein et al. 2004). Favorability of attitudes and varying levels of skepticism are also related to the amount of information consumers are presented with. Research has demonstrated that informative ad appeals hold the potential to intensify and strengthen product relevance and purchase intention (Okazaki et al., 2010). This state is, nonetheless, not achieved through more favorable attitudes, but by means of the conviction function that is inherent to the actual advertising message (Okazaki et al., 2010). Emotional appeals, by comparison, result in both more positive attitudes towards the ad and increased ad believability, also increasing purchase intention (Okazaki et al., 2010).

5.4.8 Credibility

Credibility is an essential advertising construct that increases messages' persuasive impacts (Huh et al., 2004). Hereby, credibility, as "a multi-faceted construct, is typically defined as the degree to which a consumer sees a source or medium conveying trustworthy, believable, accurate, or expert information" (Atkin and Beltramini, 2007: 177; Huh et al., 2004: 37). As such, it is closely linked to the source's expertise and competence. Credibility is aided by both message style and promotional layout, which should be engaging to mentally stimulate and draw in recipients (Salmon and Atkin, 2003): "In other words, the message's presentation should be simple, explicit, sufficiently detailed, comprehensive and comprehensible" (Salmon and Atkin, 2003: 455). Claims should not be exaggerated as messages might end up being dismissed as unbelievable or "too good to be true". Instead of being nominated or premiered, consumers should perceive adverts as "meaningful, relevant and useful" (AdWeek, 2013).

Credibility does not automatically translate into believability, which "is the appropriate measure of actual deception" (Richards, 1990); nonetheless, it is connected to believability. Already Leo Burnett, founder of the world-famous ad agency of the same name, stated that "[t]he greatest thing to be achieved in advertising is [...] believability" (Leo Burnett; cf. Atkin and Beltramini, 2007: 169). Advertising believability alludes to the extent to which an advertisement is rated as being truthful, accurate and valuable to the consumer or recipient (Maloney, 1963; Atkin and Beltramini, 2007). It is the opposite of irritation, which leads individuals to feel uncomfortable or deceived (Okazaki et al., 2010); as such, ad believability should lead consumers to consider both the message and product offering as relevant to their own lives (Beltramini and Evans, 1985).

In the case of pharmaceutical advertising, marketers are often questioned as to their adverts' information content, which are created as "powerful, emotion-arousing images [that provide] frequently unbalanced information on [drug] safety and effectiveness; [...] vague qualitative promises rather than explicit description of benefits" (Wolfe, 2002). Rarely, they provide two-sided information (on drug risks and benefits; Main et al., 2004; Koinig, 2012), even though those arguments are perceived as more believable, credible and informative than one-sided (framed) messages (Etgar and Goodwin, 1982; Kamins et al., 1989; Pechmann, 1992). One potential reason for marketers' reluctance to deploy such promotions might be by virtue of its one central benefit: one-sided arguments are easier to follow, less confusing and more comprehensible (Gilbody et al., 2005). As to ad appeal, informative and mixed/CSR appeals are assumed to be rated more credibly than their emotional counterparts. On the basis of this argumentation, the following hypothesis can be deduced:

H 2: Informative ads for pharmaceuticals score more favorable results with regard to credibility than (a) mixed or (b) CSR ads, which score even better results than (c) emotional ads in all countries.

Message features alone do not sway responses to promotional health messages; in fact, past experiences with (both prescription and non-prescription) medications, health-related knowledge (literacy and educational scores) and interpersonal resources wield significant influence on individual intentions and health decisions, further steering the degree of consumer self-empowerment. These will be discussed in the next sections.

5.4.9 Past Experiences

Patients are renowned to attribute varying degrees of importance to medications (Shoemaker and de Oliveira, 2007): while one might consider them as a suitable cure for minor medical conditions, another might regard them as necessary or – even worse – inevitable evil on the way to recovery. Perceptions of medications might be grounded in past experiences, be they positive or negative. In Social Learning Theory (Bandura, 1976), for instance, a basic premise is that people's choices and behaviors are not only informed by observing others, but also stem from their own experiences, which are difficult to discard (Kar et al., 2001: 119; Glanz and Riemer, 1997). These experiences (with either drugs and/or medical services) operate as core mechanisms and moderators of patients' responses to their illnesses (Lau-Walker, 2006), further shaping patients' judgments of their medical situations and moderating their abilities and willingness to deal with their disease (Lau-Walker, 2006).

Assuming human behaviors in the health context to be guided by past experiences stored in memory (aka schemes; Reed, 1988; Schank and Abelson, 1977; Wright et al., 2008), these are paired up with individual beliefs and expectations that exercise a "considerable influence over his or her behavior" (Wright et al., 2008: 236). So far, only a few studies have tried to evaluate medical experiences; of those, most have been linked to selected medical conditions, including asthma and hormone therapy (Adams et al., 1997; Hunter et al., 1997; Stephens et al., 2002), where patients' medication regimes and preventive behaviors have been subject to scrutiny (Carrick et al., 2004; Pound et al., 2005), while compliance with treatment regimens was explicitly addressed by Conrad (1985). In only one instance, cultural meanings and patterns associated with drug use have been explored (Lumme-Sandt et al., 2000), whilst the area of OTC drug advertising has not been included in the research corpus yet. For this reason, the present investigation wants to uncover the role of previous experiences within the self-medication domain.

5.4.10 Health Literacy | Health Education

Health reports throughout the world have given an indication of several factors impeding health implementation; unless present, they are to blame for individuals' poor health performances. The two major components responsible for rather alarming outcomes are low health literacy as well as poor health education (Grosse and Auffrey, 1989; Hohn, 1997; U.S. Department of Health and Human Services, 2000; Schillinger et al., 2002), with the former being "increasingly recognized as a crucial issue affecting communication across the continuum of healthcare" (Wright et al., 2008: 287; Davis et al., 2002). Health literacy presents one of the most important assets in health communication (Zagaria, 2004), where it is defined as "the degree to which individuals have the capacity to obtain, process, and understand basic health information and services needed to make appropriate health decisions" (U.S. Department of Health and Human Services, 2005: 15-20; Selden et al., 2000). The term is also used to refer to routine practices and activities utilized by individuals as part of their illness control mechanisms (Marks et al., 2005; Lorig and Holman, 2003; Bodenheimer et al., 2002).

In terms of the area of health promotion, health literacy is a relatively new concept that has not managed to gain a foothold yet (Nutbeam, 2000). Even though it – on a very basic level – insinuates people's abilities to read, comprehend and act in accordance with the health information they encounter (Behringer et al., 2004), it is far more than that: it also describes patients' abilities to comply with therapeutic instructions and comprehend medical information uttered by experts, on leaflets or product packages (Ad Hoc Committee of Health Literacy, 1999). It covers an additional range of skills that allow individuals to make qualified choices to reduce health risks and improve their overall quality of life simultaneously (Zarcadoolas et al., 2005). Having said that, health literacy "represents the cognitive and social skills which determine the motivation and ability of individuals to gain access to, understand and use information in ways which promote and maintain good health" (Nutbeam, 1998).

(Active) patient involvement, furthermore, presupposes health education, which presents an important asset within the health-care domain (Gastaldo, 1997). According to Green et al. (1980), health education refers to "any combination of learning experiences designed to facilitate voluntary adaptations of behavior conducive to health". It takes present knowledge as a starting point and combines it with personal attitudes and goals in an effort to overcome the gap between idealized health notions and health practice (Griffith, 1972; Simonds, 1976). Serving as a precondition to build up and strengthen health literacy, health education wants to lastingly shape and improve future health care encounters (Glanz et al., 2008). By increasing patients' say in their health care (Franklin et al., 2009) and invoking "self-autonomy and self-governance" (Bunton and Petersen, 1997: 6), it presents an intentional activity to bring about "some relatively permanent change in an individual's capability or disposition" (Berry, 2007: 90).

Low health literacy and poor health education with regard to disease treatment can be assumed to equal low patient activation, passivity or motivation to act (Paasche-Orlow and Wolf, 2007). People with marginal literacy and education rates are said to be reluctant to accept self-care tools and practices, being prone to deny any responsibility towards their bodies when it comes to medical decisions (Pignone and De Walt, 2006; Gazmararian et al., 2006). By contrast, individuals with strong levels of health literacy and higher education rates aim at increasing their access to health(-enhancing) information, strengthening their self-medication abilities and consolidating effective medication practices (Nutbeam, 1998). Thus, both health literacy and health education are understood as viable assets, enabling patients to become actively engaged and empowered in all health-related decisions (Nutbeam, 1998; Nutbeam, 2008).

Nonetheless, health literacy must not be perceived as a phenomenon per se, but rather as a concept located on a continuum that both influences and is affected by other external factors. These include health care access, drug availability, reimbursement plans and patient-physician interactions, as well as self-care practices, which are all of particular importance to the area of non-prescription and over-the-counter drug promotions (Paasche-Orlow and Wolf, 2007).

5.4.11 Social Support

Individual resources – encompassing access to adequate health care together with support from family and peer group members – also factor into a person's choice when deciding whether or not to take up a preventive behavior (Wright et al., 2008). Since people are embedded in (interpersonal) reference or social groups, alluding to "a person or group of people that significantly influences an individual's behavior" (Bearden and Etzel, 1982: 184), these networks are important points of reference in the health context, where they provide support to patients in difficult situations (Goldsmith, 2004). Interpersonal or social sources offer a form of emotional support, which is primarily concerned with taking distress to a personal level and resolving tension there

(Wright et al., 2007; Cwikel and Israel, 1987; Magen and Glajchen, 1999). Social support portends to all verbal and non-verbal forms of communication that allow individuals to manage uncertainties and needs by discussing their situation with (un-)affected peer group members. Overall, it is assigned to one of three information classes, leading "the subject to believe that he/she 1) is cared for and loved; 2) is esteemed and valued; and 3) belongs to a network of communication and mutual obligation" (Cobb, 1976: 300). Inasmuch as social support plots a safe haven, it permits individuals to experience acceptance without question and for their own sake and to return to a place where they can retreat from worldly problems and personal concerns (Cobb, 1976; Moss, 1973). This interpersonal exchange enables them to come to terms with their (health) situations as well as themselves, functioning as a means of enhancing individuals' perception of control over their illness and life experiences respectively (Albrecht and Adelman, 1987).

Social support exerts significant influence in terms of individual conformity to (social) expectations. Following SCT (Bandura, 1976), susceptibility to others presents a multi-variable construct (Bearden et al., 1989) and takes outside influence into consideration, in the course of which other peer group members offer directions as to how to improve an individual's self-image (e.g., through buying specific products) or provide guidance as to which product is considered as acceptable for use. In some instances, not only information is obtained from others, but observational learning occurs, with individuals imitating behaviors observed by watching others (Bearden et al., 1989).

In total, two types of susceptibility can be distinguished, namely normative influence or informational influence (Deutsch and Gerard, 1955). In the case of normative influence, an individual conforms to the expectations of other peers, at times to avoid punishment or isolation (Burnkrant and Cousineau, 1975); in the case of informational influence, the individual turns to (more knowledgeable) others for advice in specific situations (Deutsch and Gerard, 1955; Park and Lessing, 1977). Informational support derived from peer group members or the Internet (Wright et al., 2008) might be crucial and "is perceived as useful, [for] people with health problems may feel they have more control over their situation" (Wright et al., 2008; 77; Roter and Hall, 1992).

It is believed that reference groups expose people to behaviors and lifestyles that are regarded as desirable and, thus, trigger conformity (Bearden and Etzel, 1982). Reference groups are, thereby, consulted for varying purposes: on the one hand, they are used “as standards of comparison for self-appraisal (comparative) and […] as a source of personal norms, attitudes, and values (normative)” (Bearden and Etzel, 1982: 183; see also Kelley, 1947). Research is also indicative of interpersonal influence and (peer) group belonging strongly determining individual behavior (Bearden and Etzel, 1982; Bearden et al., 1989), with people exhibiting high degrees of compliance in most instances (Merton and Rossi, 1949; Stafford and Cocanaugher, 1977). A different set of studies has found that low-levels of self-esteem are positively related to susceptibility to others’ influence (McGuire, 1968; Stafford and Cocanaugher, 1977), while a product’s perceived risk was predicted to increase susceptibility to group influence (Bettman and Park, 1980).

5.4.12 Product Evaluation

Product evaluations refer to consumers’ conscious ratings of a promoted service or good based on the promotional information provided, comprising extrinsic and intrinsic attributes or “cues” (Olson and Jacoby, 1972; Zeithaml, 1988; Johansson, 1989; Gabbot, 1991; Baughn and Yaprak, 1993; Chao and Rajendran, 1993). Extrinsic characteristics are not part of the product itself and comprise aspects like manufacturer brand, product packaging, distribution channel, price, etc. (Blachette, 1990). Depending on the product category, intrinsic cues refer to tangible product features, such as product shape, material, color, and performance (Olsen and Jacoby, 1972) that should aid consumers with the attainment of their individual goals (Spies et al., 1997). Product evaluations can be enhanced through the inclusion of unique or novel attributes (Mukherjee and Hoyer, 2001), elevating the advertised product in relevance once its usefulness and personal value to the consumer are established (Hagtvedt, 2015).

Advertising messages can emphasize product attributes to varying degrees, thus shaping product evaluations. Informative appeals initiate a rational (logical) thinking process and build upon measurable product features, such as performance, value and quality attributes (Leonidou and Leonidou, 2009; Churchill and Peter, 1998). One extreme form are comparative claims, referring to statements contrasting two competing products in terms of relevant product specifics; while they are frequently practiced in the United States, they are frowned upon in other parts of the world (Mueller, 2011). By contrast, emotional appeals stimulate a heightened degree of arousal, with individuals being more likely to engage in certain (consumption-related) actions (Hawkins et al., 2003), alerted or called upon by positive feelings elicited through the ad (Leonidou and Leonidou, 2009).

In order to score favorable product evaluations, each form – independent of its message appeal – has to fulfill the task of strengthening "the links between product attributes and valued consequences" (McQuarrie and Langmeyer, 1985: 243f.), which is again dependent upon product category. As (rather) high involvement products, non-prescription drugs are expected to benefit from detailed information illustrating product effects and outcomes, while being rather unsuited for purely emotional promotions. This assumption results in the following hypothesis:

H 3: Informative ads for pharmaceuticals achieve higher scores with regard to product evaluation than (a) mixed or (b) CSR ads, which achieve even higher scores than (c) emotional ads in all countries.

5.4.13 Purchase Intention

Following Fishbein and Ajzen (1975: 369), "the single best predictor of an individual's behavior will be a measure of his intention to perform that behavior". So, instead of testing actual behavior – which would require a follow-up study – purchase intention will deployed in the present project. Having established itself as core construct in the marketing arena (Morrison, 1979), purchase intention is a reliable measure of advertising effectiveness that is subject to numerous factors, such as product endorser attractiveness (Ohanian, 1990; Ohanian, 1991; Laffery and Goldsmith, 1999; Chi et al., 2009) or the message's perceived value to the recipient (Dodds and Monroe, 1985; Zeithaml, 1988). It is further said to be more pronounced when corresponding with existing consumer values (Monroe and Krishnan, 1985).

In general, purchase intention measures consumers' likelihood of considering a product for trial and/or their next purchase (Dodds et al., 1991; Schiffman and Kanuk, 2000); in the case of a heightened awareness and increased interest evoked by the promotional message, the actual intention to acquire the product is said to be rather high (Dodds et al., 1991; Schiffman and Kanuk, 2000). Moreover, consumers' need for information does not only have a bearing on ad evaluation but also product purchase intention. This means that purchase intention is also dependent upon measurable product attributes and features, such as quality and (subjective) value (Monroe and Krishnan, 1985); the higher the perceived value as offered by informative accounts, the more likely it is a product will be acquired (Zeithaml, 1988). The collected evidence, hence, allows for the following supposition:

H 4: Informative ads for pharmaceuticals have a larger impact on purchase intention than (a) mixed or (b) CSR ads, which have an even larger impact than (c) emotional ads in all countries.

5.4.14 Motivation | Behavioral Intention

Norman and Conner (1996) state that social cognitive models are more appropriate for predicting human intention rather than behavior, proposing that those two concepts have to be differentiated, since intention does not automatically translate into actual behavior (Milne et al., 2002). This investigation follows a path by including three separate categories, which will be elaborated on in the following: behavior, behavioral change and behavioral intentions. While behavior describes "the actual performance of a recommended response" (Murray-Johnson and Witte, 2010: 487), behavioral change alludes to "the adoption of a new behavior, or the modification or discontinuance of a prior behavior" (Murray-Johnson and Witte, 2010: 487). In between these two, behavioral intentions are located, which "refer to the plans individuals have about whether or not they intend to perform the recommended behavior (from adoption to discontinuance)" (Murray-Johnson and Witte, 2010: 487).

Although ad stimuli are critical in creating attention, liking and personal message relevance, motivation is the one central component to evaluate and track how a message is perceived (Murray-Johnson and Witte, 2010). Motivating factors grasp a variety of aspects, "such as culture, education level, past experiences, [and] skills" (Turner et al., 2004: 33) that drive the adaptation or rejection of a specific behavioral pattern. Motivation is guided by behavioral objectives, meaning all recommended actions an audience should attend to when dealing with a particular problem situation (Schiavo, 2007); in the health domain, for instance, behavioral objectives could involve maintaining individual health, engaging in regular exercise or complying with treatment regimes.

Whilst intentions serve as a precondition for behavior (Fishbein and Ajzen, 1975), they are determined by factors such as individual beliefs and personal attitudes. In order to predict intentions (and, consequently, behavior), numerous variables need to be taken into account, including perceived Self-Efficacy, personal vulnerability, disease severity, social norms and/or perceived barriers (Schwarzer and Luszczynska, 2008). Moreover, environmental components are viewed to moderate the abovementioned relationships (Fishbein, 2008).

The stages individuals are meant to pass through until they arrive at a behavioral intention are numerous and have been extensively discussed in literature (e.g., see Lippke and Ziegelmann, 2006; Prochaska and DiClemente, 1984; Schwarzer, 1992). One model addressing these stages is the Behavioral Change Approach, which is based on the assumption that people are rational decision makers, whose actions are cognitively informed (Berry, 2007). In line with this approach, Lippke and Ziegelmann (2006) have introduced a multi-stage model (MSM) that is explicitly applicable to the health domain: They propose a two-stage-process, consisting of (1) a motivational or deliberate (goal intention) phase and (2) a post-intentional or volitional (implementation intention) phase. The first, pre-action stage, serves as a disposition for behavioral foundation, and is followed by an action stage, where thoughts get more concrete, actions are derived and plans for implementation are developed (Lippke and Ziegelmann, 2006; Wright et al., 2008). Thereby, behaviors are to be regarded as a result of people's attitudes towards a given behavior, as well as individuals' subjective norms about this behavior (Ajzen, 1985; Ajzen and Fishbein, 1980), which both impede behavioral implementation.

The process from motivation to behavioral intention comprises several steps: Once a good intention has been formed and is maintained, a transformation needs to occur: detailed instructions need to be derived from the initially formed intention, which are in turn subject to "self-regulatory skills and practices" (Schwarzer and Luszczynska, 2008: 142f.; Schwarzer, 2011). Afterwards, preferences for a particular behavior need to be manifested in form of detailed instructions on how to proceed (Schwarzer, 2011). This process is called action planning and "includes specific situation parameters ('when', 'where') and a sequence of action ('how')" (Schwarzer and Luszczynska, 2008: 143). According to research, actions are evaluated in two ways: on an executional basis (how) and a rational basis (why). In the former instance, actions are solely executed for no particular reasons, while in the latter, actions are guided by conscious thoughts about which effects or outcomes are anticipated (Vallacher and Wegner, 1989). Judged as actions, self-medication practices require appropriate OTC drugs ('how') that are used to treat bodily symptoms of disease and improve individuals' well-being ('why').

Gollowitzer (1993) and Heckhausen (1991) agree that it takes motivation to initiate and finally trigger some form of behavioral (re)enactment, and this is also the case in the health realm. During the first stage, the benefits associated with a proposed treatment are weighed against the expected costs accrued from a particular behavior: "Health beliefs influence how people estimate the likelihood of different outcomes that may be linked to the recommended behavior. If people feel competent about managing their health, they are more likely to feel optimistic about their ability to reverse negative patterns and become healthier" (Schiavo, 2007: 82). In case of highly motivated individuals, who have numerous plans and means at their disposal, health-related behavioral enactments are most likely to be carried out (Gollowitzer, 1993; Gollowitzer et al., 1990; Heckhausen, 1991; Heckhausen and Gollowitzer, 1987): when coming across promotions, highly motivated consumers might feel reassured of their self-medication skills and decide to buy the advertised product when perceiving it as meeting their needs. Individuals with low motivation rates might be less responsive to ads and refrain from becoming engaged in health-related matters.

5.4.15 Behavioral Change | Behavior

Behavior is regarded as the product of individuals' intention, which is in turn conditioned by both their beliefs and attitudes (Armitage and Conner, 2001; Fishbein and Ajzen, 1975). Specifically in the health domain, attitudes and beliefs about (health) outcomes and actions can be assumed to drive individuals to initiate a certain health-enhancing behavior (Gollowitzer, 1993; Heckhausen, 1991). Yet, health-compromising habits need to be overcome first and require the adoption of self-regulatory efforts (Schwarzer, 2008), referring to all motivational, volitional and actional processes that are meant to improve individuals' physical states (Schwarzer, 2008; Leventhal et al., 2001). Depending on which path individuals choose, their change in behavior corresponds with one of the following three (behavioral) forms: (1) cessation (getting rid of maladaptive behavior), (2) initiation (starting a new, adaptive routine) and/or (3) maintenance (continuing to implement change; Floyd et al., 2000). In case of illness, for example, considering non-prescription drugs can serve as the starting point to a new health-enhancing cycle (2) since the medication can be taken to maintain a particular health/physical state (3). Either of the two strategies is suggestive of the fact that behavior "is the actual performance of a recommended response" (Murray-Johnson and Witte, 2010: 487). In the health domain, educational measures presuppose a rational problem solving approach, in the course of which consumers seek information on preventive and adaptive behavior (McCrae, 1984). Ideally, they take up an adaptive or health-enhancing behavior (as opposed to a mal-adaptive or health-compromising behavior), which alludes to all strategies and plans to tackle the fear and ultimately overcome the initial health threat (instead of neglecting, ignoring, avoiding or even worsening it; Vincent and Dubinsky, 2005).

In general, behavioral change alludes to "the adoption of a new behavior, or the modification or discontinuance of a prior behavior" (Murray-Johnson and Witte, 2010: 487). Assuming individuals to be eager to acquire the necessary skills to become involved and perform a suggested (and desired) behavior, people's self-confidence in their coping abilities (i.e., Self-Efficacy; see section 5.4.7.1.) needs to be strengthened (Kar et al., 2001; Prochaska et al., 2009). At the same time, people's perceived (volitional) control has to be established (Ajzen and Fishbein, 1980); this process is subject to individuals' evaluations of their own capabilities to produce a change, also renowned as personal agency. Personal agency is originally conceptualized as an Action Identification Theory component (Vallacher and Wegner, 1985) and refers to a set of particular characteristics in humans that allow for a proper understanding of their behaviors and actions respectively (Vallacher and Wegner, 1987; Wegner and Vallacher, 1986). Thereby, the perceived level of personal agency operates as "an independent dimension that may distinguish just how much an individual has organized his or her actions into abstract, meaningful categories that can operate to channel behavior into dispositional tendencies" (Vallacher and Wegner, 1989: 662).

Particularly in the health domain, moves towards increasing patient agency and active consumer involvement are encouraged (Anshari et al., 2012). While most empowerment research has focused on patient-provider-exchanges and systematic perspectives so far (Anshari et al., 2012), neither the role nor the relevance of promotional material in the process has been studied to date. Hence, the present investigation intends to fill this clear research gap by determining the contribution of OTC drug promotions to the development and strengthening of consumer self-empowerment. Augmenting patients' very own autonomy (Schulz and Nakamoto, 2013) respectively participation is meant to equip them with more rights; yet, they are also burdened with more responsibility (Bhopal and White, 1993; Sherwin, 1992), put in charge of administrating their health(-care) expenses, where they are given the choice between more costly drugs and some cheaper OTC preparations (Neuhauser, 2003). Put in a nutshell, patients are empowered in that they are assumed to possess "the knowledge, skills, attitudes, and self-awareness necessary to influence their own behavior [...] to improve the quality of their lives" (Funnell et al., 1991). Empowerment is, thus, conceptualized in opposition to powerlessness (Wallerstein, 2002), which delegates responsibility for patients' health to knowledgeable experts and denies them the right to have an active say in their own care.

5.4.16 Consumer Self-Empowerment: Increasing Consumer Control and Choice

On a very basic level, empowerment is a subjective experience which presupposes consumer self-confidence and trust in their very own competencies (Eylon, 1998). Consumers are called upon to confide in their own abilities – a process to be referenced as self-empowerment: "Self-empowerment is a state in which an individual possesses a relatively high degree of actual power – that is, a genuine potential for making choices" (Tones and Tilford, 2001: 40). Self-empowerment presupposes a relatively high level of self-esteem together with a repertoire of (health-promoting) skills that enable individuals to exercise power over their lives and health respectively (Tones and Tilford, 2001). It is associated with a variety of beliefs about the causality as well as the nature of control an individual possesses and/or develops to promote states of positive health. Taking consumer involvement in the decision-making process for granted (Cole et al., 1993), self-empowerment needs to be conceptualized as a participatory process (Pardo del Val and Lloyd, 2002). The availability of information is regarded as maximizing consumer utilities and benefits (Davies and Elliott, 2006) and, as such, the degree of (self-)empowerment. The level of individual empowerment is, thereby, subject to (1) the amount of information available to the consumer and (2) their ability to make sense of this information (Newholm et al., 2006).

Empowerment builds upon personal agency and is not a completely new concept; for this reason, researchers interested in this realm do not have to reinvent the wheel but can turn to old and established theories that have already addressed this issue from varying points of view. The term's origins can be traced back to both social and behavioral sciences (Perkins and Zimmerman, 1995; Wilkinson, 1998), with first roots leading to the empowerment movement to be found in European trends calling for liberalism and individualism (Wright et al., 2006). One possibly suitable approach is the Boston's Women's Health Collective, a movement stressing the relevance of information and education to guarantee women's proper medical care (BWHC, 1973; BWHC, 1980). While this focus does not have to be taken up in the present research project, the concept of empowerment as defined at that time has not lost its validity. Back then, just like today, the goal of empowerment is "to enhance the possibility for people to control their own lives" (Rappaport, 1981: 15), affording them with the chance to "gain mastery over their own lives" (Rappaport et al., 1984), while improving their quality of life (Wallerstein, 1992). From a consumption point of view, empowerment takes control from providers and allocates it on the demand side, with consumers having more transparent information about product offerings at their disposal (Worcester and Whately, 1992).

Empowerment is, thus, associated with a shift in power, with consumers being granted more choice and variety at the expense of enterprises, which are forced to accept deductions in authority (Pires et al., 2006), particularly with the Internet gaining in relevance: "The degree of empowerment of individual consumers may increase because electronic networks are characterized by intense connectivity and are amenable to the development of virtual communities" (Pires et al., 2006: 941). Empowerment is only possible due to the availability of and access to information, which consumers may perceive as a means of achieving independence (BWHC, 1973): Hence, "information seems to be key to the sense of empowerment" (Harrison et al., 2006: 981).

In the health-care domain, it is precisely the access to information that grants people the possibility to acquire more knowledge regarding medical conditions and symptoms alike. As a result, they build up more skills and competencies, growing more self-conscious, autonomous, and stronger (BWHC, 1980; Kuhlmann and Kolip, 2005). For the OTC drug sector this implies that "[c]onsumers who are provided with useful information on products, services, and their rights are empowered to make more effective purchases and to resolve problems when they occur" (Brennan and Gallagher, 2002; Goldsmith, 2005). Consumers are familiarized with the array of products available for purchase in the health-care marketplace as well as their designated areas of application; ideally, they are also reinforced in their self-medication abilities and become empowered.

Without a doubt, no other media channel drives consumer empowerment in the health-care sector like the Internet (Bush, 2004; Wind and Mahajan, 2001; Rha and Widdows, 2002; David, 2001). Albeit health information is acquired on the Internet to the largest extent (Bush, 2004; Wind and Mahajan, 2001; Rha and Widdows, 2002; David, 2001), other sources nevertheless do not fall short (Pires et al., 2006). After 2001, a significant rise in print ads (e.g., newspapers and magazines) was reported (Adams, 2002), leading consumers to develop a new health-consciousness, paired up with a fear of attracting disease, becoming sick and aging prematurely (Moynihan and Cassels, 2005). As a consequence, patients (or consumers, when talking about the health-care marketplace) decided to become engaged, taking counter-action, which led drug sales to steadily rise over the years, for pills were perceived as a cure to those (minor) health conditions (Fitzpatrick, 2001): "The idea of health promotion has been deeply medicalized because healthy behaviors are now related to the capacity of individuals to control their risk of becoming sick" (Iriart et al., 2011: 6).

Pharmaceutical advertising's mission is to create an increased awareness for disease and medical conditions that might go unnoticed or lack public familiarity (Iriart et al., 2011), while also introducing message recipients to potential(ly new) treatment options. Advertising's goal involves educating "people to prevent the risks of becoming ill [by use of drugs] that do not require health provider mediation for their consumption" (Iriart et al., 2011: 9), granting individuals an increased say in how their bodies are treated (Iriart et al., 2011). As such, empowerment creates an increased consumer value (Turnquist, 2004), helping individuals to overcome their vulnerability and susceptibility to others in the marketplace. If consumers are not empowered, they are vulnerable, prevented the freedom of choice due to some barriers established by corporations and/or institutions (Baker et al., 2005). Thereby, "vulnerability is a condition that can be experienced by everyone; it is a transient experience situated in a specific consumption context" (Broderick et al., 2011: 4). In order to escape this vulnerability, consumers are asked to develop some coping mechanisms, which allow them to deal with the circumstances they are confronted with (Baker et al., 2005; Baker and Mason, 2012). Information (presented in form of advertising) equips them with the possibility to compensate for their lack of knowledge by directing their attention towards facts that are useful to their ultimate purchasing decisions (Broderick et al., 2011).

The extent of empowerment depends on consumers' abilities to filter out potentially useful information for product evaluation and comparison. In the process, they have to ensure that their needs are substantially satisfied and their time is not wasted (Pires et al., 2006; Byrne, 2003). Advertising then empowers consumers, "helping [them to] choose what they want, when they want it, on their own terms" (Pires et al., 2006: 939; Wind and Rangaswamy, 2001).

Figure 14: Global Caring Tendencies (de Mooij, 2011: 120)

In order for advertising messages to work and induce empowerment, they need to correspond with the cultural characteristics particular to each market: in individualistic cultures, marketers are advised to stress individual and product benefits, achievement and freedom, while advertisements in collectivistic cultures should focus on societal gain, group harmony and family values (Han and Shavitt, 1994). As indicated by Figure **14**, promotional messages in the United States, the prime example of an individualistic culture, need to grant recipients possibilities for self-enhancement; messages should confirm recipients in their self-esteem, which "is the evaluative aspect of the self-concept; it concerns how worthwhile and confident an individual feels about himself or herself" (Eysenck, 2000: 458). Similarly, Europeans pay particular attention to positive product information that is relevant to themselves and fosters their self-improvement (Kitayama et al., 1997), leading to the following hypotheses:

H 5: Informative promotions for pharmaceuticals are expected to lead to higher degrees of consumer self-empowerment than (a) mixed or (b) CSR ads, which empower consumers even more than (c) emotional ads in all countries.

H 6: Informative promotions for pharmaceuticals bring about higher degrees of consumer self-empowerment than (a) mixed, (b) CSR or (c) emotional ads in individualistic countries.

Self-enhancement is typical of individualistic cultures, where it also serves as an expression of individuals' capabilities to take care of the self (Heine and Hamamura, 2007); hence, it is less established in collective nations, where it is only deployed to "maintain face" and not threaten collective pride and belongingness that make individuals conform with group standards (Twenge and Crocker, 2000; Kurman, 2002). As advertisements depicting the end result are image-laden and well-received, the following hypothesis can be deduced:

H 7: Informative promotions for pharmaceuticals lead to lower degrees of consumer self-empowerment than (a) mixed, (b) CSR or (c) emotional ads in collectivistic cultures.

5.4.16.1 The New Consumer: Particularities of the Health Sector

> *"Health is something which lies within the control of the individual. All active citizens have a right and a duty to maintain, contribute to and ensure [...] their health" (Nettleton, 1997: 208).*

Within recent years, the empowerment of patients is advocated, who are turned into consumers conditioned by the availability of new services and products (Iriart et al., 2011). Their changing roles are facilitated by various movements in the medical sector, which primarily concern the self-care movement (Ferguson, 1980), the consumer movement (Gordon, 1980) as well as the wellness movement (Bloch, 1984). Subsequently, "better access to higher education, information sources like the Internet, and greater personal wealth" have resulted in consumers expressing a much greater interest in their medical treatment regimes (David, 2001: 1). They are encouraged to reclaim control over their bodies by taking up preventive health measures; when acquiring health products, they are turned into health consumers who – in the case of self-medication – are not dependent on experts' diagnosis alone but can consult (with) alternative practitioners or gain new insights from sympathizers concerned when exchanging opinions in online-communities (Lupton, 1997).

Empowerment is typical of contemporary health care and is driven by a dualistic goal: increasing consumer choice and promoting greater control (Asato, 2003). With these objectives in mind, power is drifting away from the established "doctor knows best" health-care model (Bosanquet, 2003: 24; Krzywicki, 2004); instead, a health partnership has developed, in which practitioners can no longer be held solely accountable for health decisions but share responsibility with knowledgeable patients and/or health-care consumers (Taylor, 2003; Evans, 2003). Apart from depending on expert diagnosis, consumers are encouraged to deploy self-care and self-management practices, which are readily used for 80 % of all (minor) health conditions (Colin-Thome, 2003). A shared approach to health recognizes consumers' sovereignty and autonomy by appealing to their self-confidence (Coulter, 2002), advising them to adopt health-enhancing beliefs and strategies, e.g., in the area of self-medication in particular (Taylor, 2003; Lorig et al., 1999). Even though practices are slowly but surely starting to catch up, self-care is still lacking acceptance globally.

As patients are no longer passive, those recent developments have led to the emergence of the health-care consumer, who is more powerful than ever before (Aspect, 2011). Statements like "customers are too smart to be fooled", "the customer is king", and "the customer is always right" have become widely used, serving as proof of this segment's rising relevance (Denegri-Knott et al., 2006: 950). From a marketing point of view, the active consumer plays a "key role in giving meaning to life through consumption" (van Raaij, 1993), repelling the supposition of consumers as passive and powerless dupes (Firat and Venkatesh, 1995; Firat and Dholakia, 1998). Instead, present-day consumption presents a process through which the individual takes care of itself (Barnett et al., 2005; Orlie, 2002): "The consumer is empowered when he or she is free to act as a rational and self-interested agent" (Denegri-Knott et al., 2006: 963).

Sources from various academic backgrounds do not neglect to emphasize empowerment's contribution to increasing individual control and responsibility (Grace, 1991; Mattila and Cranage, 2005); moreover, humans' striving for control over their own lives is seen as a conditio humana, one of the main pre-conditions of human life (Bröckling, 2003). Put simply, "to empower means to give power" (Thomas and Velthouse, 1990: 667), referring to an elevation of individual Self-Efficacy and sense of self-control (Rose, 2000). Thereby, "the idea is that consumers should be, and feel they are, in charge of their experience" (Pires et al., 2006: 943), which is said to result in a more exact match between consumers' desires and the product offerings they chose (Kreps, 1979), as well as leading to increased rates of satisfaction and contentment.

Despite being labeled "an unintended consequence of marketing" (Pires et al., 2006), empowerment accords consumers more choice, freedom and a degree of sovereignty they have not experienced before (Davies and Elliott, 2006; Taylor et al., 1992). This also holds true for the health sector, where individuals come to experience choice in form of a vast product palate of medications and treatment options, engaging and empowering self-reflexive subjects as "masters of their own fate" (Petersen, 1997: 192). Individuals have to weigh both risks and opportunities in the process (Beck, 1992) and run the risk of experiencing choice as both empowering (Wathieu et al., 2002; Schwartz, 2004) and overwhelming, thus disempowering (Davies and Elliott, 2006). Nevertheless, consumer studies have reported that the concept's potential downsides still outweigh its many benefits once choice is perceived as a privilege (Giddens, 1991), giving rise to more permanent satisfaction, overall happiness and well-being (Langer and Rodin, 1976; Langer, 1983).

The consumerization of the health realm equips patients with new, abundant choices and unprecedented degrees of freedom (Evans, 2003), clearly pushing the boundaries of empowerment by expanding customer participation (Parikh, 2013). By eliminating information asymmetry, patients become lay or 'citizen experts' (Mondry, 2014) who do not refrain from claiming a spot in health-care matters. Empowered patients are consumers who are not characterized by negligence but "take an active role in their disease management and understand a lot about the condition and the treatment options available" (Kantar Health, 2014). In order to make sense of these health matters, nonetheless, information is required, which has to be perceived as relevant and 'enabling' by consumers (HAI, 2006).

5.4.16.2 On the Relationship of Empowerment, Literacy and Education

Empowerment equals a 'responsabilization', in the course of which individuals are held accountable for their own well-being (Osborne, 1997). Portending to health as a personal responsibility (Seedhouse, 1986; Griffiths and Adams, 1991), patients rise to active agents or consumers in the health-care marketplace (Roter et al., 1988). Health empowerment presupposes consumers' active participation and pro-active behaviors, which are believed to lead to improved health outcomes, enhanced Self-Efficacy, increased medication compliance as well as consumer control (Wathieu et al., 2002; Anderson and Funnel, 2005; Michie et al., 2003). Thus, consumer self-empowerment "could be seen as synonymous with (positive) health" (Green and Tones, 2010: 12).

		Psychological Empowerment	
		Low	High
Health Literacy	High	Needlessly Dependent Patient	Effective Self-manager
	Low	High-needs Patient	Dangerous Self-manager

Figure 15: Interdependence of Literacy, Empowerment and Patient Behavior (Schulz and Nakamoto, 2013: 9)

Health empowerment must not be perceived on its own but needs to be linked to information and knowledge, which it is fostered through health literacy (see Figure **15**). Schulz and Nakamoto (2013) have detected the necessity to connect the concepts of health literacy and empowerment, whereby the degrees of psychological empowerment and health literacy result in four different types of patients. People who are health-illiterate and unengaged (low empowerment) depend on guidance and expert advice to arrive at informed health decisions (high-need patients). If they, however, feel like taking care of themselves (high empowerment), their situation becomes critical as a lack in health literacy can have fatal (health-threatening) consequences (dangerous self-managers). Only patients with high levels of health literacy can be turned into successful and effective self-managers. One type seemingly unaware of their skills (due to low empowerment rates) are needlessly dependent patients who are either reluctant to accept responsibility or long for reassurance in their judgments, which only experts can offer them. The idealistic type – the effective self-manager – knows how to utilize health-related resources and strategies in an efficient manner to achieve an improved health outcome (Schulz and Nakamoto, 2013; Wallerstein, 2002).

Empowerment presents a vital concept, enabling patients to reduce health disparities through their own efforts (Wallerstein, 2002). Non-prescription preparations are a valuable point of reference for effective self-managers, who feel competent enough to adopt preventive actions of their own accord; this drive is not well established in the needlessly dependent group, who might be literate but unaware of their skills; hence, in order to empower consumers, pharmaceutical marketers should utilize messages strengthening consumers in their self-medication abilities (UTexas, 2011).

Drawing upon a humanistic research paradigm, health empowerment requires individuals to deal with and adapt to changing circumstances in order to achieve heightened degrees of well-being, self-esteem and self-fulfillment (Warwick-Booth, 2012). Already in the early 1980s, consumer organizations recognized the possibility of advertisements to serve as a source of consumer (self-)empowerment (Critser, 2005); soon afterwards, the concept was utilized by the managed care sector, which jumped onto the bandwagon by claiming "that [only] an informed patient could make rational decisions about their health needs and [cannot] be manipulated by prescribers" (Iriart et al., 2011: 5). But is the trust put in health marketers justified?

"There are people in the medical field who want to educate people into submission and there are people in the advertising industry who only want to persuade people" (Michael Mackert, Department of Advertising, University of Texas; cf. UTexas, 2011). Both intentions, which are clearly beneficial to each party, differ significantly in their objectives: while the former is solely interested in compliance, the latter wants to convince and trigger a favorable response in recipients. This statement pinpoints the existence of a clear gap between educational and promotional efforts, which can be neither denied nor neglected (Rissel, 1994). However, it occurs at the expense of patients. So far, advertisements have been criticized for being written in a very complex, highly-theoretical language that is intended to satisfy regulating bodies but does not manage to appeal to consumers. In addressing the wrong target audience, promotions miss out on the opportunity of serving as an educational tool by raising awareness for symptoms and/or offering appropriate remedies (UTexas, 2011). In order to reach an optimum for all interest groups, they have to make ends meet by either one party sacrificing their convictions or reaching a compromise (UTexas, 2011).

When studying advertisements, consumers often struggle to find the information they are looking for. Instead of going through overwhelming and complex data or underwhelming messages listing too few details, it is recommended that information should follow three simple guidelines, referred to as the 3 Es of Effective Healthcare Advertising (Dong, 2013): Experience, Empowerment, and Efficiency. This suggests that (1) marketers are expected to lead with their experience, which establishes them as reliable (and trustworthy) sources of information; (2) they should hand over the reins by granting individuals a say in their health care and empower them; this can only be achieved once favorable reactions are elicited or provoking thoughts are formed in response to stimulating promotions; and, (3) in a fast-paced world, advertisers should keep their messages short and concise, yet efficient (Dong, 2013). At the same time, they have to ensure that ad content is translated into comprehensible pieces made accessible on a mass communication level (UTexas, 2011). For promotions, this means that selected information should be included, since consumers do not want to be flooded by lengthy text blocks that keep them from recognizing the message's gist upon first sight. In addition, advertisers could try to illustrate the OTC drug's desired end result by including an appealing image (see section 5.4.2.).

Advertisements should exploit the potential of fostering and supporting the concept of empowerment, which "is based on the idea that giving [individuals] skills, resources, authority, opportunity, motivation, as well holding them responsible and accountable for outcomes of their actions, will contribute to their competence and satisfaction" (Business Dictionary, 2014). Since the concept posits information to be present, it is specifically beneficial to the scientific health consumer, who conducts careful research, considers prospective alternatives and evaluates health and medical information objectively and with an open mind (Gould, 1988). These research activities are aided by technological developments, through which consumers become more information-savvy and engaged (Auton, 2004; Royne and Myers, 2008; Lyles, 2002). Empowerment is concerned with "ensuring that individuals and communities are able to assume the power they are entitled [to]" (WHO, 2001: 14). Nonetheless, people need to be confident enough to accept this new responsibility for their own bodies and well-being respectively; this means that people's personalities need to be strengthened and their willingness with regard to involvement has to be activated; furthermore, "[s]kill building, self-esteem development, and family strengthening must also occur" (Kar et al., 2001: 111; see also Kar et al., 1999; Pinderhughes, 1983).

5.4.16.3 Including Lay Perspectives

Empowerment evolves from the inclusion of lay perspectives – perspectives by non-expert or ordinary people (Bury, 2005; Earle, 2007; Martin, 2008). First introduced in the 1990s (Gabe et al., 1994), "lay understanding can be better defined as commonsense understandings and personal expertise, imbued with professional rationalizations" (Blaxter, 2007: 26). Since ideas about the constituents of health and illness are, above all, subjective (Williams and Calnan, 1996), ordinary people develop their own understanding of their (medical) experiences, often referred to as 'incorrect knowledge' (Health Knowledge, 2007c). These accounts expand established notions and theories of health by going "beyond common sense" or "beyond the immediately obvious" (Stacey, 1988: 142), resulting in lay knowledge often becoming discredited and stigmatized as unprofessional. Whilst lay knowledge has been criticized on the grounds of its lacking (scientific) medical foundation, it is still not as unprofessional as it might appear at first sight. Inasmuch as they center on subjective (health) experiences, lay perceptions are informed by expert (medical) knowledge (Blaxter, 2007; Shaw, 2002), acquired through practitioner-patient-encounters or online exchanges. Seeing that their relevance has also been pointed out by the Social Model of Health (Lawton, 2003), which emphasizes the relevance of heterogeneous or 'multi-factorial' illness assessments as opposed to homogenous evaluations (Popay et al., 2003; Radley, 1994; Blaxter, 1990), these common perceptions warrant inclusion in the medical discourse. There, they are meant to serve as expressions of people's perceived control over their (illness) experiences and the ways/means they utilize to counter-act harm and improve physical well-being as well as bodily comfort (Calnan, 1987).

Patient or consumer participation in their health care recognizes lay perspectives, which are nourished by both people's personal and social resources (Shearer, 2009). Personal resources describe a set of unique characteristics adults are said to possess (e.g. Self-Efficacy); in contrast, social or conceptual resources refer to sources outside the human, which might be of use in the recovery process (e.g. social support; Shearer, 2009; Dunst and Trivette, 1996). According to the Theory of Health Empowerment, empowerment can only emerge when both these competencies are activated simultaneously (Shearer, 2007). A stage of individual empowerment is entered the moment individuals purposefully participate "in a process of changing oneself and one's environment, recognizing patterns, and engaging inner resources for well-being" (Shearer and Reed, 2004).

Empowerment depends upon the existence of two environmental factors, namely public education and health literacy, which can be reinforced if individuals chose to acquire knowledge from various sources like the Internet, magazines and special interesting books (BWHC, 1980; Pires et al., 2006). To the empowerment concept, information is key, which is used to build up knowledge as, otherwise, dominant power structures, in which doctors serve as sources of authority and wisdom, cannot be altered (Kuhlmann and Kolip, 2005). As such, empowerment needs to be seen in opposition to the unquestioned acceptance of expert knowledge and is expressive of individual agency (Kozinets, 2002; Kozinets and Handelmann, 2004), closely linked to individuals and their self-perceptions. It, thus, constitutes a central facet of what Bourdieu (1984) calls 'habitus', alluding to all mental schemata that are subject to existential conditions and influence consumptions patterns and practices: "Empowerment can only be initiated or sustained by the person seeking power or self-determination" (Harrison et al., 2006: 975).

Empowerment involves taking and accepting (greater) control, affording individuals a greater say in bodily matters and awarding them the opportunity to develop "a new sense of somebodyness" (Levy Simon, 1994: 142) to overcome their "sense of powerlessness" or passivity (Foucault, 1992). Relating to drugs, the conscious purchase of a non-prescription remedy for a minor health condition serves as an act of empowerment just as the reception of the marketer's promotional message is concerned with elevating and strengthening individuals' beliefs in themselves and their skills respectively.

Advertising messages can, if executed with care, serve as sources of empowerment by appealing to and meeting recipients' health needs and can, additionally, represent the means to reassure respondents of their agency, allowing them to (re-)gain power and sovereignty as well as to find self-fulfillment (Herriger, 1997).

5.4.17 Modelling Consumer Self-Empowerment

Since the conceptual framework introduced above is very complex in nature, only a partial model comprising some core variables will be tested in the present study, aiming to determine how four distinct ad appeals are evaluated by consumers in four different cultural contexts. An additional goal is to find out to which extent the promotional message as well as the product promoted yield favorable evaluations, resulting in varying degrees of self-empowerment and purchase intention respectively. The following partial model will be contested in the investigation at hand (see Figure **16**); building upon previous theoretical discussions, the most relevant hypotheses will be deduced in a next step.

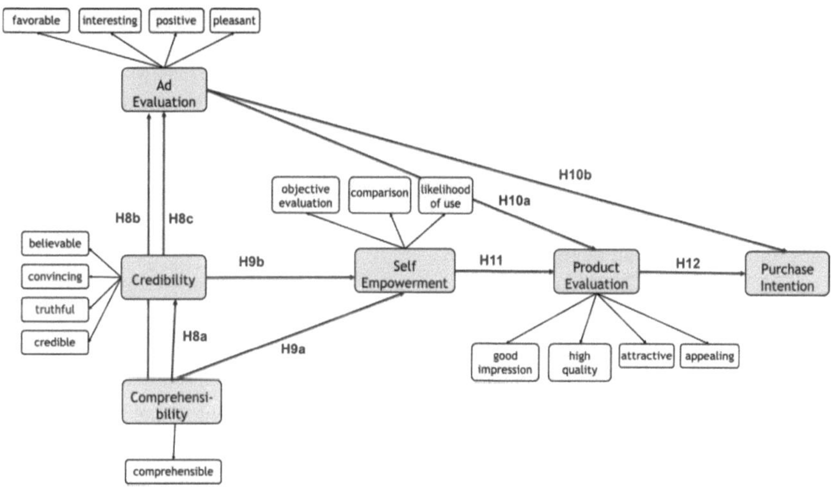

Figure 16: A Model Measuring Consumer Self-Empowerment Derived from Advertising (own illustration)

As already discussed in section 5.4.8, advertising credibility "is an important indicator of communications effectiveness" (The Wirthlin Report, 1999), for "if the advertisement is not believed, research shows that its effectiveness is restricted" (Kamins, 1989). So, which mechanisms need to be deployed for an ad to be effective, meaning credible and believable at the same time? According to research, the greatest degree of believability is achieved when advertising messages build upon already existing norms and beliefs (Maloney, 1963). Likewise, only the use of simplified, concise and comprehensible information can assist consumers in grasping the promotion's intended gist (i.e., the overall message in a nutshell), also positively influencing product and ad recall (Hoeck and Gendall, 2002). For this reason, the following can by hypothesized:

H 8a: The higher the pharmaceutical ad's comprehensibility, the more credible is its overall perception.

H 8b: The higher the pharmaceutical ad's comprehensibility, the more positive is its overall (ad) evaluation.

Constituting a highly relevant aspect in advertising research and innate to either objects or subjects (Eisend, 2002), credibility has proven to be a much-desired and striven-for communicative effect (Sternthal et al., 1978). It is dependent on the amount of information provided by marketers and, if perceived as incomplete or misleading, impedes the success of communication (Downey and Slocum 1975). Hence, advertisers are called upon to provide concise and trustworthy information to reduce consumers' uncertainties (Gemünden, 1985). As such, credibility enhances messages in general and advertisements in particular, by bringing about greater persuasive effects, as recipients do not feel tempted to question credible arguments (Sternthal and Craig, 1982). Thus, the following can be hypothesized:

H 8c: The more credible a pharmaceutical ad is perceived to be, the more positive is its overall (ad) evaluation.

The Internet and other communication forms allow for a bi-directional knowledge flow and exchange, consumer activism and shared decision making in medicinal issues (Perri and Nelson, 1987; Deshpande et al., 2004). Conditioned by those technological advances, consumers become more active and involved in their health care decisions (Auton, 2004; Royne and Myers, 2008; Lyles, 2002), whereby these communicative means "empower people by providing them with knowledge and understanding about specific health problems and interventions" (Muturi, 2005: 81). This role can also be taken up by advertising: when providing consumers with relevant and comprehensible information (Chang, 2005; Anand and Sternthal, 1990), it is capable of empowering consumers, "prompting them to seek more information about their health status and resulting in higher levels of compliance with treatment regimes" (Hoek et al., 2001: 4). Unless strengthened and reassured in their capabilities, people cannot build up enough confidence to accept responsibility for their own bodies and well-being respectively. Following Antonovsky (1997), empowerment processes should ideally strengthen individuals in their sense of coherence, i.e. their sense of life, which is closely linked to their perceived agency. This agency enables them to intervene in vital health-related decision making processes, providing them with the opportunity to shape and direct their efforts towards a desired end-state. People's sense of coherence comprises the following three aspects: comprehensibility (the ability to understand a complex problem), manageability (the belief in their own capabilities to achieve a goal by their own efforts), and meaningfulness (the reasonability behind an action; Antonovsky, 1997). As such, comprehensibility can be regarded as a pre-requisite for empowerment, allowing for the following hypothesis:

H 9a: The more comprehensible a pharmaceutical ad, the higher is the degree of self-empowerment derived therefrom.

In addition to comprehensibility, credibility does affect advertising's success (Ambler and Hollier, 2004). Credibility refers to the degree according to which message content is regarded as truthful (Lutz, 1985); however, with ads being repeatedly accused of using exaggerated claims and evoking false impressions, credibility is at stake (Obermiller et al., 2005). In order to create favorable product evaluations – and associated degrees of self-empowerment – messages need to be rated as credible (Lutz et al., 1986), whereby claims are recommended to be based on scientific research and tangible proof to enhance message credibility (van Mulken and Hornikx, 2011). As active recipients (Hirschman and Thompson, 1997), consumers do not want to be fooled but look for reassurance and guidance. They consciously process ads, pick up cues (to action) as well as draw inferences (Friestad and Wright, 1994; Meline, 1996). This argumentation is in line with Cognitive Response Theory (CRT; Petty and Cacioppo, 1986), which proclaims credible message arguments to result in more favorable ad attitudes, which are considered to moderate consumer self-empowerment. Assuming overall message perception to be positively related to ad evaluation and self-empowerment, the following can be hypothesized:

H 9b: The more credible a pharmaceutical ad, the higher is the degree of self-empowerment derived therefrom.

Research has linked ad evaluation to both product evaluation and purchase intention (Chang, 2004; Chang, 2005). Previous studies have demonstrated that those are influenced by the message appeals utilized, with hard-sell appeals holding the potential to intensify and strengthen purchase intentions (e.g., Okazaki et al., 2010). This state is, nonetheless, not achieved through more favorable attitudes or product evaluations, but by means of the ad content's conviction function (Okazaki et al., 2010). Likewise, positive affective states in consumers lead to more positive product evaluations (Chang, 2004), but only if based on hedonic (emotional) accounts (Adaval, 2001). Being based on quality claims, utilitarian messages are unable to evoke such feelings right away (Johar and Sirgy, 1991).

Nonetheless, an advertisement's success does not depend on its appeal alone, but is contingent upon recipients' affective states (e.g., mood; Pham, 1998) and needs (for respective product). The latter aspect needs to be analyzed in relation to self-congruency effects, which propose consumption to be driven by recipients' needs for self-improvement (Sentis and Markus, 1986). If products arouse the desire for self-enhancement in consumers, they are chosen over products that refrain from doing so (Sirgy, 1982). The same holds true for promotional messages: unless advertisements depict self-congruent images, they remain unnoticed (Hong and Zinkhan, 1995; Chang, 2000). Based on these rationales, the following hypothesis can be deduced:

H 10a: More positive ad evaluations will lead to more positive product evaluations.

Purchase intention is expressive of the recipient's interest in the product offering and develops on the basis of the information's perceived relevance (Zeithaml, 1988), which might be paired with a desire for additional information (Schiffman and Kanuk, 2000). It is controlled by both attitude towards the ad and attitude towards the brand (Teng and Huihuang, 2007), which can fuel consumers' heightened willingness to acquire an advertised product (Lutz et al., 1986). Product endorsers impede ad evaluations as well (Patzer, 1985; Baker and Churchill, 1977); the influence they exercise on purchase intentions is, however, subject to debate. Whilst some researchers noted little or no effects of (attractive) product endorsers (Baker and Churchill, 1977), these findings were proven wrong by others (Caballero et al., 1989), who revealed purchase frequency to moderate responses to attractiveness. Kamins' (1990) research built on this proposition, suggesting that in the case of a beauty- (or health-)enhancing product, the testimonial occupied a central role, since the product's end result was linked to (physical) attractiveness and served as a means of improving individuals' body images. As such, it confirmed consumers' preoccupation with physical attractiveness (Downs and Harrison, 1985; Harrison et al., 2001). Consequently, the following hypothesis can be derived:

H 10b: More positive ad evaluations will lead to heightened purchase intentions.

Product offerings are meant to provide consumers with benefits, suggesting that "customers are less interested in the technical features of a product or service than in what benefits they get from buying, using or consuming the product" (Hooley and Saunders, 1993: 17). According to Sheth et al. (1991), product benefits come in five forms; their list was complemented by Wenben Lai (1995), who came up with an additional three forms. For the present investigation, only a few aspects are of relevance and will be briefly discussed: Tangible product benefits are derived from the product's concrete features (e.g., the way it works), whereas social benefits are an expression of the product's status affiliation (e.g., creating acceptance due to the achievement of a desirable end result). Situational benefits, then, allude to a product meeting situational needs (e.g., when sick, OTC drugs are seen as prospective treatment options).

In order to be made aware of these benefits, consumers need to acquire knowledge on the offering (Muthukrishnan and Weitz, 1991). Studies have shown that highly knowledgeable consumers are not only familiar with the offering itself (a product or a product class) but are also familiar with product usage (Alba and Hutchinson, 1987) – a familiarity that stems from previous experiences, recommendations as well as knowledge (Raju, 1977). When introduced to a new product, knowledge develops only by and by; here, advertisements can assist consumers in accurately assessing a product and, consequently can empower them (Wang et al., 2008). If knowledge is high due to the information retained, consumers might evaluate the product as appealing and become reassured of their competencies, allowing for the following hypothesis:

H 11: The higher the perceived (consumer) self-empowerment, the more positive is the overall product evaluation.

Product evaluations occur along two dimensions, with offerings always being judged in terms of their usability (utilitarian dimension) as well as their pleasantness (hedonic dimension; Batra and Ahtola, 1990). While the former looks at the product's instrumental value in terms of its functional attributions, the latter addresses consumers' subjective evaluations of pleasure as received from the offering (Batra and Ahtola, 1990; Crowley et al., 1992). In terms of product category, hedonic aspects are more often used when promoting low-involvement products, whereas utilitarian aspects are characteristic of high-involvement products (Okazaki et al., 2010), commonly employed in both Western promotional messages (Lin, 2001; Bradley et al., 1994; Cutler and Javalgi, 1994) and in OTC drug adverts, where product specifics are said to guide consumers in their review processes. Thus, the following can by hypothesized:

H 12: The more favorable a product evaluation, the higher is the consumers' purchase intention.

6 Project Description and Design

Over the course of the past decades, the pharmaceutical industry has undergone some drastic changes, with rises in sales being predominantly attributed to so-called drug reclassifications (Rx-to-OTC), meaning drug switches from prescription (Rx) to non-prescription (OTC) status. These have not only empowered consumers but have also significantly decreased health care costs, since OTC medications present a cheap alternative to their prescription counterparts (Kittinger and Herrick, 2005). Switches usually affect medications, which hold a low potential for abuse and whose benefits outrank potential risks, whereby health conditions are self-diagnosed and treated without the assistance of doctors or physicians (DeLorme et al., 2010).

There are several important OTC drug markets worth investigating; the countries to be scrutinized in the present investigation are the United States, the largest single drug market (MarketLine, 2014), Germany, the largest representative of the European medications market (MarketLine, 2014), Austria, a second German-speaking country and the author's home market, as well as Brazil, which was chosen as a prime example of a South American emerging market in the OTC drug industry (MarketLine, 2014). While most cross-cultural research has focused on North America and European countries, other world regions have been less frequently investigated. Besides discussing established markets like Europe and the United States, the inclusion of a South American country has been recommended by Okazaki and Mueller (2007), who found data from Latin America and Asia to be quite scarce. Hence, the inclusion of a country belonging to one of those marginalized areas will help to fill an identified research gap.

6.1 Research Design and Methodology

Generally, health promotion pursues the goal of not only actively tying in people, but to also increase their participation in their own health-care and well-being (WHO, 1996). Through information, it is meant to bring about empowerment, which is "considered to be highly important [and] as a worthwhile health goal in its own right" (Tones and Tilford, 2001: 3). The project at hand is meant to scrutinize to which extent OTC drug print ads (utilizing different ad appeals) contribute to and/or foster consumer self-empowerment. As a cross-cultural research design and setting are aspired to, the project further intends to reveal if manifestations of cultural dimensions do indeed affect promotional evaluations and degrees of consumer self-empowerment respectively. Hence, the investigation explores the following two research questions:

RQ 1: How is a standardized OTC drug ad (utilizing either an informative, emotional, mixed or CSR appeal) evaluated in different cultural contexts (Germany, Austria, the United States and Brazil)?

RQ 2: Out of the four advertising appeals, which appeal leads to the highest degree of consumer self-empowerment?

For the study of cultural differences in advertising, two analytical approaches can be classified, namely content analysis and empirical ad effectiveness studies (Diehl et al., 2003). According to Okazaki and Mueller (2007), content analysis is the most prominently used methodology in the area of cross-cultural advertising research (An, 2007; Nelson and Paek, 2008), where most studies are carried out to check (confirm or reject) advertisements' degrees of similarity in form and content with regard to a priori selected cultural aspects (Cho et al. 1999; Biswas et al., 1992). Therefore, this approach is specifically qualified to establish which advertising content is expressive of a certain spirit of time (Diehl et al., 2003). While content analysis is purely observational, it does not offer any indication of consumer preferences for and acceptability of ad content, which is reserved for empirical studies. These examinations are intended to uncover consumer liking, allowing researchers to arrive at conclusions about which advertising appeals might be most beneficial to marketers (Diehl et al., 2003).

The present research project pays tribute to both forms of research: based on the results of a previously carried out extensive content analysis investigating the potential for advertising standardization in the pharmaceutical (non-prescription drug) industry (Koinig, 2012; Koinig and Diehl, 2013), the present investigation builds upon the results won therein and uses them to design appropriate (standardized) OTC drug promotions. Based on the herein conceptualized empirical investigation, these are to be evaluated in different cultural contexts in order to determine if consumer responses to standardized ads are similar around the globe, or if local adaptations are indeed required. In a second step, advertisements' contributions to consumer self-empowerment will be addressed.

To gain insights into these questions and allow for the comparability of results across countries, a standardized questionnaire was developed, which will be discussed in depth in the up-coming section.

6.1.1 Questionnaire and Variable Operationalization

A structured questionnaire is developed based on established marketing and health scales. The main categories of evaluation utilized in the questionnaire are derived from the theoretical framework (see section 5.4.) and cover: Health Consciousness, Health Information Orientation, Health Information Seeking and Sources of Information, Health Self-Efficacy, Consumers' Attitudes and Skepticism towards (Pharmaceutical) Advertising, OTC Background Information, Relevance of Pharmaceutical Products, Usage of (Non-)Prescription Medicines, Consumers' Product (Category) Involvement, Consumers' Overall Ad Evaluation, Consumers' Message Involvement, Information Processing and Affect, Perceived Susceptibility and Message Relevance, Consumers' Self-Confidence and Empowerment, Attitude towards The Product, Purchase Intention, Relevance of and Perceived Social Responsibility. For each category, items from established health and/or marketing scales are chosen (if available). In addition, each questionnaire will conclude with information on respondents' demographics.

In the following, the different variables with their corresponding questionnaire items, their theoretical origins as well as operationalization in the present project will be briefly discussed. Answers to each question were to be reported on a 7-point Likert scale, with (1) signaling the lowest agreement and (7) the highest agreement possible.

6.1.1.1 Health Consciousness

Health consciousness is grounded in individual differences and people's inclination towards the subject matter (Dutta et al., 2008), moderating health perception respectively health engagement (Moorman and Matulich, 1993). Individuals expressing high levels of health consciousness might be more prone to, e.g. search for information conducive to their well-being or engage in health-enhancing behavior; moreover, they are also more interested in and willing to self-medicate, corresponding with an increased likelihood of OTC drug use. In the following, Gould's Health Consciousness Scale (1988 and 1990) will be consulted, which shows some theoretical overlapping with a follow-up scale developed by Dutta-Bergman (2004). In the conclusion to this section, respondents are asked to indicate both their weight and height, which represent commonly reported measures indicative of respondents' overall physical shape.

A	To which degree do you agree with the following statements?	
		I do not agree at all ... I fully agree
A1	My health depends on how well I take care of myself.	❑ --- ❑ ---❑ ---❑ ---❑ ---❑ ---❑
A2	I actively try to prevent disease and illness.	❑ --- ❑ ---❑ ---❑ ---❑ ---❑ ---❑
A3	I am in good physical health.	❑ --- ❑ ---❑ ---❑ ---❑ ---❑ ---❑
A4	I reflect about my health a lot.	❑ --- ❑ ---❑ ---❑ ---❑ ---❑ ---❑
A5	I am very self-conscious about my health.	❑ --- ❑ ---❑ ---❑ ---❑ ---❑ ---❑
A6	I am constantly examining my health.	❑ --- ❑ ---❑ ---❑ ---❑ ---❑ ---❑
A7	In general, I know my health status very well.	❑ --- ❑ ---❑ ---❑ ---❑ ---❑ ---❑
A8	I am very involved with my health.	❑ --- ❑ ---❑ ---❑ ---❑ ---❑ ---❑
A9	Please indicate your weight.	_______ lbs
A10	Please indicate your height.	_______ ft

Table 3: Operationalization of Health Consciousness (adopted from Gould, 1980/1988 and Dutta-Bergmann, 2004)

6.1.1.2 Health Information Orientation

B	To which degree do you agree with the following statements?	
		I do not agree at all ... I fully agree
B1	The amount of health information available today makes it easier for me to take care of my health.	❑ --- ❑ ---❑ ---❑ ---❑ ---❑ ---❑
B2	To be and stay healthy it is critical to be informed about health issues.	❑ --- ❑ ---❑ ---❑ ---❑ ---❑ ---❑
B3	When sick, I try to get information about my disease.	❑ --- ❑ ---❑ ---❑ ---❑ ---❑ ---❑
B4	Before making a decision about my health, I find out everything I can about this issue.	❑ --- ❑ ---❑ ---❑ ---❑ ---❑ ---❑
B5	I like to get health information from a variety of sources.	❑ --- ❑ ---❑ ---❑ ---❑ ---❑ ---❑
B6	I know where to look to find the pharmaceutical product information I need.	❑ --- ❑ ---❑ ---❑ ---❑ ---❑ ---❑
B7	I feel overwhelmed with the variety of drugs available on the market.	❑ --- ❑ ---❑ ---❑ ---❑ ---❑ ---❑
B8	Choosing a pharmaceutical product takes a lot of careful thought.	❑ --- ❑ ---❑ ---❑ ---❑ ---❑ ---❑
B9	I trust my own judgment when deciding which pharmaceutical product to consider.	❑ --- ❑ ---❑ ---❑ ---❑ ---❑ ---❑

Table 4: Operationalization of Health Information Orientation (adopted from Dutta-Bergman, 2005; Maibach et al., 2006 and Kapferer and Laurent, 1985)

Consumers differ in terms of the efforts they put into finding suitable health information. Health Information Orientation is concerned with people's intended and active (information) search activities (Atkin, 1973; Griffin et al., 1999) and can be used to predict both health behaviors and health outcomes (Shim et al., 2006; van der Molen, 1999). The present study will refer to items from different health scales (Dutta-Bergman, 2005; Maibach et al., 2006), adapting them to the present study's purpose. In addition, one single item [B8] is taken from the Consumer Involvement Profile Scale in order to determine the degree of importance individuals attribute to the purchase of pharmaceutical products (Kapferer and Laurent, 1985).

6.1.1.3 Health Information Seeking and Sources of Information

Health information seeking refers to both the ways and means individuals deploy when looking for information on health-related matters. These sources can be either distinct media channels (e.g., print, broadcast or the Internet) and/or interpersonal sources (e.g., family or peer group members, doctors, or pharmacists; Niederdeppe et al., 2007), which are consulted so as to find answers to concrete health problems. Due to technological advancements and the availability of multiple points of reference, consumers are becoming better informed and information-savvier, feeling more content to arrive at qualified decisions (CHPA, 2013). Health information seeking behavior has been tested in a variety of studies, where it has been linked to positive health attitudes, an urge to search for further information as well as a need to consult (with) different sources; nonetheless, these results are somewhat inconclusive: some studies stress the importance of the Internet as a health-information vehicle, while others support the dominance of traditional sources of information (Dutta-Bergman, 2004; Maibach et al., 2006; Gollop, 1997; Tu and Hargraves, 2003). Following the Nonprescription Drug Manufacturers Association (NDMA), consumers most frequently rely on four sources of information when acquiring information on health issues in general and OTC drugs in particular: product labels, advertising, peer groups (comprising family and friends) as well as physicians and/or pharmacists (NDMA, 1992).

This notion is backed up by more recent research as well, which suggest that the most relevant sources of information are still interpersonal reference points as well as mass media channels (Kim and King, 2009). They are immediately followed by professionals, with both pharmacists and physicians functioning as the most important persons to turn to for advice concerning medical information, regardless of medication type (Kim and King, 2009). Especially recent trends are responsible for pharmacists' rising importance: increasing self-medication practices (Dinkins, 2010), more and better-informed patients, consumers' price-consciousness (Humana, 2002; French, 2011), as well as changing health-care systems throughout the world (Odler, 2010) have elevated this profession's status. Thereby, information obtained from pharmacists primarily concerns details on drugs' side effects, medication usage as well as drug interactions (Eagle and Chamberlain, 2004). Their role in drug purchasing situations is crucial, for they function as experts and/or consultants to patients who might be looking for guidance, advice or clarification (Ricks and Mardanov, 2012), particularly in the area of OTC medications (Smith et al., 2010; Bhangale, 2007), rendering them "a vital part of the consumer's word-of-mouth environment" (Ricks and Mordanov, 2012: 177).

Nonetheless, consumers might often be undecided about which information to trust or which medication to choose; for this reason, they are assumed to not only base their choices on personal preferences but are also likely to consult with other family or peer group members before implementing them. This suggests that they are susceptible to interpersonal influence besides (mass) media sources (de Mooij, 2011). Different cultures appreciate varying sources of information in decision-making processes, whereby information from the media is commonly requested in individualistic countries; in collectivistic cultures, this is not the case, for interpersonal sources are deemed more useful there (An and Kim, 2007), which also score quite high in individualistic or low-context communication countries (word-of-mouth; de Mooij, 2011). Hence, individualistic societies do not only rely on mass media messages alone, but "they also need [...] interpersonal channels and other community-specific media to reinforce mass media messages" (Schiavo, 2007: 257). While most studies have used open questions so far, the present project, following Stephens et al. (2004) as well as the NDMA (1992), explicitly listed a number of sources, which respondents could choose from.

C	**How important are the following sources when searching for health-related information?**	
		not important at all / very important
C1	family (partner, parents, children, etc.)	❑ --- ❑ ---❑ ---❑ ---❑ ---❑ ---❑
C2	friends, acquaintances/colleagues	❑ --- ❑ ---❑ ---❑ ---❑ ---❑ ---❑
C3	doctors, pharmacists or alternative practitioners	❑ --- ❑ ---❑ ---❑ ---❑ ---❑ ---❑
C4	advertising in newspapers and magazines	❑ --- ❑ ---❑ ---❑ ---❑ ---❑ ---❑
C5	advertising on TV and the radio	❑ --- ❑ ---❑ ---❑ ---❑ ---❑ ---❑
C6	advertising on social media sites (e.g., facebook)	❑ --- ❑ ---❑ ---❑ ---❑ ---❑ ---❑
C7	advertising on the Internet	❑ --- ❑ ---❑ ---❑ ---❑ ---❑ ---❑
C8	editorial content in print media	❑ --- ❑ ---❑ ---❑ ---❑ ---❑ ---❑
C9	editorial content in broadcasting	❑ --- ❑ ---❑ ---❑ ---❑ ---❑ ---❑
C10	editorial content on the Internet	❑ --- ❑ ---❑ ---❑ ---❑ ---❑ ---❑
C11	specialist literature (e.g., medical books or magazines)	❑ --- ❑ ---❑ ---❑ ---❑ ---❑ ---❑
C12	Other:________________	❑ --- ❑ ---❑ ---❑ ---❑ ---❑ ---❑

Table 5: Operationalization of Health Information Seeking and Sources of Health Information (adopted from Stephens et al., 2004 and NDMA, 1992)

6.1.1.4 Health Self-Efficacy

Self-Efficacy presents a fixed component in numerous health models, such as Protection Motivation Theory (PMT, Rogers, 1983) and the Health Belief Model (Janz and Becker, 1984; Maiman and Becker, 1974; Rosenstock, 1974), where it is used to refer to the extent to which people perceive themselves as capable of engaging in specific (health-enhancing) behaviors to attain an ideal state of health and well-being. The notion of Self-Efficacy can be traced back to Bandura's Social Cognitive Theory (Bandura, 1997; Bandura, 2001; see sections 5.1. and 5.4.7.1.) and is increasingly incorporated into health messages (Turner et al., 2006): "Individuals are not asked to rate the abilities they possess, but rather the strength of their assurance they can execute given activities under designated situational demands" (Bandura, 2007: 646).

In the health domain, Self-Efficacy is usually tested in relation to a particular disease; for this reason, the area of self-medication is emphasized in the present project. Overall questions are intended to determine individuals' (self-)confidence in executing a given behavior that is meant to be conducive to their health (Lee et al., 2008). Items were borrowed from scales developed by Lee et al. (2005), Umphrey (2004) as well as Rimal et al. (2005).

D	**To which degree do you agree with the following statements?**	
		I do not agree at all — I fully agree
D1	I consider myself capable of taking care of my body.	❑ --- ❑ ---❑ ---❑ ---❑ ---❑ ---❑
D2	I consider myself capable of finding the right information to make qualified health decisions.	❑ --- ❑ ---❑ ---❑ ---❑ ---❑ ---❑
D3	Usually, I can make sense of the health information I am presented with.	❑ --- ❑ ---❑ ---❑ ---❑ ---❑ ---❑
D4	I can use my knowledge to improve my health.	❑ --- ❑ ---❑ ---❑ ---❑ ---❑ ---❑
D5	I rely more on doctors and/or pharmacists than on self-medication.	❑ --- ❑ ---❑ ---❑ ---❑ ---❑ ---❑
D6	I am interested in self-medication.	❑ --- ❑ ---❑ ---❑ ---❑ ---❑ ---❑
D7	I consider myself capable of self-medication.	❑ --- ❑ ---❑ ---❑ ---❑ ---❑ ---❑
D8	I already practice self-medication.	❑ --- ❑ ---❑ ---❑ ---❑ ---❑ ❑
		never — very often
D9	How often do you practice self-medication?	❑ --- ❑ ---❑ ---❑ ---❑ ---❑ ---❑

Table 6: Operationalization of Health Self-Efficacy (adopted from Lee et al., 2005; Umphrey, 2004 and Rimal et al., 2005)

6.1.1.5 Attitude and Skepticism Towards (Pharmaceutical) Advertising

When investigating consumer opinions on (OTC drug) advertising and their evaluations of promotional material, two constructs are of vital importance: attitude and skepticism (Diehl et al., 2008; see section 5.4.7.4.). Comparing those two constructs, attitude is characterized by a strong emotional connection, leading respondents to "like" a product advert. As such, it is renowned to be the single-most important direct determinant of behavioral intention (Bagozzi, 1981). Skepticism requires more cognitive resources and is concerned with how the message is perceived in terms of the believability of its (informative) content (Diehl et al., 2008).

In order to test attitude towards advertising in general, the three-item scale developed by Pollay and Mittal (1993) will be applied. In the following, it will be adapted to fit the topic of non-prescription drug advertising, as suggested by Diehl et al. (2008). In a similar manner, skepticism will be measured along a scale created by Obermiller and Spangenberg (1998); their scale is, however, more focused on believability and, thus, items will be reverse-coded to offer insights into skepticism; in addition, they will be slightly altered to suit the category of medical products.

F	To which degree do you agree with the following statements?	
		I do not agree at all … I fully agree
F1	Advertisers for pharmaceuticals know how to provide the information that is needed to make a qualified decision.	❑ --- ❑ --- ❑ --- ❑ --- ❑ --- ❑ --- ❑
F2	Overall, I consider advertising for pharmaceuticals a good thing.	❑ --- ❑ --- ❑ --- ❑ --- ❑ --- ❑ --- ❑
F3	My general opinion about advertising for pharmaceuticals is unfavorable.	❑ --- ❑ --- ❑ --- ❑ --- ❑ --- ❑ --- ❑
F4	Overall, I do like advertising for pharmaceuticals.	❑ --- ❑ --- ❑ --- ❑ --- ❑ --- ❑ --- ❑
F5	I can depend on getting the truth in most advertising for pharmaceuticals.	❑ --- ❑ --- ❑ --- ❑ --- ❑ --- ❑ --- ❑
F6	Advertising for pharmaceuticals' aim is to inform the consumer.	❑ --- ❑ --- ❑ --- ❑ --- ❑ --- ❑ --- ❑
F7	I feel I have been accurately informed after viewing most advertisements for pharmaceuticals.	❑ --- ❑ --- ❑ --- ❑ --- ❑ --- ❑ --- ❑

Table 7: Operationalization of Attitude and Skepticism towards (Pharmaceutical) Advertising (adopted from Pollay and Mittal, 1993; Obermiller and Spangenberg, 1998 and Diehl et al., 2008)

6.1.1.6 OTC Background Information

Over the last decade, the pharmaceutical industry has incurred significant alterations, especially with the generic and non-prescription drug markets gaining in sales revenues (Sheppard, 2009; see section 1.1.), together with an increased demand for dietary supplements and alternative medications (Springston and Weaver Lariscy, 2010). The booming of OTC drugs does not only contribute to lower health expenses (Grunberg and Klein, 2009), but also to heightened degrees of OTC drug acceptance amongst the wider public (Brems et al., 2011). This is especially the case in the United States, the largest OTC drug market, where these preparations are preferably listed as first line treatments (Accent Health, 2014), alluding to the high degree of trust this product category enjoys (Nielsen and IMS, 2013).

Medicinal products in general are useful for fostering self-medication practices since their benefits outweigh potential risks (Vuckovic and Nichter, 1997). Most non-prescription substances available for sale are renowned to be safe and beneficial to individual health and their consumption is facilitated by previous experience and long-standing familiarity (Bissell et al., 2001): "Use of non-prescription medicines [is] seen to be a relatively ingrained and taken-for-granted activity, largely divorced from considerations of risk [and] barely worthy of much reflexive consideration" (Bissell et al., 2001: 17-23). Their accessibility and convenient availability (specifically in the United States) lead 93 % of Americans to use OTC drugs for minor medical conditions not only for themselves but also for their children (Nielsen and IMS, 2013).

While the OTC drug sector is quite similar to the retail sector in terms of regulation, the prescription drug industry is subject to more thorough review processes throughout the world (Blackett and Harrison, 2001). Yet, legal regulations vary widely across the globe: Looking at the European and U.S.-American pharmaceutical industries as examples, striking differences become clear: OTC medications can be freely sold at numerous points of sale in the U.S. but are limited to pharmacies in Europe to the largest extent (Brems et al., 2011), albeit regulations are being loosened slowly but surely (MarketLine, 2014). Additionally, in some European markets demand for OTC drugs is limited due to the existence of reimbursed prescription alternatives (Brems et al., 2011), impeding the attractiveness and appeal of non-prescription preparations. Some significant differences do, however, exist between those two product categories: OTC medications are non habit-forming, suitable for self-medication due to their low levels of toxicity and only contain compounds renowned to be safe (Hanson et al., 2005).

Another aspect influencing the acceptance of OTC drugs over both their prescription and generic counterparts are past experiences [question G3], which need to be taken into consideration, inasmuch as they are likely to increase potential risk information retention when exposed to a promotional message (Sullivan et al., 1999).

G	**The ad you are about to evaluate is for non-prescription, over-the counter (OTC) medication. So in advance, I would like to know to which degree you do agree with the following statements.**	
		I do not agree at all / I fully agree
G1	I think advertising for OTC medications is strictly regulated by the government.	❑ --- ❑ ---❑ ---❑ ---❑ ---❑ ---❑ ❑ I don't know
G2	Most OTC drug ads provide balanced information (risks and benefits).	❑ --- ❑ ---❑ ---❑ ---❑ ---❑ ---❑
G3	My previous experiences with OTC drugs were positive.	❑ --- ❑ ---❑ ---❑ ---❑ ---❑ ---❑
G4	I consider OTC drugs as effective as prescription drugs.	❑ --- ❑ ---❑ ---❑ ---❑ ---❑ ---❑

Table 8: Operationalization of OTC Background Information (adopted from Blackett and Harrison, 2001 and Sullivan et al., 1999)

6.1.1.7 Evaluation of Different Pharmaceutical Product Types

Pharmaceutical medicines do not only cover prescription and non-prescription drugs (see section 4.1.3.), but also include homeopathy and/or natural substances. While prescription-only medications require a physician's approval, both pharmacy medicines and general sales list preparations can be purchased without any kind of supervision in either pharmacies or retail stores, depending on geographic location (Bissell et al., 2001). These two forms classify as 'conventional' or 'mainstream' medicine in the Western world, where they constitute the norm. In terms of composition, they are based on hard facts and scientific evidence, proclaiming that treating or diagnosing disease is only possible by looking at either its physiological or pathological causes (Segen's Medical Dictionary, 2012).

Apart from mainstream medicine, alternative practices and preparations are starting to gain ground, with the prime example being homeopathic medicine (or homeopathy; NCCAM, 2013). Its roots can be traced back to Germany, where preparations primarily made up of substances like herbs and minerals were first introduced. In the United States, homeopathic remedies are under FDA supervision (NCCAM, 2013), while they are less strictly regulated in Europe. Despite the lack of medical evidence, these drugs are well accepted in the United States, with almost 4 million citizens having occasionally used homeopathic preparations already in 2007 (NCCAM, 2013). Also natural health products (NHPs), such as vitamins and/or supplements, present a special OTC drug category that is exclusively based on non-chemical substances or herbs (Boon et al., 2012).

H	How do you evaluate the following types of medicine?	
		not good at all — very good
H1	conventional/mainstream medicine	❑ --- ❑ ---❑ ---❑ ---❑ ---❑ ---❑
H2	homeopathic substances/homeopathy	❑ --- ❑ ---❑ ---❑ ---❑ ---❑ ---❑
H3	herbal substances	❑ --- ❑ ---❑ ---❑ ---❑ ---❑ ---❑
H4	Other_________________________	❑ --- ❑ ---❑ ---❑ ---❑ ---❑ ---❑

Table 9: Operationalization of Evaluation of Pharmaceutical Product Types (adopted from NCCAM, 2013)

6.1.1.8 *Usage of (Non-)Prescription Medicines*

While the prior set of questions measured the acceptance of several drug categories, the question at hand solely focuses on the two main drug types, namely prescription and non-prescription (OTC) drugs and their frequency of use within one year. Following previous studies, OTC remedies and/or dietary supplements "are consumed for utilitarian or functional reasons (i.e. to become healthier, to prevent illness, or to treat a medical condition)" (Main et al., 2004: 121). This is the case since these drugs are regarded as being relatively safe, curing minor conditions for which a physician does not necessarily have to be consulted. Thus, these medicines are assumed to be used more often than their prescription counterparts, which are acquired following a more complex diagnosis and hold a higher toxicity potential (Mintzes, 2006).

I	How often do you usually take the following substances within a year?	
		never — very often
I1	non-prescription/OTC medicines	❑ --- ❑ ---❑ ---❑ ---❑ ---❑ ---❑
I2	prescription medicines	❑ --- ❑ ---❑ ---❑ ---❑ ---❑ ---❑

Table 10: Operationalization of (OTC) Drug Usage (adopted from Main et al., 2004)

6.1.1.9 *Product (Category) Involvement*

Consumer involvement with the ad as well as the product (category) determine ad relevance and product involvement (Zaichowsky, 1985; Celsi and Olson, 1988), which is defined as the association of product/message characteristics as being beneficial to the achievement of consumers' goals and needs respectively (McGrath and Mahood, 2004). Previous research has observed that personally-relevant messages are processed more willingly and frequently by consumers than those considered to be of little relevance (Bell et al., 1999). Following the example of past studies (Vaughn, 1980), a block of three involvement questions is included and deemed sufficient to offer an indication of the product category's (non-prescription drug's) relevance to end users (Laurent and Kapferer, 1985).

J	To which degree do you agree with the following statements?	
		I do not agree at all — I fully agree
J1	I am interested in non-prescription (OTC) drugs.	❑ --- ❑ ---❑ ---❑ ---❑ ---❑ ---❑
J2	Non-prescription (OTC) drugs are important to me.	❑ --- ❑ ---❑ ---❑ ---❑ ---❑ ---❑
J3	I attach (great) importance to non-prescription (OTC) drugs.	❑ --- ❑ ---❑ ---❑ ---❑ ---❑ ---❑

Table 11: Operationalization of Product (Category) Involvement (adopted from Laurent and Kapferer, 1985)

6.1.1.10 Overall Ad Evaluation

Part 3: OTC Print Ad Analysis		
		not good at all — very good
K	**In general, I find the ad …**	❑ --- ❑ ---❑ ---❑ ---❑ ---❑ ---❑
L	**To which degree do you agree with the following statements?**	
	The advertisement is…	I do not agree at all — I fully agree
L1	interesting	❑ --- ❑ ---❑ ---❑ ---❑ ---❑ ---❑
L2	emotional	❑ --- ❑ ---❑ ---❑ ---❑ ---❑ ---❑
L3	pleasant	❑ --- ❑ ---❑ ---❑ ---❑ ---❑ ---❑
L4	good	❑ --- ❑ ---❑ ---❑ ---❑ ---❑ ---❑
L5	favorable	❑ --- ❑ ---❑ ---❑ ---❑ ---❑ ---❑
L6	positive	❑ --- ❑ ---❑ ---❑ ---❑ ---❑ ---❑
L7	informative	❑ --- ❑ ---❑ ---❑ ---❑ ---❑ ---❑
L8	convincing	❑ --- ❑ ---❑ ---❑ ---❑ ---❑ ---❑
L9	credible	❑ --- ❑ ---❑ ---❑ ---❑ ---❑ ---❑
L10	truthful	❑ --- ❑ ---❑ ---❑ ---❑ ---❑ ---❑
L11	believable	❑ --- ❑ ---❑ ---❑ ---❑ ---❑ ---❑
L12	comprehensible	❑ --- ❑ ---❑ ---❑ ---❑ ---❑ ---❑
L13	well structured	❑ --- ❑ ---❑ ---❑ ---❑ ---❑ ---❑
L14	clear	❑ --- ❑ ---❑ ---❑ ---❑ ---❑ ---❑

Table 12: Operationalization of Overall Ad Evaluation (adopted from Zuckermann, 1988/1991; Lane et al., 2006; Palmgreen et al., 2006; Edell and Burke, 1987)

For the overall OTC drug ad evaluation, both cognitive and emotional measures are included, borrowing from two distinct value concepts: the perceived Message Cognition Value (MCV) and the perceived Message Sensation Value (MSV; Zuckermann, 1988; Zuckermann, 1991). The first classification – the Message Cognition Value – refers to an ad's complexity and implicitness, evaluating the overall ad effectiveness by measuring how specific message features are perceived and responded to by consumers. The MCV is composed of the following three factors, namely clarity, credibility and perceived challenge (Lane et al., 2006), with only the former two aspects receiving consideration in the present investigation.

These variables are combined with items taken from the second concept, the perceived Message Sensation Value (MSV) as well as Edell and Burke's (1987) Feeling Toward

Ads scale. While the MCV is especially suited to engage audience members exhibiting high needs for cognition, the MSV and related scales are particularly useful in measuring responses by recipients with high needs for arousal (Donohew et al., 1991; Donohew et al., 1998). Two items are adopted from Palmgreen et al.'s Perceived Sensation Value scale (2002), while the remaining emotional items are derived from Edell and Burke (1987).

6.1.1.11 Message Involvement, Information Processing and Affect

Having been briefly elaborated on as part of the previous section, both the perceived Message Cognition Value (MCV) and the perceived Message Sensation Value (MSV) prove to be vital constructs to survey message involvement and information processing. Since empowerment predominantly builds on information, the former will be given preference over the latter in order to determine message involvement. Following the example of Lane et al. (2006) as well as Puto and Wells (1984), this section's first part deals with the message's degree of validity and perceived accuracy by recipients, which is then paired up with questions regarding the promotion's degree of comprehensibility and clarity.

M	To which degree do you agree with the following statements?	
		I do not agree at all / I fully agree
M1	The ad makes valid claims.	❑ --- ❑ ---❑ ---❑ ---❑ ---❑ ---❑
M2	The ad presents accurate information.	❑ --- ❑ ---❑ ---❑ ---❑ ---❑ ---❑
M3	The message was easy to follow.	❑ --- ❑ ---❑ ---❑ ---❑ ---❑ ---❑
M4	I think the ad addresses relevant product features.	❑ --- ❑ ---❑ ---❑ ---❑ ---❑ ---❑
M5	I understand the features well enough to evaluate the product.	❑ --- ❑ ---❑ ---❑ ---❑ ---❑ ---❑
M6	The ad improves my level of information regarding pharmaceuticals.	❑ --- ❑ ---❑ ---❑ ---❑ ---❑ ---❑

Table 13: Operationalization of Message Involvement, Information Processing and Affect (adopted from Lane et al., 2006 and Puto and Wells, 1984)

6.1.1.12 Perceived Susceptibility and Message Relevance

While Self-Efficacy (or recipients' evaluations of their self-medication abilities) has been tested before (see section 6.2.1.4.), one question also concerns the relevance of pain medications as a potential remedy to ease specific physical conditions. This question is included to test an OTC pain medication's perceived usefulness to recipients, whereby the higher the perceived importance, the more likely recipients are to long to purchase the advertised drug – provided the message is able to trigger their interests.

Ideally, promotions in the OTC drug sector manage to strengthen respondents' self-medication abilities and their belief therein (Maibach et al., 1991). This particular question is clustered with two more items measuring recipients' attitudes towards pain medications as well as their frequency of use within a year.

N	The ad you have seen was promoting a pain killer. To which degree do you agree with the following statements?	
		I do not agree at all ... I fully agree
N1	I have a positive attitude towards pain medications.	❑ --- ❑ ---❑ ---❑ ---❑ ---❑ ---❑
N2	I am confident that pain medications can improve my current health status.	❑ --- ❑ ---❑ ---❑ ---❑ ---❑ ---❑
		never ... very often
N3	How often do you take pain medications?	❑ --- ❑ ---❑ ---❑ ---❑ ---❑ ---❑

Table 14: Operationalization of Perceived Susceptibility and Message Relevance (adopted from Luszczynska and Schwarzer, 2005 and Schwarzer and Jerusalem, 1995)

6.1.1.13 Consumer Self-Confidence and Empowerment

Being based on Self-Efficacy, empowerment has been measured in numerous contexts with corresponding items (Kasen et al., 1992; Bandura, 1997; Lee et al., 2008; see section 5.4.6.1.); however, little has been done to come up with a unified concept, which would allow for a broader applicability. Since no suitable scale to measure empowerment could be transferred to the advertising realm, Self-Efficacy and consumer self-confidence scales (Schwarzer and Jerusalem, 1995; Bearden et al., 2001) are consulted in the process of the empowerment scale development.

Following Bandura's Social Cognitive Theory (1976; 2007: 646), Self-Efficacy can be described as "a perceived operative capability" that is grounded in individuals' very own capabilities. These comprise a person's beliefs in possessing the skills required to perform an action (so-called "resources"), together with their will and/or dedication to engage in such an action. Self-Efficacy is not concerned with people's abilities, but with the strength of their convictions of being able to achieve a goal based on specific situational needs (Bandura, 2007). As such, it captures the gist and purpose of empowerment and the role of OTC drug promotions in this matter: by use of information, advertisements hold the potential to educate consumers, involve them in their health care, and strengthen (their beliefs in) their self-medication abilities.

As the hereby derived empowerment can be traced back to information presented in commercial messages, a valuable marketing concept needs to be introduced at this point as well, namely consumer self-confidence (Bearden et al., 2001). The authors define the term as “the extent to which an individual feels capable and assured with respect to his or her marketplace decisions and behaviors” (Bearden et al., 2001: 122). Consumer self-confidence is based on message evaluations and the product knowledge acquired in the process (Bearden et al., 2001; Loibl et al., 2009), which factors into individual decision making and determines both the personal and social outcomes associated with an action (Folkes and Kiesler, 1991). In line with SCT, an increased belief in their own skills and abilities is likely to encourage individuals to take up even challenging and complex tasks (Bandura and Locke, 2003), just as it might be the case with self-medication by use of OTC drugs.

The questions developed for the present investigation measure empowerment on several levels: (1) Empowerment derived from the promotional message (Message Empowerment), (2) Empowerment in the self-medication realm, which is assumed to reassure individuals of their own Self-Medication abilities (Self-Medication Empowerment), and (3) Empowerment in one's own Health(care), granting individuals an increased say in their well-being (Health Empowerment).

O	To which degree do you agree with the following statements?	
		I do not agree at all ... I fully agree
O1	The ad allows me to objectively evaluate SENZA.	❑ --- ❑ ---❑ ---❑ ---❑ ---❑ ---❑
O2	I learned something from this advertisement that I did not know before about pain medications.	❑ --- ❑ ---❑ ---❑ ---❑ ---❑ ---❑
O3	I can now accurately compare SENZA with other competing brands on matters that are important to me.	❑ --- ❑ ---❑ ---❑ ---❑ ---❑ ---❑
O4	I would have more confidence in using SENZA now than before I saw this commercial.	❑ --- ❑ ---❑ ---❑ ---❑ ---❑ ---❑
O5	The advertisement was useful and provided me with new insights regarding pain and pain medication.	❑ --- ❑ ---❑ ---❑ ---❑ ---❑ ---❑
O6	I feel more confident in my self-medication skills/practices after having studied this ad.	❑ --- ❑ ---❑ ---❑ ---❑ ---❑ ---❑
O7	I am more interested in self-medication now than before seeing the ad.	❑ --- ❑ ---❑ ---❑ ---❑ ---❑ ---❑
O8	After seeing the ad I feel more autonomous with regard to my health.	❑ --- ❑ ---❑ ---❑ ---❑ ---❑ ---❑
O9	After seeing the ad I feel more capable with regard to my health.	❑ --- ❑ ---❑ ---❑ ---❑ ---❑ ---❑
O10	I feel like I have a greater say in my health after seeing the ad.	❑ --- ❑ ---❑ ---❑ ---❑ ---❑ ---❑
O11	The advertising message gives me stronger control over my health.	❑ --- ❑ ---❑ ---❑ ---❑ ---❑ ---❑
O12	The advertising message enables me to improve my health.	❑ --- ❑ ---❑ ---❑ ---❑ ---❑ ---❑
O13	The advertising message empowers me to make better health-related decisions.	❑ --- ❑ ---❑ ---❑ ---❑ ---❑ ---❑

Table 15: Operationalization of Consumer Self-Empowerment (own scale)

6.1.1.14 Product Evaluation

While general advertising effectiveness has already been measured before (see section 6.3.1.11), attitude towards the promoted product needs to be evaluated separately. Generally, this variable can be defined as individuals' dispositions towards a promotion and the product promoted, which can be either favorable or unfavorable and are influenced by the information included in an advertisement (Burton et al., 1998; Brakus et al., 2009; Aaker, 1997). The image won is based on the strength of both a message's emotional and rational specifics (Dobni and Zinkhan, 1990; Petty et al., 2007), which serve as a basis for the product's overall evaluation, with positive attitude being often correlated with personal relevance (Petty and Cacioppo, 1986). Evaluations are generated along the dimension of the offering's perceived quality which is meant to define the product in terms of its competitive advantage, e.g., with regard to excellence or superiority over competing brands (Zeithaml, 1988; Aaker and Jacobson, 1994). Positive attitudes are then presumed to moderate product choice and purchase intention (Fazio and Petty, 2007; Petty et al., 1995; Priester et al., 2004).

P	To which degree do you agree with the following statements?	
		I do not agree at all — I fully agree
P1	The advertised product (SENZA) makes a good impression.	❑ --- ❑ ---❑ ---❑ ---❑ ---❑ ---❑
P2	SENZA is of high quality.	❑ --- ❑ ---❑ ---❑ ---❑ ---❑ ---❑
P3	SENZA is attractive.	❑ --- ❑ ---❑ ---❑ ---❑ ---❑ ---❑
P4	SENZA is appealing.	❑ --- ❑ ---❑ ---❑ ---❑ ---❑ ---❑

Table 16: Operationalization of Attitude towards the Product (adopted from Dobni and Zinkhan, 1990; Brakus et al., 2009; Aaker, 1997)

6.1.1.15 Purchase Intention

Following numerous authors (Mittal, 1989; Dodds et al., 1991), purchase intention references an individual's willingness to buy and/or try a promoted product, which is partially based on situational involvement (Houston and Rothschild, 1977; see section 5.4.5.), offering some indication of the (temporary) relevance of a product to the recipient (Richins et al., 1992). Besides involvement, purchase intention is closely linked to the previous category, namely product attitudes formed in consequence of the promotional information received (Slama and Tashchian, 1985); when regarded as valuable, it can gear respondents towards making qualified purchase decisions (Aaker and Norris, 1982).

The relationship between ad attitudes and purchase intentions – often referred to as ad effectiveness – has found liking an ad to correlate with positive brand attitudes (Holbrook, 1978), consequently making ad effectiveness central to predicting potential outcomes (e.g., purchase intention; Haley and Baldinger, 1991). Study results, however, are inconclusive, portending that the relationship between product attitude and purchase intention is not that pronounced in the case of unfamiliar brands; yet, ad attitude and purchase intention in general are positively connected to one another (Brown and Stayman, 1992).

Q	To which degree do you agree with the following statements?	
		I do not agree at all … I fully agree
Q1	I could imagine trying SENZA.	❑ --- ❑ ---❑ ---❑ ---❑ ---❑ ---❑
Q2	I could imagine buying SENZA.	❑ --- ❑ ---❑ ---❑ ---❑ ---❑ ---❑
Q3	I could imagine SENZA being one of my most likely choices for my next purchases.	❑ --- ❑ ---❑ ---❑ ---❑ ---❑ ---❑
Q4	I am interested in more information on SENZA and will look it up online (on facebook, twitter, google+).	❑ --- ❑ ---❑ ---❑ ---❑ ---❑ ---❑

Table 17: Operationalization of Purchase Intention (adopted from Mittal, 1989; Dodds et al., 1991)

6.1.1.16 Relevance of and Perceived Social Responsibility

In the present-day, globalized marketplace, social and environmental engagements on behalf of multi-national enterprises are paramount to commercial success (Beh, 1994; Murray and Vogel, 1997) and serve as a means of establishing legitimacy (Colleoni, 2013). Even though CSR has already been discussed before (see section 5.4.1.), the concept's most relevant aspects will be emphasized once again. CSR presents "a concept whereby companies integrate social and environmental concerns in their business operations and in their interactions with their stakeholders on a voluntary basis" (European Commission, 2008). Initiatives cover all "practices that improve the workplace and benefit society in ways that go above and beyond what companies are legally required to do" (Vogel, 2006). As such, CSR allows companies to connect with their various stakeholders by informing them about (desired) benefits (Tench et al., 2007). Research in the field of CSR engagements reports a positive relationship between firms' CSR initiatives and favorable consumer attitudes toward those businesses (Brown and Dacin, 1997; Creyer and Ross, 1997; Ellen et al., 2000). Yet, not only consumer attitudes hinge on corporate CSR projects, but also behavioral intentions (Guchait et al., 2011), as half of all respondents are willing to increasingly purchase from responsible manufacturers as well as pay more for products manufactured by companies that go beyond merely obeying the law (Nielsen, 2012; Nielsen, 2013; Nielsen, 2014). This suggests that as long as message sources are perceived as (acting) in a socially responsible manner by consumers (Ross et al., 1992), positive efforts are likely to be translated into an increased likelihood of actual product purchase (Smith and Alcorn, 1991; Nan and Heo, 2007).

In this context, product-cause fit is crucial: The concept of fit looks at how compatible the product and designated cause are and is usually determined by the two concepts' commonalities (e.g., similar customer base or values; Nan and Heo, 2007). This means that the promoted brand or product ought to be congruent with the designated social cause that is supported (Nan and Heo, 2007), functioning as a moderator of consumer responses and a determinant of the promotional campaign's overall success (Rifon et al., 2004). To measure recipients' extent of involvement with corporate social behavior, three questions were taken from the survey instrument developed by Nan and Heo (2007). Two more questions were added, which were tailored to the present project, asking respondents to rate the CSR engagement on behalf of the pharmaceutical manufacturer (ProSante) as well as the perceived product-cause fit.

R	To which degree do you agree with the following statements?	
		I do not agree at all — I fully agree
R1	I think positively about enterprises which act socially responsible.	❑ --- ❑ ---❑ ---❑ ---❑ ---❑ ---❑
R2	It is important to me that enterprises increasingly consider social issues.	❑ --- ❑ ---❑ ---❑ ---❑ ---❑ ---❑
R3	I would increasingly purchase products from enterprises which act socially responsible.	❑ --- ❑ ---❑ ---❑ ---❑ ---❑ ---❑
R4	I have the impression ProSante (producer of SENZA) is a socially responsible company.	❑ --- ❑ ---❑ ---❑ ---❑ ---❑ ---❑
R5	I think that ProSante donating vaccines to reduce infant death caused by Tetanus represents a good match between the product and the cause.	❑ --- ❑ ---❑ ---❑ ---❑ ---❑ ---❑

Table 18: Operationalization of CSR Relevance (adopted from Nan and Heo, 2007)

6.1.1.17 Demographic Information

Rounding up the overall survey, the last section inquired about respondents' demographic information, including their employment status, profession, susceptibility to stress, as well as their sex, level of education, age, and marital status as well as number of children. Both nationality and student status were listed in addition in order to (1) guarantee (almost) identical sample sizes in all countries, (2) reduce student participation to a minimum, and (3) include only respondents who were residents in the country under investigation.

Part 4: Demographic Information		
S1	Are you a student?	❑ yes ❑ no
S2	Are you employed?	❑ yes ❑ no
S3	Do you work full time or part time?	❑ full time ❑ part time
S4	Please indicate your profession.	________________
T	**To which degree do you agree with the following statements?**	
	My daily activities are…	I do not agree at all … I fully agree
T1	physically demanding.	❑ --- ❑ --- ❑ --- ❑ --- ❑ --- ❑ --- ❑
T2	hectic.	❑ --- ❑ --- ❑ --- ❑ --- ❑ --- ❑ --- ❑
U1	Please indicate your sex.	❑ female ❑ male
U2	Please indicate your nationality.	________________
U3	How old are you?	______ years
V	Please indicate your (highest) level of education.	❑ no graduation ❑ primary school graduation ❑ graduation from secondary modern school ❑ graduation from high school ❑ graduation from university/ college
W1	Do you live in a domestic partnership?	❑ yes ❑ no
W2	Do you have children?	❑ yes ❑ no
W3	If yes, how many children do you have?	______ child/ren

Table 19: Operationalization of Demographic Information (own scale)

6.1.2 Study Design and Ad Development

As outlined below (see Figure **17**), the present project comprised two main studies and three distinct pre-tests, which were conducted between December 2010 and August 2014; these will be described in detail in the following sections.

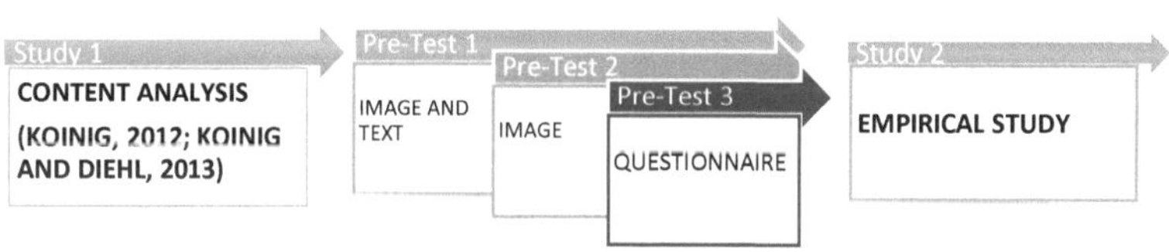

Figure 17: Study Design (own illustration)

6.1.2.1 Study 1

By use of an extensive cross-cultural content analysis, Study 1 set out to investigate the standardization potential of non-prescription drug adverts in Austria, Germany, and the United States. A high potential for unification was assumed on the basis of the countries' similarities according to GLOBE dimensions (House et al., 2004), and concerned two areas, namely product endorser and ad appeal. An in-depth analysis of 385 magazine (print) ads (Austria and Germany[1]: 183; United States: 202) collected from December 2010 to August 2011 yielded some interesting findings: in all countries, product endorsers in non-prescription drug promotions were predominantly female "Typical Person Testimonials" (Martin et al, 2008: 29; Feick and Higie, 1992), who conformed with dominant beauty standards. They were young, in good physical shape and healthy; moreover, they were usually portrayed by themselves and placed in a neutral setting. In terms of ad appeal, promotions utilized informative appeals to the largest extent in their headlines, body copies and slogans, with U.S.-American promotions taking a slightly more emotional stance (Koinig, 2012). As in all countries under investigation, both traditional gender portrayals and rational arguments prevailed, the assumption of a standardization potential of non-prescription drug ads could be confirmed.

On the grounds of the findings produced by Study 1, a second investigation was planned in an attempt to find out if standardization is indeed a fruitful concept for the pharmaceutical industry. This project at hand is, thus, meant to test consumer evaluations in four different countries when presented with one of four fictitious (yet standardized) OTC drug promotions, raising the question as to which ad is perceived most favorably and is especially suited to trigger consumer (self-)empowerment. Prior to conducting the second main study, three pre-tests were performed to ensure the suitability of the stimulus material.

6.1.2.2 (Stimuli) Ad Development

Research on promotional activities in the pharmaceutical industry has shown that in advertisements for either non-prescription medications or dietary supplements, the larger proportion of the ad is still reserved for the body copy, in which a (lengthy) message is meant to appeal to (potential) consumers. "Advertisers are relatively free to communicate any message desired in this promotional portion of the advertisement, regardless of the content of the warning information" (Main et al., 2004: 121). While

[1] German-speaking magazines are available on both the Austrian and German market.

information on both risks and adverse effects would surely be appreciated by the target audience, pharmaceutical promotions tend to be rather one-sided (Koinig, 2012), appraising a product to work its magic and evoking unrealistic expectations in recipients about drugs' potentials (Gilbody et al., 2005). As such, "OTC drug ads also focused 'on the concern of what the drug will do for the consumer, rather than on the reasons why the drug should be ingested'" (Kline, 2010: 561; Tsao, 1997: 186).

Keeping message concision in mind, ad comprehensibility is subject to the amount of information presented in the promotion, with too much information leading to an information overload, while too little information may result in trade-offs (Menon et al., 2004; Morris et al., 1989). In addition, information structure and clarity are key elements in consumers' information processing patterns (Menon et al., 2003; Menon et al., 2004) and can assist marketers in creating product awareness as well as message involvement, cautiously advising members of the target audience to comply with treatment regimens and/or seek further information (Hoek et al., 2001).

In accordance with reported trends in promotional design, the advertisements developed for the present study were based on Rossiter and Bellman's (2005) recommendations, who suggest the use of a (more or less dominant) visual in advertising (Rossiter and Percy, 1980). The image utilized could be either a product illustration or an 'emotional' picture and is recommended to occupy at least half of the ad. Ideally, as much as two thirds of the print ad can be taken up. Moreover, the actual message (the body copy) should be kept short (less than 200 words; Rossiter and Bellman, 2005; Pollay, 1985), while being removed in the case of emotional ads. With ads swaying more towards emotional approaches (Okazaki et al., 2010; Koinig, 2012), the present study also wanted to pay tribute to this development. Research has produced evidence that – in spite of informative appeals' unbroken dominance in the pharmaceutical industry (Koinig, 2012) – emotional appeals might also fulfill their duty of involving consumers. Having been developed in response to consumers' high levels of skepticisms, emotional messages present a way of circumventing audience doubtfulness (Friestad and Wright, 1994).

Following a 2012 survey, print promotions in magazines literally seem to be "a prescription for health results" (Magazine.org, 2012), allowing readers to get more involved in health-care matters when compared to other media channels. This holds especially true when it comes to acquiring a non-prescription medication; readers are highly likely to purchase an OTC drug after having come across a print ad, since these promotions are seen as being especially beneficial to health care consumers (Magazine.org, 2012; see Figure **18**).

Magazines are a prescription for **healthy results**

The MARS OTC/DTC study reveals that magazine readers are by far the most likely to take action on healthcare ads when compared to the users of any other medium.

Actions Taken Last 12 Months Due to Healthcare Advertising

	magazines	internet	television	radio	newspapers
Returned free sample card	**179**	88	168	139	117
Discussed an ad with your doctor	**148**	102	123	119	113
Called a toll free number to get additional information	**161**	118	136	112	138
Asked doctor for a prescription sample	**140**	97	118	110	104
Visited any website	**142**	139	129	100	124
Consulted a pharmacist	**133**	90	126	112	118
Switched to a different brand	**145**	96	134	120	104
Discussed an ad with a friend/relative	**150**	104	116	109	122
Asked doctor to prescribe a specific drug	**135**	116	122	108	114
Purchased a non-prescription product	**126**	99	122	107	108

Base: Top two quintiles by medium, indexed to adults 18+
Source: MARS OTC/DTC Study, April 2012

Figure 18: Actions Taken After Print-Ad Exposure in Magazines (Magazine.org, 2012: 45)

In total, four full-page print advertisements were developed, which differed considerably in their message appeals, ranging from purely informative, over mixed and CSR to purely emotional. To avoid the impact of an established and well-known brand name and the influence it exercises on product evaluations (Yin, 1999), a value-free, fictitious pain-medication brand ('Senza') was chosen for the present study.

Ad composition followed the procedure outlined by Diehl et al. (2011). First off, a suitable product category was selected; in the case of the present project, analgesics were chosen, which represent the second largest drug category in the U.S. American market (CHPA, 2012; MarketLine, 2013) and are also quite frequently used in other regions of the world (MarketLine, 2014). Second, a suitable general theme was identified. For this purpose, Aspirin – not only one of Bayer's oldest and most established brands, but also its highest-selling product [EUR 916 m./USD 1.45 bn. in 2013; Statista, 2014] – was chosen as a reference example (for example ads, see Figure **19**).

Figure 19: Aspirin Promotions by Bayer[2]

Besides the overall theme, relevant product features and the optimal setting were modeled in accordance with existing Aspirin promotions. In an attempt to come up with a suitable and matching product description, the manufacturer's websites were studied in detail in the four countries under investigation[3]. Choice of setting could also be confirmed by Study 1 (see section 6.2.2.1), which produced evidence that instead of natural or country settings, marketers have come to rely on rather neutral and reduced backgrounds (Koinig, 2012). The fictitious brand name was intended to reference the desired health-goal and, consequently, came out as "SENZA" – meaning "without" pain. The slogan was again adapted from Bayer's example, which promoted the drug

[2] Image 1 retrieved from: http://www.aspirin.at/scripts/pages/de/produkte/aspirin_c.php; Images 2 retrieved from: http://www.marketing-blog.biz/archives/70-BBDO-mit-neuem-TV-Spot-fuer-Aspirin.html; Image 3 retrieved from https://i.ytimg.com/vi/BSv1u_KluyM/hqdefault.jpg (accessed 13.02.2013)

[3] *Austria*: http://aspirin.at/scripts/pages/de/home.php; *Germany*: http://www.aspirin.de/; *United States:* http://www.aspirin.com/scripts/pages/en/home.php; *Brazil*: http://www.aspirina.com.br/index-geral.php (accessed 10.02.2013)

as leading to a reduction in pain: "Getting the best out of life despite pain – with Senza!". As in Aspirin's case, the name was deliberately included in the slogan.

The four versions of the same (thematic) ads are described in detail below[4]:

(1) The first ad pursued an **informative appeal**, which is commonly used by pharmaceutical marketers to promote OTC drugs (Koinig, 2012; Main et al., 2004). In line with previous research (DeLorme et al., 2010), it features the advertised drug as a dominant visual (~ 2/3 of the page). The slogan chosen for promotion lists the product name in a problem/solution manner: "Getting the best out of life despite pain – with Senza!". Owing to the product's similarity to Aspirin, the remaining textual elements also follow suit by emphasizing the product's effectiveness, unique composition plus its tolerance levels. The body copy is, as recommended by Rossiter and Bellman (2005), kept short and rather simple, avoiding the extensive use of medical jargon.

(2) The second ad is purely **emotional** in nature, paying tribute to promotional practices characteristic of the prescription drug industry (Wolfe, 2002). Emotional advertising "does not barrage the consumer with words, facts, or claims" (Moriarty, 1991), but woos them through images of pleasure and mood (de Mooij, 2001). For this reason, it features the same slogan, which is already utilized in the informative ad, coupled with a dominant, pleasant visual that occupies 90 % of the total page. Instead of a dominant product illustration, which is still featured yet significantly reduced in size, the image depicts a happy-looking, attractive couple corresponding to the beauty standards of all countries. In terms of emotional appeal, the choice is made in favor of happiness, claimed to be the only state universally identifiable (Russel, 1994): it can be easily recognized and is reportedly seen as the strongest human emotion, something worth striving for (Flora, 2008). It also fits the topic well, since health is regarded as a

[4] Actual-sized promotions are included in Appendix A.

pre-requisite for happiness, for "[w]ithout good health, quality of life quickly deteriorates" (Rod and Saunders, 2004: 328). By including two endorsers, the ad meant to resemble the product's intended target audience – both female and male (Martin et al, 2008; Feick and Higie, 1992).

(3) The **mixed appeal** presents a combination of the informative and emotional ad versions: while it deploys the latter's prominent visual, it also relies on complementary textual information on product specifics. As such, it builds upon Koinig's (2012) and Kroeber-Riel and Esch's (2011) recommendations to combine established approaches deployed specifically in the pharmaceutical industry (DTCA: emotional; OTC: informative; DeLorme et al., 2010; Main et al., 2004). The mixed appeal utilized herein features an emotional visual in combination with (rational) textual elements, which should get consumers to consider the promoted product on the basis of its promised gain (happiness). The inclusion of scientific evidence is meant to ensure not only subtle conviction, but also a heightened cognitive involvement through listing tangible product specifics (Rogers, 1983).

(4) One advertising appeal that has been less frequently applied in the pharmaceutical industry is the **sustainable (CSR) appeal**, in which companies proclaim their support for environmental projects and/or social causes. For pharmaceutical manufacturers, health-related causes are deemed to be the most appropriate, even though they are only attributed a moderate degree of relevance globally (e.g., improve maternal health [39 %] or reduce child mortality [38 %], according to Nielsen, 2012). Causes worth supporting, thus, especially concern the reduction of child mortality, the improvement of maternal health as well as the fight against HIV/AIDS, malaria and other terminal diseases (Nielsen, 2012).

To avoid any connotations and/or the influence of previous experiences, a fictitious CSR initiative is created, based on a successfully practiced CSR cooperation between Pampers and UNICEF (see Figure **20**). The goal of this fictitious joint mission is to create awareness and support for tetanus, a disease that can be prevented through the use of vaccines. As part of the company's overall social mission, product purchases will involve consumers directly, as every package sold provided one crucial vaccination, reducing infant and maternal morbidity considerably (Mueller, 2011).

Figure 20: CSR Promotions by Pampers and UNICEF[5]

With messages becoming more visually-oriented (Koinig, 2012), the mixed appeal is selected as design basis, to which a short 'CSR' message is added, which reads as follows: "At ProSante, we accept social responsibility. 1 sold package = 1 vaccination against tetanus".

In terms of layout and messages' structure, the ads do not considerably differ from one another. All appeals are meant to promote an un-connoted pain reliever called Senza produced by the fictitious pharmaceutical manufacturer ProSante (proHealth). A pre-test amongst 30 students showed that the names for both the product and the company were neutrally loaded (product: M = 4.7; company: M = 4.4) and seen as suitable for application in the medical domain (see Table **20**).

[5] Image 1 retrieved from http://www.unicef.at/index.php?id=412; Image 2 retrieved from http://generatoren-der-irrelevanz.de/tag/unicef (accessed 13.02.2013)

	If you think about a drug manufacturer: How would you rate the following product respectively company name?	
		positive neutral negative
P1	Senza	❑ --- ❑ --- ❑ --- ❑ --- ❑ --- ❑ --- ❑
C1	*Pro*Sante	❑ --- ❑ --- ❑ --- ❑ --- ❑ --- ❑ --- ❑
	Have you come across a similar name before in the medical field?	❑ yes ❑ no
P2	Do you think the product name is suited for application in the medical field?	❑ yes ❑ no
C2	Do you think the company name is suited for application in the medical field?	❑ yes ❑ no

Table 20: Evaluations of Product and Company Names

Not only visuals are particularly appealing and useful in generating attention, but color also aids the process (Mikellides, 1990). Primary colors (such as green, blue, red, white, etc.) are easily identifiable throughout the world (Jansson et al., 2004), yet, might differ in their associations. Hence, colors have to be selected with care: red, for instance, is linked to excitement and love, whereas blue and green – classifying as 'cold' hues – are said to invoke feelings of relaxation, peace and trust (Gorn et al., 1996). Owing to their extensive use in advertisements for pharmaceuticals (Koinig, 2012), shades of blue, green and white were deemed appropriate for the present study; additionally, their meaning is renowned to not diverge considerably across cultures (de Mooij, 2011), rendering them ideal for utilization in standardized messages.

While the product was put at the center of attention in the informative ad, the emotional version depicted the prospective addressee – either male or female – as embedded in its (closest) target group (family, partnership). Even though no explicit verbal reference was made, the slogan implicitly related to the product, by promising gains, if self-medication was deployed: health and happiness, as illustrated by the couple who was able to enjoy their time together – pain-free. It was translated into the countries' local languages (German, English and Brazilian Portuguese) for the different markets surveyed.

All ads are complemented with two more core promotional elements, namely calls to action and disclaimers. The prior is a commonly employed means of closing ads, said to create positive and favorable responses in consumers (Wells et al., 2006). Calls to action are made up of "a line at the end of an ad that encourages people to respond and gives information on how to respond" (Wells et al., 2006: 361). They are incorporated into ads to invite respondents to seek more information (online) or benefit from additional offerings, such as coupons (Wells et al., 2006). Both the digitalization of content and the advancement of the Internet in the medical realm have furnished corporations with new possibilities of initiating interactions; they can, for instance, refer to online platforms in the form of links or QR codes, allowing them to directly connect the recipient to relevant information (Okazaki et al., 2011). In order to pay tribute to these recent developments, online platforms were also referred to in the present paper: buttons referencing facebook, twitter and a QR code linking to an online project description are integrated in the fictitious OTC drug promotion.

Throughout the world, pharmaceutical advertising is subject to tight legal regulation, forcing drug marketers to include so-called “disclaimers” in public advertisements for OTC medications. These constitute warning messages and are usually represented by a detached single line placed towards the bottom of the ad (Walsh, 2012), making them easily identifiable at first sight. Their inclusion is warranted, as advertisers need to ensure consumers’ proper medicinal treatment, advising them to consult with experts if unsure of how to self-medicate. In the countries selected for study, disclaimers have to contain the following information:

United States	These statements have not been evaluated by the Food and Drug Administration. This product is not intended to diagnose, treat, cure, or prevent any disease (FDA, 2009)
Germany/Austria	Zu Risiken und Nebenwirkungen lesen Sie die Packungsbeilage und fragen Sie Ihren Arzt oder Apotheker.[6]
Brazil:	Estas declarações não foram avaliadas pela ANVISA. Este produto não se destina a diagnosticar, tratar, curar ou prevenir qualquer doença.[7]

In order to create authentic promotional messages, these disclaimers were included in all ads under investigation, with the final ad being professionally designed by a graphic designer. A more complete and in-depth description of the individual sub-studies is offered in the next paragraphs, describing the three pre-tests and the second main study.

---

[6] Translation: *For risks and side effects read the package insert and refer to your physician or pharmacist.*

[7] Translation: *These statements have not been evaluated by ANVISA [Agência Nacional de Vigilância Sanitária]. This product is not intended to diagnose, treat, cure, or prevent any disease.*

6.1.2.3 Pre-Test 1

First of all, the four fictitious advertisements to be used in this study had to undergo several extensive pre-tests to prove their suitability for the project at hand. The pre-tests' objectives were to determine (1) the clarity of the ad appeal used, together with (2) the advertisement's comprehensibility, (3) believability, as well as (4) the image's general appeal (see Table **21**).

	You are about to see four ad versions. For each advertisement, please choose the most appropriate answer. (1 answer maximum) **To which degree do you agree with the following statements?**	
		I do not agree at all … I fully agree
A1	The ad is informative.	❑ --- ❑ ---❑ ---❑ ---❑ ---❑ ---❑
A2	The ad is emotional.	❑ --- ❑ ---❑ ---❑ ---❑ ---❑ ---❑
A3	The ad is both informative and emotional.	❑ --- ❑ ---❑ ---❑ ---❑ ---❑ ---❑
A4	The ad is sustainably oriented.	❑ --- ❑ ---❑ ---❑ ---❑ ---❑ ---❑
	To which degree do you agree with the following statements?	
		I do not agree at all … I fully agree
B1	The ad is realistic.	❑ --- ❑ ---❑ ---❑ ---❑ ---❑ ---❑
B2	The ad is trustworthy.	❑ --- ❑ ---❑ ---❑ ---❑ ---❑ ---❑
B3	The ad is credible.	❑ --- ❑ ---❑ ---❑ ---❑ ---❑ ---❑
B4	The ad is believable.	❑ --- ❑ ---❑ ---❑ ---❑ ---❑ ---❑
B5	The ad is comprehensible.	❑ --- ❑ ---❑ ---❑ ---❑ ---❑ ---❑
B6	The ad is well-structured.	❑ --- ❑ ---❑ ---❑ ---❑ ---❑ ---❑
	Please rate the length of the body copy by choosing the most appropriate answer. (1 answer maximum)	
		I do not agree at all … I fully agree
C1	The body copy is too long.	❑ --- ❑ ---❑ ---❑ ---❑ ---❑ ---❑
C2	The body copy is of right length.	❑ --- ❑ ---❑ ---❑ ---❑ ---❑ ---❑
C3	The body copy is too short.	❑ --- ❑ ---❑ ---❑ ---❑ ---❑ ---❑

Table 21: Pre-Test 1 Questionnaire (Excerpt)

A total of 28 subjects – students from a mid-sized European university; male (n= 13), female (n= 15) – participated in the pre-test in return for credit-points. Results clearly indicated that each ad version was associated with its intended appeal (informative: M = 5.5; emotional: M = 5.0; mixed: M = 4.6; CSR: M = 4.2; answers ranging from 1 to 7, with 7 being the highest score). Moreover, the ads were regarded as being realistic (M = 4.8), trustworthy (M = 4.7), sufficiently credible (M = 4.2), comprehensible (M = 4.9) and well-structured (M = 4.0). Thus, findings underscored the ads' overall suitability. In total, only one minor change had to be applied: the body copy was deemed too long by respondents and was, as a consequence, shortened to aid the text's readability, comprehensibility and overall structure.

6.1.2.4 Pre-Test 2

The second pre-test examined the suitability of the visual stimulus material. In order to offer students some choices, six distinct images that were filtered out beforehand by the research team were put up for vote. Following Aspirin's example, all three images for the informative ad featured a dominant product illustration (a drug package with a row of pills sticking out). For the emotional visual – in line with Bayer's ad campaign at that time (2012/2013) – a happy Western looking couple was selected. For each version, the 22 student respondents (m = 9; f = 13) were asked to indicate their perceived degree of applicability on a 7-point scale, with 1 suggesting a very low degree of suitability, while 7 was indicative of a high suitability (see Table **22**). A clear preference for one particular product image emerged right away (M = 5.3), whereas two emotional images were up almost evenly in terms of liking (M = 5.2 vs. M = 5.0). Because of this tie, an additional group of 5 students (m = 3; f = 2) was consulted, who voted 4:1 in favor of the final emotional image, which was then utilized for the mixed and CSR versions respectively.

	You are about to see three different ad versions. Please indicate your degree of linking for each image on a 7-point scale.	
		I do not like it at all / I like it a lot
A1	Ad #1	❑ --- ❑ ---❑ ---❑ ---❑ ---❑ ---❑
A2	Ad #2	❑ --- ❑ ---❑ ---❑ ---❑ ---❑ ---❑
A3	Ad #3	❑ --- ❑ ---❑ ---❑ ---❑ ---❑ ---❑

Table 22: Pre-Test 2 Questionnaire (Excerpt)

6.1.2.5 Pre-Test 3

The questionnaire was pre-tested in Austria (n = 16), Germany (n = 5) and the United States (n = 5), where it did not raise any issues of concern amongst respondents (see Table **23**). Its length was deemed appropriate for the topic under investigation, guaranteeing extensive and comprehensive results that would be of use to numerous areas of research, including marketing, advertising and behavioral sciences. Difficulties in either comprehending or answering the questionnaires were neither anticipated nor reported in any of the three countries and, hence, the originally conceptualized questionnaire was utilized. A translation/back-translation procedure commonly applied in cross-cultural surveys was also used in the present project: questionnaires were translated by a group of bilingual speakers, while the back-translation was made by a different group of bilingual speakers.

	You are about to be handed a questionnaire. Please read through it thoroughly and answer the following questions afterwards.	
		I do not like it at all ... I like it a lot
A1	The questionnaire is well-structured.	❑ --- ❑ --- ❑ --- ❑ --- ❑ --- ❑ --- ❑
A2	The questionnaire is comprehensible.	❑ --- ❑ --- ❑ --- ❑ --- ❑ --- ❑ --- ❑
A3	The questionnaire is confusing.	❑ --- ❑ --- ❑ --- ❑ --- ❑ --- ❑ --- ❑
A4	The questionnaire is too long.	❑ --- ❑ --- ❑ --- ❑ --- ❑ --- ❑ --- ❑
A5	The questionnaire is appropriate in length.	❑ --- ❑ --- ❑ --- ❑ --- ❑ --- ❑ --- ❑
A6	How long did it take you to answer the questionnaire?	_____ minutes
A7	**Comments:**	

Table 23: Pre-Test 3 Questionnaire

6.1.2.6 Study 2

The study was conducted in spring and summer of 2014. In each of the four chosen countries (Austria, Germany, the United States and Brazil) ~ 60 people were presented with one of the four ad versions (described in section 6.2.2.2.), amounting to a total sample size of around 240 subjects per country. Student participation was kept at a low range (> 25 %) in response to a critique uttered against the use of student samples (Wells, 1993; Winer, 1999). However, student involvement could not be rejected entirely (Lynch, 1999), for this target group was considered useful in providing meaningful insights during the study's pre-test phase.

In advance, participants were informed about the study's overall purpose. They were told that the study constituted a cross-cultural doctoral project supervised by the Department of Media Communications of the Alpen-Adria-Universität Klagenfurt, Austria. The same information was also provided in the study's introductory text, which constituted the questionnaire's initial paragraph. In the United States, where data collection was carried out in cooperation with the San Diego State University, recipients were, additionally, provided with an informed consent statement on official SDSU letterhead.

Participants were made aware that the project set out to determine how their overall health behaviors and their attitudes towards advertising impacted their evaluations of pharmaceutical adverts. After completing some general questions regarding their health and self-medication interests respectively abilities, participants were presented with an ad (one out of four versions; between-subject design) and were advised to read through the ad carefully. The average viewing time ranged between 15 to 25 seconds. Afterwards, they were asked to return the ad and continue answering questions relating to selected categories, such as ad evaluation, message involvement, product evaluation, purchase intention, as well as the empowerment derived from the promotion. Answers to each question were determined by use of a 7-point scale ranging from (1) 'I do not agree at all' to (7) 'I fully agree'.

Subjects were asked to either fill in the questionnaires by themselves or were assisted by a trained interviewer. To ensure almost identical situations of inquiry in all countries, interviewers were provided with instructions on how to proceed in the data collection process. They received a standardized text which they should cite when approaching prospective subjects, who were usually encountered in public places, e.g., along public streets, in walking or jogging parks, the beach (in the case of the U.S.), on public transportation or in cafés and restaurants. When selecting respondents, interviewers were cautioned to not appear too persistent; rather, they were advised to ask for participation in a polite manner, informing subjects that their participation was completely voluntary and that their answers would remain anonymous. In most cases, respondents chose to fill in the questionnaire on their own, with interviewers staying in the immediate surrounding to answer questions (if necessary). This procedure also ensured that interviewer influence was kept at a minimum.

6.1.3 Introductory Remarks

Before study results will be elaborated on in detail, some general remarks on the methodological approach used herein need to be included, with selected aspects being discussed in depth (e.g., Structural Equation Modeling, Model Fit and Measurement Invariance, etc.).

6.1.3.1 Structural Equation Modeling (SEM)

Behavioral sciences research has become known to utilize latent variable modeling (Baumgartner and Homburg, 1996) or structural equation modeling (SEM) as a norm (Hooper et al., 2008). In recent years, it has established itself as a reliable and frequently used method in the marketing and consumer behavior domain, where it has grown into a valuable technique to statistically test and validate theoretically profound assumptions (Bentler and Chou, 1987). Due to the project's focus on consumer behavior, the present project can be allocated in this category and will, thus, follow the same path.

Generally, SEM is used to (1) estimate dependence relationships, (2) visually represent theoretical concepts in the form of a structural model and correct (as well as improve) those interconnections, (3) conceptualize a model to explain and assess proposed relationships, and (4) test and validate hypotheses (Hair et al., 2006). As it is grounded in statistical correlations (Baumgartner and Homburg, 1996), SEM presents a confirmatory approach to analysis that is bound to follow six stages (Hair et al., 2006):

(1) Construct Definition and Conceptualization
(2) (Measurement) Model Development
(3) Study Purpose Definition (incl. Empirical Results)
(4) Assessment of Measurement Model Validity
(5) Structural Model Specification
(6) Assessment of Structural Model Validity

In the course of stage 1, the constructs to be evaluated have to be defined together with their proper measurement instrument or scale. For the present study, a standardized questionnaire was developed, which was composed of established scales to the largest extent. The utilization of renowned measurement instruments is proclaimed for research topics of high interest; only for marginalized research areas, scales should be composed from scratch (Hair et al., 2006). General measurement bias was eliminated as all questions included in the questionnaire were to be answered on 7-item Likert scales, reducing confusion amongst respondents by sticking with a single format type (Hair et al., 2006). Constituting a cross-cultural research project, the material's linguistic equivalence had to be established beforehand as well (Hair et al., 2006), pointing to the verification of the scales' linguistic meaning across cultures. This step implied following the established procedure of translation|back-translation by different native speakers (Harkness, 2003).

Once constructs have been defined and conceptualized, the measurement model should be developed in the course of stage 2. This process involves the definition of constructs (latent variables) to be tested on the one hand and the selections of items (indicator variables) specifying said constructs on the other hand (Hair et al., 2006). A (operationalized) latent variable refers to any construct that is not directly measured by a single item but is composed of numerous single indicators (Hair et al., 2006). Latent variables are rarely composed of single item-measures as preference is given to constructs combining multiple items or survey questions (Anderson and Gerbing, 1984). Albeit the exact amount of single variables making up one latent construct is hardly clarified, it remains uncontested that each additional variable contributes to the datasets' overall complexity (Baumgartner and Homburg, 1996). However, the minimum-item rule of three to four indicators per item should not be broken (Hair et al., 2006; Jarvis et al., 2003; Bollen, 1989).

Model development includes specifying model causality, too, whereby frameworks can be grouped into two big causal categories, namely reflective or formative factor models (Hair et al., 2006). In behavioral sciences, reflective measurement theory is quite frequently encountered, e.g., when surveying attitudes, personality traits and behavioral inhibitions (Bollen and Lennox, 1991). Formative models, conversely, are based on the assumption that measured items cause or specify larger constructs (Hair et al., 2006). By extensively surveying consumer attitudes and responses towards pharmaceutical advertising, the model conceptualized clearly qualifies as belonging to reflective measurement theory, where latent constructs are supposed to consist of multiple items representing the same concept.

Stage 3 addresses questions of both research design and model estimation and is especially concerned with three areas, namely sample size and missing data and the choice of estimates. First, sample size has to be addressed, which is dependent upon the measurement procedure chosen. For the present study, the Maximum-Likelihood-Estimation (MLE) was used as a standard (Bollen, 1989), which is suited for small as well as large samples (Hair et al., 2006); for the latter classification, it is expected to bring about more stable, reliable and valid results (Baumgartner and Homburg, 1996; Hair et al., 2006). MLE is also the one procedure recommended by numerous researchers, making it the most commonly applied estimation procedure when testing parameters and working with quantitative data (95 % following Baumgartner and Homburg, 1996). Second, for model estimates to be accepted, all potential coding errors in the tested data-set need to be eliminated in advance; in addition, missing values need to be substituted (Kaplan, 1990), especially if their distribution is non-random and they constitute more than 10 % of the complete corpus (Hair et al., 2006). In the total data set, all missing values were substituted with the mean values for each item (mean imputation), following the suggestion by Gelman and Hill (2006), as missing values amounted to a minimum (1.8 %). Third, a measurement procedure has to be chosen, whereby both correlations and covariances can serve as points of reference for data analysis (Hair et al., 2006). Even though the use of correlations is often advocated, especially in causal models, they are not useful for comparing means and groups, which are at the core of the present investigation. For this reason, covariances will be consulted, which are the pillars a Confirmatory Factor Analysis (CFA) is built upon. CFA is deployed to test the extent to which a proposed theory is applicable in reality (Hair et al., 2006) and assesses a construct's validity as represented by numerous single (measured) variables (Hair et al., 2006). Hence, it benefits researchers by granting them insights into their measures' quality.

During stage 4, the conceptualized model's validity is assessed (for a detailed discussion, see sections 6.2.3.3. and 6.2.3.4.) and, afterwards (during stage 5), model specification takes place. Hereby, theoretically deduced relationships between the different constructs are added to the proposed conceptual framework. Finally, attention to the structural model's overall validity is given in stage 6. In a cross-cultural research endeavor like the present project, the equivalence of scales and scores cannot be assumed automatically. As soon as numerous groups or countries are examined, Measurement Invariance (MI) needs to be established to guarantee that the different items and consecutive factors are equivalent across groups or countries, as otherwise composite variables lose their validity (Hair et al., 2006).

Before a detailed description of and systematic approach to Measurement Invariance will be provided, the next section will give an account of the SEM procedure carried out in the present study, which will be immediately followed by the previously mentioned areas of Model Fit and Measurement Invariance.

6.1.3.2 SEM Procedure

Once a study's theoretical foundation has been established, the model can be conceptualized by use of a suitable SEM software. In the present project, the most recent version of AMOS (AMOS 22) was used. A set of latent variables respectively questions (indicators) representative of the two main research questions was selected and visually depicted. By putting the focus on the evaluation of fictitious OTC drug promotions and the resulting degrees of empowerment gained therefrom, the following latent constructs were chosen to be of value to the present investigation: Ad Evaluation, Ad Credibility, Ad Comprehensibility, Self-Empowerment, Product Evaluation, and Purchase Intention. All constructs are not measured directly (Hair et al., 2006; Anderson and Gerbing, 1984) but are made up of several single items, meaning single questions taken from the questionnaire (see section 6.2.1.).

Moreover, the number of factors included in the conceptualized framework as well as the individual items defining each single construct have to be chosen in advance (Hair et al., 2006). Following established recommendations (Hair et al., 2006; Jarvis et al., 2003; Bollen, 1989), latent variables should combine at least three items and this rule was abided to with one exception (comprehensibility; in italics). The following latent variables and their indicators were integrated into the conceptual framework (see section 6.1.1.):

- **Ad Evaluation** (favorable, interesting, positive, pleasant; Zuckermann, 1988/1991; Lane et al., 2006; Palmgreen et al., 2006; Edell and Burke, 1987)
- **Credibility** (believable, convincing, truthful, credible; Zuckermann, 1988/1991 and Lane et al., 2006)
- **Comprehensibility** (comprehensible; Lane et al., 2006)
- **Self-Empowerment** (objective evaluation, comparison, increased likelihood of use; own scale)
- **Product Evaluation** (good impression, high quality, attractive, appealing; Dobni and Zinkhan, 1990; Brakus et al., 2009; Aaker, 1997)
- **Purchase Intention** (trial, likelihood of purchase, consideration for purchase; Mittal, 1989; Dodds et al., 1991)

After the structural framework had been visually drawn, theoretically sound pathways were added. In SEM, proposed relations present regressional equations that are depicted in the form of arrows linking constructs – comprising both dependent (endogenous) and independent (exogenous) variables – and indicators (measured items; Hair et al., 2006). When straight arrows are used, a relation of dependence between the different items is assumed (Nunnally, 1978); if two-headed arrows are utilized, a correlation rather than a direct impact between two exogenous constructs is suggested (Hair et al., 2006; Backhaus et al., 2011). Thereby, some variables might be independent (e.g., comprehensibility), while others can serve as both an independent factor in one hypothesis and a dependent construct in another (e.g., ad evaluation, self-empowerment; Hair et al., 2006), portending that a construct's status is free to change for the purpose of testing proposed hypotheses. The way constructs are linked with one another has a bearing on model fit as well, which will be addressed next.

6.1.3.3 Model Fit

Any proposed model does not have to be based on theoretical constructs alone (Hair et al., 2006), it also has to reflect the underlying data set (Hooper et al., 2008). For this reason, model fit becomes crucial and is guided by fit indices, referencing "interpretative value[s] in assessing model fit" (Hooper et al., 2008: 53). Model fit describes the extent according to which a proposed model (based on its factor structure) is representative of correlations and covariances between selected variables in a data set. If the major correlations are accounted for, model fit will be good; if relationships are not captured or wrongly assumed, model fit will be poor and indicative of these discrepancies. Consensus on the number and mix of appropriate fit indices is, nonetheless, not reached (Ping, 2004; Viera, 2011).

A proposed model's goodness of fit is dependent upon sample size as well as the number of variables used in SEM, with large samples impeding model fit (Hooper et al., 2008). This suggests that great fit is hard to achieve for a large data corpus, meaning 300 samples and above. In order to evaluate the fit of structural equation models, numerous parameters can be consulted. In practice, the Chi-Square measure (x^2) remains the most commonly consulted fit index (Bagozzi and Heatherton, 1994; Baumgartner and Homburg, 1996), determining the fit between the assumed model and the underlying data-set (Bagozzi and Heatherton, 1994; Baumgartner and Homburg, 1996). However, as it is affected by sample size (Baumgartner and Homburg, 1996), additional fit indices are recommended for reporting, whereby absolute and incremental fit indices need to be distinguished. Besides the Chi-Square measure, which is this category's most prominent example, absolute fit indicators evaluate the general model fit for the data-set on which the model is based (Hair et al., 2006; McDonald and Ho, 2002): this means that these scores test for how well the conceptual framework matches the underlying data set (Hair et al., 2006) and are fundamentally useful in indicating the overlapping between a proposed model and the data. Usually, one or more of the four additional measures can be reported (Hair et al., 2006; Weiber and Mühlhaus, 2014): the relative Chi-Square goodness-of-fit test, which takes the proposed model's degrees of freedom into account (x^2/df or DMIN/DF), the Root Mean Squared Error of Approximation (RMSEA), the Goodness-of-Fit Index (GFI) as well as the Adjusted Goodness-of-Fit Index (AGFI). Incremental fit indices, by contrast, compare the proposed model with a basic or independence model (referred to as the baseline model; Weiber and Mühlhaus, 2014), in which the observed variables are uncorrelated even if they are correlated (Baumgartner and Homburg, 1996). Incremental fit measures, thus, offer some indication of improvement by contrasting the conceptualized model with a restricted or nested model (Hair et al., 2006) and can take two forms, namely the comparative fit index (CFI) or the non-normed fit or Tucker-Lewis index (NNFI or TLI; Hooper et al., 2008).

Taking up those recommendations, the present investigation will deploy a selected set of the indices proposed, which will be described briefly:

- **CHI-SQARE or x^2:** As it presupposes normal data-distribution (Yuan, 2005), the Chi-Square index is commonly cited when assessing model fit. Labeled as the "traditional measure" of model fit (Hooper et al., 2008: 53), the x^2 is devoted to evaluate "the magnitude of discrepancy between the sample and fitted covariances matrices" (Hu and Bentler, 1999: 2). Notwithstanding its wide acceptance (McIntosh, 2006), it is conditioned by sample size (Schumacker and Lomax, 2004), with large data sets being almost always immediately rejected (Bentler and Bonnet, 1980). Including the Chi-Square is only meaningful if the scores' respective degrees of freedom (DF) are reported as well (Baumgartner and Homburg, 1996). Lower x^2 scores are said to be expressive of a better model fit and should not exceed a score twice or three times the model's degrees of freedom (Carmines and McIver, 1981).
- **CMIN/DF or x^2/df:** The Relative or Normal x^2 value (CMIN/DF) refers to the generated x^2 divided by the model's degrees of freedom (df; Wheaton, 1987). As a fit index controlling for sample size, it should be incorporated when testing for model fit (Wheaton et al., 1977) and, as a rule, scores between 2 and 5

are commonly listed as qualifying as more or less acceptable in literature (Marsh and Hocevar, 1985).

- **RMR and SRMR:** The Root Mean square Residual (RMR) and its Standardized counterpart (SRMR) contrast residual scores of the samples' covariance matrix with the hypothesized model (Hooper et al., 2008). While the RMR often hinders interpretations and, thus, is not recommended for use (Kline, 2005), the SRMR is more meaningful, even though it is affected by both sample size and the model's number of parameters. Ideally, it should achieve scores below .05 (Byrne, 1998; Diamantopoulos and Siguaw, 2000), while in some instances, values up to .08 are agreed on (Hu and Bentler, 1999).

- **GFI**: The Goodness-of-Fit Index (GFI) presents the most popular alternative to the Chi-Square test (Jöreskog and Sorbom, 1996) and was developed to account for the variance proportion in estimated population covariances (Tabachnick and Fidell, 2007). Increased values are normally reported for models based on large samples (Hooper et al., 2008; Bollen, 1990; Miles and Shevlin, 1998); on the other hand, the fit score decreases as more parameters are added (MacCallum and Hong, 1997). GFI scores between .9 and .95 are regarded as indicating a good model fit (Miles and Shevlin, 1998).
- **AGFI**: Building on the previous measure, the Adjusted Goodness-of-Fit Index (AGFI) corrects for degrees of freedom and reduces fit especially for saturated models (Tabachnick and Fidell, 2007). Just like other measures in this category, it is sensitive to sample size and increases for large data corpuses (Hooper et al., 2008). Overall, scores greater than .8 are widely accepted (Tabachnick and Fidell, 2007).
- **CFI**: The CFI (Comparative Fit Index; Bentler, 1995) is an incremental fit index modeled after the Normed Fit Index (NFI; Bentler and Bonnet, 1980), improving the latter by controlling for sample size (Byrne, 1998; Tabachnick and Fidell, 2007). This measure presupposes all latent variables to be uncorrelated and compares the won sample covariance matrix with a null-model, where all parameters are set to 0 and all variables are assumed to be independent. The CFI ranks amongst the most frequently reported fit indices (Fan et al., 1999),

with scores close to 1.0 suggesting a good model fit, whilst scores of .95 and beyond are deemed acceptable (Hu and Bentler, 1999).

- **TLI**: As a comparative or relative fit index (Miles and Shevlin, 2007; McDonald and Ho, 2002), the TLI (Tucker-Lewis Index) utilizes the Chi-square score for comparative purposes, meaning that a model's x^2 manifestation is contrasted with a baseline model (McDonald and Ho, 2002). The TLI is especially useful when contesting large samples and estimation methods other than the Maximum Likelihood Estimation (Hu and Bentler, 1998; Hu and Bentler, 1999); yet, it is predominantly used for rather simple models (Bentler, 1990; Kline, 2005; Tabachnick and Fidell, 2007). Scores can range from .80 to .95 (Bentler and Hu, 1999).
- **RMSEA**: Owing to insights on how well the model, whose parameters are unknown but chosen to an optimum, fits the covariance matrix (Byrne, 1998) and its sensitivity to model parameters (Diamantopoulos and Siguaw, 2000), the Root Mean Squared Error of Approximation (RMSEA) has become renowned as being amongst the "most informative fit indices" (Diamantopoulos and Siguaw, 2000: 85). By taking population-based measures into account, the RMSEA (first introduced by Steiger, 1989) was added to numerous research areas as a reliable fit measure. Generally, it gives preference to the model utilizing the fewest parameters (MacCallum et al., 1996). Values between 0.05 and 0.08, ideally even below the first score, are approved (Browne and Cudeck, 1993), deeming scores below .08 to be of good fit (MacCallum et al., 1996). Scores between .00 and .05, hence, allude to a close and almost perfect fit (Hair et al., 2006).

In the process of assessing goodness of fit for a SEM, the x^2 methodology has been applied at the highest frequency, often on the basis of its robustness to violations (Baumgartner and Homburg, 1996; Bentler, 1990). But, like numerous other fit indices, it is subject to flaws as well, prompting the application of a variety of fit measures as advantageous. If indices are meant to be used by themselves, meaning as stand-alone-indices, only the GFI, AGFI and RMR are recommended for use (Baumgartner and Homburg, 1996). In all other cases, the RMSEA, CFI, and the TLI or NNFI could be utilized additionally (Tanaka, 1993).

Research on which model fit indices are used is contradictory. Agreement is only reached as to the necessity of listing numerous fit measures (Crowley and Fan, 1997), which take different aspects of model fit into consideration. The x^2 score as well as its respective degrees of freedom (df) have to reported at all times (Kline, 2005; Hayduk et al., 2007), while additional measures are subject to variations. According to McDonald and Ho (2002), the most commonly cited indices are the NFI, NNFI, GFI, and CFI. Kline (2005) insists on including the CFI, SRMR, and RMSEA besides the x^2 test, while Hu and Bentler (1999) favor the SRMR, TLI, CFI, and RMSEA. On the other hand, the RMSEA, TLI or AIC (Akaike Information Criterion) are highly commended by Williams and Holahan (1994). The most recent contribution by Hooper et al. (2008), however, expands these recommendations by listing the x^2, RMSEA, SRMR, CFI and a PNFI (Parsimony Normed Fit Index). This last measure belongs to the group of parsimony fit indices, which reduce model complexity and adjust degrees of freedom (Mulaik et al., 1989).

For the study at hand, Hair et al.'s (2006) recommendation will be followed, who suggest to use at least three to four fit indices. Besides giving the obligatory x^2 and its degrees of freedom (df), they propose to include one badness-of-fit or parsimony index, one incremental fit index respectively one absolute fit index (Hair et al., 2006). Out of the parsimony fit indices section, the RMSEA is the undefeated forerunner for use (Hu and Bentler, 1999), whose success can be attributed to it not being dependent upon sample size; however, it is criticized for increasing with model complexity. Routinely, it is combined with the CFI, the one incremental index recommended for application (Gerbing and Anderson, 1993). For absolute fit indices, both the GFI and AGFI will be reported, which, in combination, are neither sensitive to sample size nor model complexity (Hair et al., 2006).

Once a preliminary model has been drawn, these indices can be turned to to gradually enhance model fit until reasonable scores are met. Model fit can be improved by looking at different measures, such as path estimates, standardized residuals, as well as modification indices (Hair et al., 2006), whereby path estimates and modification indices were consulted in the project at hand. Path estimates are useful in that their estimated loadings (linking indicators and constructs) offer some guidelines regarding which items can potentially be dropped (below .5; Hair et al., 2006). While items loading above .7 should be kept by all means, items with scores of .5 and below are recommended to be dropped. Modification indices, expressing every possible (fixed) path in a model, can also be consulted in the process of improving model fit (Baumgartner and Homburg, 1996), whereby each constrained parameter is assigned a modification index of its own. For better model fit, parameters – as reported in the AMOS output material (Baumgartner and Homburg, 1996) – can be either constrained or freed (Steenkamp and Baumgartner, 1998). Starting with the highest scores, improvements to modification indices might be able to resolve potential discrepancies, usually by adding covariances, drawn between items belonging to the same factor. Ultimately, fit values can be corrected and adapted to arrive at more plausible and sound conclusions that can be backed up by the quantitative data corpus (Baumgartner and Homburg, 1996).

In the present project, the model conceptualization was proceeded by slight improvements in fit, which did not violate Baumgartner and Homburg's (1996) recommendation. Confirmatory factor analyses were conducted for 3 distinct groups, comprising a 2-group model (Individualistic/Collectivistic), a 3-group model (Individualistic countries: Austria, Germany, and the U.S.), and a 4-group model (Austria, Germany, the U.S., and Brazil). The final model fit for the different groups and individual countries has been summarized below, including an immediate evaluation of model fit scores for each group separately and by use of symbols (👍 for acceptable; 👎 for unacceptable; see Tables **24** and **25**).

Fit Indices	**Group 1** **2 groups** **(IND/COLL)**	**Group 2** **4 groups** **(COUNTRIES)**	**Group 3** **3 groups (INDIV. COUNTRIES)**
CMIN **(up to DF*3)**	827.887 👎	1255.146 👍	919.785 👍
DF	270	540	405
CMIN/DF **(between 2 and 5)**	3.006 👍	2.324 👍	2.271 👍
GFI **(between .9 and .95)**	.918 👍	.880 👎	.885 👎
AGFI **(above .8)**	.884 👍	.832 👍	.838 👍
CFI **(between .9 and .95)**	.969 👍	.961 👍	.962 👍
RMSEA **(below .08)**	.046 👍	.037 👍	.042 👍

Table 24: Model Fit - Group Scores

Fit indices		Group 2			
	Group 1		Group 3		
	Individualistic	Collectivistic/Brazil	Austria	Germany	United States
CMIN (up to DF*3)	492.167 👍	335.360 👍	271.438 👍	377.923 👍	270.427 👍
DF	135	135	135	135	135
CMIN/DF (between 2 and 5)	3.646 👍	2.484 👍	2.011 👍	2.799 👍	2.003 👍
GFI (between .9 and .95)	.935 👍	.868 👎	.899 👎	.861 👎	.896 👎
AGFI (above .8)	.909 👍	.814 👍	.857 👍	.804 👍	.853 👍
CFI (between .9 and .95)	.973 👍	.959 👍	.968 👍	.949 👍	.971 👍
RMSEA (below .08)	.060 👍	.079 👍	.065 👍	.086 👎	.065 👍

Table 25: Model Fit - Cluster and Country Scores

In their article, a meta-analytic analysis on Structural Equation Modeling (SEM) in marketing and consumer behavior, Baumgartner and Homburg (1996) pointed out that models rarely manage to achieve the scores desired (e.g., CFI > .9 or RMSEA > .05 or .08 respectively). For this reason, acceptable thresholds levels have been developed (Hooper et al., 2008), offering researchers some range in determining their model's appropriateness. These are given in brackets in the fit indices column (see Tables 24 and 25).

The values won for the Individualistic/Collectivistic cluster, the four different countries and the Individualistic cluster alone suggest that the herein conceptualized model exhibits a reasonable fit for the different groups and countries, allowing for a utilization of the suggested models for each country and cultural cluster. For all groups, CMIN and CMIN/DF scores are highly acceptable (ranging between 2 and 3.6). The GFI is slightly below the proposed mark, which can be explained by the large sample size used herein, which decreases the score. Correcting for sample size, the AGFI is above the suggested overall value (above .814); so is the CFI (above .949) and, apart from one instance, the RMSEA also yields fairly reasonable results (below .079). Albeit some scores do not meet the acceptability margin, they are still located within the threshold range, proposing a highly acceptable model fit for the conceptualized framework.

In conclusion, it is important to mention that a good overall model fit does not automatically suggest the validity of the theory contested (Duncan, 1975; Fornell, 1983) nor does it necessarily validate the model as being true or false (Breckler, 1990); rather, it is only expressive of the model being a potential and plausible account of the data collected (Baumgartner and Homburg, 1996).

6.1.3.4 Establishing (Construct) Validity

Before designing a conceptual model, factor items need to be tested for both their validity and reliability to ensure they load on the same factor and present a significant contribution to said factor. The validity of individual constructs is, thereby, assessed by two distinct concepts, namely convergent validity and discriminant validity (Hair et al., 2006). First, convergent validity is judged, insinuating that all indicators assigned to a construct should share some commonalities (Hair et al., 2006). Thereby, high (or at least, statistically significant) factor loadings serve as a core indicator of such validity (Anderson and Gerbing, 1988). Factor loadings exceeding .7 are desirable (Hair et al., 2006) and Average Variance Extracted scores of .5 and above for each featured latent construct indicate a high level of convergent validity (Fornell and Larcker, 1981; Hair et al., 2006).

	Ad Evaluation		**Credibility**		**Self Empowerment**		**Product Evaluation**		**Purchase Intention**	
	CR	**AVE**	**CR**	**AVE**	**CR**	**AVE**	**CR**	**AVE**	**CR**	**AVE**
Individualism	.881	.649	.921	.746	.877	.706	.940	.797	.916	.784
Collectivism	.914	.727	.921	.744	.891	.733	.947	.819	.925	.805

Table 26: Composite Reliability and Average Variance Extracted for Cultural Clusters

	Ad Evaluation		**Credibility**		**Self Empowerment**		**Product Evaluation**		**PurchaseIntention**	
	CR	**AVE**	**CR**	**AVE**	**CR**	**AVE**	**CR**	**AVE**	**CR**	**AVE**
Austria	.853	.593	.917	.735	.867	.786	.940	.799	.955	.877
Germany	.903	.699	.904	.805	.871	.693	.940	.797	.954	.874
United States	.873	.634	.941	.801	.899	.748	.942	.804	.875	.706
Brazil	.914	.727	.921	.744	.891	.733	.947	.819	.925	.805

Table 27: Composite Reliability and Average Variance Extracted for Individual Countries

In line with this, construct reliability – computed as factor loadings' squared sum – can be consulted to measure this validity type (Bacon et al., 1995), whereby scores of .6 and higher are deemed acceptable (Hair et al., 2006; Tseng et al., 2006). Tables **26** and

27 summarize the scores obtained from the procedure outlined by Hair et al. (2006). Meaningful results were obtained for all categories for both the clustered and individual data sets.

The numbers above clearly indicate no convergent validity issues (Hair et al., 2006), meaning that the variables chosen to explain the different latent constructs do indeed only correlate well within the construct they have been assigned to, suggesting that the factor is well represented by the set of variables chosen. Since scores below the recommended .5 level do not exist, both individual variable and construct reliability are given (Anderson and Gerbing, 1985; Dillon and Goldstein, 1984; Bagozzi, 1991).

Second, discriminant validity needs to be assessed. It is concerned with interconstruct variance, in the process of which variance extracted measures are compared against squared interconstruct correlations (Hair et al., 2006). Alluding to the construct's distinctiveness from its counterparts, high discriminant validity scores reference the construct's unique character and set it apart from other measures (Hair et al., 2006). To calculate validity scores, construct correlations have to be fixed to one; afterwards, model fit has to be assessed, whereby an increased Chi^2 value (of 3.841 and beyond) would serve as proof of sufficient discriminant validity (Anderson and Gerbing, 1988; Bagozzi and Phillips, 1982). It is established by use of Chi^2 difference tests as exemplified by the U.S.-American scores below (Segars, 1997; see Table **28**).

	Comprehensibility	**Ad Evaluation**	**Credibility**	**Self Empowerment**	**Product Evaluation**	**Purchase Intention**
Comprehensibility	---	279.634	291.480	301.799	310.287	362.193
Ad Evaluation		---	282.207	290.038	300.888	352.842
Credibility			---	280.788	289.177	341.140
Self Empowerment				---	278.603	330.794
Product Evaluation					---	323.000
Purchase Intention						---
Original Chi^2 Value: 270.427 **Requirement: Chi^2 Difference Value $\geq$ 3.841**						

Table 28: Discriminant Validity[8] (Established by Chi^2-Tests)

[8] Tables listing results from Austria, Germany and Brazil can be found in Appendix E.

	Compre-hensibility	Ad Evaluation	Credibility	Self Empower-ment	Product Evalua-tion	Purchase Intention
AVE	**1.000**	**.634**	**.801**	**.748**	**.804**	**.706**
Comprehensi-bility	---	.631	.612	.521	.527	.473
Ad Evaluation		---	.798	.649	.726	.645
Credibility			---	**.762**	.759	.687
Self Empow-erment				---	.599	.765
Product Evalu-ation					---	**.721**
Purchase In-tention						---
Requirement: AVE ≥ Squared Correlations						

Table 29: Discriminant Validity (Established by Fornell-Larcker-Criterion)

One additional criteria used to explore discriminant validity is the Fornell-Larcker criterion (1981), which has been used in approximately three quarters of all cases by researchers (Hair et al., 2012). This methodology is based on AVE values (as derived from convergent validity tests), whereby "discriminant validity is assessed by comparing the shared variance (squared correlation) between each pair of constructs against the average of the AVEs for these constructs" (Bove et al., 2009). Hence, to confirm discriminant validity, squared correlations of connected constructs should not exceed the Average Variance Extracted score of the original factor (Fornell and Larcker, 1981). Again, U.S.-American results are included below as an example (see Table **29**), while results for the remaining countries are to be found in Appendix E.

In general, indicators meet the discriminant validity criteria almost in full; the Chi^2 contrast test did produce evidence of validity in measures across countries (see Table 28), suggesting that individual items do not overlap but do indeed measure diverse constructs (Bagozzi and Philips, 1982). Likewise, the Fornell-Larcker-Criterion could be established sufficiently, with only two values slightly exceeding the proposed values: in the case of the United States, self-empowerment as well as purchase intention came in fractionally above the suggested scores (see Table 29). Nonetheless, they still achieve very high manifestations and do not present any severe issues, also by virtue of the constructs' highly pronounced CR and AVE scores.

6.1.3.5 Measurement Invariance

When comparing findings from different national backgrounds, the necessity of cross-validity has been emphasized in literature for the longest time (MacCallum et al., 1992), where it is proclaimed as a way of eliminating theoretical doubt (Horn and McArdle, 1992). Research is indicative of the fact that some constructs might be more acceptable for testing in one country than in others, since some items are renowned to be 'etic' (i.e. similar across countries) whereas others are 'emic' (i.e. divergent across countries; Berry, 1969). Differences might stem from cultural particularities characteristic of each country – as explained by House et al. (2004) – or variations in response to specific categories (Steenkamp and Baumgartner, 1998). For this reason, the reliability and similarity of underlying constructs and items needs to be confirmed before arriving at conclusions (Hayduk, 1996), because both results and conclusions can only become valid and acceptable across countries and cultures (Horn, 1991), if invariances are investigated and accounted for. can.

To test this assumption, Measurement Invariance (MI) has to be assessed (Steenkamp and Baumgartner, 1998), referring to "whether or not, under different conditions of observing and studying phenomena, measurement operations yield measures of the same attribute" (Horn and McArdle, 1992: 117). Meredith (1993) perceives Measurement Invariance as a set of parameters that are subject to group belongingness; this implies that equally established characteristics in one model (in the form of latent constructs and/or factor structures) are leveled across groups to establish invariance, which is required to ensure meaningful plus comparative results (MacCallum and Austin, 2000; Kim et al., 2006). As a rule, Measurement Invariance follows the following procedure: a series of tests is conducted to account for model equality in between groups, whereby a free (unconstrained) model is compared against a restricted (constrained) other; results are then meant to uncover whether the gradually imposed restrictions (e.g., on intercepts, factor loadings, etc.; Hair et al., 2006) have a negative impact on model fit (Horn, 1991).

Invariance can be either established in full or partially. While full invariance suggests all constructs to be identical for all groups, it is solely a utopian state (Milfont and Fischer, 2010), "a condition to be striven for, not one expected to be fully realized" (Horn, 1991: 125). Partial invariance presents a far more realistic scenario (Byrne et al., 1989) and assumes only a few constructs (or a sub-set of parameters) to be comparable across cultural segments (Steenkamp and Baumgartner, 1998; Griffin et al., 2000), further proposing that some parameters might be invariant across some but not all groups examined (Vandenberg and Lance, 2000).

In order to assess and establish equivalence across the different groups, several research methods can be utilized (Fischer and Fontaine, 2009), of which the Confirmatory Factor Analysis (CFA) is by far the most widely deployed (Milfont and Fischer, 2010). Generally reflective of the construct and its theoretical assumptions, it is intended to measure scale reliability by putting a model's theoretical foundation to the test (Hair et al., 2006; Raykov, 2001; van de Schoot et al., 2012). Hence, this analytical method sets out to confirm the model's overall factor structure with regard to its validity and model fit, granting researchers the liberty to model relationships (Hair et al., 2006).

In cross-national surveys, data from numerous independent national corpuses is analyzed along the same dimensions (Jöreskog, 1971) in a pursuit of the following three objectives: (1) comparing and examining construct validity, (2) testing quantitative equivalence, and (3) determining (structural) relationships. All these goals presuppose different degrees of invariance (Steenkamp and Baumgartner, 1998). Thereby, invariance needs to be established on several (interrelated) levels, resulting in four distinct forms: *Configural Invariance, Metric Invariance, Scalar Invariance*, and *Factor Covariance Invariance* (Steenkamp and Baumgartner, 1998).

- **Configural Invariance** is met once the basic model structure is found to be invariant across the different groups or countries (Milfont and Fischer, 2010). To test this assumption and establish configural invariance, individual CFAs are conducted for each group, whereby special attention is paid to indicators' validity. In the case of construct validity, which is concerned with unraveling whether constructs are similar in meaning and/or structure across nations, it is sufficient to determine the same pattern as to factor loadings (zero vs. non-zero; Horn et al., 1983).

  Afterwards, model fit for the different groups is examined when combining the individual models and running them freely (i.e. without constraints). This means that after the model is drawn in AMOS, meaningful groups are identified in the data set, for which model fit is levied. If the achieved model fit for the split corpus is decent, then Configural Invariance is given, meaning the individual groups are equivalent with regard to factor structure in either cluster, suggesting constructs to be perceived in an almost identical manner by respondents in different groups.

- Once configural invariance has been confirmed, the second invariance type (**Metric Invariance**) needs to be passed. Hereby, the relationship between a specific item and the construct it has been assigned to in advance is subject to inquiry (Vandenberg and Lance, 2000). For this, not the construct itself but responses to the construct (indicators) are matched across groups (Milfont and Fischer, 2010; van de Schoot et al., 2012), as results are meant to provide some indication of construct meanings and scale usage amongst members of different cultural groups (Cheung and Rensvold, 2002). For this purpose, a Chi-Square difference test between the split groups needs to be executed, in the course of which the original x^2 score is contrasted with its counterpart derived from an ever-more constrained model. Differences between the two scores and their respective degrees of freedom (df) are expressed in the form of the p-value or p-score. This measure estimates the rejection of the assumed null-hypothesis and, if the p-score won from the test is below the standard of .05, no deviation (or no variance) is noteworthy, leveling results are deemed acceptable. This insinuates that in the case of invariance, answers to items are not manifested distinctively but equally for constructs in all groups. If metric invariance can be confirmed, no significant differences between the groups under investigation exist, allowing for a (meaningful) multi-group comparison of results (Hair et al., 2006). Metric invariance, thereby, presupposes both configural invariance and factor loading equivalence; in the course of the latter, loading estimates are leveled for each group (Cheung and Rensvold, 2002).
- After at least partial metric invariance is accounted for, (partial) scalar invariance has to be ascertained (Steenkamp and Baumgartner, 1998). **Scalar Invariance** is based on a comparison of latent constructs and is concerned with the degree of interconnectedness between latent and observed variables (Milfont and Fischer, 2010). It, thus, scrutinizes whether respondents' answers to the latent construct can be related to their scores for one or more observed con-

struct(s). Thereby, intercepts for each item are constrained to be equal across groups, suggesting that not only the construct (i.e. by means of factor loadings) but also the underlying items are equally manifested for all sub-groups. In a second step, latent scores can be compared across groups. In case zero-intercept vectors are not distinct amongst both groups, full scalar invariance does exist; for partial scalar invariance, only two items per construct need to be invariant (Steenkamp and Baumgartner, 1998).

While configural invariance does not produce any indication of how people respond to constructs across groups, metric invariance tries to fill this gap by looking at the extent to which item scores are indeed comparable across clusters (Rock et al., 1978). Scalar invariance adds even more depth to the investigation by conducting an intercept comparisons across the sub-data sets investigated (Meredith, 1993). Thereby, the underlying construct's meaning to respondents is determined for each group, unveiling potential discrepancies or consistencies in individual perceptions (Steenkamp and Baumgartner, 1998). If scalar and metric invariance pertain in parts, at a minimum, a strong factorial invariance can be assumed as well, which facilitates the comparison of means as well as relationships across clusters (Cheong and Rensvold, 2002).

- Discovering factor correspondence across groups presupposes **Factorial (Co)Variance Invariance** (Alwin and Jackson, 1981), in the process of which intercepts are leveled for all groups under investigation. This specification implies that latent constructs, as defined through variable measurements, are conceptualized in the same way for every cluster. If invariance of intercepts respectively factor loadings is given, construct means are comparable for all samples under investigation (Reise et al., 1993).

Measurement Invariance is commonly used to compare groups of individuals regarding personal characteristics and/or psychological factors (Milfont and Fischer, 2010). In the present project, it will be consulted to examine to which degree individual responses from four selected countries overlap or diverge by comparing their score loadings. This analysis represents a necessity as, before conducting in-depth analyses, it is crucial to safeguard that instrument measures are perceived in an equal manner by all respondents (Milfont and Fischer, 2010), irrespective of their nationalities, as otherwise results cannot be interpreted in any meaningful way. Hence, establishing measurement invariance serves the purpose of offering meaningful comparisons across groups or cultures.

In the present study, the corpus was split into the two cultural groups (Individualistic/Collectivistic), the four countries (Austria, Germany, the U.S., and Brazil) as well as the individualistic countries alone (Austria, Germany, and the U.S.). Next, invariance will – in line with model fit – be assessed for the three distinct groups (see Table **30**).

	Group 1 **2 groups** **(IND/COLL)**	**Group 2** **4 groups** **(COUNTRIES)**	**Group 3** **3 groups** **(Ind. Countries)**
Initial Scores	**CMIN: 827.887** **DF: 270**	**CMIN: 1255.146** **DF: 540**	**CMIN: 919.785** **DF: 405**
CONFIGURAL INVARIANCE	**full configural invariance**	**full configural invariance**	**full configural invariance**
METRIC INVARIANCE			
- ***Ad evaluation***	CMIN: 830.565/DF: 273 (2.678) | Q = .44	CMIN: 1266.990/DF: 549 (11.844) | Q = .23	CMIN: 929.212/DF: 411 (9.427) | Q = .15
- ***Credibility***	CMIN: 837.556/DF: 276 (9.669) | Q = .14	CMIN: 1269.572/DF: 552 (14.426) | Q = .28	CMIN: 931.376/DF: 413 (11.591) | Q = .17
- ***Self-Empowerment***	CMIN: 837.995/DF: 278 (10.108) | Q = .26	CMIN: 1277.679/DF: 558 (22.533) | Q = .21	CMIN: 933.775/DF: 415 (13.99) | Q = .17
- ***Product Evaluation***	CMIN: 840.601/DF: 281 (12.714) | Q = .31	CMIN: 1290.078/DF: 567 (34.932) | Q = .14	CMIN: 940.432/DF: 419 (20.647) | Q = .11
- ***Purchase Intention***	CMIN: 840.936/DF: 283 (13.049) | Q = .44	No metric invariance	No metric invariance
	full metric invariance	**partial metric invariance**	**partial metric invariance**
SCALAR INVARIANCE			
- ***Ad evaluation***	CMIN: 845.685/DF: 285 (43.059) | Q = .00	CMIN: 1293.123/DF: 570 (37.954) | Q = .15	CMIN: 945.411/DF: 423 (25.626) | Q = .11
- ***Credibility***	No scalar invariance	No scalar invariance	No scalar invariance
- ***Self-Empowerment***	No scalar invariance	No scalar invariance	CMIN: 946.802/DF: 425 (27.017) | Q = .14
- ***Product Evaluation***	No scalar invariance	No scalar invariance	CMIN: 948.877/DF: 427 (29.092) | Q = .14
- ***Purchase Intention***	No scalar invariance	No scalar invariance	No scalar invariance
	no scalar invariance	**no scalar invariance**	**partial scalar invariance**
FACTORIAL INVARIANCE - ***Comprehensibility***			**no factorial invariance**

Table 30: Measurement Invariance – Cluster and Country Scores

For all groups, Configural Invariance could be confirmed in full, confirming that the overall model structure does not differ significantly across groups with regard to their indicator reliability. Group 1 even achieved full Metric Invariance, while this measure could only be partially established for groups 2 and 3. There, a minimum of two constructs was constrained for every latent variable (Byrne et al., 1989; Meredith, 1993), with the exception of Purchase Intention, for which parameters could not be fixed as p-values would have exceeded the reported threshold values. Hence, Metric Invariance – alluding to indicators' being equal in terms of factor loading – is given for each group. Finally, Scalar Invariance was subject to inquiry and could not be established for all groups. Only one item is invariant across all groups in the Individualism/Collectivism and country groups (Ad Evaluation) and, thus, did not allow for the establishment of (partial) Scalar Invariance. The non-existence of scalar invariance then hints at group differences at a model level, where paths might vary in significance across clusters and/or countries. Group 3 – the Individualistic cluster – yielded slightly better results: with the exception of Credibility and Purchase Intention, a minimum of two intercepts could be equaled for all other latent variables, lending support to partial Scalar Invariance of results in individualistic countries. Lastly, Factorial Invariance was scrutinized but could be affirmed for neither group; however, since it did not present a necessity and only looked at path manifestations, the existence of scalar invariance was sufficient when comparing mean values across countries. Hence, as Scalar Invariance could only be established for the individualistic country cluster, meaningful comparisons of results across (individualistic) countries are ensured. Nevertheless, Brazilian results will not be neglected, but will be discussed on their own terms, without drawing a comparison between the collectivistic and individualistic clusters.

6.2 Study Results and Test of Hypotheses

Throughout the investigation's theoretical part, two main research questions have been emphasized, which aim to investigate (1) whether advertising is evaluated similarly or distinctively in four countries and (2) whether advertising deploying four distinct appeals can be conducive to consumer self-empowerment. The study is not limited to one single culture, but will shed some light on responses from two very diverse cultural backgrounds, namely three individualistic cultures (comprising Austria, Germany, and the United States) and one collectivistic culture (Brazil). In the following, consumer responses to questions in the areas of health and pharmaceutical marketing will be contrasted, focusing on the previously introduced research questions and hypotheses (for a summary, see Table **31**):

RESEARCH QUESTIONS	
RQ 1	**How is a standardized OTC drug ad (utilizing either an informative, emotional, mixed or CSR appeal) evaluated in different cultural contexts (Germany, Austria, the United States and Brazil)?**
RQ 2	**Out of the four advertising appeals, which appeal leads to the highest degree of consumer self-empowerment?**
HYPOTHESES (THEORY-DEDUCED)	
P 1a	Externally-oriented individuals (e.g., Brazilians) are less interested in self-medication practices than internally-oriented nations (e.g., Austria, Germany, and the U.S.).
P 1b	Externally-oriented individuals (e.g., Brazilians) delegate responsibility for health-related matters to experts, which is less common in internally-oriented countries (e.g., Austria, Germany, and the U.S.).
P 1c	Internally-oriented individuals (e.g., respondents from Austria, Germany, and the U.S.) hold a more attitude towards self-medication practices than their externally-oriented counterparts (e.g., respondents from Brazil).
H 1	Informative ads for pharmaceuticals yield better results with regard to ad evaluation than (a) mixed or (b) CSR ads, which yield even better results than (c) emotional ads in all countries.
H 2	Informative ads for pharmaceuticals score more favorable results with regard to credibility than (a) mixed or (b) CSR ads, which score even better results than (c) emotional ads in all countries.
H 3	Informative ads for pharmaceuticals achieve higher scores with regard to product evaluation than (a) mixed or (b) CSR ads, which achieve even higher scores than (c) emotional ads in all countries.
H 4	Informative ads for pharmaceuticals have a larger impact on purchase intention than (a) mixed or (b) CSR ads, which have an even larger impact than (c) emotional ads in all countries.
H 5	Informative promotions for pharmaceuticals are expected to lead to higher degrees of consumer self-empowerment than (a) mixed or (b) CSR ads, which empower consumers even more than (c) emotional ads in all countries.
H 6	Informative promotions for pharmaceuticals bring about higher degrees of consumer self-empowerment than (a) mixed, (b) CSR or (c) emotional ads in individualistic countries.
H 7	Informative promotions for pharmaceuticals lead to lower degrees of consumer self-empowerment than (a) mixed, (b) CSR or (c) emotional ads in collectivistic cultures.
HYPOTHESES (MODEL-DEDUCED)	
H 8a	The higher the pharmaceutical ad's comprehensibility, the more credible is its overall perception.
H 8b	The higher the pharmaceutical ad's comprehensibility, the more positive is its overall (ad) evaluation.
H 8c	The more credible a pharmaceutical ad is perceived to be, the more positive is its overall (ad) evaluation.

H 9a	The more comprehensible a pharmaceutical ad, the higher is the degree of self-empowerment derived therefrom.
H 9b	The more credible a pharmaceutical ad, the higher is the degree of self-empowerment derived therefrom.
H 10a	More positive ad evaluations will lead to more positive product evaluations.
H 10b	More positive ad evaluations will lead to heightened purchase intentions.
H 11	The higher the perceived (consumer) self-empowerment, the more positive is the overall product evaluation.
H 12	The more favorable a product evaluation, the higher is consumers' purchase intention.

Table 31: Overview of Hypotheses (continued)

6.2.1 Study Population

While all three pre-tests were conducted amongst a student population, the main investigation wanted to break with this tradition. Instead, a non-student sample comprising 967 respondents constituted the study's population (Austria: 240; Germany: 244; USA: 242; Brazil: 241). In terms of age, respondents were between 18 and 93 years old, with an average age of 35.9 years in the four countries scrutinized (Austria: 33.1 yrs.; Germany: 36.1 yrs.; USA: 41.0 yrs.; Brazil: 33.4 yrs.). In all countries, subjects were recruited in mid-size cities and were representatives across a broad range of professions, including teachers, doctors, secretaries, union workers and craftsmen. Female/male participation was almost equally distributed amongst the sexes (f = 50.6 %; m = 49.4 %).

Before providing answers to the proposed hypotheses, some general questions leading into the topic will be discussed, covering respondents' overall attitudes towards health, their self-medication skills as well as their evaluations of different drug types, their health information seeking and most commonly consulted sources of health information, together with their attitudes and skepticism towards (pharmaceutical) advertising.

6.2.2 Individual Opinions of and Attitudes Towards Health

The general notion of health being a personal responsibility (Rose, 1990; du Gay, 1996), an endeavor individuals are required to take, seems to have become readily accepted in all countries as respondents agreed that their health was dependent upon how well they looked after themselves and/or the energy they invested in maintaining their bodies (Total: 5.961; AUT: 5.854; GER: 5.721; USA: 6.132; BRA: 6.137). Survey scores offered an impressive range and were more pronounced in the United States (an individualistic culture; Hall, 1976) and in Brazil (a collectivistic culture), lending support to highly significant differences between the groups, especially when contrasting the two European countries with the Americas (F= 8.238, p= .000). ANOVAs and consecutive contrast tests revealed highly significant distinctions regarding health involvement to exist solely between Germany and the U.S. (F= .924, p= .000) and Brazil (F= .457, p= .000), while differences between Austria and the U.S. (F= .461, p= .007) and Brazil (F= 4.922, p= .007) were significant. For all other country comparisons, no relevant variations were confirmed.

Individual tendencies to look after and care for their bodies go hand in hand with them taking up preventive steps to counteract the development of disease, while ensuring conformity with the status quo at the same time, may it be through a balanced diet, regular exercise or self-medication (Total: 5.358; AUT: 5.150; GER: 5.131; USA: 5.789; BRA: 5.361). When questioned about precautions and preventive measures, very strong differences in value manifestations between the countries examined surfaced (F= 10.731, p= .000). As to individuals' willingness to take care of their bodies, variations could be traced back to U.S. American scores, which were responsible for highly significant differences between the North Americas and Austria (F= 3.732, p= .000), Germany (F= 2.658, p= .000) and Brazil (F= 2.061, p= .001). Comparisons with other countries, e.g. between the European countries and Brazil, did not indicate any significant distinctions as to health engagements.

Both individual concerns for their health and the preoccupation with their health status could be related to high levels of health consciousness (Gould, 1988), defined as individuals' deep-rooted concerns for their well-being. The inclusion of health consciousness in the present study is warranted, as individuals exhibiting a high degree thereof are regarded to be more involved in the evaluation of health information. This variable was measured by use of five distinct constructs, which were factorized into the single item Health Consciousness (KMO: .798; Significance according to Bartlett: .000; Cronbach α: .841): (1) "I reflect a lot about my health", (2) "I am very self-conscious about my health", (3) "I am constantly examining my health", (4) "In general, I know my health status very well", and (5) "I am very involved with my health". Overall findings portended to individual respondents being highly health-conscious, regardless of their respective cultural backgrounds (T: 4.997; AUT: 5.1435; GER: 4.8613; USA: 5.0341; BRA: 4.9259[9]). Factor scores did not significantly discern among the four countries (F= 2.597, p= .051[10]) and comparative tests only revealed consumers' health consciousness in Germany and Austria to vary highly distinctively (F= .337, p= .006). Figure **21** summarizes respondents' answers to the three questions.

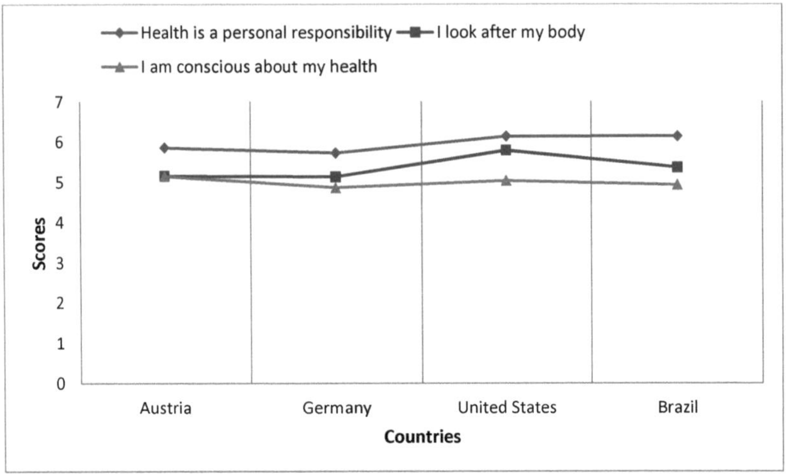

Figure 21: Individual Health Perceptions

6.2.3 *Self-Medication Practices and Abilities*

Increasingly, health issues are being attributed to individual self-management, of which monitoring is a prominent and commonly practiced form (Snyder, 1974). It is used to ensure appropriate behavior and conformity and is, not infrequently, closely related to the self-medication practices, in the course of which individuals claim responsibility over health-related issues (Snyder, 1974). When asked about their own capabilities, recipients considered themselves capable of taking care of their bodies (Total: 5.901; AUT: 6.154; GER: 5.967; USA: 6.095; BRA: 5.386), as well as being in the position of finding appropriate information to make qualified health decisions (To-

[9] An overview of mean scores for both individual questions and factorized items can be found in Appendix C.
[10] Tables listing T-Test results can be found in Appendix D.

tal: 5.466; AUT: 5.712; GER: 5.492; USA: 5.839; BRA: 4.822). While the highest scores could not be assigned regionally, the lowest scores were reported for Brazil, a collectivistic society, resulting in highly significant differences on a country-level (F= 23.380, p= .000 respectively: F= 28.951, p= .000). As to taking care of their bodies as well as claiming responsibility for their health, Brazilian values were considerably lower than those of their North American respectively European counterparts, lending support to highly significant differences between the Latin American country and Austria (F= 51.191, p= .000), Germany (F= 39.562, p= .000), as well as the United States (F= 34.037, p= .000). Individuals' information search capabilities in the health realm were also the least pronounced in South America, and consequently, highly distinct manifestations were reported between Brazil and Austria (F= 33.866, p= .000), Germany (F= 37.040, p= .000) and the United States (F= 49.807, p= .000); in addition, German and U.S. American scores exhibited highly developed variations (F= 2.135, p= .000).

Proposition 1a claimed that externally-oriented individuals – in the present study, this comprises the respondents from Brazil – were interested in self-medication practices to a lesser extent than respondents from internally-oriented nations, such as Austria, Germany, and the United States. The interest was, thereby, seen as being impacted by individuals' evaluations of their own self-management skills. For the present study, these were measured by four questions, whose scores were factorized into the item Self-Medication Ability (KMO: .781; Significance according to Bartlett: .000; Cronbach α: .817): (1) "I consider myself capable of taking care of my body", (2) "I consider myself capable of finding the right information to make qualified health decisions", (3) "Usually, I can make sense of the health information I am presented with", and (4) "I can use my knowledge to improve my health". Total scores indicated respondents' quite high beliefs in those "empowering" practices (T: 5.6465; AUT: 5.7362; GER: 5.5446; USA: 5.8013; BRA: 5.5048), whereby the existence of highly significant differences amongst the individual countries could not be denied (F= 5.714, p= .000). Variations in self-medication abilities were highly established between the United States and Germany (F= 1.450, p= .000) as well as Brazil (F= 35.913, p= .000); they were also present to a significant extent between Austria and Brazil (F= 24.421, p= .005) respectively Germany (F= .130, p= .006). Results brought about by the present study confirmed that, while respondents generally believed themselves to be capable of self-medication across countries, Brazilian scores were slightly less strongly established, resulting in the confirmation of **Proposition 1a**.

Proposition 1b proclaimed externally-oriented (Brazilian) individuals to be more likely to delegate responsibility for health-related matters to experts (e.g., doctors and/or pharmacists), which was less likely in internally-oriented countries (e.g., Austria, Germany, and the U.S.). The notion of health and personal well-being as an individual task seemed to have been grasped slowly but surely. However, one question arose in this context: does the consciousness for individual health matters automatically translate into a willingness to take action and take up self-medication practices? Results of the present study were somewhat ambiguous: Albeit individual responsibility was readily accepted by respondents displaying a high involvement in health-related issues (T: 5.308; AUT: 5.621; GER: 5.610; USA: 5.201; BRA: 4.796), scores diverged very significantly across countries (F= 18.131, p= .000). With Austrian and German scores being reasonably in line, highly distinct variations surfaced between Austria and the U.S. (F= .085, p= .001) respectively Brazil (F= 5.174, p= .002). Moreover, highly significant differences with regard to respondents' health responsibilities were also noted between Germany and the U.S. (F= 1.240, p= .001) respectively Brazil (F= 10.817, p= .000) as well as the United States and Brazil (F= 4.230, p= .003). Lower Brazilian scores were suggestive of sovereignty for health-matters not yet having been claimed by individuals. In spite of the strong relevance attributed to self-medication across the board, Brazilian scores still ranked below those of the three individualistic countries, resulting in the confirmation of **Proposition 1b**.

Propositions 1c suggested respondents from Austria, Germany, and the U.S. (i.e. internally-oriented individuals) to be more likely to take up self-medication practices, which is explained by the more positive attitudes they express towards self-medication; hence, Brazilian subjects (i.e. externally-oriented individuals) were predicted to be less likely to engage in self-medication due to their less favorable attitudes towards this practice. In the present study, respondents' general attitudes towards self-medication were measured by three distinct questions that were summarized into the factor Attitude towards Self-Medication (KMO: .742; Significance according to Bartlett: .000; Cronbach α: .885): (1) "I am interested in self-medication", (2) "I consider myself capable of self-medication", and (3) "I already practice self-medication". In line with moderate attitudes (T: 4.1027; AUT: 4.1402; GER: 4.3014; USA: 4.3152; BRA: 3.6510), numbers also suggested that actual self-medication practices are not commonplace (T: 3.911; AUT: 3.837; GER: 4.019; USA: 4.616; BRA: 3.884).

Striking and highly distinct differences for self-medication attitudes scores were manifested on a country-level (F= 8.245, p= .000) but did not translate into equally developed variations in terms of self-medication practices (F= .368, p= .776). Below-average Brazilian scores for self-medication attitude were responsible for highly significant differences between Brazil and Austria (F= .007, p= .002), Germany (F= 2.609, p= .000) plus the United States (F= 7.000, p= .000). With regard to self-medication practices, scores were not distinct for any country combination. Based on the above-average values and slightly more established self-medication attitudes in the three individualistic countries, **Proposition P1c** could be validated. Responses to Propositions 1a-1c questions are visually depicted in Figure **22**.

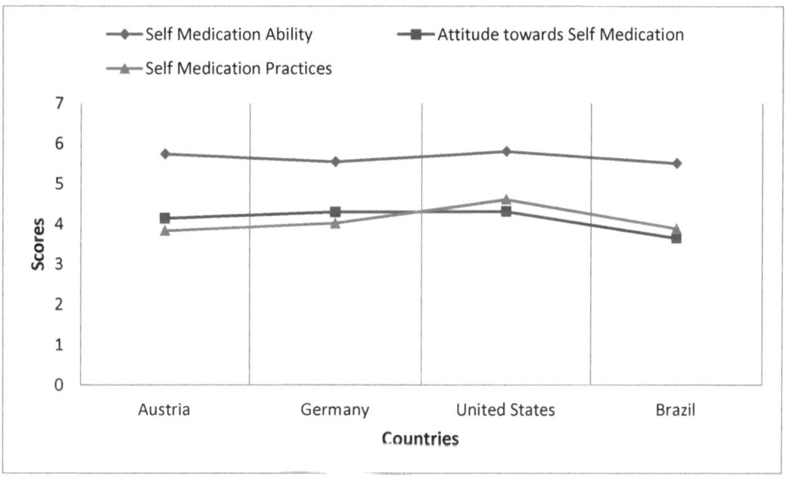

Figure 22: Self-Medication Evaluations

6.2.4 *Opinions Towards Different Drug Types*

One important question needed to be answered before reporting answers to the individual hypotheses: Does the assumption of non-prescription drugs being as effective as prescription preparations also impede medications' general evaluations? Overall, conventional (or Western) medicine, comprising medications that have been scientifically developed and tested, seemed to be most accepted across the board (Total: 5.567; AUT: 5.542; GER: 5.586; USA: 5.236; BRA: 5.905). In second and third place, herbal remedies (Total: 4.927; AUT: 5.066; GER: 4.777; USA: 4.491; BRA: 5.377) and homeopathic substances (Total: 4.698; AUT: 4.733; GER: 4.443; USA: 4.532; BRA: 5.087) were listed, with scores indicating their increasing relevance.

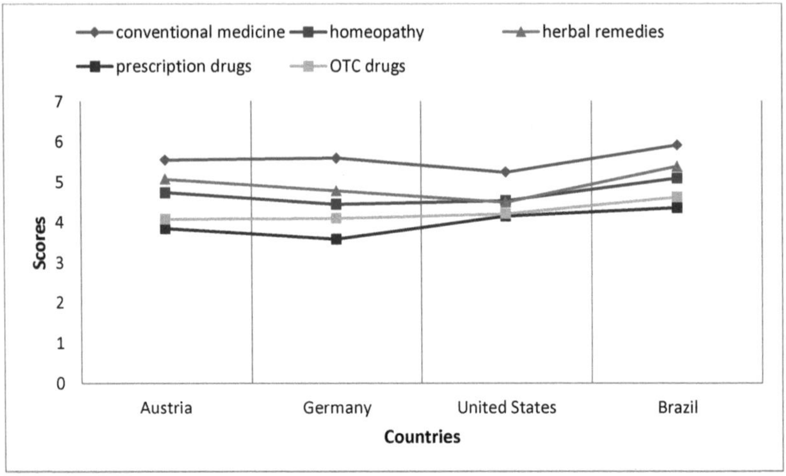

Figure 23: Acceptance of Different Drug Types

Since Brazilian scores were clearly more developed for all medication types than in their individualistic counterparts, the utilization of herbal medicines was highly distinct across countries (F= 9.182, p= .000), while this was neither the case for mainstream (F= 2.506, p= .058) nor for homeopathic medicine (F= 1.519, p= .208). The most distinct ratings of conventional medicine were noted between Brazil and Austria (F= 3.007, p= .001), Germany (F= .768, p= .003) and the United States (F= 5.045, p= .000) as well as between Germany and the United States (F= 2.492, p= .002). Differences were less pronounced for homeopathic substances, with scores only being marked by highly significant manifestations between Brazil and Germany (F= 7.854, p= .000) as well as the U.S. (F= .122, p= .000); for herbal preparations, U.S. American values differed significantly from those of Austria (F= .550, p= .000) respectively Brazil (F= .582, p= .000), as well as between Germany and Brazil (F= .034, p= .000). A summary of scores can be found below (see Figure **23**).

When questioned about their usage behavior within a year, response patterns established some significant variations: over-the-counter medications were more often (T: 4.248; AUT: 4.078; GER: 4.096; USA: 4.207; BRA: 4.614) consumed than their prescription counterparts (T: 3.994; AUT: 3.846; GER: 3.582; USA: 4.148; BRA: 4.353). For both drug classes, significant differences manifested themselves on a country-basis (OTC: F= 5.377, p= .001; DTC: F= 8.930, p= .000). Differences in non-prescription drug evaluations were most significant between Brazil and its European counterparts (Austria: F= 1.024, p= .000; Germany: F= 3.963, p= .000), while distinctions between Brazil and Austria (F= .008, p= .002) respectively Germany (F= 4.605, p= .000) as well as between Germany and the U.S. (F= 50.970, p= .000) were most striking for prescription drugs. Generally, non-prescription drugs might be met with more good will, due to the above-cited advantages, which primarily concern their convenient availability, efficacy as well as their affordability and safe use (Accent Health, 2014; see section 6.1.1.6.).

After having evaluated the relevance of different drug types to individual health and its maintenance, consumers' attitudes towards non-prescription medications were investigated. For this purpose, three separate questions were combined into the factor Attitude towards OTC drugs (KMO: .721; Significance according to Bartlett: .000; Cronbach α: .882): (1) "I am interested in non-prescription (OTC) drugs", (2) "Non-prescription (OTC) drugs are important to me", and (3) "I attach (great) importance to non-prescription (OTC) drugs". In total, the attitude developed was slightly above average in all societies (T: 4.0157; AUT: 3.8692; GER: 3.9121; USA: 4.0854; BRA: 4.1964), revealing significant differences at a 10 % level across countries (F= 2.389, p= .067).

The fictitious OTC drug SENZA was adapted from the market leader in this drug category, Bayer's Aspirin (see section 6.1.1.2.) and the adverts designed resembled the brand's thematic orientation. Assuming pain medications to be a part of every household's inventory, "versatile" uses were emphasized, with drugs being suited to treat a variety of medical symptoms, such as fever, cold symptoms, body pain (affecting muscles, back, joints), headaches, etc. Hence, recipients' general attitudes towards pain medications were examined, which achieved average scores (T: 4.384; AUT: 3.929; GER: 3.973; USA: 4.649; BRA: 4.988). Results were characterized by highly significant differences between the individual countries (F= 22.600, p= .000). Austrian and German answers affirmed this product category to be of little relevance to respondents and, with the two countries' scores being almost equally low, distinctions were most pronounced between Austria and the U.S. (F= 1.545, p= .000) respectively Brazil (F= 10.283, p= .000) as well as between Germany and the U.S. (F= .762, p= .000) respectively Brazil (F= 7.902, p= .000).

While numerous health conditions can be eased by pain medications, a high need for those preparations could not be detected for the sample investigated (T: 3.803; AUT: 3.475; GER: 3.434; USA: 3.781; BRA: 4.527); nevertheless, Brazilian results stood out, where self-medication by use of analgesics was regarded as more essential when compared to other parts of the world. Hence, highly significant differences between the countries under investigation could be confirmed (F= 18.711, p= .000), whereby variations were highly pronounced between Brazil and Austria (F= 3.348, p= .000), Germany (F= 6.860, p= .000) as well as the U.S. (F= .900, p= .000).

In line with this result, the frequency of pain medication use within a year offered some variation as well: for the total sample, moderate usage rates could be noted (M = 3.385) but allowed for clear differences on a country scale (F= 30.909, p= .000): in individualistic countries (Austria, Germany, the United States) values were rather ill pronounced (T: 3.119; AUT: 2.942; GER: 3.018; USA: 3.398), whereas scores in Brazil were comparatively high (M = 4.187), with the heightened awareness for quality of life driving usage rates. In detail, differences as to pain medication usage were highly developed between Brazil and Austria (F= 5.618, p= .000), Germany (F= 6.877, p= .000), and the U.S. (F= .046, p= .000) as well as between the United States and Austria (F= 4.790, p= .002) and Germany (F= 5.976, p= .008).

6.2.5 *Sources of Health Information*

The sources available to consult for health information are plenty, ranging from people sources (experts and non-expert) to media sources (see section 6.1.1.3.), which enjoy varying degrees of trust. The present study revealed the highest degree of relevance to be assigned to doctors, alternative practitioners and/or pharmacists (Total: 6.367; AUT:

6.232; GER: 6.221; USA: 6.512; BRA: 6.502), followed by family members such as parents, the partner and/or children (Total: 5.621; AUT: 5.837; GER: 5.765; USA: 5.512; BRA: 5.369). Friends respectively acquaintances ranked last in the interpersonal source category (Total: 4.780; AUT: 4.958; GER: 4.955; USA: 4.620; BRA: 4.587), lending support to the assumption that health constitutes an important matter that is primarily discussed in a professional or private environment. Opinions uttered by health professionals, by virtue of their expertise and status, were met with the highest degrees of trust but were marked by highly significant differences between the different countries (F= 6.060, p= .000; see Figure **24**). With European scores being almost identically pronounced in terms of experts' importance, highly significant differences surfaced between Austria and the U.S. (F= 4.121, p= .002) respectively Brazil (F= .971, p= .001) as well as Germany and the U.S. (F= 3.245, p= .001) respectively Brazil (F= .659, p= .004).

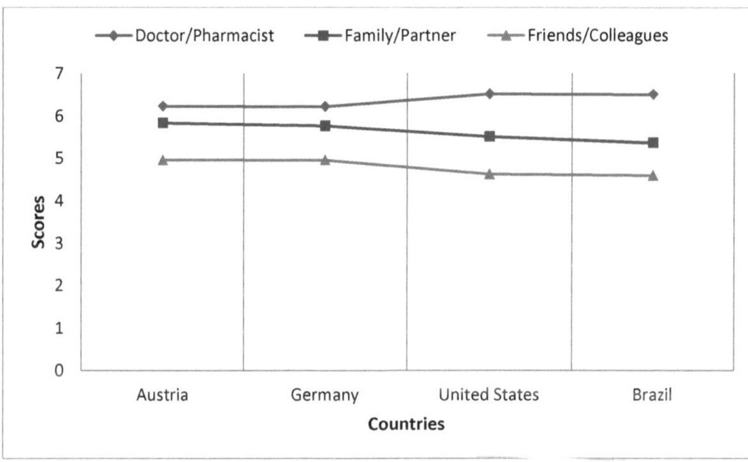

Figure 24: Sources of Health Information – Interpersonal Sources

The second place was occupied by family members, alluding to health matters being primarily of personal interest. This rationale could be confirmed for all countries, where scores are marked by highly significant differences (F= 5.137, p= .002). Ranking slightly behind were acquaintances and colleagues, with whom health concerns are obviously discussed to a far lesser extent in all states. Country-wise, pronounced differences became obvious (F= 3.882, p= .009) and only a handful of significant distinctions with regard to family consultations were found (BRA/AUT: F= 21.516, p= .005; BRA/GER: F= 23.608, p= .004), while none were reported for friends and colleagues.

In terms of media sources, both advertising or editorial content can be referred: The first form presents a rather complex communication form that follows pre-defined objectives and sets out to create affective responses in consumers (Wells et al., 2006). It qualifies as a text genre that is guided by clear (promotional) intentions (Behrens, 2001; Forceville, 1996) and utilizes the mass media on a personal and interactive level, where adverts are placed on behalf of identified sponsors with the intention of creating a need and/or desire for the product; at the same time, advertising can serve educational purposes by providing detailed information on product features and specifics (Wind, 1994). The second form, the editorial, is quite distinct from advertising, described as a leading article usually written by the senior editor or publisher. It presents an opinion piece that is reflective of the source's (e.g., a magazine's and/or TV station's) mind-set, making it more subjective (Business Dictionary, 2014).

Compared to the previously-listed interpersonal sources of information, media channels were attributed far lesser degrees of relevance: while advertising in newspapers and magazines received relatively low scores (Total: 3.061; AUT: 2.863; GER: 2.680; USA: 3.227; BRA: 3.477), both TV and radio advertising were even less popular (Total: 2.961; AUT: 2.708; GER: 2.520; USA: 3.145; BRA: 3.473). The last rank was occupied by online promotional channels, namely the Internet in general (Total: 2.601; AUT: 2.390; GER: 2.078; USA: 3.015; BRA: 2.926) and Social Media in particular (Total: 2.488; AUT: 2.231; GER: 2.045; USA: 2.818; BRA: 2.861). All these statements lend support to source credibility theory, which describes the extent to which plausibility is attributed to different sources of information; thereby, a low degree of credibility is said to be characteristic of advertising messages (Salmon et al., 1985). Highly pronounced variations were clearly noteworthy across countries for all promotional forms (see Figure **25**).

Print advertising evaluations (F= 10.314, p= .000) were most distinct between Brazil and Austria (F= 7.032, p= .000) as well as Germany (F=30.163, p= .000); the latter's scores were also marked by highly distinct manifestations when compared to U.S. results (F= 12.632, p= .000). Due to lower Austrian and German values, TV and radio advertising ratings (F= 15.209, p= .000) exhibited highly pronounced variations between Austria and the U.S. (F= .089, p= .005) respectively Brazil (F= 6.308, p= .000) as well as between Germany and the U.S. (F= 13.777, p= .000) respectively Brazil (F= 33.622, p= .000). A similar picture could be painted for Internet advertising (F= 16.352, p= .000) and Social Media advertising (F= 14.264, p= .000), where once again European and American scores were very diverse from one another: highly pronounced variations were reported between Austria and the U.S. (Internet: F= 2.444, p= .000; Social Media: F= 5.752, p= .000) respectively Brazil (Internet: F= 1.697, p= .000; Social Media: F= 8.645, p= .000), as well as between Germany and the U.S. (Internet: F= 34.260, p= .000; Social Media: F= 29.742, p= .000) respectively Brazil (Internet: F= 30.425, p= .000; Social Media: F= 33.625, p= .000).

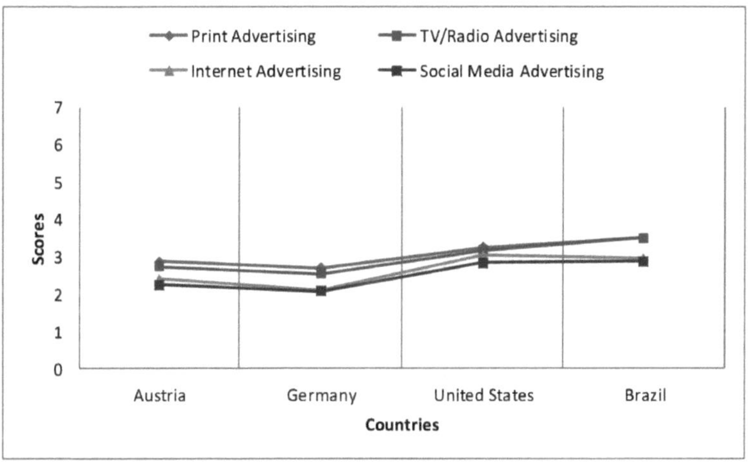

Figure 25: Sources of Health Information – Media Sources (Advertising)

Editorial content, which can match recipients' thought profiles and does not possess an inherent sales intention, scored slightly more favorable evaluations, with two media vehicles receiving quite similar scores: the low-paced print media (Total: 3.385; AUT: 3.349; GER: 3.250; USA: 3.698; BRA: 3.242) and the interactive Internet (Total: 3.336; AUT: 3.025; GER: 3.178; USA: 3.753; BRA: 3.387). In third place, editorial broadcasting content could be found, which was perceived as less reliable due to its fleeting nature (Total: 3.179; AUT: 3.000; GER: 2.881; USA: 3.574; BRA: 3.261). In addition, specialist literature was awarded quite high degrees of importance (Total: 4.676; AUT: 4.643; GER: 4.340; USA: 4.977; BRA: 4.746). Overall reported values for editorial content, independent of media vehicle, were marked by (highly) significant differences across countries (see Figure **26**).

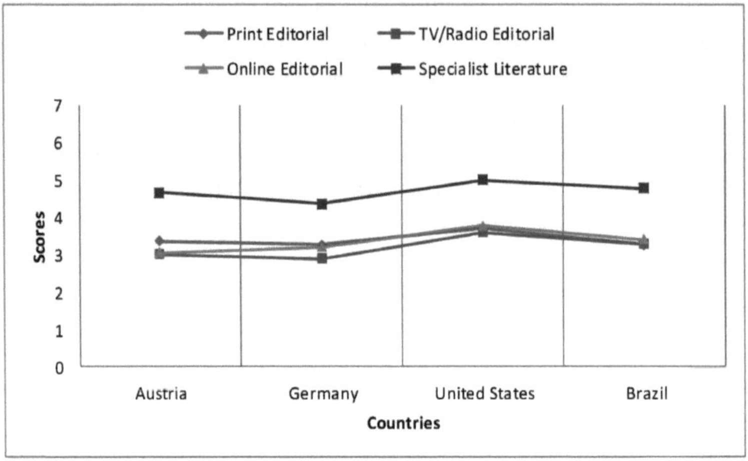

Figure 26: Sources of Health Information – Media Sources (Editorials)

For print content (F= 3.501, p= .015) only two significant distinctions between the U.S. and Germany (F= .000, p= .004) respectively Brazil (F= 4.057, p= .006) could be reported; likewise, editorial broadcasting content received quite distinct evaluations across countries (F= 7.281, p= .000), leading to highly pronounced differences between the U.S. and Austria (F= .257, p= .000) respectively Germany (F= .075, p= .000). In the Internet content category more differences surfaced (F= 7.146, p= .000), where these country groupings also exhibited highly distinct manifestations (USA/AUT: F= .347, p= .000; USA/GER: F= .681, p= .000), while for specialist literature the only highly developed differences were observed between Germany and the United States (F= 3.171, p= .000).

6.2.6 *Self-Medication and Advertising*

Self-medication practices and individuals' beliefs in their own capabilities to engage therein are nourished by information. In the process, various resources can be consulted. For the purpose of the present investigation, however, special attention will be given to advertisements. Before establishing the value of the current study's stimuli ads, individual attitudes towards advertising in general and pharmaceutical advertising in particular need to be substantiated. *Attitude towards Advertising* (KMO: .616; Significance according to Bartlett: .000; Reliability: .750) was measured with the following three items: (1) "Advertisers know how to provide the information that is needed to make a qualified decision"; (2) "Overall, I consider advertising a good thing"; and (3) "Overall, I do like advertising". In a similar manner, respondents' *Attitudes towards Pharmaceutical Advertising* (KMO: .670; Significance according to Bartlett: .000; Reliability: .820) were determined via the following three items: (1) "Advertisers for pharmaceuticals know how to provide the information that is needed to make a qualified decision "; (2) "Overall, I consider advertising for pharmaceuticals a good thing"; and (3) "Overall, I do like advertising for pharmaceuticals". For both attitude categories, KMO values of slightly above .6 indicate a reasonable potential for factorization. Overall results reveal Attitude towards Advertising (Total: 3.7824; AUT: 3.8715; GER: 3.6487; USA: 3.6120; BRA: 4.000) to be more negative than Attitude towards Pharmaceutical Advertising (Total: 3.4520; AUT: 3.5527; GER: 3.2702; USA: 3.3636; BRA: 3.6262).

Across the spectrum, attitude towards advertising scores significantly varied, manifesting highly developed variations between Brazil and Germany (F= 1.789, p= .007) as well as the United States (F= .882, p= .003). Differences between Austria and the United States were only significant at a 5 % level (F= .006, p= .041), while results were distinct at a 10 % level between Austria and Germany (F= .096, p= .074). In line with this, attitudes towards pharmaceutical advertising exhibited significant distinctions when comparing answers from Germany and Brazil (F= 17.907, p= .007). Scores for Germany and Austria were characterized by variations at a 5 % level (F= 1.702, p= .019), while they varied at a 10 % level between the United States and Brazil (F= 3.611, p= .058).

Taken together, these scores suggest a below-average approval of this promotional technique (see Figure **27**). One potential explanation for these rather low ratings can be found in recipients' skepticism towards (pharmaceutical) advertising, for which the following questions were factorized into two distinct categories: *Skepticism towards*

*Advertis*ing (KMO: .782; Significance according to Bartlett: .000; Reliability: .867) respectively *Skepticism towards Pharmaceutical Advertising* (KMO: .816; Significance according to Bartlett: .000; Reliability: .872). They comprised the following items, all of which were reverse coded to offer insights into consumers' levels of skepticism: (1) "I can depend on getting the truth in most advertising (for pharmaceuticals)", (2) "Advertising (for pharmaceuticals)'s aim is to inform the consumer", and (3) "I feel I have been accurately informed after viewing most advertisements (for pharmaceuticals)".

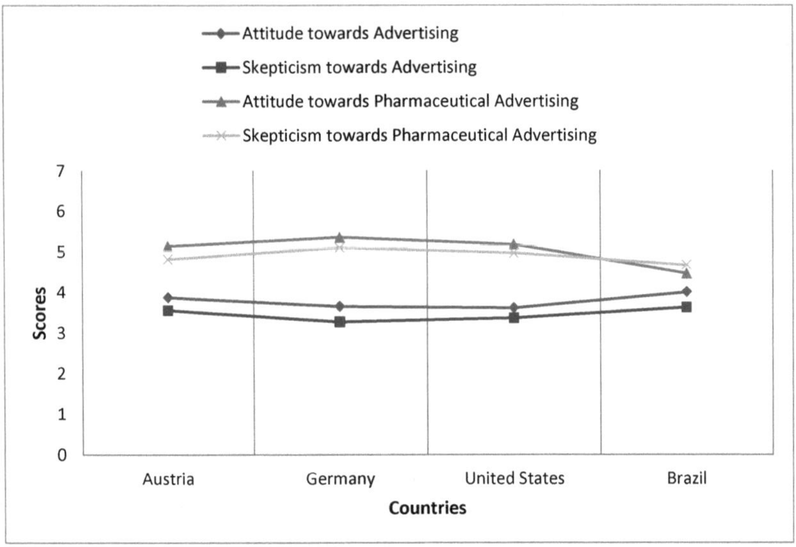

Figure 27: Attitudes and Skepticism towards Advertising in General and Pharmaceutical Advertising in Particular

Skepticism scores for promotions in general were rather high (T: 5.1336; AUT: 5.1336; GER: 5.3514; USA: 5.1736; BRA: 4.4583; see Figure 27). Due to low Brazilian manifestations, results were marked by high distinctions, especially when comparing answers from Brazilian respondents with those of Austria (F= 1.839, p= .000), Germany (F= 10.243, p= .000) and the U.S. (F= 7.048, p= .008). Results between Austria and Germany differed at a 10 % level (F= 3.831, p= .098). In terms of *Skepticism towards Pharmaceutical Advertising*, overall scores tended to be lower across countries (T: 4.8799; AUT: 4.8037; GER: 5.0944; USA: 4.9542; BRA: 4.6624). Once again, Brazilian results were the least pronounced, explaining significant distinctions in scores between Brazil and Germany (F= 5.447, p= .002). In addition, results varied on a 5 % level between the United States and Brazil (F= 2.041, p= .036) as well as between Austria and Germany (F= 3.520, p= .029).

For the present project, ad execution was controlled, meaning that four different yet cohesive print ad versions deploying either informative, emotional, mixed or CSR appeals were put to the test. In the next section, core topics of advertising research will be addressed, followed by the degree of consumer self-empowerment derived from each ad version. The evaluation of different ad elements is suggested to operate as a mediator of the information obtained and, consequently, influences the degree of empowerment obtained from the actual ad (Chaffee and Schleuder, 1986).

6.2.7 Consumer Responses to Different Advertising Styles

Ad evaluation is based upon the respondent "lik[ing] the ad execution" and their evaluation of "how the brand claims are made" (Keller, 1991: 43). By implication, promotions need to be perceived and evaluated favorably by recipients with regard to four distinct categories, namely attitude towards the ad, credibility, product evaluation and consequent purchase intention (Kroeber-Riel and Esch, 2011; Grewal et al. 1997). Evaluations, which were predicted to vary with regard to the ad appeal being chosen, were put into four core hypotheses (H 1 – H 4), whose results will be discussed in the next sections.

Both ad appeal and product category are said to shape ad evaluations (DeLorme et al., 2009). So far, the pharmaceutical industry has relied on a factual information-provision strategy (Main et al., 2004; DeLorme et al., 2010; Koinig, 2012), assuming that people are entitled to information to make qualified decisions. Conditioned by OTC drugs' product class (rather high-involvement products; see section 4.3.6.), this rationale has apparently paid off: consumers claim to look for product indicators when selecting a non-prescription drug (75 %; Accent Health, 2014) and since symptom alleviation is put first, choice of medication is, in most instances, driven by the product's symptom-relief abilities (89 %; CHPA, 2013). The one exception is represented by the direct-to-consumer-advertising (DTCA) domain, where emotional appeals have been utilized with great success (Wolfe, 2002). Hence, the present investigation raised the question whether the OTC drug industry should try to change its promotional activities accordingly by adopting a more visual and story-driven tactic instead of a fact and data-loaded approach.

6.2.7.1 Ad Evaluations, Credibility and Comprehensibility

A useful variable in judging advertising effectiveness and consumers' responsiveness is the involvement construct, whereby consumer involvement with the product (category) on the one hand and advertising message involvement on the other hand need to be taken into consideration. Consumer involvement determines ad and product relevance (Zaichowsky, 1985; Celsi and Olson, 1988), defined as the association of product characteristics as being beneficial to the achievement of consumers' goals and fulfillment of their needs respectively (McGrath and Mahood, 2004). Consumer involvement is rather cognitive (Zaichkowsky, 1994) and closely related to product involvement, which is said to lead to (advertising) message involvement in turn (Laczniak et al., 1999). The latter is conceptualized as an individual's motivational state, which is likely to trigger message processing (Laczniak et al., 1989) and is, according to the Elaboration Likelihood Model of persuasion (Petty and Cacioppo, 1981; see section 5.2.1.), dependent upon the ad appeal used: "When the elaboration likelihood is high, the central route to persuasion should be particularly effective, but when the elaboration likelihood is low, the peripheral route should be better" (Petty et al., 1983: 137; see also Petty and Cacioppo, 1981). So, while a central route would be pursued for informative appeals (requiring cognitive processing capacities), an emotional promotion would require less resources but would appeal to consumers' feelings (peripheral route). Mixed and CSR promotions then would require the activation of both paths simultaneously.

The strongest predictor of ad effectiveness is attitude towards the ad (also referred to as ad evaluation), an affective response variable (MacKenzie et al., 1986). **Hypothesis 1** set out to investigate which promotional form yielded the most favorable responses in terms of attitude towards the ad, proposing that – conditioned by product category – informative appeals were expected to outrank not only mixed or CSR appeals, but especially emotional approaches. Answers to this hypothesis will be provided in the form of (1) a single question and (2) a more complex, multi-item construct.

Single-answer results won by the current survey revealed that in terms of ad liking (ad evaluation), neither ad appeal in its purity reached the highest scores. Contrary to expectations, both informative and emotional ads were outranked by the mixed version, which combines the best of both worlds (rational arguments with atmospheric images; Kroeber-Riel and Esch, 2011). Mixed approaches received the most favorable ratings amongst respondents in almost all countries (T: 4.534; AUT: 4.371; GER: 4.303; USA: 4.167; BRA: 5.308), followed by plain informative (T: 4.344; AUT: 4.212; GER: 4.311; USA: 4.036; BRA: 4.817) and CSR appeals (T: 3.954; AUT: 4.207; GER: 3.583; USA: 4.056; BRA: 3.984); the latter were identical to the mixed ad but contained an additional CSR statement. Being short of textual elements, emotional ads only scored low in the present research project (T: 3.884; AUT: 3.831; GER: 3.970; USA: 3.229; BRA: 4.506; see Figure **28**).

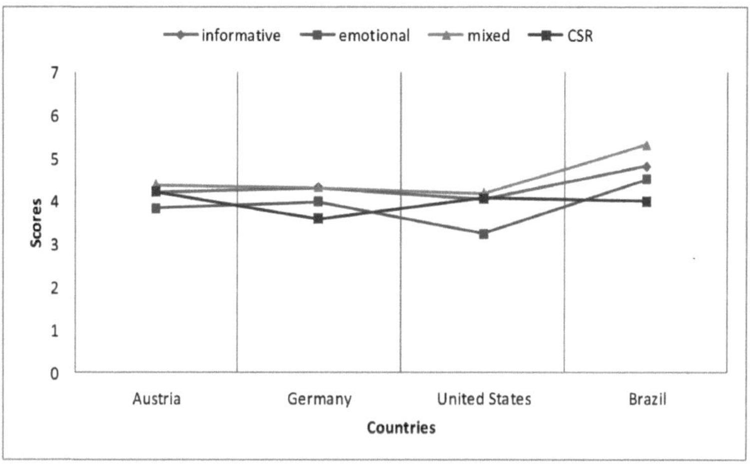

Figure 28: Attitude towards the Ad (single Question)

When contrasting findings from the different countries, variations in responses were seen to be dependent upon ad appeal (F= 11.077, p= .000) as well as the country of inquiry (F= 12.864, p= .000), resulting in highly pronounced interactive effects between the two grouping variables (F= 5.603, p= .005). As a consequence of Brazilian scores being significantly higher than those in both Europe and North America, contrast tests indicated highly distinct ad evaluations in Brazil (F= 7.684, p= .000), especially with regard to rating informative and CSR ads on the one hand (F= 1.513, p= .007) as well as mixed and emotional ads on the other hand (F= 4.838, p= .002). Similarly, results from Germany (F= 3.699, p= .012) and the United States (F= 5.324, p= .001) displayed some highly pronounced differences, the former concerning their evaluations of informative and CSR ads (F= 1.780, p= .008), while the latter produced highly developed scores for the mixed/emotional (F= .170, p= .001), the CSR/emotional (F= .126, p= .003), and informative/emotional comparisons (F= 3.152, p= .002). No such variations could be confirmed for the Austrian sample (F= 1.610, p= .188).

In the present study, emotional involvement (being equal to general ad evaluation) and cognitive involvement (comprising rational/thinking components) were both factorized for analysis. Emotional Involvement or Ad Evaluation (KMO: .813; Significance according to Bartlett: .000; Cronbach α: .889) included items like "interesting", "pleasant", "favorable", and "positive". While the highest scores for emotional involvement were anticipated for the emotional ad, followed by the mixed and CSR versions alike, results did not completely point in the expected direction. In terms of scores, the mixed promotion came in highest (T: 4.4642; AUT: 4.0257; GER: 4.3042; USA: 4.3843; BRA: 5.1542) and was preceded by the informative ad (T: 4.2575; AUT: 4.0583; GER: 4.2746; USA: 3.9635; BRA: 4.7333). The emotional ad reached the third highest score (T: 4.0241; AUT: 4.1308; GER: 3.8852; USA: 3.7994; BRA: 4.2820), outranking the CSR version with the total lowest score (T: 3.8256; AUT: 4.2136; GER: 3.3185; USA: 3.8330; BRA: 3.9541). Differences came out highly significant for the countries under investigation (F= 8.378, p= .000), where highly pronounced distinctions for the different ad appeals could be noted (F= 9.041, p= .000). These results also suggested very significant interactive effects amongst ad version and country (F= 2.538, p= .007; see Figure **29**). ANOVAs revealed highly significant differences with regard to ad evaluation in Germany (F= 6.249, p= .000) and Brazil (F= 7.295, p= .000). In the case of the United States, differences solely surfaced on a 10 % level (F= 2.214, p= .087), whereas no significant distinction was reported for Austria (F= .223, p= .880).

Contrast tests conducted for the German data set disclosed highly different evaluations of the informative respectively CSR ads (F= 1.087, p= .000), which were also reported for Brazil (F= .233, p= .004), besides significant variations in ratings for mixed and emotional ads (F= 10.022, p= .002). While Brazilian respondents perceived all ad appeals significantly more positively than their European and/or North American counterparts, they were the least responsive to CSR appeals. Those were, however, slightly better received in the United States, where they outranked emotional appeals commonly used in Direct-to-Consumer-Advertising (Wolfe, 2002; Main et al., 2004).

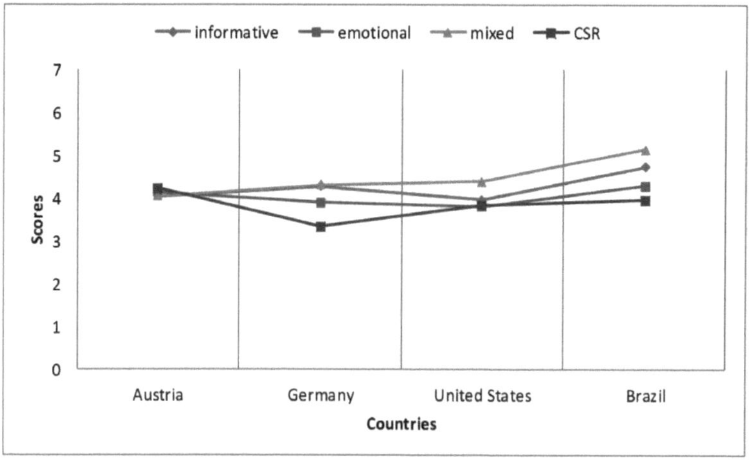

Figure 29: Attitude towards the Ad (Factorized Questions)

Contrary to expectations, mixed appeals yielded even better results than informative advertisements, which have been used to promote pharmaceutical products for the longest time (Main et al., 2004). CSR and emotional approaches fought a close battle for the last spot: in Brazil, CSR ads lost to their emotional counterparts, which performed very poorly in the United States. As the highest degrees of liking were not reported for informative but mixed appeals and emotional messages were received least favorably in three out of four countries, **Hypothesis 1** could only be partially confirmed.

Involvement, however, is not only emotional, but also comprises cognitive elements (see section 5.4.5.). As such, it is concerned with thinking aspects and logical argumentation, with its major goal being the achievement of comprehensibility and credibility. For high involvement products like (non-)prescription drugs, the provision of information is emphasized, assisting consumers in arriving at qualified decisions. **Hypothesis 2** expected informative ads to receive more positive ratings in terms of credibility than mixed, CSR and emotional promotions, which were assumed to occupy the last rank.

Cognitive involvement measures were split into two distinct categories, namely Cognitive Involvement I (or Credibility; KMO: .831; Significance according to Bartlett: .000; Cronbach α: .924), which covered the items "convincing", "credible", "truthful", and "believable", and Cognitive Involvement II (or Comprehensibility), which consisted of the single item "comprehensible". On the two cognitive involvement scales, scores diverged slightly. With regard to Cognitive Involvement I (Credibility; see Figure **30**), the promotion utilizing the mixed appeal was received most positively (T: 3.7953; AUT: 3.3832; GER: 3.6037; USA: 3.3333; BRA: 4.8789), narrowly outranking its informative complement (T: 3.7265; AUT: 3.7245; GER: 3.7150; USA: 3.2667; BRA: 4.2000). The last respectively second to last spots in this category were reserved for the CSR and emotional ad editions (CSR: T: 3.2548; AUT: 3.5610; GER: 2.9756; USA: 3.3083; BRA: 3.1834; emotional: T: 3.1397; AUT: 3.2061; GER: 3.2049; USA: 2.3325; BRA: 3.8185).

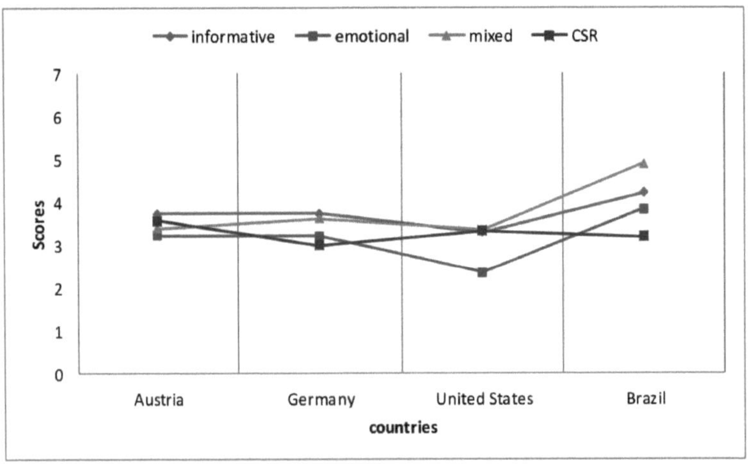

Figure 30: Cognitive Involvement I (Credibility) Scores

Once again, highly significant differences were noted amongst countries (F= 17.800, p= .000) and for the different ad versions (F= 12.208, p= .000), for which interaction effects were highly pronounced (F= 4.358, p= .000). In Austria, no significant differences in credibility scores were brought about (F= 1.367, p= .254); in Germany, they existed on a 5 % level (F= 3.782, p= .011), where the informative ad received significantly higher credibility ratings than the CSR version (F= .120, p= .004). In the United States (F= 6.953, p= .000), the credibility of the emotional ad was significantly below that of the informative (F= .324, p= .000), the mixed (F= .194, p= .000) as well as the CSR promotion (F= 6.564, p= .001). In Brazil, credibility values were highly distinct for the informative/CSR comparison (F= 1.383, p= .000) together with the emotional/mixed comparison (F= 2.404, p= .001).

In line with findings from the ad evaluation category, the highest credibility manifestations were reported for the mixed respectively informative ad, whose scores almost coincided in a tie. The overall lowest values manifested for the emotional ad, which was not perceived as credible at all. Yet, it had a direct face-off for favor in Germany, where it lost to its CSR counterpart. With mixed and informative ad editions being in the lead and emotional messages being rated as the least credible in the majority of countries, **Hypothesis 2** has to be partially rejected.

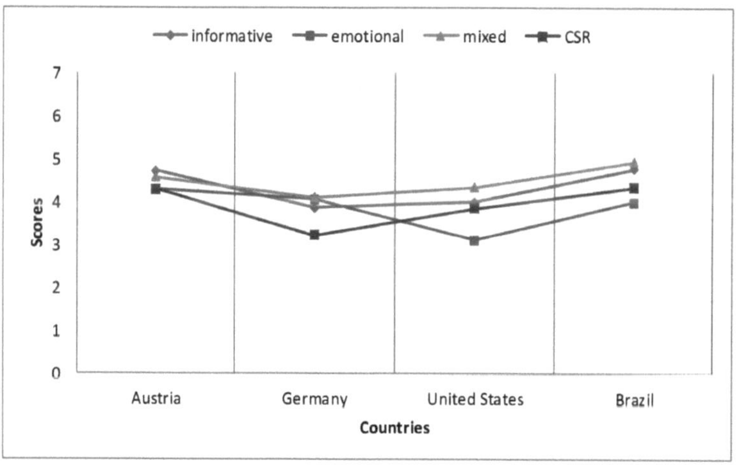

Figure 31: Involvement II (Comprehensibility) Scores

Cognitive Involvement II or Comprehensibility yielded (slightly) more profitable results (see Figure **31**). In this category, the mixed promotion managed to be in the lead once again by reaching above-average manifestations (T: 4.482; AUT: 4.569; GER: 4.102; USA: 4.333; BRA: 4.932). It was immediately preceded by the informative advertisement (T: 4.328; AUT: 4.717; GER: 3.852; USA: 3.983; BRA: 4.767), with both the CSR (T: 3.910; AUT: 4.283; GER: 3.210; USA: 3.838; BRA: 4.333) and the emotional ad (T: 3.850; AUT: 4.283; GER: 4.049; USA: 3.097; BRA: 3.986) staying behind.

Highly significant differences in credibility could be noted for the different ad versions ($F = 7.269$, $p = .000$) as well as between the different countries ($F = 11.622$, $p = .000$); nonetheless, significant interaction effects between ad version and country could only be manifested on a 10 % level ($F = 1.848$, $p = .056$). Credibility scores for the different ad versions did not diverge considerably in Austria ($F= .881$, $p= .452$), but they were marked by variations at a 5 % level in both Germany ($F= 3.293$, $p= .021$) and Brazil ($F= 3.407$, $p= .018$): in the former case, emotional ads outperformed their CSR counterpart ($F= .076$, $p= .008$) while in the latter case emotional promotions were assigned less credibility than the mixed appeal ($F= 11.831$, $p= .004$). Similarly, emotional ads ranked last in terms of credibility in the U.S., manifesting strong differences when compared against mixed ($F= 1.253$, $p= .000$) or informative adverts ($F= .004$, $p= .007$).

6.2.7.2 Product Evaluation

Advertising messages, if perceived as both useful and positive, also play into individual product evaluation (McQuarrie and Langmeyer, 1985). Product evaluation usually takes core aspects into consideration, such as consumer value, price as well as qualitative aspects (Dodds and Monroe, 1985). These specifics should convince consumers, aiding them in their decision finding processes. The higher the perceived value and its associated benefits (Thaler, 1985; Monroe and Krishnan, 1985), the more likely are consumers to acquire the favorably evaluated product (Zeithaml, 1988; Dickson and Sawyer, 1990). At the same time, competitive claims (unless prohibited by law; see section 4.2.1.) might lead to positive product evaluations (Heskett et al., 1994; Ravald and Grönroos, 1996; Treacy and Wiersema, 1993). Product evaluation is heavily dependent upon the ad appeal utilized. Informative appeals initiate a rational (logical) thinking process, stressing measurable product attributes and features, such as performance, value and quality attributes (Leonidou and Leonidou, 2009; Churchill and Peter, 1998). By contrast, emotional appeals stimulate a heightened level of arousal in consumers, who are then more likely to engage in certain consumption-related actions (Hawkins et al., 2003), alerted or called upon by feelings elicited through the ad (Leonidou and Leonidou, 2009). By virtue of their high-involvement character, Hypothesis 3 expected informative ad appeals to bring about the most favorable product evaluations for OTC drugs, followed by mixed and CSR appeals. The last rank was assumed to be taken by the low-information emotional ad.

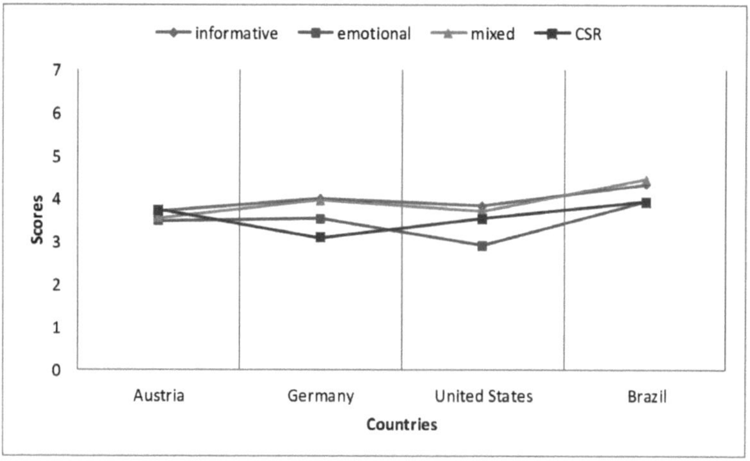

Figure 32: Product Evaluation Scores

For the present study, this category was measured by use of four items introduced by Dobni and Zinkhan (1990), Brakus et al. (2009) as well as Aaker (1997; see section 6.1.1.14): (1) "The advertised product (SENZA) makes a good impression", (2) "SENZA is of high-quality", (3) "SENZA is attractive", and (4) "SENZA is appealing". Items were, in a second step, combined into one single factor called Product Evaluation (KMO: .835; Significance according to Bartlett: .000; Cronbach α: .943). Results showed that the most favorable product evaluation was obtained for the mixed ad (T: 4.0353; AUT: 3.5446; GER: 3.9625; USA: 3.7042; BRA: 4.9449), whilst the runner-up position in this category was reserved for the informative edition (T: 3.9621; AUT: 3.7083; GER: 3.9877; USA: 3.8186; BRA: 4.3333). The second-to-last respectively last ranks were held by the CSR (T: 3.5580; AUT: 3.7237; GER: 3.0868; USA: 3.5330; BRA: 3.9042) and its emotional counterpart (T: 3.4502; AUT: 3.4833; GER: 3.5337; USA: 2.8629; BRA: 3.9234; see Figure **32**).

As to product evaluation, responses exhibited highly significant variations across the four countries (F = 12.667, p = .000) that were, further, dependent upon the ad appeal utilized (F = 8.472, p = .000). Nonetheless, an interactive effect between ad appeal and country origin could only be confirmed at a 5 % level for product evaluation (F = 2.322, p = .014). While product evaluations did not discern in Austria (F = .381, p = .767), they did so to a highly significant extent in Germany (F = 5.576, p = .001), the United States (F = 4.200, p = .006) and Brazil (F = 5.181, p = .002). In Germany, the informative ad scored far more favorable product evaluations than the CSR promotion (F = .181, p = .001); in the U.S., by contrast, the emotional ad failed to compete with regard to positive evaluation with both the informative (F = .375, p = .001) and the mixed promotions (F = .084, p = .004), whilst the mixed ad achieved more appealing evaluations than the emotional advert in Brazil (F = .7687, p = .001). By virtue of their factual and extracting style, both informative and mixed promotions were seen to offer beneficial accounts in terms of product information. CSR ads came in third, while emotional ads were seen as providing the fewest account of product specifics. Since emotional ads reported the overall lowest scores in all but one country and informative and mixed promotions received equally high scores, **Hypothesis 3** was only verified in parts.

6.2.7.3 Purchase Intention

Both positive ad evaluation and favorable product evaluation alike have the potential of influencing and directing purchase intention (Fishbein and Ajzen, 1975), meaning the probability of a consumer either trying or purchasing an advertised product (Whitlark et al., 1993). Heightened degrees of consumer satisfaction as derived from the product (Fournier, 1998) are said to increase the likelihood of purchase (Dodds, et al., 1991; Schiffman and Kanuk, 2000), as product offerings are always evaluated in terms of their usability (utilitarian dimension) as well as their pleasantness (hedonic dimension; Batra and Ahtola, 1990) and are acquired with the intention of aiding consumers with the attainment of their individual goals (Spies et al., 1997). Purchase intentions are initiated once a product purchase is seen as a means of meeting consumers' objectives. Previous research has demonstrated that informative appeals hold the potential to intensify and strengthen purchase intentions (Okazaki et al., 2010). Emotional appeals, on the other hand, result in both more positive attitudes towards the ad and ad believability, as such indirectly increasing the likelihood of purchase (Okazaki et al., 2010). In the case of non-prescription as well as prescription drugs, the classical hierarchy-of-affects sequence is expected to apply (see section 5.2.): the provision of information on behalf of an advertising party is followed by a stage of awareness; then, knowledge about the product and its usability is generated, which results in liking and preference before, finally, a purchase intention originates and an actual purchase takes place (Vaughn, 1986). For non-prescription drugs, information is regarded as being vital, whereby marketers are called upon to point out the product's main advantages to meet consumers' needs and wants. If these aspects are addressed in promotions, purchase intentions should be manifested as a result. Hence, **Hypothesis 4** proposed informative ads to be especially suited to bring about an increased purchase intention for OTC drugs, followed by the mixed respectively the CSR promotion. The last spot was expected to be occupied by the more image-based emotional advertisement.

Following Mittal (1989) and Dodds et al. (1991; see section 6.1.1.15.), trial likelihood and purchase intention were explored using the following three items: (1) "I could imagine trying SENZA", (2) "I could imagine buying SENZA", as well as (3) "I could imagine SENZA being one of my most likely choices for my next purchases". Since the individual items were highly correlated and provided answers to a similar construct, they were merged into the factor Purchase Intention (KMO: .749; Significance according to Bartlett: .000; Cronbach α: .952). The highest likelihood of purchase was reported for the mixed promotion, which also yielded the highest scores for ad evaluations (T: 3.4868; AUT: 2.6944; GER: 3.3667; USA: 3.2722; BRA: 4.6328). The second highest purchase intention was noted for the informative version, which obviously managed to convince and draw in respondents on the basis of its rational argumentation (T: 3.2540; AUT: 2.9333; GER: 3.3798; USA: 3.0563; BRA: 3.6444). With almost equally low scores, the emotional (T: 2.8966; AUT: 3.0278; GER: 3.1045; USA: 2.2366; BRA: 3.2252) and the CSR promotions (T: 2.8898; AUT: 2.9611; GER: 2.3978; USA: 2.6444; BRA: 3.5722) shared the last rank (see Figure **33**).

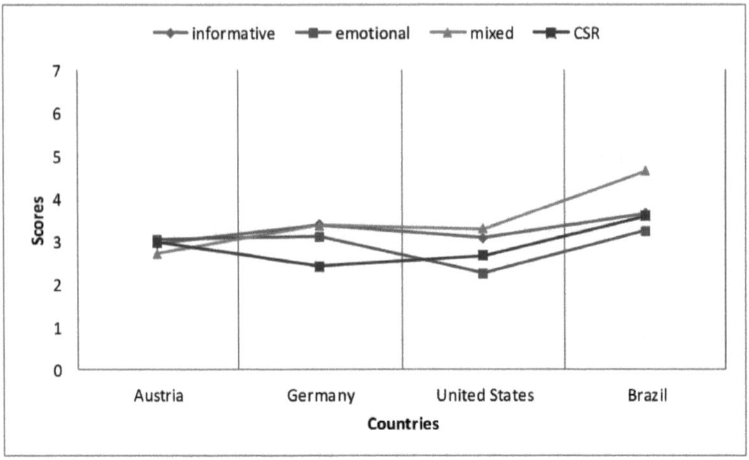

Figure 33: Purchase Intention Scores

The degree of purchase intention, as mentioned before, is subject to fluctuation and dependent on the information received on behalf of marketers. Information on drug performance and product benefits was stressed in three out of four promotions, which were rated quite favorably and more positively than the emotional edition. Responses varied significantly across countries (F = 14.803, p = .000) as well as with regard to the ad appeal utilized (F = 6.618, p = .000), leading to a highly significant interaction between the two variables (F = 3.047, p = .001). Differences in purchase intention were not reported in Austria (F = .396, p = .756) but were highly significant for all other countries (Germany: F = 4.501, p = .004; USA: F = 4.994, p = .002; Brazil: F = 5.866, p = .001). In Germany, the informative respectively CSR promotions manifested highly distinct purchase intentions (F = .417, p = .001), whereas in the U.S. the informative respectively mixed ads yielded significantly better scores than their emotional counterpart (informative: F = 1.569, p = .004; mixed: F = 9.377, p = .001). The last category (mixed/emotional) also produced striking values in Brazil (F = 10.243, p = .000) alongside highly diverse purchase likelihoods for the mixed/informative comparison (F = 3.697, p = .002).

Looking at the scores in detail, the informative respectively mixed and informative ads obtained the highest ratings in all countries except for Austria, where the mixed appeal did not create the desire to acquire the promoted product. Different versions shared the last spot: in Germany, respondents were not sold on the CSR version, whereas in both the U.S. and Brazil, the lowest purchase intention was reported for the emotional promotion. This suggests that adverts based on rational arguments seemingly increased the likelihood of purchase as compared against their emotional counterpart, which, nonetheless, did not achieve the lowest evaluations in all countries. As a consequence, **Hypothesis 4** is partially backed up.

Together with product evaluations and purchase intentions, another aspect was explored, namely respondents' interest in additional product information or the 'calls to action' (i.e. icons referring to social networks and a QR code, which – when scanned – would direct the respondent to the product website) integrated into the promotional material. This question was intended to determine product relevance while establishing promotional information sufficiency. In general, interest in additional product specifics and features seemed to be meagerly pronounced, independent of advertising appeal. If appeals were to be taken into account, the highest scores for additional information were – quite contrary to expectations – reported for the informative (T: 2.945; AUT: 2.429; GER: 2.705; USA: 3.350; BRA: 3.300) and the mixed ads (T: 2.812; AUT: 2.517; GER: 2.783; USA: 3.233; BRA: 2.712), which already contained a considerable amount of information. The CSR version came in last (T: 2.507; AUT: 2.617; GER: 2.113; USA: 2.933; BRA: 2.379), exceeded in values by its emotional counterpart (T: 2.652; AUT: 2.433; GER: 2.508; USA: 2.097; BRA: 3.560). Thereby, interactive effects of ad appeal and country were highly significant ($F = 3.353$, $p = .000$). Responses were subject to ad appeal alone at a 10 % level ($F = 2.535$, $p = .056$), whilst country of origin very significantly impacted answers ($F = 4.486$, $p = .004$). Nationality did not have a bearing on results in either Austria ($F = .151$, $p = .929$) or Germany ($F = 1.800$, $p = .148$), but did do so in the Americas (USA: $F = 5.770$, $p = .001$; Brazil: $F = 4.254$, $p = .006$). In North America, respondents exposed to emotional promotions exhibited far less established needs for additional information than those encountering informative ($F = 13.321$, $p = .000$), mixed ($F = 22.949$, $p = .001$) or CSR adverts ($F = 12.365$, $p = .007$). The opposite trend was observed in Brazil, where higher emotional scores suggested that subjects harbor more defined information needs when contrasted with the CSR appeal ($F = 13.054$, $p = .003$).

6.2.8 *Advertising's Contribution to Consumer Self-Empowerment: The case of OTC drugs*

Given their capacity to empower consumers, the relevance of as well as the reliance on OTC drugs has already been pointed out previously (see sections 1.1. and 2.4.). Thereby, empowerment is especially fostered by education: "The more consumers educate themselves about their OTC treatment choices – and continue to talk with their physicians and pharmacists about their healthcare options – the better that is for improving the health of all Americans and delivering healthcare savings throughout the healthcare system" (CHPA, 2013). In the process, consumers' lay knowledge is supplemented with information received from a credible expert source, be this a doctor, pharmacist, etc. (Wilson, 2001; see section 5.4.15.3.). This role can also be taken up by advertisements, which – regardless of the vivid criticism about their biased and too positive reporting (Coulter, 2003; HAI, 2009) – can fulfil their 'duty' of involving patients: "Informed patient participation in health care choices is impossible without access to accurate, comprehensive, unbiased information about thc pros and cons of all available treatment options" (Coulter, 2003: 39). For this reason, pharmaceutical companies are called upon to disseminate "information that is accurate and medically sound" (Kantar Health, 2014) or provide additional links to such sources. Hence, **Hypothesis 5** sought to test the degree of consumer self-empowerment derived from each ad, postulating that informative promotions would grant the highest degree of empowerment, followed by mixed and CSR versions, which were assumed to outrank emotional advertisements. Conditioned by the countries' allocation to different cultural clusters (House et al., 2004; Hofstede, 1980), **Hypotheses 6 and 7** investigated whether the rationale of consumers from different cultural backgrounds preferring different ad appeals also applied to the self-empowerment realm: here, individualistic cultures (Austria, Germany, and the U.S.) were presumed to favor informative and mixed/CSR pharmaceutical ads over emotional promotions, which respondents from Brazil (i.e. a collectivistic culture) were expected to prioritize over informative or mixed/CSR ads.

In the present study, empowerment was measured for three distinct categories, namely Message Empowerment (i.e. individuals' increased or heightened belief that the promoted product can be of personal use), Self-Medication Empowerment (i.e. individuals' increased trust in their very own self-medication abilities) and Health Empowerment (i.e. individuals' convictions of having a greater say in their health(-care) in general). As the project's title suggests, the investigation is primarily concerned with advertising as a source of consumer self-empowerment. For this reason, the very first category will be put at the discussion's center.

6.2.8.1 Message Empowerment

Albeit several individual questions addressed empowerment as derived from the message, there was a clear potential to factorize them into one single item called Message Empowerment (KMO: .729; Significance according to Bartlett: .000; Cronbach α: .866). The factor combined the answers to the following three questions: (1) "The ad allows me to objectively evaluate SENZA", (2) "I can now accurately compare SENZA with other competing brands on matters that are important to me", and (3) "I would have more confidence in using SENZA now than before I saw this commercial". In line with results from previous categories, mixed ad appeals obtained the highest total scores (T: 3.5662; AUT: 2.9167; GER: 3.3278; USA: 3.2222; BRA: 4.8192), with Brazilian results being significantly more distinct than those of the three individualistic countries. The second highest values were reported for the informative promotion (T: 3.3638; AUT: 3.2056; GER: 3.0546; USA: 3.2333; BRA: 3.9667), while the CSR edition occupied the third place (T: 3.0801; AUT: 3.4282; GER: 2.7204; USA: 2.9393; BRA: 3.2444). The least degree of message empowerment was accounted for by the emotional promotion (T: 2.6845; AUT: 2.5504; GER: 2.4809; USA: 2.2043; BRA: 3.4946). These numbers were expressive of highly significant differences between countries ($F = 54.291$, $p = .000$) and, furthermore, portended responses to vary significantly depending upon the ad version used ($F = 15.010$, $p = .000$), explaining highly pronounced interactive effects between ad appeal and country ($F = 3.371$, $p = .000$; see Figure **34**).

With regard to message empowerment, ANOVAs indicated highly significant differences in two out of four countries (USA: $F = 5.506$, $p = .001$; BRA: $F = 10.735$, $p = .000$), while differences in Europe were significant (AUT: $F = 3.775$, $p = .011$; GER: $F = 4.168$, $p = .007$). In the United States, the emotional ad did not manage to empower consumers, especially when compared against the informative ($F = 4.639$, $p = .000$) respectively mixed promotions ($F = .615$, $p = .000$). Distinct degrees of empowerment also surfaced in Brazil, where the mixed advert led to significantly more pronounced degrees of message empowerment than both the informative (F = 7.860, p = .002) and emotional appeals (F = 18.789, p = .000). Fewer distinctions could be manifested in Austria as well as Germany: in the former case, the emotional version was outperformed by the CSR ad (F = .020, p = .000), while in the latter, the mixed promotion yielded significantly higher scores than its CSR counterpart (F = 5.413, p = .000).

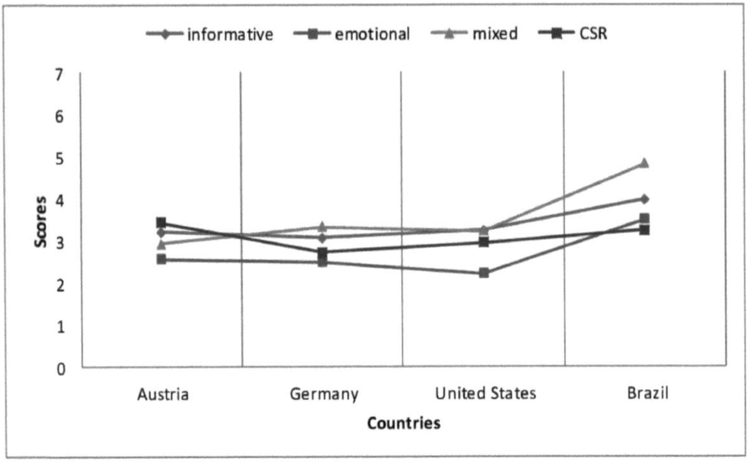

Figure 34: Message Empowerment Scores

The lowest manifestations of consumer self-empowerment were reported for two ad versions: the poorest performances of the emotional edition were seen in Austria, Germany, and the United States; the CSR promotion did not succeed in Brazil, though. Recipients reported to have gained the highest extent of message empowerment from the informative ad in all but one country; in Austria, where both the CSR and informative appeals proved to empower respondents more than their mixed equivalent. Hence, the assumption of information being beneficial to consumer self-empowerment (as granted by the actual promotional message) seemed to prevail in all countries, since all ad versions containing factual text blocks clearly outranked their emotional counterpart. With the informative promotion receiving the most favorable evaluation and the emotional ad being outranked by all other versions in two respectively three out of four countries, **Hypothesis 5** was only partially supported.

6.2.8.2 *Self-Medication Empowerment*

The promoted product was clearly identified as an over-the-counter drug and, thus, the advertisement was also meant to strengthen recipients in their self-medication abilities. In order to measure this second form of empowerment, individuals were asked to provide answers to the following two questions: (1) "I feel more confident in my self-medication skills after having studied this ad" and (2) "I am more interested in self-medication now than before seeing the ad". With regard to self-medication confidence, the highest (yet still below-average) scores were found for the mixed ad (T: 3.007; AUT: 2.730; GER: 2.850; USA: 3.167; BRA: 3.288), followed by its almost identical CSR counterpart (T: 2.830; AUT: 2.717; GER: 2.710; USA: 3.213; BRA: 2.683) as well as the informative ad version (T: 2.850; AUT: 2.750; GER: 2.607; USA: 2.996; BRA: 3.050), whose scores only differed marginally. Even lower scores were produced by the emotional edition (T: 2.437; AUT: 2.500; GER: 2.164; USA: 2.032; BRA: 3.048; see Figure **35**).

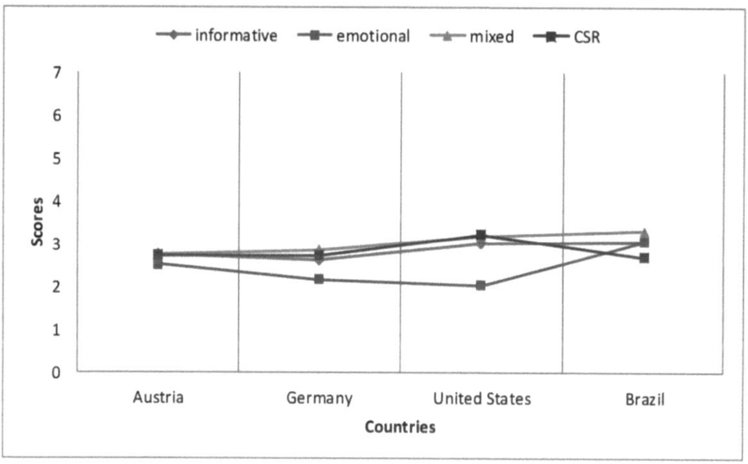

Figure 35: Self-Medication Confidence Scores

As far as significant variations could be noted regarding ad appeal (F = 4.843, p = .002), respondents respectively countries of origin seemingly only impacted the degree of self-medication empowerment at a 5 % level (F = 3.026, p = .029) as well; thus, an interaction of ad appeal with country allocation could not be confirmed (F = 1.597, p = .111). Differences were distinct in neither Austria (F = .281, p = .839) nor Brazil (F = 1.020, p = .384); while variations diverged significantly on a 10 % level in Germany (F = 2.243, p = .084), they were highly pronounced in the United States (F = 6.325, p = .000), where self-medication empowerment could be affirmed least for the emotional appeal, resulting in significantly diverging scores between the emotional promotion and its informative (F = 12.482, p = .001), mixed (F = 8.266, p = .000) and CSR counterparts (F = 23.970, p = .000).

The second question explicitly referred to respondents' empowerment with regard to their self-medication interest, which was assumed to have increased after having been exposed to the Senza promotion. Whilst the mixed ad was the forerunner in almost all other categories, results slightly differed here, since the mixed (T: 2.724; AUT: 2.417; GER: 2.583; USA: 2.750; BRA: 3.153) respectively the CSR adverts (T: 2.665; AUT: 2.800; GER: 2.129; USA: 3.150; BRA: 2.600) almost came out at a tie. The plain informative promotion ranked third in terms of its potential to strengthen recipients in their self-medication interests (T: 2.577; AUT: 2.433; GER: 2.279; USA: 2.633; BRA: 2.967), whereas the purely emotional edition occupied the fourth and last place (T: 2.370; AUT: 2.300; GER: 2.197; USA: 1.871; BRA: 3.106).

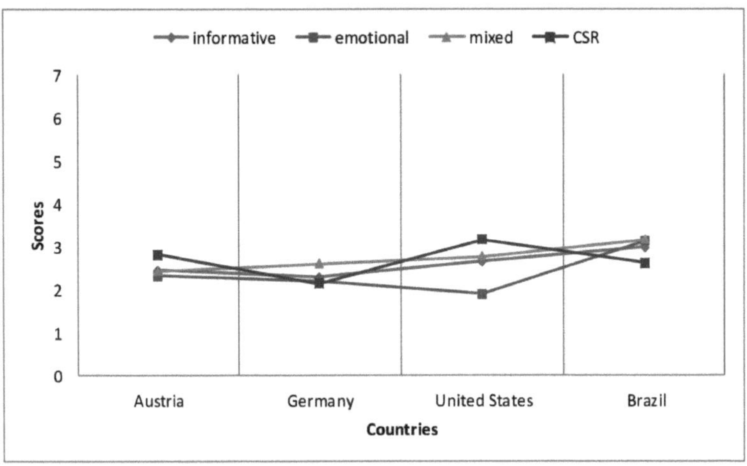

Figure 36: Self-Medication Interest Scores

Overall, below average scores could be noted (see Figure **36**), indicating that neither promotion was able to substantially increase respondents' interest in self-medication; thereby, highly significant disparities had to be highlighted between the individual countries (F = 6.618, p = .000). Variations in responses could be ascribed to the different ad appeals on a 10 % level (F = 2.130, p = .095) and also allude to the existence of significant interaction effects between the promotional appeals and the countries under investigation (F = 2.435, p = .010). Provided that answers in Austria, Germany and Brazil were characterized by low differences (Austria: F = .986, p = .400; Germany: F = 1.063, p = .365; Brazil: F = 1.079, p = .359), a different trend could be observed in the United States (F = 6.678, p = .000): there, emotional promotions triggered self-medication interest in respondents to a lesser extent than the informative (F = 4.896, p = .006;), mixed (F = 3.548, p = .001) respectively CSR ad versions (F = 15.426, p = .000).

It is noteworthy that in terms of advertising's influence on people's self-medication confidence, Brazilian scores were the highest for all except the CSR ad version, for which the United States was in the lead. Otherwise, this highly individualistic nation seemed to be least convinced by the emotional promotion; German respondents were reluctant to accept information from CSR adverts, which were also not positively received in South America, but yielded the highest scores in both Austria and the United States. While in both self-medication categories emotional promotions led to the lowest extent of empowerment, the highest boost in confidence respectively interest was registered by the mixed and CSR ads, followed at a distance by the informative promotion.

6.2.8.3 Health Empowerment

Across countries, respondents' health empowerment as won from the promotion was also investigated. Independent questions were grouped into one single factor labelled Health Empowerment (KMO: .913; Significance according to Bartlett: .000; Cronbach α: .966), which included the following six items: (1) "After seeing the ad I feel more autonomous with regard to my health", (2) "After seeing the ad I feel more capable with regard to my health", (3) "I feel like I have a greater say in my health after seeing the ad", (4) "The advertising message gives me stronger control over my health", (5) "The advertising message enables me to improve my health", and (6) "The advertising message empowers me to make better health-related decisions". Thereby, the mixed promotion was met with the highest degree of content (T: 2.834; AUT: 2.6985; GER: 2.5586; USA: 2.7583; BRA: 3.5696) right before the informative (T: 2.6816; AUT: 2.5032; GER: 2.3553; USA: 2.8214; BRA: 3.0519) and the CSR promotions (T: 2.5093; AUT: 2.5452; GER: 2.4047; USA: 2.8047; BRA: 2.2861). The emotional advertisement came in last concerning health empowerment (T: 2.4349; AUT: 2.3322; GER: 2.1694; USA: 2.1237; BRA: 3.1067; see Figure **37**).

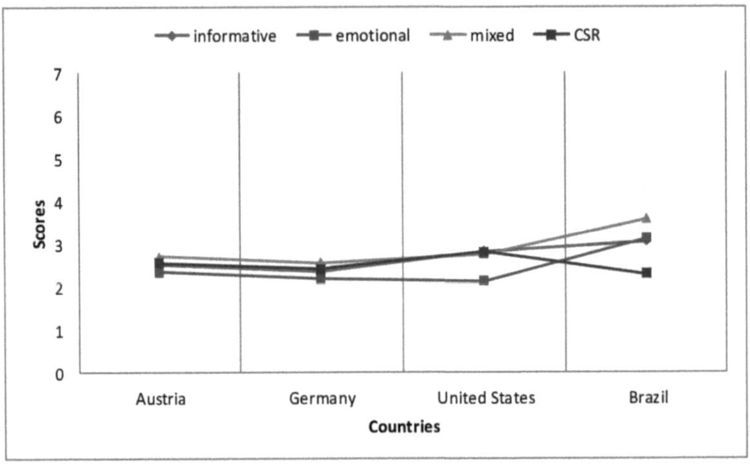

Figure 37: Health Empowerment Scores

Answers for health empowerment varied highly significantly amongst countries (F = 7.597, p = .000), for which significant differences in answers could be attributed to the ad appeal utilized (F = 4.405, p = .004); overall scores were also indicative of a reasonable interaction between ad appeal and country (F = 2.393, p = .011; 5 % level). Health Empowerment scores did not vary significantly in Europe (Austria: F = .538, p = .656; Germany: F = .801, p = .495), but were marked by highly developed differences in South America (F = 6.469, p = .000) and in North America (F = 3.186, p = .025; 5 % level), where answers implied that respondents feel less empowered when being shown the CSR version over the informative (F = 2.148, p = .006) respectively emotional ads (F = 9.266, p = .008).

Health Empowerment scores were biased, too. Brazilian values indicated that respondents felt all but the CSR ad version offered them a greater say in their health, whereas Austrian, German, and U.S. recipients were the most rejective of the emotional ad; at the same time, Americans were sold most on its CSR counterpart, which might stem from the country's philanthropic orientation (Cone Communications, 2013). For all three empowerment categories, a clear trend could be identified: the mixed appeal was rated to have made the largest contribution to individual self-empowerment and was followed by the informative edition; at times, the CSR promotion even barged in between, whilst the emotional ad was placed at the bottom in most instances. As a result, **Hypothesis 5** was partially verified for Message Empowerment; it could also be confirmed in parts for Self-Medication Empowerment respectively Health Empowerment.

Hypotheses 6 and **7** were concerned with the question of which ad version resulted in the largest degree of empowerment in individualistic and collectivistic countries respectively. The former category is renowned to be more responsive to ads providing insights into product features, uses and benefits (explicit communication); the latter, in contrast, are more image-oriented and, thus, predicted to favor emotional stimuli (implicit communication; see section 5.4.2.). Study results suggested that respondents from individualistic nations like Austria, Germany, and the United States, clearly preferred information-based ads, giving priority to informative, mixed and CSR ads at alternating ranks for the different empowerment categories. As they repeatedly outperformed the emotional ad and purely informative promotions did not claim the top spot alone, **Hypothesis 6** could be partially confirmed. Collectivistic countries were claimed to rely on information to a far lesser extent; consequently, information contained in ads was seen as less conducive to empowerment. As overall findings allude to emotional ads surpassing some but not all informative ad editions, **Hypothesis 7** had to be rejected.

6.2.9 Testing for Interactive Effects: Model-Deduced Hypotheses

The study's second part tested for causal relations of the previously designed and modelled conceptual framework (see sections 5.4. and 5.4.17.). By use of Structural Equation Modeling (SEM), causal interconnections derived from established theories were put to the test by use of the SEM-software AMOS, which allows for a simultaneous test of hypotheses respectively effects of interdependence.

While the **structural model** illustrates the hypothesized relations of dependence between latent (unobserved) variables, the **measurement model** specifies and assigns indicator items to each latent variable (Homburg and Baumgartner, 1998; Hair et al., 2006), thus, enabling construct validity estimation. The previously introduced hypotheses (H 8 to H 12) are illustrated below; parameters were, in a second step, measured by use of the Maximum-Likelihood-Estimation (Backhaus et al., 2011; Hair et al., 2006). The operationalization of variables followed a standardized procedure (see section 6.1.1.), whereby all items utilized in the causal model were measured on a 7-point Likert scale, with higher scores indicating larger extents of approval with regard to the questions posed.

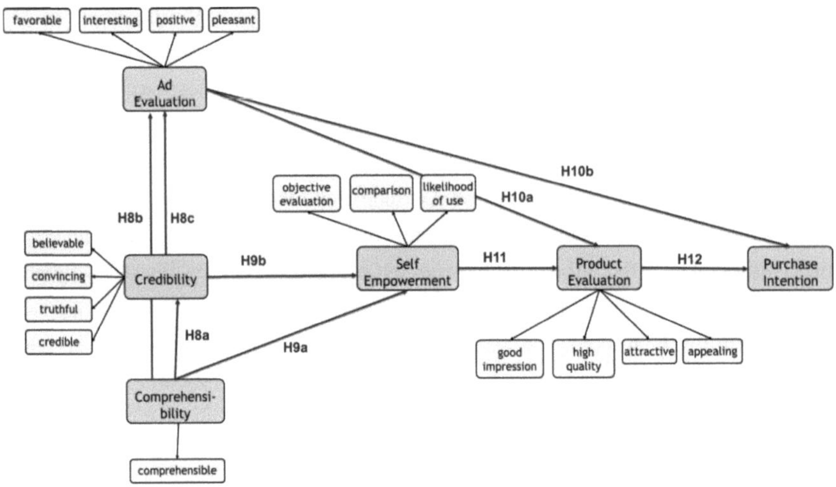

Figure 38: Conceptual Framework incl. all Hypotheses

Figure **38** offers an overview of the hypotheses deduced in section 5.4.17. **Hypothesis 8** proposed an advertisement's comprehensibility (Co) to be positively linked to (**a**) the ad's overall credibility (Cr) and (**b**) its overall evaluation (AE; i.e. more positive attitude towards the ad). The variables were operationalized as follows: ad comprehensibility was measured by a single item ('comprehensible'), while credibility comprised several items, namely 'believable', 'convincing', 'truthful', and 'credible' (Cronbach α: .924). Both items were taken from the previously introduced Perceived Message Cognition Value Scale and related to the scale's two dimensions of credibility and clarity (Lane et al., 2006; see sections 6.1.1.10 and 6.1.1.11). Results proposed that comprehensibility did indeed have an impact on the ad's perceived credibility (AUT: .54; GER: .64; USA: .61; BRA: .68) as predicted for high involvement products, for which information was seen as beneficial. On the other hand, the influence of credibility on attitude towards the ad could not be confirmed due to low score manifestations (AUT: .12; GER: .15; USA: .23; BRA: .09). Values were more pronounced in individualistic countries, were comprehensibility seemed to exercise a larger influence on overall ad evaluation. Variations in scores can most likely be ascribed to the country's diverging preferences for communication styles (see section 5.4.2.): While low-context, individualistic cultures (like the United States but particularly Austria and Germany) rely on direct, explicit and structured communication (Hall, 1976; de Mooij, 2011), comprehensibility seems to be taken for granted, aiding consumers in grasping the ad's gist. In a high context or collectivistic culture like Brazil, meaning is often disguised, counting on respondents to dismantle the promotion's intended message (de Mooij, 2011). Specifically in the health context, credibility might be dependent upon the way information is transmitted (see section 5.4.8.). In line with common advertising practice in the OTC drug industry (Koinig, 2012), the present ad provided one-sided information; yet, it might impede credibility as consumers demand transparency and balanced information. With comprehensibility being positively linked to credibility, **Hypothesis 8a** can be confirmed for all countries. But as the favorable connection between Comprehensibility and Ad Evaluation did not prevail, particularly in Austria and Brazil (see Table **32**), **Hypothesis 8b** has to be rejected for the complete data set.

Path	Hypothesis	Path Coefficient	Critical Ratio	p	Path Coefficient	Critical Ratio	p
		Austria			Germany		
Co-Cr	H 8a	.54	9.242	***	.64	11.748	***
Co-AE	H 8b	.02	.393	.694	.15	2.901	.004
Cr-AE	H 8c	.86	12.303	***	.79	12.352	***
		United States			Brazil		
Co-Cr	H 8a	.61	10.708	***	.68	12.043	***
Co-AE	H 8b	.23	3.650	***	.09	1.438	.150
Cr-AE	H 8c	.65	9.348	***	.80	10.718	***

Table 32: Path Coefficients and Critical Ratios (H 8a, H 8b, H 8c)

Hypothesis 8c tested for an ad's perceived credibility respectively its impact on the promotion's general evaluation, suggesting that credible messages score more favorable evaluations (Sternthal and Craig, 1982). In the present investigation, this assumption seemed to have come to pass in all countries (AUT: .86; GER: .79; USA: .65; BRA: .80[11]), solely exhibiting slight variations in scores amongst individualistic nations, where the lowest total scores were reported for the United States. There, credibility might fuel evaluations to a lesser extent, for respondents might be won over as a consequence of the promotional messages' overall evaluation. Yet, message credibility seems to be of advantage to marketers; if perceived as authentic, it can lead to heightened ad evaluations. Overall high scores, thus, allow for the affirmation of **Hypothesis 8c**. In this context, it is important to note that while Comprehensibility did not have a direct influence on Ad Evaluation (H 8b), it did so indirectly: comprehensible ads are obviously rated as being more credible and, as a result, higher credibility rates positively control Ad Evaluation (H 8c).

Advertisements' contributions to consumers' Self-Empowerment (SE) were examined through **Hypothesis 9**. Information was seen as a precondition for Self-Empowerment (Kuhlmann and Kolip, 2005), fostering health education and the development of medical knowledge. Hence, two items were assumed to control this variable, namely (**a**) Comprehensibility (Co) and (**b**) Credibility (C). Empowerment is a subjective experience, which presupposes consumer self-confidence and trust in their very own competencies (Eylon, 1998). It presupposes a dual(istic) conceptualization: as a process, it demands that individuals develop suitable competencies to tackle the problem they face; as an outcome, it is linked to a sense of subjective control (Pires et al., 2006). The degree of individual empowerment is subject to the amount of information available to the consumer on the one hand and their abilities to make sense of this information on the other hand (Newholm et al., 2006). As a consequence, empowerment is closely linked to the two variables of comprehensibility and credibility: only if individuals are able to understand information and follow directives, as well as believe the information they are presented with, can they become empowered.

Path relations between Comprehensibility and Self-Empowerment, however, did not suggest any significant interaction effects between the two variables (AUT: -.03; GER:

[11] A detailed illustration of path estimates respectively interactive effects can be found in Appendix E.

-.04; USA: .04; BRA: .05), while in some instances even a negative effect could be noted (characteristic of the Americas). Self-Empowerment, however, seemed to be closely linked to Credibility, with paths exhibiting highly significant (and almost equal) manifestations across countries (AUT: .74; GER: .72; USA: .78; BRA: .72). These findings are expressive of one interesting aspect: as long as messages are evaluated as credible, they are positively related to consumers' sense of Self-Empowerment, irrespective of their comprehensibility (see Table **33**). The latter might be explained by the fact that the promoted product constitutes a non-prescription drug for whose promotion respondents might expect advertisers to use medical and scientific terminology they themselves lack familiarity with. The proposed relationship between Comprehensibility and Self-Empowerment could not be confirmed by the present study, leading to the rejection of **Hypothesis 9a**. Inasmuch as credibility seemingly acted as an antecedent to consumer Self-Empowerment, **Hypothesis 9b** was backed up by substantial evidence.

Path	Hypothesis	Path Coefficient	Critical Ratio	p	Path Coefficient	Critical Ratio	p
		Austria			Germany		
Co-SE	H 9a	-.03	-.458	.647	-.04	-.549	.583
Cr-SE	H 9b	.74	9.966	***	.72	8.718	***
		United States			Brazil		
Co-SE	H 9a	.04	.809	.418	.05	.738	.460
Cr-SE	H 9b	.78	10.462	***	.72	8.906	***

Table 33: Path Coefficients and Critical Ratios (H 9a, H 9b)

Hypothesis 10 took Ad Evaluation (AE; or attitude towards the ad) as a starting point and set out to demonstrate the variable's influence on (**a**) Product Evaluations (PE) and (**b**) consumers' Purchase Intentions (PI). Ad evaluation, which describes a person's overall response to a stimulus and the resulting attitude towards said stimulus (Verdurme and Viaene, 2003), was tested by four items derived from the Perceived Sensation Value Scale (Palmgreen et al., 2002) as well as MacKenzie and Lutz (1989; see section 6.1.1.10.), comprising the items 'favorable', 'interesting', 'positive' and 'pleasant' (Cronbach α: .889). Study results hinted at Ad Evaluation indeed having a direct impact on Product Evaluation (AUT: .58; GER: .63; USA: .32; BRA: .22), whereby values were significantly more pronounced in Europe than in the United States or Brazil, allowing for significant distinctions between the individual countries under examination. Different manifestations in Ad Evaluation scores and the effect they have on Product Evaluations might be conditioned by various aspects, including expert statements, which are prominently used in Brazil (and other collective cultures), but are deployed on a less frequent basis in other countries (Huh et al., 2004); these, however, might be able to explain discrepancies in results. Even though European countries exhibited path estimates that were twice as high when compared to their (North and South) American counterparts, these significant differences did not affect results but could be read in favor of **Hypothesis 10a**, which was verified.

Ad Evaluations were, furthermore, expected to have a bearing on Purchase Intentions, with favorable evaluations being assumed to lead to a heightened willingness in consumers to acquire the advertised product. Nevertheless, this assumption could not be confirmed by the present investigation, as counter-effects were noted for all countries (AUT: -.39; GER: -.43; USA: -.05; BRA: -.03). Once again, European countries produced more similar results (see Table **34**), while U.S. scores resembled those of Brazil to a larger extent. Contrary to expectations, purchase intentions were not formed in consequence of favorable ad evaluations. It appears as if product attributes had a larger impact, convincing recipients by means of rational arguments. Overall reverse scores in all countries lead to the rejection of **Hypothesis 10b**.

Path	Hypothesis	Path Coefficient	Critical Ratio	p	Path Coefficient	Critical Ratio	p
		Austria			Germany		
AE-PE	H 10a	.58	7.670	***	.63	9.855	***
AE-PI	H 10b	-.39	-1.654	.098	-.43	-2.587	.010
		United States			Brazil		
AE-PE	H 10a	.32	5.137	***	.22	3.381	***
AE-PI	H 10b	-.05	-.506	.613	-.03	-.394	.694

Table 34: Path Coefficients and Critical Ratios (H 10a, H10b)

According to **Hypothesis 11**, Self-Empowerment (SE) was also predicted to be linked to Product Evaluation (PE): a favorable and beneficial product message packaged into an advertisement was expected not only to appeal to consumers' skills, but also to equip them with relevant information on how the product either matched or even extended their very own capabilities. The scope of empowerment would then depend on consumers' abilities to filter out potentially useful information for product evaluation and comparison, whilst ensuring that their needs were (substantially) satisfied and their time was not wasted (Pires et al., 2006; Byrne, 2003). In the present model, Self-Empowerment was only related to the empowerment derived from the actual promotion and included the following three items: (1) "The ad allows me to objectively evaluate SENZA", (2) "I can now accurately compare SENZA with other competing brands on matters that are important to me", and (3) "I would have more confidence in using SENZA now than before I saw this commercial" (Cronbach α: .886). Study findings proposed Self-Empowerment to actually control Product Evaluations, even though manifestations varied significantly across countries (AUT: .29; GER: .36; USA: .63; BRA: .66).

Path	Hypothesis	Path Coefficient	Critical Ratio	p	Path Coefficient	Critical Ratio	p
		Austria			Germany		
SE-PE	H 11	.29	4.058	***	.36	5.775	***
		United States			Brazil		
SE-PE	H 11	.63	8.416	***	.66	8.203	***

Table 35: Path Coefficients and Critical Ratios (H 11)

Yielding contradictory results, the present study identified two sub-groups: European countries (Austria and Germany), which were characterized by rather low Self-Empowerment manifestations, and the Americas with the United States and Brazil, whose scores almost ended in a draw and were twice as high as those of their European counterparts (see Table **35**). Self-Empowerment's positive influence on product evaluation could serve as an indication of the relevance of information: promotional messages that convince and/or reassure individuals of their skills respectively the product's contribution to strengthening them can be read in support of this relationship. Regardless of varying manifestations, path estimates were positive for all countries, leading to the confirmation of **Hypothesis 11**.

Finally, Product Evaluations (PE) were said to drive consumers' Purchase Intentions (PI), especially when scoring a very positive assessment. **Hypothesis 12** thus assumed a positive interdependence between the two variables, whereby Product Evaluation covered the following four questions: (1) "The advertised product (SENZA) makes a good impression", (2) "SENZA is of high-quality", (3) "SENZA is attractive", and (4) "SENZA is appealing" (Cronbach α: .943). Scores won from the investigation suggested a high interdependence in all countries (AUT: 1.30; GER: 1.28; USA: .95; BRA: .93). As was the case with Self-Empowerment and Product Evaluation, findings can be clustered in two sub-groups: higher interactive effects were noteworthy for the two European countries, while lower yet highly significant effects were also reported for the Americas. Overall, findings supported **Hypothesis 12**, which could, thus, be affirmed (see Table **36**).

		Path Coefficient	Critical Ratio	p	Path Coefficient	Critical Ratio	p
Path	**Hypothesis**	**Austria**			**Germany**		
PE-PI	H 12	1.30	4.504	***	1.28	6.765	***
		United States			**Brazil**		
PE-PI	H 12	.95	8.360	***	.93	8.763	***

Table 36: Path Coefficients and Critical Ratios (H 12)

In total, the majority of hypotheses stood the test, meaning that only a handful of paths had to be rejected (see Figure **39**). While Comprehensibility was significantly linked to Ad Evaluation (H 8a), it only exercised an indirect influence (via Credibility), since no direct path to this variable could be confirmed (H 8c). The same held true for the relationship between Comprehensibility and Self-Empowerment: while Comprehensibility did not directly wield any influence on Self-Empowerment (H 9a), it did have an affect once Credibility was introduced (H 9b). Self-Empowerment, then, fueled Product Evaluations (H 11). Ad Evaluations, moreover, acted as a source of influence on Product Evaluations (H 10a), but failed to bring about an increased Purchase Intention (H 10b); they only did so indirectly: if Product Evaluations were favorable, these resulted in heightened Purchase Intentions (H 12).

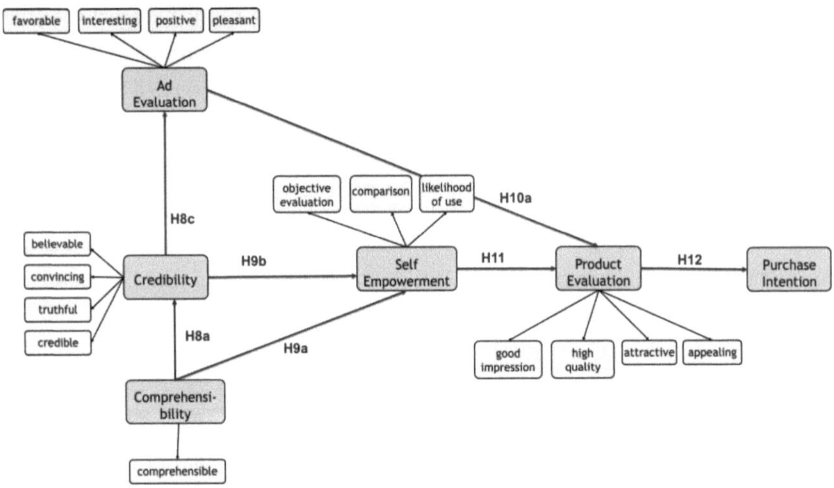

Figure 39: Conceptual Framework incl. Confirmed Hypotheses

7 Conclusion: Discussion of Results, Implications, Limitations, and Recommendations

In conclusion, this investigation's main findings will be discussed in detail, also working out their implications and contributions to academic research and marketing practices around the globe. Afterwards, the study's main limitations will be discussed, before arriving at some final recommendations.

7.1 Discussion of Results

Despite being quite highly pronounced in all countries, the notions of health as a personal responsibility respectively a topic of personal relevance were slightly less developed in both Germany and Austria; the highest scores, by contrast, were reported for the United States (see section 6.2.2.). While respondents in Austria and the United States expressed marginally higher scores of health consciousness, German answers were more in line with those of Brazil. One cultural criteria that might explain distinctions in agreement is **Performance Orientation** (AUT: 4.47; GER: 4.29; USA: 4.45; BRA: 4.11; House et al., 2004), according to which higher-scoring societies (Austria and the U.S.; Band A) put individuals in charge of their experiences and encourage them to take personal initiative; lower scoring nations, such as Germany and Brazil (Band B), give utterance to traditional schemes of operation and though they value the quality of life, they do encourage personal action and involvement to a lesser extent (Javidan, 2004). Representing environments where individuals were likely to work on their health and invest efforts towards its maintenance to secure personal success, respondents from Austria and the United States seemed to be more keen on accepting their share in health matters; individuals in Germany and especially Brazil apparently wanted to be held liable to a lesser degree, but rather chose to devolve responsibility unto health professionals instead.

Especially U.S. American health consciousness results were striking, alluding to the country's high individualistic orientation, which is confirmed by the GLOBE **In-Group Collectivism** value (AUT: 4.89; GER: 4.38; USA: 4.22; BRA: 5.16; House et al., 2004). In collectivistic nations like Brazil, the self's self-worth is rather defined in relation to the group, while in individualistic countries, the self is autonomous and independent, judged on its own terms. Individual well-being is stressed and people are held accountable for their success and failure alike. This also holds true for the health domain, where individuals are called upon to take preventive action and become engaged. By weight of numbers, responsibility for health-related decisions was more developed in the three individualistic nations (Austria, Germany, and the United States) where individuals have seemingly started to declare that "what happens to me is my own doing" (Nelson and Shavitt, 2002: 450). Besides **Power Distance**, distinctive health consciousness scores might be attributable to diverging Uncertainty Avoidance scores across the board (AUT: 5.10; GER: 5.27; USA: 4.15; BRA: 3.74; House et al., 2004), explaining an over-reliance on established norms and procedures in the case of Brazil (Band C). This dependence also seems to involve the health-care realm, with respondents being prone to delegate responsibility for their bodies to other parties, such as doctors, refusing to accept the newly gained autonomy and sovereignty.

In addition, a conviction that individuals can make a valuable contribution to their health by stepping up and taking active care of their bodies could be identified in all countries, expressed through respondents' high manifestations with regard to their self-medication abilities (see section 6.2.4.). Results amongst individualistic countries were consistent, whereby low variances might stem from divergences in the Individualism/Collectivism dimension: individualistic countries are said to be internally-oriented, encouraging personal involvement and action in health matters, e.g., through self-medication practices in general and the use of OTC drugs in particular. People in collectivistic nations like Brazil, which reported slightly lower scores, are regarded to be more externally-oriented, relying on a more hierarchical approach towards health in which diagnosis and treatment are left to experts (Rabinow, 1984; Rouse and Haas, 2003). As to illness prevention, both cultural groups were presumed to take precautions for different reasons: following Cultural Theory, individualistic nations engage in preventive activities to express their capabilities of attending to bodily and health needs respectively (Heine and Hamamura, 2007); in collectivistic countries, individuals care for their bodies out of fear of punishment, if they fail to conform to established group standards, rendering self-medication a "maintaining face" tactic (Twenge and Crocker, 2000; Kurman, 2002).

The initially introduced **Proposition 1** served as an introductory question to the research topic at hand and examined respondents' attitudes towards self-medication, which was seen as a prime determinant of both individual responses to the advertising message and the degree of self-empowerment obtained therefrom. Overall, individuals' self-medication attitudes were only moderately pronounced despite high ratings for self-medication skills. Significant differences surfaced when comparing responses from individualistic nations with their collective counterpart: Austrian, German, and American subjects did not only consider themselves to possess slightly higher self-medication abilities, but also held a far more favorable attitude towards self-medication. Brazilian respondents, nonetheless, reported to deploy self-medication practices far more frequently. Variations in answers might stem from the countries' different cultural orientations as explained by the **Individualism/Collectivism** dimension: individualistic nations stress achievement, for which a healthy body is seen as a necessity; consequently, individuals from those countries are considered to be more interested in ensuring health through the use of self-medication substances. Collectivistic Brazilian citizens, on the other hand, might feel tempted to self-medicate as it ensures conformity with established group norms and makes them fit in (Twenge and Crocker, 2000).

Self-Medication attitudes could also be related to the cultural dimension of **Performance Orientation** (AUT: 5.00; GER: 5.59; USA: 4.92; BRA: 5.24; House et al., 2004). Exhibiting higher manifestations, the two individualistic countries of Austria and Germany (Band A respectively B) presume individuals to be in charge: these societies encourage individuals to take a personal initiative in order to achieve pre-defined (health) goals; thus, they emphasize the use of self-medication substances. Despite being a country with slightly more moderate manifestations, the United States stresses individuals' very own health involvement as well: By virtue of its **Gender Egalitarianism** values (AUT: 4.83; GER: 5.02; USA: 5.03; BRA: 4.91; House et al., 2004), which are considerably higher than its Gender Egalitarianism practices (AUT: 3.18; GER: 3.21; USA: 3.36; BRA: 3.44; House et al., 2004), both the U.S. and Brazil stress the relevance of an increased quality of life and promote individual health engagement through self-care practices.

Besides, distinctions with regard to self-medication could be traced back to non-cultural reasons, including varying health-care systems and reimbursement schemes (see section 5.4.9.): while some countries (especially in Europe) attempt to decrease health expenses by providing extensive reimbursement plans, other countries – with the U.S. leading the way – are unable to offer such coverage but are eager to cut down costs in other ways. Due to steadily rising health-care costs, citizens might look for more inexpensive yet effective alternatives and are likely to turn to non-prescription drugs; the government endorses these medications by continuously extending the list of substances regarded as safe (see discussion of Rx-to-OTC switches in section 4.2.1.).

A general preference for different medication types might be subject to a society's relationship with nature as introduced by Kluckhohn und Stodtbeck (1961) and applied to the pharmaceutical sector by Diehl et al. (2008). Some cultures entertain a harmonious relationship with nature (e.g., Chinese and South American cultures), others prefer to be subjugated by nature or to dominate it (e.g., United States, Western Europe). The United States is an example for the last category, whereas Latin American countries are assumed to bow down to nature's rules (McCarty and Hattwick, 1992), explaining differences in responses towards herbal as well as homeopathic substances, which received more favorable evaluations there.

In terms of information sources consulted for health matters, a clear preference for traditional channels – comprising both interpersonal and media sources – was noted across the board (Dutta-Bergman, 2004; Maibach et al., 2006; Gollop, 1997; Tu and Hargraves, 2003). In first place, experts (either doctors and/or pharmacists) were to be found and were immediately followed by family members and friends respectively colleagues, who achieved third place. This ranking suggested that in terms of their health, individuals still confide in experts to the largest extent, regardless of their cultural allocation. Occupying second place, the trust put in individuals' closest peer group (i.e., partners, children, etc.) can be interpreted as health still being a highly private topic and, consequently, it is discussed with colleagues less frequently. From the media sources category, respondents put most stock in specialist literature, whilst relying on both editorial content and advertising at lower rates. When looking at the different media channels, print advertising was best received over advertising diffused by other media channels; in the editorial section, print split the first spot with online coverage, which scored high ratings in both the United States and Brazil. Reliance on the latter could be explained by the two countries' low Uncertainty Avoidance rates (AUT: 5.10; GER: 5.27; USA: 4.15; BRA: 3.74; House et al., 2004) according to which technological advancements and new communication channels are more readily embraced than in higher scoring countries.

By focusing on (print) advertising as a source of consumer self-empowerment, attitudes towards advertising in general and pharmaceutical advertising in particular also had to be examined. Building on results brought about by an earlier study relating to the pharmaceutical industry (Diehl et al., 2008), consumers' attitudes towards (pharmaceutical) advertising were predicted to be rather negative. By and large, study results support Diehl et al.'s (2008) findings, who found that albeit attitude towards advertising was negative, consumers' attitudes towards pharmaceutical advertising were slightly more negative. For skepticism, scores were reversed and suggested skepticism to be less pronounced for promotions in general, while it was more established for pharmaceutical promotions in particular. These findings were also consistent with Mueller (2006), whose study revealed people to be highly likely to believe ads for health-care related products. The present investigation was, however, unable to confirm the intercultural differences uncovered by Diehl et al. (2008), who discovered U.S. American consumers to exhibit lesser degrees of skepticism towards (pharmaceutical) advertising when compared to German respondents (Diehl et al., 2008). Reasons for skepticism or negative connotations were not inquired about in detail but could be grounded in promotions' complex message structures or consumers' overall distrust in message content (Steyr, 1999; Leavitt, 1996).

Whether these aspects had a bearing on either ad evaluation or consumer self-empowerment derived from a fictitious OTC drug promotion was scrutinized in a next step. By virtue of the product's (rather) high-involvement character (see section 5.4.6.), **Hypothesis 1** to **4** proposed non-prescription drug promotions utilizing an informative ad appeal to be perceived more favorably than their mixed or CSR counterparts, which were predicted to yield even more positive scores than the emotional ad edition. Evaluations were raised for four distinct variables, namely overall Ad Evaluation (H 1), Credibility (H 2), Product Evaluation (H 3), and Purchase Intention (H 4).

The origin of the striking distinctions in pharmaceutical ad evaluations (also in terms of credibility) across countries can be traced back to varying preferences for ad appeals (see section 5.4.2.): Brazilian respondents perceived all ad versions significantly more positively than their European and/or North American counterparts, but were the least responsive to CSR adverts. These were slightly better judged in the United States, where they outscored emotional appeals commonly used in Direct-to-Consumer-Advertising (Wolfe, 2002; Main et al., 2004). In some instances, mixed appeals yielded even better results than informative advertisements, which have been used for the longest time (Main et al., 2004). CSR and emotional promotions fought a close battle for the last spot: in Brazil, CSR ads lost in all areas but purchase intention, while emotional adverts performed very poorly in the United States. Total findings suggested that information was appreciated most for this high-involvement product category and in the case of the mixed ad, a combination of two promotional techniques was in the lead: it indicated that even though information presented an important personal and social asset, emotional approaches came to deploy more subtle techniques of conviction, which could also prove to be powerful in achieving conviction (Okazaki et al., 2010).

Preferences for distinct ad execution styles can be explained by two cultural dimensions, namely **Power Distance** (AUT: 5.00; GER: 5.59; USA: 4.92; BRA: 5.24; House et al., 2004) and **Uncertainty Avoidance** (AUT: 5.10; GER: 5.27; USA: 4.15; BRA: 3.74; House et al., 2004; see section 5.4.2.), which allude to Austrian and German individuals being more comfortable with direct and explicit data-based messages; the same is seen to apply in the United States, even though the country's Uncertainty Avoidance scores are relatively low when compared to its European counterparts. Brazilian citizens, however, are said to be more visually oriented and favor implicit, indirect and image-centered messages (see section 5.4.2.). These preferences can be used to explain differences in the scores obtained by the present thesis: The overall lowest values were accounted for by the emotional ad in three out of four countries, which was not able to create positive ad evaluations. Only in Germany did it have a direct face-off for favor, but nevertheless lost to its CSR counterpart. One reason for this different CSR perception might lie in distinct German legal regulations for "what would be marketed in other countries as 'CSR' is mandatory […] in Germany" (Cone Communications, 2013: 45). In this European country, CSR efforts are not necessarily promoted, since marketers run the risk of being discredited due to inauthentic sustainable communication. If they decide to deploy this appeal regardless, their messages need to be fact-based and less romantic, for Germans are not sold on "flashy campaigns" (Cone Communications, 2013: 45).

Hypothesis 5 looked at the degrees of consumer self-empowerment gained from the different promotions respondents were exposed to. Empowerment was, thereby, perceived as "providing [individuals] with knowledge and understanding about specific health problems and interventions" (Muturi, 2005: 81), allowing them to "arrive at their own understanding of issues, to consider and discuss ideas, to negotiate, and to engage in public debates at community and national levels" (UN Food and Agriculture Organization, 2011: 1). As health communication in general and pharmaceutical advertising in specific depend on the availability of information to "advance the health of the public" (Bernhardt, 2004: 2051), informative advertisements were presumed to lead to higher extents of empowerment than mixed/CSR or emotional ad editions. Two additional assumptions (**Hypotheses 6** and **7**) predicted respondents from individualistic countries to be more empowered when encountering informative or mixed/CSR ads than emotional promotions. On the other hand, these ad versions were expected to lead to lower levels of consumer self-empowerment in collectivistic societies where emotional promotions were regarded to match respondents' preferences to a larger degree.

Findings somewhat point in the expected direction: for all three forms of empowerment (Message Empowerment, Self-Medication Empowerment and Health Empowerment), responses to the mixed respectively informative promotion gave account of the largest degree of self-empowerment. This assumption particularly held true for individualistic countries, but was only met in parts in collectivistic cultures, where the emotional ad was able to hit a cord with regard to self-medication empowerment. One possible explanation for the ad's success story in South America might lie in the fact that collectivistic nations are more accepting of emotional advertising stimuli than individualistic countries, which respond to information more readily (see section 5.4.2.). The favorable reception with which mixed promotions were met in all countries seemed to recognize the necessity of information for obtaining consumer engagement with self-medication practices: recipients seemingly need to be made aware of their own capabilities as well as OTC medications' ease of use and low side effects (Accent Health, 2014), which should be stressed in promotional messages.

Empowerment gained from the actual advertising message presented the one main focus of the current study, where cultural differences did indeed seem to exist. In terms of advertising's influence on people's self-medication abilities as well as interests, individualistic nations seemed to be the least convinced by the emotional promotion, which generated the lowest total scores. Brazilian scores were the highest for all except the CSR ad version, where the United States was in the lead. Health Empowerment scores were somewhat biased as well: Brazilian values indicated that respondents felt all but the CSR ad version offered them a greater say in their health. On the other hand, U.S. recipients were the most rejective of the emotional ad and, at the same time, were the most susceptible to its CSR counterpart, which might stem from the country's philanthropic orientation (Cone Communications, 2013). North American consumers were especially receptive to sustainable promotions, renowned to feel the "need to perceive a personal and societal value from their actions" (CONE Communications, 2013: 37). These high degrees of empowerment reaped from CSR messages could be grounded in the country's high **Humane Orientation** practices (AUT: 3.77; GER: 3.38; USA: 4.18; BRA: 3.76; House et al., 2004), according to which individuals are willing to make a sustainable contribution in an attempt to ensure personal and social well-being (House et al., 2004). Having turned CSR into an essential business aspect, U.S. American customers have grown "more sophisticated about who and what deserves their hard-earned dollars. [...] They want to understand their individual and collective impact before purchasing" (CONE Communications, 2013: 37). In exhibiting the total lowest acceptance rates for CSR appeals and the least pronounced Humane Orientation scores, respondents from Germany (Band D) did not share this notion: despite the fact that the "concept of social responsibility is entrenched in the German cultural landscape, [there] is a certain reluctance to communicate about it" (Cone Communications, 2013: 45).

Having provided answers to the individual hypotheses, only the two research questions remain to be addressed. **Research Question 1 (RQ 1)** raised the question of which standardized OTC drug promotion scored the most favorable evaluation amongst subjects in different cultural contexts. For all four evaluation categories (ad evaluation, credibility, product evaluation, and purchase intention) mixed promotions yielded the highest scores, suggesting that when taking information and emotion as two opposites, the best option is not one or the other, but both. **Research Question 2 (RQ 2)** took this evaluation one step further, exploring which advertisement offered consumers the highest degree of self-empowerment. The mixed promotion reported the most pronounced self-empowerment scores besides the informative ad, alluding to the power of information in reaching self-empowerment. Consisting of a dominant visual coupled with a short factual text block, the mixed appeal received the most favorable assessments with regard to attitudes and self-empowerment, making it the ideal candidate for a standardized OTC drug promotion in a cross-cultural setting.

Table **37** provides an overview of two major research questions and the theory-deduced hypotheses respectively their results.

	RESEARCH QUESTIONS	
RQ 1	**How is a standardized OTC drug ad (utilizing either an informative, emotional, mixed or CSR appeal) evaluated in different cultural contexts (Germany, Austria, the United States and Brazil)?**	
RQ 2	**Out of the four advertising appeals, which appeal leads to the highest degree of consumer self-empowerment?**	
	HYPOTHESES (THEORY-DEDUCED)	
P 1a	Externally-oriented individuals (e.g., Brazilians) are less interested in self-medication practices than internally-oriented nations (e.g., Austria, Germany, and the U.S.).	☑
P 1b	Externally-oriented individuals (e.g., Brazilians) delegate responsibility for health-related matters to experts, which is less common in internally-oriented countries (e.g., Austria, Germany, and the U.S.).	☑
P 1c	Internally-oriented individuals (e.g., respondents from Austria, Germany, and the U.S.) hold a more positive attitude towards self-medication practices than their externally-oriented counterparts (e.g., respondents from Brazil).	☑
H 1	Informative ads for pharmaceuticals yield better results with regard to ad evaluation than (a) mixed or (b) CSR ads, which yield even better results than (c) emotional ads in all countries.	☐
H 2	Informative ads for pharmaceuticals score more favorable results with regard to credibility than (a) mixed or (b) CSR ads, which score even better results than (c) emotional ads in all countries.	☐
H 3	Informative ads for pharmaceuticals achieve higher scores with regard to product evaluation than (a) mixed or (b) CSR ads, which achieve even higher scores than (c) emotional ads in all countries.	☐
H 4	Informative ads for pharmaceuticals have a larger impact on purchase intention than (a) mixed or (b) CSR ads, which have an even larger impact than (c) emotional ads in all countries.	☐
H 5	Informative promotions for pharmaceuticals are expected to lead to higher degrees of consumer self-empowerment than (a) mixed or (b) CSR ads, which empower consumers even more than (c) emotional ads in all countries.	☐

H 6	Informative promotions for pharmaceuticals bring about higher degrees of consumer self-empowerment than (a) mixed, (b) CSR or (c) emotional ads in individualistic countries.	☐
H 7	Informative promotions for pharmaceuticals lead to lower degrees of consumer self-empowerment than (a) mixed, (b) CSR or (c) emotional ads in collectivistic cultures.	☒
Legend:	☑ **Hypothesis is confirmed** ☒ **Hypothesis is rejected** ☐ **Hypothesis is partially confirmed**	

Table 37: Research Questions and Theory-Deduced Hypothesis - Overview of Results

So far, hypotheses have only been concerned with statistically testing assumptions across countries to determine consumers' preferences for selected ad appeals; the second set of hypotheses took a more complex stance by addressing relationships between the different variables as well as the interactive effects between these items. Albeit solely representing the core of the originally conceptualized theoretical framework (see section 5.4.), the model proposed Comprehensibility to affect Credibility (H 8a) as well as Ad Evaluation (H 8b); Credibility was also said to have a bearing on Ad Evaluation (H 8c). Moreover, Self-Empowerment was perceived as being (positively) linked to both Comprehensibility (H 9a) and Credibility (H 9b), whereas attitudes towards the ad were expected to factor into Product Evaluations (H 10a) and Purchase Intentions (H 10b) alike. Product Evaluations were also said to be subject to Self-Empowerment (H 11) and expected to influence Purchase Intentions (H 12). To test these assumptions, the hypotheses were graphically depicted and computed using a well-established structural-equation modelling software (AMOS 22). While the model achieved a reasonable fit in all four countries (see section 6.1.3.3.), Measurement Invariance – testing for similarities amongst countries or groups – produced evidence of significant differences between the three individualistic countries and their collectivistic counterpart, Brazil. Since invariances for the herein conceptualized model could only be confirmed for the individualistic cluster (see section 6.1.3.5.) a direct cross-cultural comparison was not possible by virtue of scalar invariance's non-existence, leading collectivistic results to be analyzed in isolation. Path coefficients were equally pronounced in all countries and did not differ significantly for the individualistic and collectivistic data sets.

Results proclaim that Comprehensibility was positively related to Credibility (Hoeck and Gendall, 2002) but did not have a bearing on Ad Evaluation, which might be explained by the fact that the terminology utilized in OTC drug adverts is expected to be highly scientific ('medical jargon'; Steyr, 1999; Paasche-Orlow and Wolf, 2007). Even though surveys have reported comprehensibility issues with regard to understanding medical terminology, complex sentence structures and the absence of explanations and definitions (Zarcadoolas et al., 2005), these might make promotions qualify as credible, which was confirmed to positively impact Ad Evaluation. So, while Comprehensibility did not directly have an effect on Ad Evaluation, it did via a detour (Credibility; H 8c). Comprehensibility also failed to influence Self-Empowerment, demonstrating that Self-Empowerment was not dependent upon information clarity. This finding came as a surprise, for in the health context, health literacy – referencing individuals' abilities to comply with therapeutic instructions and comprehend medical information (Ad Hoc Committee of Health Literacy, 1999) – is seen as a prerequisite for Self-Empowerment (see section 5.4.16.). It did produce an effect: Credibility was positively related to Self-Empowerment as soon as Comprehensibility was introduced, indirectly impacting Self-Empowerment (H 9b). As proposed by Chang (2004 and 2005), favorable ad evaluations did fuel more positive Product Evaluations (H 10a), but refrained from triggering increased Purchase Intentions (H 10b). Nonetheless, as positive Ad Evaluations led to favorable Product Evaluations (H 10a), which also increased the likelihood of purchase amongst respondents, an indirect effect could also be noted in this case. With regard to Self-Empowerment, knowledge introduced by the actual promotion was seen to positively shape Product Evaluations (Wang et al., 2008; H 11), which then translated into an increased Purchase Intention (H 12).

In total, three proposed relations had to be rejected for all groups (see Table **38**).

HYPOTHESES (MODEL-DEDUCED)		
H 8a	The higher the pharmaceutical ad's comprehensibility, the more credible is its overall perception.	☑
H 8b	The higher the pharmaceutical ad's comprehensibility, the more positive is its overall (ad) evaluation.	☒
H 8c	The more credible a pharmaceutical ad is perceived to be, the more positive is its overall (ad) evaluation.	☑
H 9a	The more comprehensible a pharmaceutical ad, the higher is the degree of self-empowerment derived therefrom.	☒
H 9b	The more credible a pharmaceutical ad, the higher is the degree of self-empowerment derived therefrom.	☑

H 10a	More positive ad evaluations will lead to more positive product evaluations.	☑
H 10b	More positive ad evaluations will lead to heightened purchase intentions.	☒
H 11	The higher the perceived (consumer) self-empowerment, the more positive is the overall product evaluation.	☑
H 12	The more favorable a product evaluation, the higher is consumers' purchase intention.	☑
Legend:	**☑ Hypothesis is confirmed** **☒ Hypothesis is rejected** **☐ Hypothesis is partially confirmed**	

Table 38: Model-Deduced Hypothesis - Overview of Results

In the present project, empowerment was seen as being determined by respondents' cultural backgrounds, whereby several cultural dimensions were assumed to come into play, such as **Individualism/Collectivism**, which was said to shape individual responses to ad stimuli – and it did: Extracting communication styles (covering informative and mixed message appeals) arrived at the highest rankings for both Ad Evaluation and consumer Self-Empowerment, underlining that information was best suited to not only increase consumers' health literacy rates but also empower them, granting them the right to "participate in and take responsibility for their health care" (Schulz and Nakamoto, 2013: 4). Empowerment, thus, means allocating power with those who are most affected by health decisions, namely active health care consumers, who want to see an increase in "feelings of power, control, and self-esteem that lead the patient to value autonomy—and thus [evoke] interest in and desire to participate in healthcare decisions" (Schulz and Nakamoto, 2013: 5).

By appealing to individuals' very own competencies and skills, empowerment is also closely linked to the **Individualism/Collectivism** continuum (Hofstede, 1980). In stressing individual achievement and self-responsibility (House et al., 2004), communicative measures address formerly passive patients, trying to evoke a "will to self-care" in active consumers (Illich, 1975) and invoking them to "effectively reclaim [their] own control over medical perception, classification, and decision-making" (Illich, 1975). For this reason, empowerment might be attributed more relevance in individualistic nations, where emphasis is put on personal interests and needs (Hofstede, 1980; House et al., 2004). These societies regard health as an individual responsibility, with a larger share of individual incomes being directed towards health care services and medications (Hofstede, 2005).

Attention towards health concerns was seen as being particularly dependent upon the **Locus of Control** dimension, which is nourished by both **Uncertainty Avoidance** and **Power Distance** (see section 5.4.1.). If individuals regard themselves as active agents who can positively shape their health (e.g., by taking up health-enhancing behaviors), they are internally oriented; if they perceive themselves not to play a role in their health, but regard it as being subject to external forces, they hold an external Locus of Control (Wallston, 1982). Believing individualistic cultures to be more internally oriented, people in Austria, Germany and the United States were predicted to claim responsibility for health-related matters more frequently while collectivistic nations like Brazil were said to delegate responsibility to more knowing experts due to their more external orientation (see section 5.4.1.). Individualistic members were not only assumed to actively look for information but were supposed to exhibit a heightened interest in self-medication, which serves as way of enhancing individuals' bodies, restoring physical health and boosting their self-worth. For the pharmaceutical industry, this implies that marketers should not only promote their product alone but also appeal to consumers' capabilities and self-medication skills (see Figure **40**). Information can assist recipients in building up and strengthening their health literacy rates, increasing their knowledge and Self-Efficacy rates at the same time. Once again, this underlines the interdependence of health literacy and empowerment (Schulz and Nakamoto, 2013), with adverts holding the potential to turn consumers into competent self-managers.

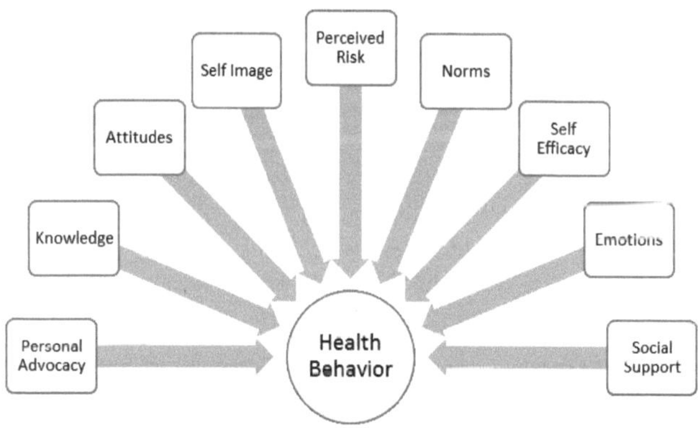

Figure 40: Factors Influencing Health Behaviors (Schiavo, 2014: 47; own illustration)

In collectivistic cultures, the tendency to look after the group is more pronounced and individual wishes respectively concerns take a backseat. People direct their efforts towards the collective well-being in order to not endanger in-group ties and belongingness (Hofstede, 2005). Responsibility for social topics, such as health, is not assigned to the individual but to an acclaimed expert, whose role is upheld and praised (An and Kim, 2007; Lin, 2001); if individuals choose to become engaged, they do it not for their own sake, but for fear of being excluded from their social group (Gelfand et al., 2004).

Finally, concern for health is also impacted by Gender Egalitarianism. Across-the-board, countries exhibit rather low **Gender Egalitarianism** scores (AUT: 3.18; GER: 3.21; USA: 3.36; BRA: 3.44; House et al., 2004), alluding to the prevalence of rather masculine social values, such as assertiveness, success, ambition, and independence; feminine qualities, which are concerned with ensuring a heightened quality of life (i.e. health), fall short. However, all nations expressed an interest in achieving a more feminine orientation following GLOBE (AUT: 4.83; GER: 5.02; USA: 5.03; BRA: 4.91; House et al., 2004), denoting individuals' pursuit of an increased quality of life, which would explain more pronounced efforts to maintain individual health and become empowered.

In summary, the purpose of this investigation was to add to the body of knowledge regarding the influence of culture on consumer responses to standardized OTC drug ads and their respective degrees of Self-Empowerment derived therefrom[12]. Study results demonstrated that with regard to Ad Evaluation only slight differences could be found: in both Brazil and the United States, the mixed appeal turned out to be the most successful in three out of four ad evaluation categories. The reasons for this appeal's favorable evaluation might lie in the fact that, in addition to product information, the desired health-outcome (i.e. the emotion of happiness as portrayed in the ad) possibly triggered positive association. Study results further portend that the choice of ad appeal can have an impact on consumers' sense of Self-Empowerment. Taking the three

[12] The proposed conceptual framework that combined elements from advertising evaluation and health models, was supported by the individualistic data corpus, but not for the individualistic-collectivistic data, where it failed to achieve Scalar Invariance. The non-existence of Scalar Invariance could stem from translational problems, as terminological differences might exist on the South-American continent. Hence, the author refrained from arriving at generalized interpretations that might not be justified, but interpreted findings independently for both hypotheses and path relations.

individualistic countries (Austria, Germany and the U.S.) together, perceived self-empowerment did not differ considerably regardless of the ad appeal used; however, it was lowest for the emotional message. In Brazil, a collectivistic country, the mixed appeal was also superior to both the emotional and the CSR ads in respect to fostering Self-Empowerment. When Ad Evaluation and Self-Empowerment are considered, the mixed appeal seems to be the most fruitful approach for cross-cultural application. Advertisers might be well advised to refrain from using emotional OTC drug ads, as they led to lower Self-Empowerment than all other ad appeals (in three out of four countries), and they also scored rather negative Ad Evaluations in two countries.

After having summarized the study's core findings, their implications will be explored next, deducing some recommendations for international (pharmaceutical) marketers and policy makers, while also discussing some future research potentials for academics.

7.2 Implications and Recommendations

In a fast advancing and converging business world, advertisers are faced with severe competition and ever-new technological innovations, forcing them to reach a maximum payout in a short amount of time. For this reason, they might opt to create standardized advertising campaigns, targeting consumers with almost identical messages in diverse national settings (Levitt, 1983). With cultural differences shrinking due to globalizing tendencies (Mueller, 2011; Diehl and Karmasin, 2013), this step might yield some profit and success in the long run.

The investigation at hand endeavored to produce findings that are of relevance to different parties. On the one hand, it intended to provide some insights for **international (pharmaceutical) advertisers**: first, it wanted to prove that a standardized communication campaign might be of advantage; second, it tried to determine which ad appeal was best perceived by consumers in four distinct markets that are characterized by similarities, pinpointing that changes to established practices (utilizing predominantly informative appeals) might be overdue; third, it introduced them to the concept of consumer self-empowerment, revealing the extent to which an advertisement was able to strengthen consumers in their own skills and competencies.

On the other hand, findings are relevant to **health-care providers** and **governmental parties**. In a time of increasing health expenses and decreasing reimbursements (Paasche-Orlow and Wolf, 2007; Brems et al., 2011), individuals might refrain from seeking medical treatment altogether, since they are unable to cover accruing medical bills. As they might not be familiar with changing legal regulations and drug switches, the government and pharmaceutical manufacturers should act in concert to improve health messages' overall acceptance and positively shape demand for non-prescription drugs (UTexas, 2011). Advertisers should make use of the chance to redeem themselves from accusations of misleading consumers and neglecting their educational missions: they should not lead consumers on, but should lead by providing them with adequate and relevant information on new and improved products that might be the right remedy for a (minor) medical condition.

The project at hand set out to demonstrate how four distinct (yet standardized) advertising appeals were rated and contributed to consumer-self empowerment in a cross-cultural setting, contrasting findings from Austria, Germany and the U.S. with those of Brazil. This standardized approach was taken as – in the age of globalization – advertisers are increasingly choosing to target consumers in a similar fashion throughout the world for various reasons (e.g., converging consumer values or cost efficacy purposes; Mueller, 2011). This investigation's objective was to unravel the question if culture – seen as moderating and shaping individual responses to different communication styles (Markus and Kitayama, 1991; Hofstede, 2005) – took its toll on advertising evaluations as well as consumer Self-Empowerment. The investigation at hand was able to pinpoint that a mixed message appeal seems to be a fruitful candidate for standardized application, as neither appeal in isolation (informative vs. emotion) managed to score the most favorable Ad Evaluations nor the highest degree of Self-Empowerment.

7.3 Limitations and Directions for Future Research

Without question, there are numerous limitations to the present study. First and foremost, only parts of the initially developed framework were put to the test, leaving out some core variables such as attitude and skepticism towards advertising, attitudes towards self-medication respectively pain medications as well as previous drug experiences. Future research should, thus, not neglect to include those variables and test e.g., to what extent attitudes and skepticism towards advertising in general or the ad in particular moderate responses to an OTC drug ad or the degree of empowerment derived therefrom. Follow-up investigations could also control for attitudes towards non-prescription drugs or pain medications.

While the study was able to produce results indicating how promotions for an OTC drug were evaluated in three Western (Germany, Austria, and the United States) and one South American country (Brazil), more countries (especially along the collective continuum) should be investigated. Hence, future examinations on the effectiveness of OTC drug advertisements should not neglect to include countries characterized by even more significant differences (as expressed by their scores on the GLOBE or Hofstede cultural scales; House et al. 2004; Hofstede, 1980). In a next step, studying responses to an OTC drug promotion in an Asian country might seem worthwhile, where the pharmaceutical markets of both China and India could present fruitful territories for examination.

The present research project was interested in uncovering advertising's (potential) contribution to consumer Self-Empowerment along three dimensions, namely Message Empowerment, Self-Medication Empowerment and Health Empowerment. Limitations in scope only allowed for a more detailed discussion of empowerment as derived from the message, blending out the impact of potential predecessors, such as the role of health literacy or trust in respondents' self-medication abilities. Follow-up research should definitely try to accommodate those variables and examine their moderating role in consumers' OTC medication choices.

Some limitations with regard to the product promoted have to be pointed out as well. The use of a fictitious product has been put forward by previous research, allowing consumers to approach advertisements with open eyes and minds, not distorting their judgment through previous experiences (Yin, 1999). Nonetheless, skepticism towards unfamiliar brands is also seen as an obstacle to both product evaluations and purchase intentions, particularly for (rather) high-involvement and experience products such as OTC drugs (Diehl et al., 2008). For future research endeavors, a cooperation with a pharmaceutical manufacturer might prove profitable in order to win some valuable insights into the perception of an established pain-medication brand like Aspirin or Aleve. Research could also benefit from expanding the present project to other product categories, e.g., remedies treating flu-like symptoms (e.g., coughs and colds) as well as preparations for digestive problems or heart burn, which might yield different results.

In the present study, emotional appeals produced the most unfavorable results with regard to message-induced consumer self-empowerment. Even though they have been successfully utilized as persuasive tools in public health campaigns (95 %; Frosch et al., 2007), the use of emotion might have some counter-effects, if regarded as inauthentic or exaggerated (Rains and Turner, 2007); at times, they might even run the risk of being judged as being inappropriate for specific (sensitive) topics or audiences (Turner, 2012). In the health-care context, positive emotional or gain-framed appeals that stress product benefits and advantages are utilized more frequently than negative emotional or loss-framed messages, which invoke fear by focusing on disadvantages or counter-effects (O'Keefe, 2012). While gain-framed appeals are favored in the health-realm, since they are predicted to lead to preventive behavior (Salovey et al., 2002), negative emotional (fear) appeals have re-emerged recently (author's observation), with pharmaceutical marketers taking a problem-solution (before-after) approach to promote their medical products. These might warrant consideration in future investigations.

The herein conceptualized OTC drug print promotion followed recent advertising trends. Print ads, which allow for self-paced examination while also being frequently consulted by respondents (Chaiken and Eagly, 1976; Accent Health, 2014), were used as stimuli in the present study; in terms of product endorser and setting, typical person testimonials (Martin et al, 2008: 29; Feick and Higie, 1992) together with a minimum (neutral) setting were given preference over unconventional promoters and environments (Koinig, 2012). For future studies, nevertheless, it might be worthwhile to challenge present-day advertising conventions by depicting new role models and relationship types (e.g., business women and patchwork families), taking a progressive stance and standing apart from the advertising clutter. In addition, new and interactive promotional channels (e.g., social media) should be investigated with regard to their effectiveness and empowerment potential.

Of course, the present examination built upon quantitative data alone, which should be complemented by additional research: for instance, qualitative interviews could be conducted to find out what consumers demand from advertisers, which would provide some viable starting points for how marketers can counter-act negative attitudes and high levels of skepticism towards advertising in general and pharmaceutical advertising in particular (see sections 5.4.7.4. and 6.2.6.). In a subsequent step, strategies and recommendations could be developed that could help advertisers to tackle those unfavorable responses and establish their promotional messages as reliable points of reference for future encounters.

The Internet is growing in importance as a source for drug and health-related information (Friedman and Gould, 2007; Menon et al., 2002), responsible for extending "the scope of health care beyond its traditional boundaries" (Eysenbach, 2001: 20; Viswanath, 2005). To marketers, it has not only widened companies' scopes of reaching prospective customers (Buckley, 2004), but also allows them to accommodate their audience's needs for specific information offered via different, interactive channels (Friedman and Gould, 2007). Extending the functionalities of traditional media vehicles, the Internet offers several benefits to consumers, such as enabling them to actively participate in their health care, delivering a vast range of health-related information and guaranteeing consumer anonymity when debating illnesses as well as their treatment options respectively (Bischoff and Kelley, 1999; Spain et al., 2001). Past surveys have indicated that of all people surveyed, almost two thirds browsed the Internet for health-related information (Twibell and Anzalone, 2001), making it the sixth most researched issue online (Henkel, 2002). Recent surveys have produced further evidence of the Internet's growing importance as a source of information for people's healthcare decisions and drug choices (Fox, 2005; Rice, 2004; Fox and Rainie, 2002; Cassil, 2008), being attributed an even higher degree of credibility and reliability than other sources (family, friends and/or health professionals; Atkinson et al., 2009).

In the advent of eHealth (electronic health; Eysenbach, 2001) and mHealth (mobile health; Abidi, 2015), health has emerged as "a field in the intersection of medical informatics, public health and business, referring to health services and information delivered or enhanced through the Internet and related technologies" (Eysenbach, 2001: 20). In 2015, the concept of the wired patient has been identified as one of the core health topics (Makovsky, 2015; see Figure **41**).

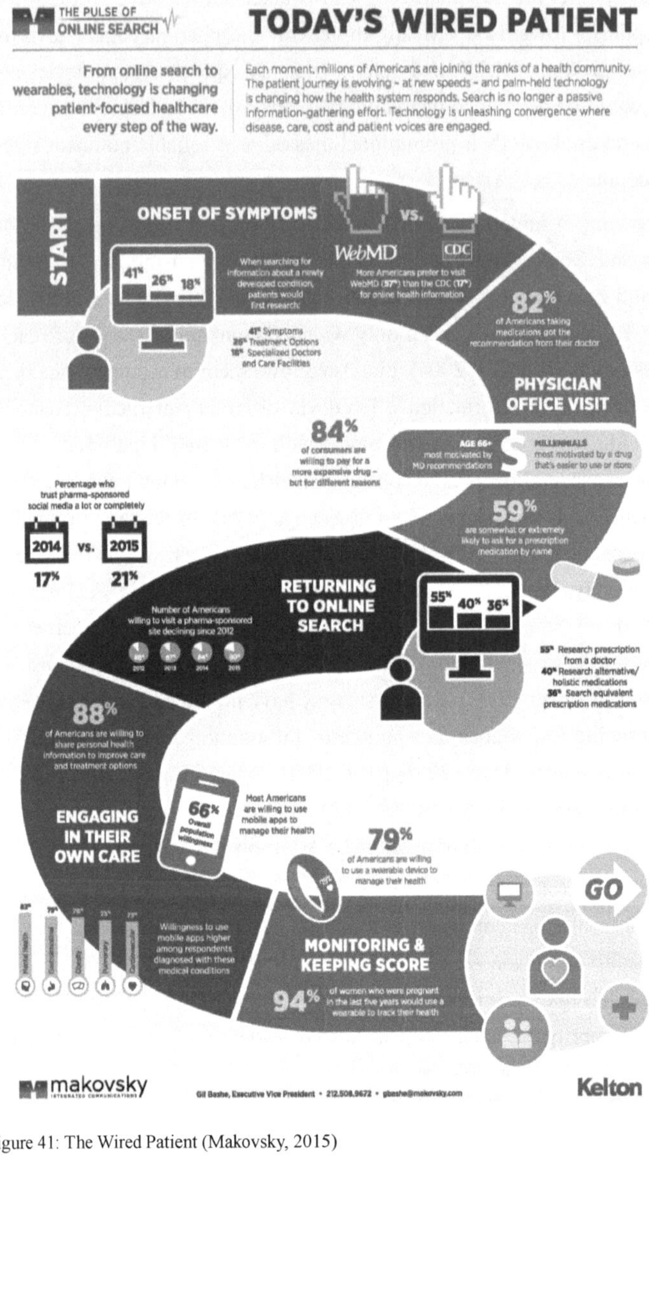

Figure 41: The Wired Patient (Makovsky, 2015)

Through interactive as well as mobile health technologies, consumers can become more involved in and empowered regarding their health-care, agreeing to disclose their online health records to receive more precisely tailored treatments (Makovsky, 2015); moreover, the availability of online-services is meant to guarantee a faster delivery of care and increased participation (Street, 2003). Despite being burdened by already heightened health-care costs, Americans would still leverage technology, even expressing a high willingness to pay for innovative services (Makovsky, 2015), as these new tools have some clear benefits: they "have the potential to improve communication with clinicians, access to personal health information, and health education with the goal of preparing patients to take a more active role in their care" (Franklin et al., 2009: 169f.). With changing health-care environments, the different media channels involved in present-day medical encounters might be worth studying, too.

There is one final limitation to the present study: the present investigation provided a rather generalized account of ad evaluations and consumer self-empowerment as gained from the promotional message; results might, though, be characterized by significant differences that could be traced back to consumer demographics and personality traits, including sex/gender, age as well as educational background.

Individuals are emotionally invested in their health; having unlearned to take action themselves, they might need some guidance on how to unlearn their passivity and become pro-active and empowered again. Taking interventional measures themselves, the use of non-prescription drugs presents an empowering act, whereby advertisers should not neglect to incorporate those precise (empowering) aspects into their promotional messages (UTexas, 2011). Thus, both marketers and their adverts need to be given the benefit of the doubt, allowing messages to unfold their full potential. By providing useful and adequately-prepared information, often paired up with personal recounts, recipients might become invested cognitively and emotionally and opt to acquire the product on their next pharmacy or supermarket visit. However, information is still key in those decisions (Harrison et al., 2006): Unless respondents are not strengthened in the convictions that they hold, the belief that their actions can make them achieve results, advertisements cannot have an effect and yield (desirable) outcomes. Respondents should look at ads with fresh eyes and open minds. However, these have to conform to the marketer's educational duties, to render consumer doubts and disbeliefs unwarranted.

Due to the availability of new services and an abundance of health-care products brought about by constant switches in drug categories, patients are turned into consumers in the contemporary health-care marketing place (Roter et al., 1988), who are put in charge of their own health. Thinking of health as a metaphor, consumers are asked to take the driver's instead of the passenger's seat, where they are involved only marginally. They have to take the wheel, steering and shaping their own health-care experiences. Taking the car image one step further, health itself can be pictured as a car, which needs to be maintained and looked after. It needs to be taken for a drive and serviced on a regular basis, with negligence bringing about undesired outcomes, such as bad health, etc. Health is no longer about sitting back, relaxing, and enjoying the ride, while someone else is in charge, driving the car (e.g., a medical expert). Rather, it involves consumers claiming a pro-active stance, stepping up and taking the (steering) wheel themselves.

8 Bibliography

Aaker, D. A./Batra, R./Myers, J. G. (1992). Advertising management. 4th ed. Englewood Cliffs, NJ: Prentice-Hall.

Aaker, D.A. and Jacobson, R. (1994). The financial information content of perceived quality. In: Journal of Marketing Research. Vol. 31 (May). 191-201.

Aaker, D.A. and Norris, D. (1982). Characteristics of TV Commercials Perceived as Informative. In: Journal of Advertising Research. Vol. 22. 61-70.

Aaker, J. (1997). Dimensions of Brand Personality. In: Journal of Marketing Research. Vol. 34. 347-356.

Abidi, S. (ed.) (2015). Mobile Health: A Technology Road Map. Wiesbaden: Springer.

Abraham, C. and Sheeran, P. (2000). Understanding and changing health behavior: From health beliefs to self-regulation. In: Norman, P./Abraham, C./Conner, M. (eds.). Understanding and changing health behavior. Amsterdam: Harwood. 3-24.

Abraham, J. (2010). Pharmaceuticalization of Society in Context: Theoretical, Empirical and Health Dimensions. In: Sociology. Vol. 40. 603-622.

Accent Health. (2014). The Value of Physicians in the OTC Marketplace. White Paper. Retrieved from http://www.accenthealth.com/AccentHealth/media/Documents/AH_OTC_whitepaper_2014.pdf (accessed 11.12.2014)

Ad Hoc Committee (1999). Health Literacy: Report of the Council on Scientific Affairs. American Medical Association. In: Journal of the American Medical Association. Vol. 281. 552-557.

Adams, C. (2002). FDA is inundated trying to assess drug ad pitches. Retrieved from http://online.wsj.com/news/articles/SB1016053991820089240 (accessed 18.01.2014)

Adams, S./Pill, R./Jones, A. (1997). Medication, chronic illness and identity: The perspective of people with asthma. In: Social Science and Medicine. Vol. 45(2). 189–201.

Adaval, R. (2001). Sometimes it just feels right: The differential weighting of affect-consistent and affect-inconsistent product information. In: Journal of Consumer Research. Vol. 28. 1-17.

Adler, R. and Elmhorst, J.M. (2008). Communicating at Work: Principles and Practices for Business and the Professions. 9th ed. Tuas Basin Link, Singapore: McGraw-Hill.

Adoni, H. and Mane, S. (1984). Media and the construction of reality: Toward an integration of theory and research. In: Communication Research. Vol. 3. 323-340.

AdWeek. (2013). Do Ad Messages Have a Credibility Problem? Retrieved from http://www.adweek.com/news/advertising-branding/do-ad-messages-have-credibility-problem-152818 (accessed 17.08.2014)

Agarwal, M. (1995). Review of a 40-Year-Debate in International Advertising. In: International Marketing Review. Vol. 12(1). 26-48.

Aggleton, P. (1990). Health. London: RKP.

Aghadiuno, M. and Dowrick, C. (2010). Soul Matters: The Spiritual Dimension within Healthcare. Oxon, UK: Radcliffe.

Ajzen, I. (1985). From intentions to actions: A theory of planned behavior. In: Kuhl, J. and Beckmann, J. (eds.). Action control: From cognition to behavior. Berlin: Springer. 11-40.

Ajzen, I. (2002). Perceived Behavioral Control, Self-Efficacy, Locus of Control, and the Theory of Planned Behavior. In: Journal of Applied Social Psychology. Vol. 32(4). 665–683.

Ajzen, I. and Fishbein, M. (1980). Understanding Attitudes and Predicting Social Behavior. Englewood Cliffs, NJ: Prentice Hall.

Alba, J./Hutchinson, J.W./Lynch, J. (1991). Memory and Decision Making. In: Kassarjian, H. H. and Robertson, T. S. (eds.). Handbook of Consumer Theory and Research. Englewood Cliffs, NJ: Prentice Hall.

Alba, J.W and Hutchinson, J.W. (1985). A Framework for Understanding Consumer Knowledge II. Comparison and Inference Process. Working Paper. University of Florida: Center for Consumer Research.

Albrecht, T.L. and Adelman, M.B. (1987). Communicating Social Support: A theoretical perspective. In: Albrecht, T.L. and Adelman, M.B. (eds.). Communicating Social Support. Newbury Park, CA: SAGE. 18-39.

Ali, N. (2002). Prediction of coronary heart disease preventive behaviors in women: A test of the Health Belief Model. In: Women and Health. Vol. 35(1). 83-96.

Allison, K.R./Dwyer, J.M./Makin, S. (1999). Perceived barriers to physical activity among high school students. In: Preventive Medicine. Vol. 28. 608-615.

Allison, K.R./Dwyer, J.M./Makin, S. (1999). Self efficacy and participation in vigorous physical activity by high school students. In: Health Education and Behavior. Vol. 26. 12-24.

Alwin, D.F. and Jackson, D.J. (1981). Applications of simultaneous factor analysis issues of factorial invariance. In: Jackson, D.D. and Borgotta, E.P. (eds.). Factor analysis and measurement in sociological research: a multidimensional perspective. Beverly Hills, CA: Sage. 249-280.

Ambler, T. and Hollier, E. (2004). The Waste in Advertising Is the Part That Works. In: Journal of Advertising Research. Vol. 44(4). 375-389.

American Medical Association (2005). Partnership for Clear Health Communication. Retrieved from http://www.npsf.org/pchc2/ (accessed 13.10.2012)

An, D. (2007). A content analysis of multinational advertisers' localization strategy in web advertising. In: International Journal of Internet Marketing and Advertising. Vol. 3. 120-141.

An, D. and Kim, S. (2007). Relating Hofstede's masculinity dimension to gender role portrayals in advertising: A cross-cultural comparison of Web advertisements. In: International Marketing Review. Vol. 24. 181-207.

Anand, P. and Sternthal, B. (1990). Ease of message processing as a moderator of repetition effects in advertising. In: Journal of Marketing Research. Vol. 27. 343-353.

Anderson, J.C. and Gerbing, D.W. (1983). Some Methods for Respecifying Measurement Models to obtain Unidimensional Construct Measurement. In: Journal of Marketing Research. Vol. 19 (November). 453-460.

Anderson, J.C. and Gerbing, D.W. (1988). Structural Equation Modeling in Practice: A Review and Recommended Two-Step Approach. In: Psychological Bulletin. Vol. 103. 411-423.

Anderson, J.R. (2004). Cognitive psychology and its implications. 6th ed. London: Palgrave MacMillan.

Anderson, L.A. and Dedrick, R.F. (1990). Development of the Trust in Physician Scale: A Measure to assess interpersonal trust in patient-physician relationships. In: Psychological Reports. Vol. 67. 1091-1100.

Anderson, R.M. and Funnel, M.M. (2005), Patient empowerment: reflections on the challenge of fostering the adoption of a new paradigm. In: Patient Education and Counseling, Vol. 57(2).

Andrews, J.C./Durvasula, S./Ahker, S.H. (1990). A framework of conceptualizing and measuring the involvement construct in advertising. In: Journal of Advertising. Vol. 19(4). 27-40.

Angel, M.D. (2000). The Pharmaceutical Industry – To whom is it accountable? In: New England Journal of Medicine. Vol. 342(25). 1902-1904.

Antil, J.H. (1984). Conceptualization and Operationalization of involvement. In: Advances in Consumer Research. Vol. 11. 203-209.

Antonovsky, A. (1985). Health, Stress, and Coping. 1st ed. San Francisco: Jossey-Bass.

Antonowsky, A. (1996). The salutogenetic model as a theory to guide health promotion. In: Health Promotion International. Vol. 11. 11-18.

Armitage, C. J. and Conner, M. (2000). Social cognition models and health behavior. In: Psychology and Health. Vol. 15. 173-189.

Armstrong, D. (1983). Political Anatomy of the Body: Medical Knowledge in Britain in the Twentieth Century. Cambridge: Cambridge University Press.

Arney, W.R. and Bergen, B. (1984). Medicine and the Management of Living: Taming the Last Great Beast. London: University of Chicago Press.

Arnould, E. and Thompson, C. (2005). Consumer culture theory (CCT): Twenty years of research. In: Journal of Consumer Research. Vol. 31(4). 868-882.

Ashkanasy, N./Gupta, V./Mayfield, M. S./Trevor-Roberts, E. (2004). Future Orientation. In: House, R.J./Hanges, P.J./Javidan, M. (eds.). Culture, Leadership, and Organizations: The GLOBE Study of 62 Societies. Thousand Oaks, CA: Sage. 282-342.

Aspect. (2011). Connecting to the Empowered Customer: How the right customer strategy can help companies succeed in the age of the empowered consumer. Retrieved from http://in.aspect.com/Documents/Papers/Aspect_ConnectingEmpoweredCust_WP.pdf (accessed 15.04.2014)

Assael, H. (1981). Consumer Behavior. New York: Wadsworth.

Assael, H. (2004). Consumer Behavior: A Strategic Approach. Boston: Houghton Mifflin.

Atkin, C. K. (1973). Instrumental utilities and information seeking. In: Clarke, P. (ed.). New models for communication research. Beverly Hills, CA: Sage. 205–242.

Atkin, J.L. and Beltramini, R.F. (2007). Exploring the Perceived Believability of DTC Advertising in the US. In: Journal of Marketing Communications. Vol. 13(3). 169-180.

Atkinson, N.L./Saperstein, S.L./Pleis, J. (2009). Using the Internet for Health-Related Activities: Findings from a National Probability Sample. In: Journal of Medical Internet Research. Vol. 11(1).

Austin, E.W. and Johnson, K.K. (1997). Effects of general and alcohol-specific media literacy training on children's decision making about alcohol. In: Journal of Health Communication. Vol. 2. 17-42.

Austin, E.W. and Knaus, C.S. (2000). Predicting the potential for risky behavior among those "too young" to drink, as the result of appealing advertising. In: Journal of Health Communication. Vol. 5. 13-27.

Austin, E.W. and Meili, H.K. (1994). Effects of interpretations of televised alcohol portrayals on children's alcohol beliefs. In: Journal of Broadcasting and Electronic Media. Vol. 38. 417-435.

Austin, E.W./Miller, A.C.-R./Silva, J./Guerra, P./Geisler, N./Gamboa, L./Phakakayai, O./Juechle, B. (2002). The Effects of Increased Cognitive Involvement in College Students' Interpretations of Magazine Advertisements for Alcohol. In: Communication Research. Vol. 29(2). 155-179.

Austin, E.W./Pinkleton, B./Fujioka, Y. (1999). Assessing prosocial message effectiveness: Effects of message quality, production quality, and persuasiveness. In: Journal of Health Communication. Vol. 4. 195-210.

Austin, E.W./Pinkleton, B./Fujioka, Y. (2000). The role of interpretation processes and parental discussion in the media's effect on adolescents' use of alcohol. In: Pediatrics. Vol. 105. 343-349.

Austin, E.W./Roberts, D.F./Nass, C.I. (1990). Influences of family communication on children's television interpretation processes. In: Communication Research. Vol. 17. 545-564.

Auton, F. (2004). The advertising of pharmaceuticals direct to consumers: A critical review of the literature and debate. In: International Journal of Advertising. Vol. 23(1). 5-52.

Backhaus, K. and van Doorn, J. (2007). Consumer perceptions of Advertising Standardization: A Cross-Country Study of Different Categories. In: International Management Review. Vol. 3(4). 37-49.

Backhaus, K./Erichson, B./Plinke, W./Weiber, R. (2011). Multivariate Analysemethoden: Eine anwendungsorientierte Einführung. 13th ed. Heidelberg: Springer.

Backhaus, K./Muhlfeld, K./van Doorn, J. (2001). Consumer perspectives on standardization in international advertising: a student sample. In: Journal of Advertising Research. Vol. 41(5). 53-61.

Baer, H./Singer, M./Johnson, J. (1986). Toward a critical medical anthropology. In: Social Science and Medicine. Vol. 23(2). 95-98.

Bagozzi, R.P. (1981). And Examination of the Validity of Two Models of Attitude. In: Multivariate Behavioral Research. Vol. 16. 323-359.

Bagozzi, R.P. (1981). Attitudes, Intentions, and Behavior: A Test of Some Key Hypotheses. In: Journal of Personality and Social Psychology. Vol. 41(4). 607-626.

Bagozzi, R.P. (1991). Further thoughts on the validity of measures of elation, gladness, and joy. In: Journal of Personality and Social Psychology. Vol. 61. 98–104.

Bagozzi, R.P. and Burnkrant, R.E. (1979). Attitude Organization and the Attitude-Behavior Relationship. In: Journal of Personality and Social Psychology. Vol. 37. 913-929.

Bagozzi, R.P. and Heatherton, T.F. (1994). A general approach to representing multifaceted personality constructs: application to state self-esteem. In: Structural Equation Modeling. Vol. 1(1). 35–67.

Bagozzi, R.P. and Warshaw, P.R. (1990). Trying to consume. In: Journal of Consumer Research. Vol. 17. 127–140.

Bagozzi, R.P./Tybout, A.M./Craig, S./Strenthal, B. (1979). The Construct Validity of Tripartite Classification of Attitudes. In: Journal of Marketing Research. Vol. 16. 88-95.

Baker, M.J. and Churchill, G.A. (1977). The Impact of Physically Attractive Models on Advertising Evaluations. In: Journal of Marketing Research. Vol. 14 (November). 538-555.

Baker, S.M. and Mason M. (2012). Toward a Process Theory of Consumer Vulnerability and Resilience: llluminating its Transformative Potential. In: David, G.M./Pettigrew, S./Pechmann, C./Ozanne, J.L. (eds.). Transformative Consumer Research for Personal and Collective Well Being. New York, NY: Routledge. 543-563.

Baker, S.M./Gentry, J.W./Rittenburg, T.L. (2005). Building Understanding of the Domain of Consumer Vulnerability. In: Journal of Macromarketing. Vol. 25(2). 128-139.

Ball-Rokeach, S.J. and DeFleur, M.L. (1976). A dependency model or mass-media effects. In: Communication Research. Vol. 3. 3-21.

Balog, J. E. (1978). The concept of health and the role of health education. In: The Journal of School Health. Vol. 9. 462-464.

Bandura, A. (1976). Social learning perspective on behavior change. In: Burton, A. (ed.). What makes behavior change possible? New York: Brunner/Mazel. 34-57.

Bandura, A. (1977). Self-efficacy: Toward a unifying theory of behavioral change. In: Psychological Review. Vol. 84. 191-215.

Bandura, A. (1982). Self-efficacy mechanisms in human agency. In: American Psychologist. Vol. 37. 122-147.

Bandura, A. (1986). Social foundations of thought and action. Englewood Cliffs, NJ: Prentice Hall.

Bandura, A. (1987). Self-Efficacy: The Exercise of Control. New York: Freeman.

Bandura, A. (1992). Exercise of personal agency through the self-efficacy mechanism. In: Schwarzer, R. (ed.). Self-efficacy. Thought control of action. Washington, DC. Hemisphere. 3-38.

Bandura, A. (1997). Self-efficacy: The exercise of control. New York: Freeman.

Bandura, A. (2001). Self-efficacy and health. In: Smelser, N.J. and Baltes, P.B. (eds.). International encyclopedia of the social and behavioral sciences. Vol. 20. Oxford: Elsevier Science. 13815-13820.

Bandura, A. (2001). Social cognitive theory: An agentic perspective. In: Annual Review of Psychology. Vol. 52. 1-26.

Bandura, A. (2007). Much ado over a faulty conception of perceived self-efficacy grounded in faulty experimentation. In: Journal of Social and Clinical Psychology. Vol. 26(6). 641-658.

Bandura, A., and Locke, E. A. (2003). Negative self-efficacy and goal effects revisited. In: Journal of Applied Psychology. Vol. 88. 87–99.

Banerjee, A. (1994). Transnational advertising development and management: An account planning approach and a process framework. In: International Journal of Advertising. Vol 13(2). 95-124.

Banton, M. (1965). Roles: An Introduction to the study of social relations. London: Tavistock.

Barnett, C./Cloke, P./Clarke, N./Malpass, A. (2005), Consuming ethics: articulating the subjects and spaces of ethical consumption. In: Antipode. Vol. 37. 23-45.

Barry, A.-M. and Yuill, C. (2008). Concepts of Health and Medicine. In: Barry, A.-M. and Yuill, C. (eds.). Understanding the Sociology of Health: An Introduction. Thousand Oaks, CA: Sage. 20-30.

Barry, A.-M. and Yuill, C. (2012). Understanding the Sociology of Health. 3rd ed. London: SAGE.

Bass, S.B./Ruzek, S.B./Gordon, T.F./Fleisher, L./McKeown-Conn, N./Moore, D. (2006). Relationship of internet health information use with patient behavior and self-efficacy. Experiences of newly diagnosed cancer patients who contact the National Cancer Institute's Cancer Information Service. In: Journal of Health Communication. Vol. 11(2). 219-236.

Batra, R. and Ahtola, O.T. (1990). Measuring the Hedonic and Utilitarian Sources of Consumer Attitudes. In: Marketing Letters. Vol. 2(2). 159-170.

Batra, R. and Ahtola, O.T. (1990). Measuring the Hedonic and Utilitarian Sources of Consumer Attitudes. In: Marketing Letters. Vol. 2(2). 159-170.

Batra, R. and Ray, M. (1985). How Advertising Works at Contact. In: Alwitt, L.F. and Mitchell, A.A. (eds.). Psychological Processes and Advertising Effects. Hillsdale, NJ: Lawrence Erlbaum Associates. 13-44.

Batra, R./Myers, J.G./Aaker, D.A. (1996). Advertising Management. 5th ed. Upper Saddle River, NJ: Prentice Hall.

Bauer, H.H./Heinrich, D./Hampel, S. (2012). Mit hochveredelten Printmedien ein Leseerlebnis schaffen. In: Bauer, H.H./Heinrich, D./Samak, M. (eds.). Erlebniskommunikation. Heidelberg: Springer. 251-273.

Baughn, C.C. and Yaprak, A. (1993). Mapping Country-of-Origin Research: Recent Developments and Emerging Avenues. In: Papadopoulos, N. and Heslop, L.A. (eds.). Product-Country Images: Impact and Role in International Marketing. , Binghamton, NY: International Business Press. 89-115.

Baumgartner, H. and Homburg, C. (1996). Applications of structural equation modeling in marketing and consumer research: a review. In: International Journal of Research in Marketing. Vol. 13. 139-161.

BBC. (2015). Pharmaceutical Industry gets high on fat profits. Retrieved from http://www.bbc.com/news/business-28212223 (accessed 01.03.2015)

Beard, F.K. (2004). Hard Sell 'Killers' and Soft Sell 'Poets': Modern Advertising's Enduring Message Strategy Debate. In: Journalism History. Vol. 30(3). 141-149.

Bearden, W.O. and Etzel, M.J. (1982). Reference Group Influence on Product and Brand Purchase Decisions. In: Journal of Consumer Research. Vol. 9 (September). 183-194.

Bearden, W.O./Hardesty, D.M./Rose, R.L. (2001). Consumer Self-Confidence: Refinements in Conceptualization and Measurement. In: Journal of Consumer Research. Vol. 28(1). 121-134.

Bearden, W.O./Hardesty, D.M./Rose, R.N. (2001). Consumer Self-Confidence: Refinements in Conceptualization and Measurement. In: Journal of Consumer Research. Vol. 28 (June). 121-134.

Bearden, W.O./Netemeyer, R.G./Teel, J.E. (1989). Measurement of Consumer Susceptibility to Interpersonal Influence. In: Journal of Consumer Research. Vol. 15 (March). 473-481.

Beck, U. (1992). Risk society: Towards a new modernity. London: Sage.

Becker, C.M./Glascoff, M.A./Felts, W.M. (2010). Salutogenesis 30 Years Later: Where do we go from here? In: International Electronic Journal of Health Education. Vol. 13, 25-32.

Becker, M.H. (ed.) (1974). The health belief model and personal health behavior. In: Health Education Monographs. Vol. 2(4). 324-508.

Becker, M.H./Maiman, L.A./Kirscht, J.P./Haefner, D.P./Drachman, R.H. (1977). The Health Belief Model and prediction of dietary compliance: A field experiment. In: Journal of Health and Social Behavior. Vol. 18. 348-366.

Beh, H. (1994). Going Green is not optional. In: Asian Business. Vol. 30(9). 70.

Behrens, G./Esch, F-R./Leischner, E./Neumaier, M. (eds.) (2001). Gabler-Lexikon Werbung. Wiesbaden: Gabler.

Behringer, M.B. et al. (2004). Medical Home Health Literacy: Bringing Health to Life. Alabama Medicaid Agency.

Belch, G.E. and Belch, M.A. (1993). Introduction to Advertising and Promotion: An integrated marketing communications perspective. Homewood, IL: Irwin.

Belcher, L./Sternberg, M.R./Wolotski, R.J./Halkitis, P./Hoff, C. (2005). Condom use and perceived risk of HIV transmission among sexually active HIV positive men who have sex with men. In: AIDS Education and Prevention. Vol. 17(1). 79-89.

Bell, R.A./Kravitz, R.L./Wilkes, M.S. (1999). Direct-to-consumer prescription drug advertising and the public. In: Journal of General Internal Medicine. Vol. 14(11). 651-657.

Beltramini, R.F. and Evans, K.R. (1985). Perceived believability of research results information in advertising. In: Journal of Advertising. Vol. 14(3). 18-24.

Bennett, P. and Murphy, S. (1997). Psychology and health promotion. Buckingham: Open University Press.

Bentler, P.M. (1990). Comparative Fit Indexes in Structural Models. In: Psychological Bulletin. Vol. 107(2). 238-246.

Bentler, P.M. (1995). EQS, Structural Equations Program Manual. Program Version 5.0. Encino, CA: Multivariate Software.

Bentler, P.M. and Bonnet, D.C. (1980). Significance Tests and Goodness of Fit in the Analysis of Covariance Structures. In: Psychological Bulletin. Vol. 88(3). 588-606.

Bentler, P.M. and Chou, C.P. (1987). Practical issues in structural modeling. In: Sociological Methods and Research. Vol. 16(1). 78-117.

Bereiter, C. (2002). Education and Mind in the Knowledge Age. Mahwah, NJ: Lawrence Erlbaum Associates.

Berger, P. and Luckmann, T. (1971). The Social Construction of Reality: A Treatise in the Sociology of Knowledge. London: Penguin.

Berkowitz, L. and Lundy, R.M. (1957). Personality Characteristics related to Susceptibility to Interpersonal Influence by Peers or Authority Figures. In: Journal of Personality. Vol. 25(1). 306-316.

Bernhardt, J. M. (2004). Communication at the Core of Effective Public Health. In: American Journal of Public Health. Vol. 94(2). 2051-2053.

Berry, D. (2006). Health Communication: Theory and Practice. Buckingham, GBR: Open University Press.

Berry, D. (2007). Health Communication. Theory and Practice. New York: Open University Press.

Berry, J.W. (1969). On cross-cultural comparability. In: International Journal of Psychology. Vol. 4(2). 119-238.

Betancourt, J. R. (2006). Cultural competence and medical education: many names, many perspectives, one goal. In: Academic Medicine. Vol. 81(6). 499-501.

Bettman, J.R. (1979). Memory Factors in Consumer Choice: A review. In: Journal of Marketing. Vol. 43 (Spring). 37-53.

Bettman, J.R. and Park, C. W. (1980). Effects of Prior Knowledge and Experience and Phase of the Choice Process on Consumer Decision Processes: A Control Analysis. In: Journal of Consumer Research. Vol. 7 (December). 243-248.

BHMA. (2014). Holistic healthcare today. Retrieved from http://www.bhma.org/pages/about/holistic-healthcare.php (accessed 22.08.2014)

Bilton, T./Bonett, K./Jones, P./Lawson, T./Skinner, D./Stansworth, M./Webster, A. (1996). Introductory Sociology. 3rd ed. London: Macmillan.

Bischoff, W.R. and Kelley, S.J. (1999). 21st century house calls: The Internet and the world wide web. In: Holistic Nursing Practices. Vol. 13(4). 42–50.

Bissell, P./Ward, P.R./Noyce, P.R. (2001). The Dependent Consumer: Reflections on Accounts of the Risks of Non-Prescription Medicines. In: Health. Vol. 5(1). 5-30.

Biswas, A./Olsen, J./Carlet, V. (1992). A comparison of print advertisements from the United States and France. In: Journal of Advertising. Vol. 21(4). 73-81.

Blackett, T. and Harrison, T. (2001). Brand Medicine: Use and Future Potential of Branding in Pharmaceutical Markets. In: Journal of Medical Marketing. Vol. 2. 33-49.

Blanchette, D.M. (1990). Schematic Associations in Information Processing and Their Influence on Extrinsic Attribute Cue Acquisition, Utilization, and Multi-Attribute Attitude Modeling for a Novel Service Seminar. Ann Arbor, MI: Bell and Howell Information Company.

Blaxter, M. (1990). Health and Lifestyles. London: Routledge.

Blaxter, M. (2004). Health. Cambridge: Polity.

Blaxter, M. (2007). How is health experienced? In: Douglas, J./Earle, S./Handsley, S./Lloyd, C.E./Spurr, S. (eds.). A Reder in promoting public Health. London: Sage. 26-32.

Blaxter, M. (2010). Health. 2nd ed. Cambridge: Polity.

Blaxter, M. and Paterson, S. (1982). Mothers and daughters: A three-generation study of health, attitudes and behavior. London: Heinemann Educational.

Bloch, P.H. (1981). An Exploration into the Scaling of Consumers' Involvement with a Product Class. In: Advances in Consumer Research. Vol. 8. 61-65.

Bloch, P.H. (1984). The Wellness Movement: Imperatives for Health Care Marketers. In: Journal of Health Care Marketing. Vol. 4(1). 348-366.

Blosser, B.J. and Roberts, D.F. (1985). Age differences in children's perceptions of message intent: Responses to TV news, commercials, educational spots, and public service announcements. In: Communication Research. Vol. 12. 455-484.

Blumer, H. (1969). Symbolic Interaction. Englewood Cliffs, NJ: Prentice Hall.

Boase, J./Horrigan, J.B./Wellman, B./Rainie, L. (2006). The Strength of Internet Ties The internet and email aid users in maintaining their social networks and provide pathways to help when people face big decisions. Retrieved from http://www.pewinternet.org/files/old-media/Files/Reports/2006/PIP_Internet_ties.pdf.pdf (accessed 20.12.2014)

Boddewyn, J.J./Soehl, R./Picard, J. (1986). Standardization in international marketing: is Ted Levitt in fact right? In: Business Horizon. Vol. 29(6). 69-75.

Bodenheimer, T./Lorig, K./Holman, H./Grumbach, K. (2002). Patient self-management of chronic disease in primary care. In: Journal of the American Medical Association. Vol. 19/20(288). 2469-2475.

Bollen, K. and Lennox, R. (1991) Conventional wisdom on measurement: A structural equation perspective. In: Psychological Bulletin. Vol. 110(2). 305-314

Bollen, K.A. (1989). Structural equations with latent variables. New York: Wiley.

Bollen, K.A. (1990). Overall Fit in Covariance Structure Models: Two Types of Sample Size Effects. In: Psychological Bulletin. Vol. 107(2). 256-259.

Bolton, L.E./Cohen, J.B./Bloom, P.N. (2006). Does Marketing Products as Remedies Create "Get Out of Jail Free Cards"? In: Journal of Consumer Research. Vol. 33. 71-81.

Bond, G. G./Aiken, L. S./Somerville, S. C. (1992). The health belief model and adolescents with insulin-dependent diabetes mellitus. In: Health Psychology. Vol. 11(3). 190-198.

Boon, H./Kachan, N./Bocker, A.. (2012). Use of Natural Health Products: How does being 'natural' affect choice? In: Medical Decision Making. Vol. 33. 282-297.

Boruchovitch, E. and Mednick, B. (2002). The meaning of health and illness: some considerations for health psychology. In: Psico-USF. Vol. 7(2). 175-183.

Bottomore, T. and Rubel, M. (1963). Karl Marx: Selected Writings in Sociology and Social Philosophy. Harmondsworth: Penguin.

Bourdieu, P. (1977). Outline of a Theory of Practice. Cambridge: Cambridge University Press.

Bourdieu, P. (1984). Distinction: A Social Critique of the Judgment of Taste. Routledge: London.

Bourdieu, P. (1986). The Forms of Capital. In: Richardson, J. (ed.). Handbook of Theory and Research for the Sociology of Education. New York: Greenwood Press. 241-258.

Boush, D.M./Friestad, M./Rose, G.M. (1994). Adolescent skepticism toward TV advertising and knowledge of advertiser tactics. In: Journal of Consumer Research. Vol. 21/No. 1. 165-175.

Bove, L.L./Pervan, S.J./Beatty, S.E./Shiu, E. (2009). Service worker role in encouraging customer organizational citizenship behaviors. In: Journal of Business Research. Vol. 62(7). 698-705.

Bovee, C.L. (1992). Contemporary Advertising. Boston: McGraw-Hill.

Bradley, L.R. and Zito, J.M. (1997). Direct-to-consumer prescription drug advertising. In: Medical Care. Vol. 35. 86-92.

Bradley, S./Hitchon, J./Thorson, E. (1994): Hard Sell Versus Soft Sell: A Comparison of American and British Advertising. In: Englis, B.G. (ed.). Global and Multinational Advertising, Hillsdale, NJ: Psychology Press. 141-159.

Brakus, J.J./Schmitt, B.H./Zarantonello, L. (2009). Brand Experience: What is it? How is it measured? Does it affect Loyalty? In: Journal of Marketing. Vol. 73 (May). 52-68.

Braverman, H. (1974). Labour and Monopoly Capital. New York: Monthly Review Press.

Breckler, S.J. (1990). Applications of Covariance Structure modeling in psychology: Cause for Concern? In: Psychological Bulletin. Vol. 107. 260-273.

Brems, Y./Seville, J./Baeyens, J. (2011). The expanding world market of generic pharmaceuticals. In: Journal of Generic Medicines – the Business Journal for the Generic Medicine Sector. Vol. 8. 227-239.

Brennan, C. and Gallagher, K. (2002). Consumer Support Networks: improving consumer advice in the UK. In: International Journal of Consumer Studies. Vol. 26(3). 227-238.

Brickman, P./Rabinowitz, V.C./Karuza, J. Jr./ Coates, D./Cohn, E./Kidder, L. (1982). Models of Helping and Coping. In: American Psychologist. Vol. 37(4). 368-384.

Bröckling, U. (2003). You are not responsible for being down, but you are responsible for getting up. Über Empowerment. In: Leviathan. Vol. 31(3). 323-344.

Broderick, A.J./Demangeot, C./Ross Adkins, N./Ferguson, N.S./Herderson, G.R./Johnson, G./Kipnis, E./Mandiberg, J.M./Mueller, R.D./Pullig, C./Roy, A./Zúniga, M.A. (2011). Consumer Empowerment in Multicultural Marketplaces: Navigating Multicultural Identities to Reduce Consumer Vulnerability. In: Journal of Research for Consumers. Vol. 19. 1-13.

Bronn, P.S. and Vrioni, A.B. (2001). Corporate social responsibility and cause-related marketing: an overview. In: International Journal of Advertising. Vol. 20(2). 207-222.

Brown, B./Crawford, P./Carter, R. (2007). Evidence Based Health Communication. New York: McGraw-Hill.

Brown, S.P. and Stayman, D.M. (1992). Antecedents and Consequences on Attitude toward the Ad: A Meta-Analysis. In: Journal of Consumer Research. Vol. 19. 34-51.

Brown, T.J. and Dacin, P.A. (1997). The Company and the Product. Corporate Associations and Consumer Product Responses. In: Journal of Marketing. Vol. 61. 68-84.

Browne, M.W. and Cudeck, R. (1993). Alternative ways of assessing model fit. In: Bollen, K.A. and Long, L.S. (eds.). Testing structural equation models. Newbury Park, CA: Sage. 36-162.

Bruner, J. (1990). Acts of Meaning. Cambridge, MA: Harvard University Press.

Buchanan, D.R. (2000). An Ethic for Health Promotion: Rethinking the Sources of Human Well-Being. New York: Oxford University Press.

Buckley, J. (2004). Pharmaceutical Marketing – Time for Change. In: Electronic Journal of Business Ethics and Organization Studies. Vol. 9(2). 4-11.

Bunton, R. (1997). Popular health, advanced liberalism and Good Housekeeping magazine. In: Petersen, A. and Bunton, R. (eds.). Foucault, Health and Medicine. London: Routledge. 223-248.

Bunton, R. and Burrows, R. (1995). Consumption and health in the 'epidemiological' clinic of late modern medicine. In: Bunton, R./Nettleton, S./Burrows, R. (eds.). The Sociology of Health Promotion. London: Routledge.

Bunton, R. and Petersen, A. (1997). Foucault's medicine. In: Petersen, A. and Bunton, R. (eds.). Foucault, Health and Medicine. London: Routledge. 1-11.

Bunton, R./Murphey, S./Bennett, P. (1991). Theories of behavioral change change and their use in health promotion. In: Health Education Research: Theory and Practice. Vol. 6(2). 153-162.

Burawoy, M. (1979). Manufacturing Consent. Chicago: University of Chicago Press.

Burke, M. and Edell, J. (1989). The Impact of Feelings on Ad-Based Affect and Cognition. In: Journal of Marketing Research. Vol. 26. 69-83.

Burnkrant, R.E. and Cousineau, A. (1975). Informational and Normative Social Influence in Buyer Behavior. In: Journal of Consumer Research. Vol. 2 (December). 206-2015.

Burr, V. (2003). Social Constructionism. London: Routledge.

Burton, S./Lichtenstein, D.R./Netemeyer, R.G./Garretson, J.A. (1998). A scale for measuring attitude toward private label products and an examination of its psychological and behavioral correlates. In: Journal of the Academy of Marketing Science. Vol. 26(4). 293-306.

Bury, M. (2005). Health and Illness. London: Polity.

Bush, J. (2004), Consumer Empowerment and Competitiveness. London: National Consumer Council.

Business Dictionary. (2014). Empowerment. Retrieved from http://www.businessdictionary.com/definition/empowerment.html (accessed 21.08.2014)

BWHC. (1973). Our Bodies, Ourselves. New York: Simon and Schuster.

BWHC. (1980). Unser Körper, unser Leben : ein Handbuch von Frauen für Frauen. Reinbek near Hamburg: Rowohlt.

Byrne, B.M. (1998), Structural Equation Modeling with LISREL, PRELIS and SIMPLIS: Basic Concepts, Applications and Programming. Mahwah, NJ: Lawrence Erlbaum Associates.

Byrne, B.M./Shavelson, R.J./Muthen, B.O. (1989). Testing for equivalence of factor covariance and mean structures: The issue of partial measurement invariance. In: Psychological Bulletin. Vol. 105. 456–466.

Byrne, D. (2003), European commissioner for health and consumer protection. Brussels: Consumer General Assembly. 28 October 2003.

Cacioppo, J.T. and Petty, R. (1985). Central and Peripheral Routes to Persuasion: The Role of Message Repetition. In: Alwitt, L.F. and Mitchell, A.A. (eds.). Psychological processes and advertising effects: Theory, research, and applications. Hillsdale, NJ: Erlbaum. 91–111.

Caillat, Z. and Mueller, B. (1996). The Influence of Culture on American and British Advertising: An Exploratory Comparison of Beer Advertising. In: Journal of Advertising Research. Vol. 36(3). 79-87.

Calfee, J.E. and Ringold, D.J. (1994). The 70 % majority: Enduring consumer beliefs about advertising. In: Journal of Public Policy and Marketing. Vol. 13. 228-238.

Callow, M. and Schiffman, L.G. (2004). Sociocultural Meanings in Visually Standardised Print Ads. In: European Journal of Marketing. Vol. 38(9/10). 1113-1128.

Calnan, M. (1987). Health and illness: The lay perspective. London: Tavistock.

Carl, D./Gupta, V./Javidan, M.(2004). Power Distance.In: House R.J./Hanges, P.J./Javidan, M. (eds.). Culture, Leadership, and Organizations: The GLOBE Study of 62 Societies. Thousand Oaks, CA: Sage. 513-563.

Carmines, E.G., and McIver, J.P. (1981). Analyzing Models with Unobserved Variables. In: Bohrnstedt, G.W. and Borgatta, E.F. (eds.). Social Measurement: Current Issues. Beverly Hills, CA: Sage.

Carrick, R./Mitchell, A./Powell, R./Lloyd K. (2004). The quest for well-being: a qualitative study of the experience of taking antipsychotic medication. In: Psychology and Psychotherapy. Vol. 77. 19–33.

Carver, C. and Scheier, M.F. (1998). Attention and Self-Regulation: A Control Theory Approach to Human Behavior. New York: Springer.

Cassil, A. (2008). Rising Rates of Chronic Health Conditions: What Can Be Done? Issue Brief No. 125. Retrieved from http://www.hschange.com/CONTENT/1027/ (accessed 20.10.2013)

Cavusgil, S.T./Zou, S./Naidu, G.M. (1993). Product and Promotion Adaptation in Export Ventures: An Empirical Investigation. In: Journal of International Business Studies. Vol. 24(3). 479-506.

CDC. (2001). What is Health Communications? Retrieved from http://www.cdc.gov/healthcommunication/healthbasics/whatishc.html (accessed 21.06.2014)

Celsi, R.L. and Olson, J.C. (1988). The Role of Involvement in Attention and Comprehension Processes. In: Journal of Consumer Research. Vol. 15 (September). 210-224.

Centers for Disease Control and Prevention. (2004). Program Operations Guidelines for STD Prevention: Community and Individual Behavior Change Interventions. Retrieved from http://www.cdc.gov/std/program/community.pdf (accessed 01.12.2013)

Chaffee, S.D. and McLeod, L.M. (1973). Consumer Decisions and Information Use. In: Ward, S. and Robertson, T.S. (eds.). Consumer Behavior: Theoretical Sources. Englewood Cliffs, NJ: Prentice-Hall.

Chaffee, S.H. and Schleuder, J. (1986). Measurement and Effects of Attention to Media News. In: Human Communication Research. Vol. 13(1). 76-107.

Chaiken, S. and Eagly, A.H. (1976). Communication Modality as a determinant of message persuasiveness and message comprehensibility. In: Journal of Personality and Social Psychology. Vol. 34. 605-614.

Chang, C. (2000). The Role of Self in Processing Advertising Messages—An Exploration of Gender Schema. Paper presented at the annual meeting of the Association for Education in Journalism and Mass Communication, Phoenix, AZ.

Chang, C. (2004). How Mood and Ad-self-congruency Affect the Relative Influence of Hedonic Ad Appeals and Utilitarian Ad Appeals on Product Evaluations. In: Advances in Consumer Research. Vol. 31. 721-727.

Chang, C. (2005). Ad and Brand Evaluations in a Competitive Processing Context: The Effects of Number of Attributes and Repetition Strategies. In: Advances in Consumer Research. Vol. 32. 548-553.

Chao, P. and Rajendran, K.N. (1993). Consumer Profiles and Perceptions: Country-of-Origin Effects. In: International Marketing Review. Vol. 10(2). 22-39.

Cheah, E.T./Chan, W.L./Chieng, C.L.L. (2007). The Corporate Social Responsibility of Pharmaceutical Product Recalls: An Empirical Examination of U.S. and U.K. Markets. In: Journal of Business Ethics. Vol. 76. 427-449.

Chen, S. and Chaiken, S. (1999). The heuristic-systematic model in its broader context. In: Chaiken, S. and Trope, Y. (eds.). Dual-process theories in social psychology. New York: Guilford. 73-96.

Cheng, H. and Schweitzer, J.C. (1996). Cultural Values Reflected in Chinese and US Television Commercials. In: Journal of Advertising Research. Vol. 36(3). 27-45.

Cheung, G.W. and Rensvold, R.B. (2002). Evaluating Goodness-of-Fit Indexes for Testing Measurement Invariance. In: Structural Equation Modeling. Vol. 9(2). 233-255.

Chi, H. K./Yeh, H. R./Huang, M. W. (2009). The Influences of advertising endorser, brand image, brand equity, price promotion on purchase intention: The mediating effect of advertising endorser. In: The Journal of Global Business Management. Vol. 5(1). 224-233.

Chi, H. K./Yeh, H. R./Yang, Y. T. (2009). The impact of brand awareness on consumer purchase intention: The mediating effect of perceived quality and brand loyalty. In: Journal of International Management Studies. Vol. 4(1). 135-144.

Chiu, L./Tang, K.Y./Liu, Y.H./Shyu, W.C./Chang, T.P. (1998). Willingness of Families Caring for Victims of Dementia to pay for Nursing Home Care: Results of Pilot Study in Taiwan. In: Journal of Management in Medicine. Vol. 12(6). 349-360.

Cho, B./Kwon, U./Gentry, J.W./Jun, S./Kropp, F. (1999). Cultural values reflected in theme and execution: a comparative study of US and Korean television commercials. In: Journal of Advertising. Vol. 28(4). 60–73.

Cho, H. (2012). Health Communication Message Design: Theory and Practice. Los Angeles, CA: Sage.

CHPA. (2012). The Value of OTC Medicine to the United States. Retrieved from http://www.chpa.org/ValueofOTCMeds2012.aspx (accessed 21.01.2015)

CHPA. (2013). New Data Shows Reliability and Efficacy Fuel Trust and Preference for OTC Options. Retrieved from http://www.chpa.org/03_06_13.aspx (accessed 01.04.2014)

CHPA. (2013). Understanding Trust in OTC Medicines: Consumer and Healthcare Provider Perspectives. White Paper. Retrieved from http://www.yourhealthathand.org/images/uploads/CHPA_OTC_Trust_Survey_White_Paper.pdf (accessed 11.12.2014)

CHPA. (2014). Rx-to-OTC Switch. RETRIEVED FROM http://www.chpa.org/switchpp.aspx (accessed 02.12.2014)

CHPA. (2014). Statistics on OTC Use. Retrieved from http://www.chpa.org/marketstats.aspx (accessed 01.04.2014)

Christensen, L.T./Morsing, M./Thyssen, O. (2010). The polyphony of corporate social responsibility: deconstructing transparency and accountability and opening for identity and hypocrisy. In: Cheney, G./May, S./Mumby, D. (eds). The Handbook of Communication Ethics. New York, NY: Routledge. 457-473.

Churchill, G.A. and Peter, J.P. (1998). Marketing: Creating Value for Customers. 2nd ed. Boston: Irwin/McGraw-Hill.

Churchill, G.A. and Peter, J.P. (1998). Marketing: Creating Value for Customers. Boston: Irwin/McGraw-Hill.

Cialdini, R.B./Petty, R.E./Cacioppo, J.T. (1981). Attitude and Attitude Change. In: Annual Review of Psychology. Vol. 32. 357-404.

Clarke, S. (2008). Culture and Identity. In: Bennett, T. and Frow, J. (eds.). The SAGE Handbook of Cultural Analysis. London: Sage. 510-529.

Clift, E. and Freimuth, V. (1995). Health Communication: What is it and what can it do for you? In: Journal of Health Education. Vol. 26(2). 68-74.

Clutterbuck, D. and Crainer, S. (1988). The Decline and Rise of British Industry. London: W.H. Allen.

Cobb, S. (1976). Social Support as a moderator of life stress. In: Psychosomatic Medicine. Vol. 38(5). 300-314.

Cockerham, W.C. (2006). Medical Socioly and Sociological Theory. In: Cockerham, W.C. (ed.). The Blackwell Companion to Medical Sociology. Oxford: Blackwell. 3-22.

Cockerham, W.C. (2013). Social Causes of Health and Disease. Cambridge: Polity Press.

Cockerham, W.C. (ed.) (2006). The Blackwell Companion to Medical Sociology. Oxford: Blackwell.

Cohen, J. (1982). Involvement: Separating the State from its Causes and Effects. Unpublished Paper. University of Florida.

Cole, R.E./Bacdayan, P./White, B.J. (1993). Quality, participation and competitiveness. In: California Management Review. Vol. 35(3). 68-81.

Colleoni, E. (2013). CSR communication strategies for organizational legitimacy in social media. In: Corporate Communications: An International Journal. Vol. 18(2). 228-248.

Collier, J. and Iheanacho, I. (2002). The pharmaceutical industry as an informant. In: The Lancet. Vol. 360(9343). 1405-1409.

Cone Communications. (2011). 2011 Cone/Echo Global CR Opportunity Study. Retrieved from http://www.clearlyso.com/uploads/2011_cone_echo_global_cr_opportunity_study.pdf (accessed 04.04.2014)

Cone Communications. (2013). Global CSR study. Retrieved from https://www.energystar.gov/ia/partners/downloads/2013_cone_communicationsecho_global_csr_study.pdf (accessed 04.04.2014)

Conner, M. and Sparks, P. (2005). Theory of Planned Behavior and health behavior. In: Conner, M. and Norman P. (eds.). Predicting Health Behavior: research and practice with social cognition models. Buckingham, UK: Open University Press. 170-222.

Conrad, P. (1975). The discovery of hyper-hinesis: notes on the medicalization of deviant behavior. In: Social Problem. Vol. 23. 12-21.

Conrad, P. (1985). The meaning of medication: another look at compliance. In: Social Science and Medicine. Vol. 20. 29–37.

Conrad, P. (1992). Medicalization and Social Control. In: Annual Review of Sociology. Vol. 18 (August). 209-232.

Contoyannis, P./Jones, A.M./Rice, N. (2004). The dynamics of health in the British Household Panel Survey. In: Journal of Applied Econometrics. Vol. 19(4). 473-503.

Cook, T.D. and Flay, B.R. (1978). The persistence of experimentally induced attitude change. In: Berkowitz, L. (ed.). Advances in experimental social psychology. New York: Academic Press. 1–57.

Cooley, C.H. (1902). Human nature and the social order. New York: Scribner.

Copjec, J. (1994). Read my desire: Lacan against the Historicists. Harvard, MIT Press.

Corstjens, M. (1992). Marketing Strategy in the Pharmaceutical Industry. London: Chapman and Hall.

Coulter, A. (2003). Slander: Liberal Lies about the American Right. New York, NY: Three Rivers Press.

Cox, D. and Bauer, R.A. (1964). Self-Confidence and Persuasibility in Women. In: Public Opinion Quarterly. Vol. 28 (Fall). 453-466.

Crawford, R. (1994). The boundaries of the self and the unhealthy other: reflections on health, culture and AIDS. In: Social Science and Medicine. Vol. 38(10). 1347-1365.

Creyer, E.H. and Ross, W. (1997). The influence of Firm behavior on purchase intention: do consumers really care about business ethics? In: Journal of Consumer Marketing. Vol. 14(6). 421-432.

Critser, G. (2005). Generation Rx: How prescription drugs are Altering American Lives, Minds and Bodies. New York, NY: Houghton Mifflin Co.

Cronin de Chavez, A./Backett-Milburn. K./Parry, O./Platt, S. (2005.) Understanding and researching wellbeing: its usage in different disciplines and potential for health research and health promotion. In: Health Education Journal. Vol. 64(1). 70-87.

Crossley, M.L. (2003). Would you consider yourself a healthy person? Using focus groups to explore health as moral phenomenon. In: Joural of Health Psychology. Vol. 8(5). 501-514.

Crowley, A.E./Spangenberg, E.R. and Hughes, K.R. (1992). Measuring the Hedonic and Utilitarian Dimensions of Attitudes toward Product Categories. In: Marketing Letters. Vol. 3(3). 239-249.

Crowley, S.L. and Fan, X. (1997). Structural Equation Modeling: Basic Concepts and Applications in Personality Assessment Research. In: Journal of Personality Assessment. Vol. 68(3). 508-531.

Cutler, B.D. and Javalgi, R.G: (1994). Comparison of Business to Business Advertising. In: Industrial Marketing Management. Vol. 23(2). 117-125.

Cwikel, J.M. and Israel, B.A. (1987). Examining the mechanisms of social support and social networks: A review of health-related intervention studies. In: Public Health Review. Vol. 15. 159-193.

Czaja, S.J./Schulz, R./Lee, C.C./Belle, S.H. (2003). A methodology for describing and decomposing complex psychosocial and behavioral interventions. In: Psychology and Aging. Vol. 18. 385–395.

d'Houtaud, A. and Field, M.G. (1984). The Image of Health. Variation in Perception by Social Class in a French Population. In: Sociology of Health and Illness. Vol. 6. 30-59.

Daneski, K./Higgs, P./Myfanwy, M. (2010). From gluttony to obesity: moral discourses on apoplexy and stroke. In: Sociology of Health and Illness. Vol. 32(5). 730-744.

Darby, M. and Karni, E. (1973). Free Competition and the Optimal Amount of Fraud. In: Journal of Law and Economics. Vol. 16(1). 67-88.

David, C. (2001). Marketing to the consumer: perspectives from the pharmaceutical industry. In: Marketing Health Services, Vol. 21(1). 5-11.

Davidson, A.I. (2005). Ethics as Ascetics: Foucault, the History of Ethics, and Ancient Thought. In: Gutting, G. (ed.). The Cambridge Companion to Foucault. 2nd ed. Cambridge: Cambridge University Press. 123-148.

Davies, A. and Elliott, R. (2006). The evolution of the empowered consumer. In: European Journal of Marketing. Vol. 40(9/10). 1106-1121.

Davis, E./Kay, J./Star, J. (1991). Is Advertising Rational? In: Business Strategy Review. Vol. 2 (Fall. 1-23.

Davis, R.E. and Rexnicoow, K. (2012). The Cultural Variance Framework for Tailoring Health Messages. In: Cho, H. (ed.). Health Communication Message Design: Theory and Practice. Thousand Oaks, CA: SAGE. 115-135.

Davis, T.C./Williams, M.V./Marin, E./Parker, R.M./Glass, J. (2002). Health Literacy and Cancer Communication. In: CA: A Cancer Journal for Clinicians. Vol. 52(3). 134-149.

de Certeau, M. (1984). The Practice of Everyday Life. London: University of California Press.

de Luque, S. and Javidan, M. (2004). Uncertainty Avoidance. In: House, R.J./Hanges, P.J./Javidan, M. (eds.). Culture, Leadership, and Organizations: The GLOBE Study of 62 Societies. Thousand Oaks, CA: Sage. 602-653.

de Mooij, M. (1994). Advertising worldwide. 2nd ed. New York: Prentice Hall.

de Mooij, M. (1998). Global Marketing and Advertising: Understanding Cultural Paradoxes. Thousand Oaks, CA: Sage.

de Mooij, M. (2001). The Impact of Culture on Advertising. In: Kloss, I. (ed.). Advertising worldwide. Berlin: Springer. 1-24.

de Mooij, M. (2005). Global Marketing and Advertising: Understanding Cultural Paradoxes. 2nd ed. Thousand Oaks, CA: Sage.

de Mooij, M. (2011). Consumer Behavior and Culture: Consequences for Global Marketing and Advertising. Los Angeles, CA: SAGE.

de Mooij, M. and Hofstede, G. (2010). The Hofstede model: Applications to global branding and advertising strategy and research. In: International Journal of Advertising. Vol. 29(1). 85-110.

de Wit, J.B.F./Vet, R./Schutten, M./van Steenbergen, J. (2005). Social-cognitive determinants of vaccination behavior against hepatitis B: An assessment among men who have sex with men. In: Preventive Medicine. Vol. 40(6). 795-802.

DeLorme, D.E./Huh, J./Reid, L.N. (2009). Direct-to-consumer advertising skepticism and consumers' use and usefulness of prescription drug sources. In: Health Marketing Quarterly. Vol. 26. 293-314.

DeLorme, D.E./Huh, J./Reid, L.N./An, S. (2010). The state of public research on over-the-counter drug advertising. In: International Journal of Pharmaceutical and Healthcare Marketing. Vol. 4(3). 208-231.

Den Hartog, D.N. (2004). Assertiveness. In: House, R.J./Hanges, P.J./Javidan, M. (eds.). Culture, Leadership, and Organizations: The GLOBE Study of 62 Societies. Thousand Oaks, CA: Sage. 395-436.

Denegri-Knott, J./Zwick, D./Schroeder, J.E. (2006). Mapping consumer power: an integrative framework for marketing and consumer research. In: European Journal of Marketing. Vol. 40(9/10). 950-973.

DeRuiter, J. and Holston, P. (2012). Drug Patent Expirations and the "Patent Cliff". In: U.S. Pharmacist. Vol. 37(6). Generic Supplement. 12-20.

Derzon, J. H. and M. W. Lipsey (2002). A Meta-Analysis of the Effectiveness of Mass-Communication for Changing Substance-use: Knowledge, Attitudes and Behavior. In: Crano, W.D. and Burgoon, M. (eds.). Mass Media and Drug Prevention: Classic and Contemporary Theories and Research. Mahwah, London: Lawrence Erlbaum Associates: 231-258.

Deutsch, J. and Gerard, H.B. (1955). A study of normative and informational social influence upon individual judgment. In: The Journal of Abnormal and Social Psychology. Vol. 51(3). 629-636.

DeVito, J.A. (2003). Human Communication: The Basic Course. 9th ed. New York: Allyn and Bacon.

Diamantopoulos, A. and Siguaw, J.A. (2000). Introducing LISREL. London: SAGE.

Dickson P.R. and Sawyer, A.G. (1990). The Price Knowledge and Search of Supermarket Shoppers. In: Journal of Marketing. Vol. 54(July). 42–53.

Diehl, S./Mueller, B./Terlutter, R. (2007). Skepticism toward pharmaceutical advertising in the U.S. and Germany. In: Advances in International Marketing. Vol. 18. 31-60.

Diehl, S./Mueller, B./Terlutter, R. (2008). Consumer responses towards non-prescription and prescription drug advertising in the US and Germany: They don't really like it, but they do believe it. In: International Journal of Advertising. Vol. 27(1). 99-131.

Diehl, S./Mueller, B./Terlutter, R. (2014). The Usefulness of GLOBE Dimensions in Analyzing Consumer Perceptions of Advertising: Results from Multinational Studies. LEWI Working Paper Series. Retrieved from http://lewi.hkbu.edu.hk/WPS/126%20Diehl.pdf (accessed 20.8.2014)

Diehl, S./Terlutter, R./Mueller, B. (2011). Factors Influencing Consumer Attitudes toward Non-Prescription Drug Advertising. Paper presented at the 11th Icoria in Berlin, Germany. June 2011.

Diehl, S./Terlutter, R./Weinberg, P. (2003). Advertising Effectiveness in different cultures: results of an experiment analyzing the effects of individualistic and collectivistic advertising on Germans and Chinese. In: European Advances of Consumer Research. Vol. 6. 128-136.

Dillon, W. and Goldstein, M. (1984). Multivariate analysis: Methods and applications. New York:Wiley.

Dmoch, T. (1999). Der Einfluss der Kultur auf die Standardisierbarkeit erlebnisbetonter Werbung - Eine empirische Untersuchung in Deutschland, Frankreich und der Schweiz. In: Marketing ZFP. Vol. 3. 179 – 195.

Dobni, D. and Zinkhan, G.M. (1990). In search of brand image: a foundation analysis. In: Advances in Consumer Research. Vol. 17. 110-119.

Dodds, W. B. and Monroe, K. B. (1985). The effect of brand and price information on subjective product evaluations. In: Advances in Consumer Research. Vol. 12(1). 85-90.

Dodds, W. B./Monroe, K. B./Grewal, D. (1991). Effect of price, brand and store information on buyers' product evaluations. In: Journal of Marketing Research. Vol. 28(3). 307-319.

Doherty, G. and Ennew, C.T. (1995). The Marketing of pharmaceuticals: standardization or customization? In: Journal of Marketing Practice. Vol. 1(3). 39-50.

Doktoruz. (2007). OTC Policies and Market Structures in the USA, the European Union and Turkey. Retrieved from http://www.istanbul-ekonomi.com/en/yayinlar/Recetesiz%20ilac%20raporu_ENG.pdf (accessed 19.11.2013)

Dong, B. (2013). 3 'E's of Effective Healthcare Advertising: Experience, Empowerment, and Efficiency. Retrieved from http://www.mediapost.com/publications/article/205955/3-es-of-effective-healthcare-advertising-experi.html (accessed 26.01.2014)

Donohew, L./Lorch, E. P./Palmgreen, P. (1991). Sensation seeking and targeting of televised antidrug PSAs. In: Donohew, L./Sypher, H.E./Bukoski, W.J. (eds.). Persuasive communication and drug abuse prevention. Hillsdale, NJ: Lawrence Erlbaum. 209–226.

Donohew, L./Lorch, E. P./Palmgreen, P. (1998). Applications of a theoretic model of information exposure to health interventions. In: Human Communication Research. Vol. 24. 454–468.

Douglas, M. (1980). Purity and Danger: an Analysis of Concepts of Pollution and Taboo. London: Routledge.

Dowling, G. (2006) Communicating corporate reputation through stories. In: California Management Review. Vol. 49 (Fall). 82-100.

Downey, H.K. and Slocum, J.W. (1975). Uncertainty: Measures, Research and Sources of Variation. In: Academy of Management Journal. Vol. 18(3). 562-578.

Downs, A.C and Harrison, S.K. (1985). Embarrassing Age Spots or Just Plain Ugly? Physical Attractiveness Stereotyping as an Instrument of Sexism in American T.V Commercials. In: Sex Roles. Vol. 13. 9-19.

Drum Beat. (2005). Health Communication vs. Related Disciplines. The Communication Initiative. Retrieved from http://forums.comminit. com/viewtopic.php?t=63257&style=2 (accessed 11.02.2014)

du Gay, P. (1996). Consumption and Identity at Work. London: SAGE.

Du Pré, A. (2000). Communicating About Health: Current Issues and Perspectives. Mountain View, CA: Mayfield Publishing Company.

Dubin, R. (1962). Industrial Workers' Worlds: a study of the central life interests of industrial workers. In: Rose, A. (ed.). Human Behaviour and Social Processes. London: Routledge. 247-266.

Dubos, R. (1959). Mirage of Health. New York: Harper and Row.

Dunbar-Jacob, J./Gemmell, L.A./Schlenk, E.A. (2009). Predictors of Patient Adherence: Patient Characteristics. In: Shumaker, S.A./Ockene, J.K./Riekert, K.A. (eds.). The Handbook of Health Behavior Change. New York: Springer. 397-410.

Duncan, O.D. (1975). Introduction to structural equation models. New York: Academic Press.

Dunst, C.J. and Trivette, C.M. (1996), Empowerment, effective helpgiving practices and family-centered care. In: Paediatric Nursing. Vol. 22(4). 334-343.

Durkheim, E. (1950). The Rules of Sociological Method. New York: Free Press.

Dutta, M.J. (2008). Communicating Health: A Culture-Centered Approach. Malden, MA: Policy.

Dutta, M.J./Bodie, G.D./Basu, A. (2008). Health disparity and the racial divide among the nation's youth: Internet as a site for change? In: Everett, A. (ed.). Learning race and ethnicity: Youth and digital media. Cambridge, MA: The MIT Press. 175-198.

Dutta-Bergman, M. (2004). Health attitudes, health cognitions and health behaviors among Internet health information seekers: Population-based survey. In: Journal of Medical Internet Research. Vol. 6(2). 15.

Dutta-Bergman, M. (2004). Primary sources of health information: Comparison in the domain of health attitudes, health cognitions, and health behaviors. In: Health Communication. Vol. 16. 273-288.

Dutta-Bergman, M. (2005). Developing a profile of consumer intention to seek out additional information beyond a doctor: The role of communicative and motivation variables. In: Health Communication. Vol. 17. 1–16.

Dutton, K.R. (1995). The Perfectible Body: The Western Ideal of Physical Development. London: Cassell.

Earle, S. (2007). Exploring Health. In: Earle, S./Lloyd, C.E./Sidell, M./Spurr, S. (eds.). Theory and Research in Promoting Public Health. London: Sage. 37-66.

Earle, S. (2007). Promoting public health: Exploring the Issues. In: Earle, S./Lloyd, C.E./Sidell, M./Spurr, S. (eds.). Theory and Research in Promoting Public Health. London: Sage. 1-36.

Eckermann, L. (1997). Foucault, embodiment and gendered subjectivities: The case of voluntary self-starvation. In: Petersen, A. and Bunton, R. (eds.). Foucault, Health and Medicine. London: Routledge. 151-169.

Edell, J.A. and Burke, M.C. (1987). The power of feelings in understanding advertising effects. In: Journal of Consumer Research. Vol. 14 (December). 421-433.

Edell, J.A. and Staelin, R. (1983). The information processing of pictures in print advertisements. In: Journal of Consumer Research. Vol. 10(1). 45-61.

Edwards, W. (1954). The theory of decision making. In: Psychological Bulletin. Vol. 51. 380-471.

Eisend, M. (2002). Dimensions of Credibility in Marketing Communication. In: AP - Asia Pacific Advances in Consumer Research. Vol. 5. 366-373.

Ellen, P.S./Mohr, L.A./Web, D.J. (2000). Charitable programs and the retailer: do they mix? In: Journal of Retail. Vol. 76(3). 393-406.

Emrich, C.G./Denmark, F.L./Den Hartog, D.N. (2004). Cross-Cultural Differences in Gender Egalitarianism. In: House, R.J./Hanges, P.J./Javidan, M. (eds.). Culture, Leadership, and Organizations: The GLOBE Study of 62 Societies. Thousand Oaks, CA: Sage. 343-394.

Eng, T.R. and Gustafson, D.H. (1999). Wired for Health and Well-Being The Emergence of Interactive Health Communication. Science Panel on Interactive Communication and Health. Washington, DC.: Office of Disease Prevention and Health Promotion US Department of Health and Human Services.

Engel, G.L. (1979). Resolving the Conflict between medicine and psychiatry. In: Research Staff Physician. Vol. 196. 129-136.

Engel, J.P./Kollat, D.T./Blackwell, R.D. (1973). Consumer Behavior. 2nd ed. New York: Holt, Rinehart and Winston.

Engel, James F. and Blackwell, Rodger D. (1982). Consumer Behavior. 4th ed. New York: The Dryden Press.

Epp, L. (1986). Achieving Health for all. A Framework for Health Promotion in Canada. Toronto: Health and Welfare Canada.

Ericson, J. (2014). A Pill for every Ill. In: Newsweek. 6 February 2014. Retrieved from www.newsweek.com/.../pill-every-ill-245476.html (accessed 17.06.2014)

Esch, F.-R. (2008). Werbewirkungsforschung. In: Hermann, A./Homburg, C./Klarmann, M. (eds.). Handbuch Marktforschung. 3rd ed. Wiesbaden: Springer. 1147-1196.

Esch, F.-R. (2011). Wirkung integrierter Kommunikation: Ein verhaltenswissenschaftlicher Ansatz für Werbung. 5th ed. Wiesbaden: Forschungsgruppe Konsum und Verhalten.

Esteban, D. (2008). Strengthening corporate social responsibility in the pharmaceutical industry. In: Journal of Medical Marketing. Vol. 8(1). 77-79.

Etgar, M. and Goodwin, S.A. (1982). One-sided versus two-sided comparative message appeals for new brand introductions. In: Journal of Consumer Research. Vol. 10(1). 460-466.

Eurobarometer. (2002). The attitudes of Europeans towards the environment. Retrieved from http://ec.europa.eu/public_opinion/archives/ebs/ebs_180_en.pdf (accessed 28.01.2014)

Eurobarometer. (2008). Attitudes of European citizens towards the environment. Retrieved from http://ec.europa.eu/public_opinion/archives/ebs/ebs_295_en.pdf (accessed 28.01.2014)

Eurobarometer. (2009). Public Opinion in the European Union. Retrieved from http://ec.europa.eu/public_opinion/archives/eb/eb72/eb72_vol1_en.pdf (accessed 28.01.2014)

European Commission. (2008). Definition of Corporate Social Responsibility. Retrieved from http://ec.europa.eu/enterprise/policies/sustainable-business/corporate-social-responsibility/index_en.htm (accessed 02.04.2014)

Ewles, L. and Simnett, I. (2003). Promoting Health: A Practical Guide. 5th ed. Edinburgh: Bailliere Tindall.

Eylon, D. (1998). Understanding empowerment and resolving its paradox. In: Journal of Management History. Vol. 4(1). 16-28.

Eysenbach, G. (2001). What is eHealth? In: Journal of Medical Internet Research. Vol. 3(2).

Eysenck, M. W. (2000). Psychology: A student's handbook. Hove, East Sussex, UK: Psychology Press.

Falk, P. (1994). The Consuming Body. London: Sage.

Faltermeier, T. (2005). Gesundheitspsychology. Stuttgart: Kohlhammer.

Fan, X./Thompson, B./Wang, L. (1999). Effects of Sample Size, Estimation Methods, and Model Specification on Structural Equation Modeling Fit Indexes. In: Structural Equation Modeling. Vol. 6 (1). 56-83.

Faulkner, S.L. and Hecht, M.L. (2007). Tides in the ocean: A layered approach to culture and communication. In: Whaley, B.B. and Samter, W. (eds.). Explaining communication: Contemporary theories and exemplars. Mahwah, NJ: Lawrence Erlbaum. 393-402.

Fazio, R. H. and Petty, R. E. (2007). Attitudes: Their structure, function and consequences. Vol. 1. Philadelphia, PA: Psychology Press.

Featherstone, M. (1991). Consumer Culture and Postmodernism. London: Sage.

Feick, L. and Higie, R.A. (1992).The Effects of Preference Heterogeneity and Source Characteristics on Ad Processing and Judgments about Endorsers. In: Journal of Advertising. Vol. 21(2). 16-21.

Ferguson, T. (1980). Medical-Self Care: Self-Responsibility for Health. In: Hastings, A.C./Fadiman, J.F./Gordon, J.S. (eds.). Health for the Whole Person. Boulder, CO: Westview. 87-99.

Festinger, L. and Maceoby, N. (1964). On Resistance to Persuasive Communications. In: Journal of Abnormal and Social Psychology. Vol. 68. 359-366.

Findlay, S.D. (2001). Direct-to-consumer promotion of prescription drugs: economic implications for patients, payers and providers. In: Pharmoeconomics. Vol. 19(2). 109-119.

Finkelstein, J. (1990). Bio-medicine and technocratic power. In: Hastings Center Report. Vol. 20(4). 13-16.

Firat, A. and Dholakia, N. (1998). Consuming People: From Political Economy to Theatres of Consumption. London: Routledge.

Firat, A.F. and Venkatesh, A. (1995). Liberatory postmodernism and the reenchantment of consumption. In: Journal of Consumer Research. Vol. 22. 239-267.

Fischer, R. and Fontaine, R.J.R. (2009). Methods for investigating structural equivalence. In: Matsumoto, D. and Van der Vijver, F.J.R. (eds.). Cross-cultural research methods. New York: Oxford University Press. 179-215.

Fischhoff, B. and Quadrel, M.M. (1991). Adolescent alcohol decisions. In: Alcohol Health and Research World. Vol. 15(1). 43-51.

Fishbein, M. (2008). A Reasoned Action Approach to Health Promotion. In: Medical Decision Making. Vol. 28(6). 834-844.

Fishbein, M. and Ajzen, I. (1975). Belief, attitude, intention and behavior. An introduction to theory and research. Reading, MA: Addison-Wesley.

Fishbein, M. and Yzer, I. (2003). Using theory to design effective health behavior interventions. In: Communication Theory. Vol. 13. 164-183.

Fitzpatrick, M. (2001). The tyranny of health, doctors, and the regulation of lifestyle. London: Routledge.

Fletcher, C.M. (1973). Communication in Medicine. London: Nuffield Provincial Hospitals Trust.

Flora, C. (2008). The Pursuit of Happiness. Retrieved from https://www.psychologytoday.com/articles/200812/the-pursuit-happiness (accessed 01.03.2014)

Floyd, D. L./Prentice Dunn, S./Rogers, R. W. (2000). A meta-analysis of research on protection motivation theory. In: Journal of Applied Social Psychology. Vol. 30. 407-429.

Folkes, V. S. and Kiesler, T. (1991). Social Cognition: Consumers' Inferences about the Self and Others. In: Robertson, T.S. and Kassarjian, H.H. (eds.). Handbook of Consumer Behavior. Englewood Cliffs, NJ: Prentice-Hall. 281-315.

Fontanarosa, P.B./Rennie, D./DeAngelis, C.D. (2004).Postmarketing Surveillance-Lack of Vigilance, Lack of Trust. In: Journal of the American Marketing Association. Vol. 292. 2647-2650.

Forceville, C. (1996). Pictoral Metaphor in Advertising. New York: Routledge.

Ford, G.T./Smith, D.B./Swasy, J.L. (1988). An Empirical Test of the Search, Experience, and Credence Attributes Framework. In: Advances in Consumer Research. Vol. 15. 239-243.

Ford, L.A., and Yep, G.A. (2003). Working along the margins: Developing community-based strategies for communicating about health with marginalized groups. In: Thompson, T.L./Dorsey, A.M./Miller, K.I./Parrot, R. (eds.). Handbook of health communication. Mahwah, NJ: Lawrence Erlbaum Associates. 241–261.

Ford, L.A./Babrow, A.S./Stohl, C. (1996). Social support messages and the management of uncertainty in the experience of breast cancer: An application of problematic integration theory. In: Communication Monographs. Vol. 63. 189-207.

Fornell, C. (1983). Issues in the application of covariance structure analysis: A comment. In: Journal of Consumer Research. Vol. 9(4). 443-448.

Fornell, C. and Larcker, D.F. (1981). Evaluationg Structural Equation Models with Unobservable Variables and Measurement Error. In: Journal of Marketing Research. Vol. 18 (February). 39-50.

Foucault, M. (1973). The Birth of the Clinic: An Archaeology of Medical Perception. London: Random House.

Foucault, M. (1975). Discipline and Punish. New York: Vintage Books.

Foucault, M. (1976). Birth of the Clinic: An Archeology of Medical Perception. London: Tavistock.

Foucault, M. (1977). Discipline and Punish: The Birth of the Prison. London: Penguin.

Foucault, M. (1977). Theatrum Philosophicum. In: Bouchard, D.F. (ed.). Language, Counter-Memory, Practice. Oxford: Blackwell.

Foucault, M. (1979). Discipline and Punish: The Birth of the Prison. Harmondsworth: Peregrine.

Foucault, M. (1980). The eye of power. In: Gordon, C. (ed.). Power/Knowledge. Brighton: Harvester Press.

Foucault, M. (1980). The Politics of Health in the 18th century. In: Gordon, C. (ed.). Power/Knowledge. Selected Interviews and Other Writings: 1972-1977. Brighton: The Harvester Press. 166-182.

Foucault, M. (1984). Truth and Power. In: Rabinow, P. (ed.). The Foucault Reader. New York: Pantheon.

Foucault, M. (1988). Social security. In: Kritzman, L. (ed.). Michel Foucault: Politics, Philosophy, Culture. London: Routledge.

Foucault, M. (1990). The History of Sexuality. Vol. 1: An Introduction. New York: Vintage.

Foucault, M. (1991). Discipline and Punish – The Birth of the Prison. London: Penguin.

Foucault, M. (1992). Was ist Kritik? Berlin: Merve.

Foucault, M. (1994). An Interview with Michel Foucault. In: Faubion, J.D. (ed.). Power. Vol. 3. New York: The New Press. 239-297.

Foucault, M. (1995). Discipline and Punish. 2nd ed. New York: Vintage Books.

Foucault, M. (1996). Foucault Life: Interviews 1961-1984. New York: Semiotext(e).

Fox, N.J. and Ward, K.J. (2008). Pharma in the bedroom ... and the kitchen.... The pharmaceuticalisation of daily life. In: Sociology of Health and Illness. Vol. 30(6). 856-868.

Fox, S. (2005). Health Information Online. Washington, DC: Pew Internet and American Life Project. 1–16.

Fox, S. and Rainie, L. (2002). The online health care revolution: How the Web helps Americans take better care of themselves. Washington, DC: Pew Internet and American Life Project.

Frank, A. (1990). Bringing bodies back in: a decade review. In: Theory, Culture and Society. Vol. 7(1). 131-162.

Frank, D./Swedmark, J./Grubbs, L. (2004). Colon cancer screening in African American women. In: ABNF Journal. Vol. 15(4). 67-70.

Frankish, C.J./Lovato, C.Y./ Poureslami, I. (1999). Models, theories, and principles of health promotion and their use with multicultural populations. In: Huff, R.M./Kline, M.V./Peterson, D.V. (eds.). Health Promotion in Multicultural Populations. Thousand Oaks, CA: Sage.

Franklin, P.D./Farzanfar, R./Thompson, D. (2009). E-Health Strategies to Support Adherence. In: Shumaker, S.A./Ockene, J.K./Riekert, K.A. (eds.). The Handbook of Health Behavior Change. New York: Springer. 169-190.

Franzen, G.. (1994). Advertising Effectiveness. London: NTC.

Freidson, E. (1970). Professional Dominance: The Social Structure of Medical Care. Chicago: Aldine.

Freimuth, V./Linnan, H.W./Potter, P. (2000). Communicating the Threat of Emerging Infections to the Public. In: Emerging Infectious Diseases. Vol. 6(4). 337-374.

French, D./West, R./Elander, J./Wilding, J.M. (1992). Decision making style, driving style and self-reported involvement in road traffic accidents. In: Ergonomics. Vol. 36(6). 627-644.

Friedman, M. and Gould, J. (2007). Consumer attitudes and behaviours associated with direct-to-consumer prescription drug marketing. In: Journal of Consumer Marketing. Vol. 24(2). 100–109.

Friestad, M. and Wright, P. (1994). The persuasion knowledge model: how people cope with persuasion attempts. In: Journal of Consumer Research. Vol. 21(1). 1-31.

Frith, K. and Mueller, B. (2004). Advertising and Societies: Global Issues. New York: Peter Lang.

Frith, K.T. (1998). Undressing the ad: Reading culture in advertising. New York: Peter Lang.

Frith, K.T. and Sengupta, S. (1991). Individualism and advertising: A cross-cultural comparison. In: Asian Mass Communication Research and Information. Vol. 18(4). 191-197.

Frosch, D.L./Krueger, P.M./Hornik, R.C./Cronholm, P.F./Barg, R.K. (2007). Creating demand for prescription drugs: A content analysis of television direct-to-consumer advertising. In: Annals of Family Medicine. Vol. 5. 6-13.

Fuchs, V.R. (1986). The Health Economy. Cambridge, Mass: Harvard University Press.

Gabbott, M. (1991). The Role of Product Cues in Assessing Risk in Second-hand Markets. In: European Journal of Marketing. Vol. 25(9). 38-50.

Gabe, J./Kelleher, D./Williams, G. (1994). Challenging Medicine. London: Routledge.

Gafni, A./Charles, C./Whelan, T. (1998). The Physician-Patient Encounter: the physician as a perfect agent for the patient versus the informed treatment decision-making model. In: Social Science and Medicine. Vol. 47. 347-354.

Galanti, G.A. (1991). Caring for Patients from Different Cultures. Philadelphia: University of Pennsylvania Press.

Galvin, R. (2002). Disturbing notions of chronic illness and individual responsibility: towards a genealogy of morals. In: Health. Vol. 6(2). 107-137.

Gardner, M.P. (1983). Criteria Recalled and Those Used for Brand Evaluation. In: Journal of Consumer Research. Vol. 10(December). 310-318.

Gardner, M.P./Mitchell, A.A./Russo, J.E. (1985). Low Involvement Strategies for Processing Advertisements. In: Journal of Advertising. Vol. 14(2). 4-12.

Garfinkel, H. (1967). Studies in Ethnomethodology. London: Prentice Hall.

Gastaldo, D. (1997). Is health education good for you? Re-thinking health education through the concept of bio-power. In: Petersen, A. and Bunton, R. (eds.). Foucault, Health and Medicine. London: Routledge. 113-133.

Gazmarian, J. A./Kripalani, S./Miller, M.J./Echt, K.V./Ren, J./Rask, K. (2006). Factors associated with medication refill adherence in cardiovascular-related diseases: a focus on health literacy. In: Journal of General Internal Medicine. Vol. 21(12). 1215-1221.

Gebbie, K./Rostenstock, L./Hernandez, L.M. (2003). Who will keep the public healthy? Educating public health professionals for the 21st century. Washington, DC: National Academies Press.

Gelfand, M.J./Bhawuk, D.P.S./Nishii, L.H./Bechthold, D.J. (2004). Individualism and collectivism. In: House, R.J./Hanges, P.J./Javidan, M. (eds.). Culture, Leadership, and Organizations: The GLOBE Study of 62 Societies. Thousand Oaks, CA: Sage. 437-512.

Gelman, A. and Hill, J. (2006). Missing Data Imputation. In: Gelman, A. and Hill, J. (eds.). Data Analysis Using Regression and Multilevel/Hierarchical Models. Cambridge: Cambridge University Press. 529-544.

Gemünden, H.G. (1985). Perceived Risk and Information Search. A Systematic Meta-Analysis of the Empirical Evidence. In: International Journal of Research in Marketing. Vol. 2. 79-100.

Gerbing, D.W. and Anderson, J.C. (1993). Monte Carlo Evaluations of Goodness of Fit indices for Structural Equation models. In: Bollen, K.A. and Long, J.S. (eds.). Testing Structural Equation Models. Beverly Hills, CA: Sage. 40-65.

Gergen, K.J. (2000). An Invitation to Social Construction. London: Sage.

Gerhardt, U. (1989). Ideas about Illness. London: Macmillan.

Gibson, C.H. (1991). A concept analysis of patient empowerment, In: Journal of Advanced Nursing, Vol. 16. 354-361.

Giddens, A. (1991). Modernity and Self Identity: Self and Society in the Late Modern Age. London: Polity.

Giddens, A. (1992). The Transformation of Intimacy: Sexuality, Love and Eroticism in Modern Societies. Cambridge: Polity Press.

Giddens, A. (2009) Sociology. 6th ed. Cambridge: Polity.

Gilbody, S./Wilson, P./Watt, I. (2005). Benefits and Harms of Direct to Consumer Advertising: A Systematic Review. In: Quality and Safety in Healthcare. Vol. 14. 246-250.

Giles, H. and Franklyn-Stokes, A. (1989). Communicator Characteristics. In: Asante, M.K. and Gudykunst, W.B. (eds.). The Handbook of Intercultural Communication. Newbury Park, CA: Sage.

Gillam, S.J. (1991). Understanding the uptake of cervical cancer screening: The contribution of the Health Belief Model. In: British Journal of General Practice. Vol. 41(353). 510-513.

Gitlin, T. (1990). On drugs and mass media in America's consumer society. In: Resnik, H./Gardner, Stephen E./Lorion, Raymond P./Marcus, Carol E. (eds.). Youth and Drugs: Society's Mixed Messages. Rockville, MD: DIANE Publishing. 31-52.

Glanz, K. and Riemer, B. (1997). Theory at a glance: A guide for health promotion practice. National Institutes of Health/National Cancer Institute. Retrieved from http://oc.nci.nih.gov/services/Theory_at_glance/HOME.html (accessed 21.02.2014)

Glanz, K./Rimer, B.K./Lewis, F.M. (eds.) (2002). Health Behavior and Health Education. 3rd ed. San Francisco: Jossey-Bass.

Glanz, K./Rimer, B.K./Viswanath, K. (eds.). (2008). Health Behavior and Health Education. 4th ed. San Francisco: Jossey-Bass.

Glassner, B. (1992). Bodies: The Tyranny of Perfection. Los Angeles: Lowell House.

Glassner, B. (1995). In the name of health. In: Bunton, R./Nettleton, S./Burrows, R. (eds.). The Sociology of Health Promotion. London: Routledge.

Goffman, E. (1967). Interaction Ritual. New York: Pantheon.

Goffman, E. (1968). Asylums: Essays on the Social Situation of Mental Patients and other Inmates. Harmondsworth: Penguin.

Goffman, E. (1968). Stigma: Notes on the Management of Spoiled Identity. Harmondsworth: Penguin.

Golden, L.L. and Johnson, K.A. (1983). The Impact of Sensory Preference and Thinking versus Feeling Appeals on Advertising Effectiveness. In: Advances in Consumer Research. Vol. 10. 203-208.

Goldman, M./Brown, S./Christiansen, B. (1987). Expectancy theory: Thinking about drinking. In: Blane, H. and Leonard, D. (eds.). Psychological theories of drinking and alcoholism. New York: Guilford.

Goldsmith, D.J. (2004). Communicating Social Support. Cambridge: Cambridge University Press.

Goldsmith, E.B. (2005), Consumer empowerment: public policy and insurance regulation. In: International Journal of Consumer Studies, Vol. 29. 86-92.

Goldthorpe, J.H./Lockwood, D./Bechhofer, F./Platt, J. (1969). The Affluent Worker in the Class Structure. Cambridge: Cambridge University Press.

Gollop, C. J. (1997). Health information-seeking behavior and African American women. In: Bulletin of Medical Library Association. Vol. 85(2). 141–146.

Gollowitzer, P. M. (1993). Goal achievement: The role of intentions. In: European Review of Social Psychology. Vol. 4. 141-185.

Gollowitzer, P. M./Heckhausen, H./Steller, B. (1990). Deliberative vs. implemental mind-sets: Cognitive turning towards congruous thoughts and information. In: Journal of Personality and Social Psychology. Vol. 59. 1119-1127.

Gollwitzer, P. M. and Sheeran, P. (2007). Implementation intentions and goal achievement: A meta-analysis of effects and processes. In: Advances in Experimental Social Psychology. Vol. 38. 69–119.

Gonzales, V.M./Goeppinger, J./Lorig, K. (1990). Four psychosological theories and their application to patient education and clinical practice. In: Arthritis Care. Vol. 3. 132-143.

Goodstein, R.C. (1993). Category-Based Applications and Extensions in Advertising: Motivating More Extensive Ad Processing. In: Journal of Consumer Research. Vol. 20(1). 89-99.

Gordon, C. (1987). The soul of the citizen: Max Weber and Michel Foucault on rationality and government. In: Whimster, S. and Lash, S. (eds.). Max Weber: Rationality and Modernity. London: Allen and Unwin. 293-316.

Gordon, C. (1991). Governmental rationality: an introduction. In: Burchell, G./Gordon, C./Miller, P. (eds.). The Foucault Effect: Studies in Governmentality. Hemel Hempstead: Harvester Wheatsheaf.

Gordon, C. (ed.) (1980). Power/Knowledge. Brighton: Harvester Press.

Gordon, J.S. (1980). The Paradigm of Holistic Medicine. In: Hastings, A.C./Fadiman, J.F./Gordon, J.S. (eds.). Health for the Whole Person. Boulder, CO: Westview. 1-27.

Gorn, Gerald J./Chattopadhyay, Amitava/Yi, Tracey/Dahl, Warren W. (1996). Effects of Color as an Executional Cue in Advertising. They're in the Shade. In: Management Science. Vol. 43(10). 1387-1400.

Gould, S.J. (1988). Consumer attitudes toward health and health care: A differential perspective. In: Journal of Consumer Affairs. Vol. 22(1). 96-118.

Gould, S.J. (1990). Health Consciousness and Health Behavior: The Application of a New Health Consciousness Scale. In: American Journal of Preventive Medicine. Vol. 6(4). 228-237.

Grace, V. M. (1991) The marketing of empowerment and the construction of the health consumer: a critique of health promotion. In: International Journal of Health Services. Vol. 21. 329-343.

Graham, M. E. (2002). Health beliefs and self breast examination in in black women. In: Journal of Cultural Diversity. Vol. 9(2). 49-54.

Greco, M. (1993). Psychosomatic subjects and the 'duty to be well': personal agency within medical rationality. In: Economy and Society. Vol. 22(3). 357-372.

Green, J. and Tones, K. (2010). Health Promotion: Planning and Strategies. 2nd ed. Thousand Oaks, CA: SAGE.

Green, L. and Kreuter, M. (1991). Health Promotion Planning: An Educational and Environmental Approach. Mountain View, CA: Mayfield.

Greenwald, A.G./Brock, T.C./Ostrom, T.M. (eds.) (1968). Psychological Foundation of Attitude. New York: Academic Press.

Greenwald, G.A. (1968). On Defining Attitude and Attitude Theory. In: Greenwald, A.G./Brock, T.C./Ostrom, T.M. (eds.). Psychological Foundation of Attitude. New York: Academic Press.

Griffin, M./Babin, B.J./Modianos, D. (2000). Shopping Values of Russian Consumers: The Impact of Habituation in a Developing Economy. In: Journal of Retailing. Vol. 76(Spring). 33-52.

Griffin, R. J./Dunwoody, S./Neuwirth, K. (1999). Proposed model of the relationship of risk information seeking and processing to the development of preventive behaviors. In: Environmental Research. Vol. 80. 230–245.

Griffiths, J. and Adams, L. (1991). The new health promotion. In: Draper, P. (ed.). Health through Public Policy. London: Grenn Print.

Grosse, R. N. and Auffrey, C. (1989). The myth of medical breakthrough: Smallpox, vaccination and Jenner reconsidered. In: Annual Review of Public Health. Vol. 10. 281-297.

Grunberg, N.E. and Klein, L.C. (2009). Biopsychological obstacles to adoption and maintenance of a healthy lifestyle. In: Shumaker, S.A./Ockene, J.K./Riekert, K.A. (eds.). The handbook of health behavior change. 3rd ed. New York, NY: Springer. 411– 426.

Guchait, P./Anner, M./Wu, L. (2011). Consumer perceptions of corporate social responsibility of service firms: impact on customer attitudes and behavioral intentions. Retrieved from http://scholarworks.umass.edu/cgi/viewcontent.cgi?article=1034&context=gradconf_hospitality (accessed 02.04.2014)

Gudykunst, W.B./Gao, G./ Nishida, T./Bond, M.H./Leung, K./Wang, G./Barraclough, R.A. (1989). A cross-cultural comparison of self-monitoring. In: Communication Research Reports. Vol. 6. 7-12.

Guido, G. (2001). The Salience of Marketing Stimuli: An incongruity-salience hypothesis on consumer awareness. Boston, MA: Kluwa Academic Publishers.

Gully, P.R. (2008). Foreword. In: Parker, J. and Thorson, E. (eds.). Health Communication in the new media landscape. New York: Springer. xxvii-xxix.

Gutman, J. (1983). A means-end chain model based on consumer categorization process. In: Journal of Marketing. Vol. 46(2). 60-72.

Habermas, J. (1975). Legitimation Crisis. Boston: Beacon Press.

Hagtvedt, H. (2015). Promotional phrases as questions versus statements: An influence of phrase style on product evaluation. In: Journal of Consumer Psychology. In Press. Retrieved from http://dx.doi.org/10.1016/j.jcps.2014.12.005 (09.02.2015)

HAI. (2009). Understanding and Responding to Pharmaceutical Promotion. Retrieved from http://www.haiweb.org/11062009/drug-promotion-manual-CAP-3-090610.pdf (accessed 26.11.2014)

Hair, J.F. jr./Black, W.C./Babin, B.J./Anderson, R.E./Tatham, R.L. (2006). Multivariate Data Analysis. 6th ed. Upper Saddle River, NJ: Pearson/Prentice Hall.

Hair, J.F./Sarstedt, M./Ringle, C.M./Mena, J.A. (2012a). An assessment of the use of partial least squares structural equation modeling in marketing research. In: Journal of the Academy of Marketing Science. Vol. 40(3). 414–433.

Haley, Russel I. and Baldinger, Allan L. (1991). The ARF Copy Research Validity Project. In: Journal of Advertising Research. Vol. 31. 11-32.

Hall, E.T. (1966). The hidden Dimension. Garden City, NY: Anchor/Doubleday.

Hall, E.T. (1976). Beyond culture. Garden City, NY: Anchor/Doubleday.

Hall, E.T. and Hall, M.H. (1987). Hidden differences: Doing business with the Japanese. Garden City, NY: Anchor/Doubleday.

Han, S. and Shavitt, S. (1994). Persuasion and culture: Advertising appeals in individualistic and collectivistic societies. In: Journal of Experimental Social Psychology. Vol. 30. 326-350.

Hannerz, U. (1990). Cosmopolitans and Locals in World Culture. In: Featherstone, M. (ed.). Global Culture: Nationalism, Globalization and Modernity. Thousand Oaks, CA: Sage. 295-310.

Harding, J. (1997). Bodies at risk: Sex, surveillance and hormone replacement therapy. In: Petersen, A. and Bunton, R. (eds.). Foucault, Health and Medicine. London: Routledge. 134-150.

Harkness, J.A. (2003). Questionnaire translation. In: Harkness, J.A./van de Vijver, F./Mohler, P.P. (eds.). Cross-cultural survey methods. Hoboken, NJ: John Wiley and Sons. 35-56.

Harris, A.A. and Moran, R.T. (1987). Managing Cultural Differences. 2nd ed. Houston: Gulf Publishing Co.

Harris, D. and Gluten, S. (1979). Health Protective Behavior: An Exploratory Study. In: Journal of Health and Social Behavior. Vol. 20(1). 17-29.

Harris, G. and Attour, S. (2003). The international advertising practices of multinational companies: a content analysis study. In: European Journal of Marketing, Vol. 37(1/2). 154-168.

Harris, W.S./Gowda, M./Kolb, J.W./Strychacz, C.P./Vacek, J.L./Jones, P.G./Forker, A./O'Keefe, J.H./McCallister, B.D. (1999). A randomized, controlled trial of the effects of remote, intercessory prayer on outcomes in patients admitted to the coronary care unit. In: Archives of Internal Medicine. Vol. 159(19). 2273–2278.

Harrison, G./Juric, B./Cornwell, T.B. (2001). The Relationship of Advertising Model Attractiveness and Body Satisfaction to Intention to Purchase an Exercise Product. In: AP - Asia Pacific Advances in Consumer Research. Vol. 4. 217-222.

Harrison, T./Waite, K./Hunter, G.L. (2006). The internet, information and empowerment. In: European Journal of Marketing. Vol. 40(9/10). 972-993.

Hartog, D.N. (2004). Assertiveness. In: House, R. J./Hanges, P.J./Javidan, M./Dorfman, P.W./Gupta, V. (eds.). Culture, leadership, and organizations. The GLOBE study of 62 societies. Thousand Oaks, CA: Sage. 395-436.

Harvey, M.G. (1993). Point of view: A model to determine standardization of the advertising process in international markets. In: Journal of Advertising Research. Vol. 33(4). 57-64.

Havitz, M.E. and Mannell, R.C. (2005). Enduring Involvement, Situational Involvement, and Flow in Leisure and Non-leisure Activities. In: Journal of Leisure Research. Vol. 37(2). 152-177.

Hawkins, D. I./Best, R. J./Coney, K. A. (2003). Consumer behavior: Building marketing strategy. New York: McGraw Hill.

Hayduk, L./Cummings, G.G./Boadu, K./Pazderka-Robinson, H./Boulianne, S. (2007). Testing! Testing! One, Two, Three – Testing the theory in structural equation models! In: Personality and Individual Differences. Vol. 42 (2). 841-850.

Hayduk, L.A. (1996). LISREL issues, debates and strategies. Baltimore: Johns Hopkins University Press.

Health Communication Partnership. (2005). Introduction to Theories of Communication Effects: Social Learning Theory. Retrieved from http://www.hcpartnership.org/Topics/Communication/theory/256,1,Slide 1. (accessed 08.03.2014)

Health Communication Unit. (2006). Developing health communication campaigns. Retrieved from http://www.nccmt.ca/registry/view/eng/75.html (accessed 18.03.2014)

Health Knowledge. (2007a). Concepts of Health and Illness: Section 1. The Sociological Perspective. Retrieved from http://www.healthknowledge.org.uk/public-health-textbook/medical-sociology-policy-economics/4a-concepts-health-illness/section1 (accessed 13.07.2014)

Health Knowledge. (2007b). Concepts of Health and Illness: Section 2: Sociological Conceptualisation of Medical Knowledge and Power. Retrieved from http://www.healthknowledge.org.uk/public-health-textbook/medical-sociology-policy-economics/4a-concepts-health-illness/section2 (accessed 13.07.2014)

Health Knowledge. (2007c). Concepts of Health and Illness: Section 4. Lay Health Beliefs and Illness Behaviour. Retrieved from http://www.healthknowledge.org.uk/public-health-textbook/medical-sociology-policy-economics/4a-concepts-health-illness/section4 (accessed 13.07.2014)

Hecht, M.L. and Choi, H.J. (2012). The Communication Theory of Identity as a Framework for Health Message Design. In: Cho, H. (ed.). Health Communication Message Design: Theory and Practice. Thousand Oaks, CA: SAGE. 137-152.

Hecht, M.L./Jackson, R.L./Ribeau, S. (2003). African American communication: Exploring identity and culture. 2nd ed. Mahwah, NJ: Lawrence Erlbaum.

Hecht, M.L./Warren, J./Jung, J./Krieger, J. (2004). Communication theory of identity. In: Gudykunst, W.B. (ed.). Theorizing about intercultural communication. Newbury Park, CA: SAGE. 257-278.

Heckhausen, H. (1991). Motivation and action. Berlin: Springer.

Heckhausen, H. and Gollowitzer, P. M. (1987). Thought contents and cognitive functioning in motivational versus volitional states of mind. In: Motivation and Emotion. Vol. 11. 101-120.

Heine, S.J. and Hamamura, T. (2007). In search of East Asian self-enhancement. In: Personality and Social Psychology Review. Vol. 11. 4-27.

Helmer, S.M./Krämer, A./Mikolajczyk, R.T. (2012). Health-related locus of control and health behaviour among university students in North Rhine Westphalia, Germany. In: BMC Reseach Notes. Vol. 5. 703.

Hendershot, C./Stoner, S./Pantalone, D./Simoni, J. (2009). Alcohol Use and antiretroviral adherence: review and meta-analysis. In: Journal of Acquired Immune Deficiency Syndromes. Vol. 52. 180–202.

Henkel, J. (2002). Buying drugs on-line: It's convenient and private, but beware of 'rouge sites'. FDA Consumer Magazine. Retrieved from http://www.fda.gov/Drugs/EmergencyPreparedness/BioterrorismandDrugPreparedness/ucm137269.htm (accessed 12.05.2013)

Herriger, N. (1997). Empowerment in der Sozialen Arbeit. Eine Einführung. Stuttgart: Kohlhammer.

Herzenstein, M./Misra, S./Posavac, S.S. (2004). How consumers'attitudes towards direct-to-consumer advertising of prescription drugs influence ad effectiveness, and consumer and physician behavior. In: Marketing Letters. Vol. 15(4). 201-212.

Heskett, J.L./Jones, T.O./Loveman, G.W./Sasser, E.W./Schlesinger, L.A. (1994). Putting the Service-Profit Chain to Work. In: Harvard Business Review. Vol. 72(2). 164-174.

Hill, R.P. and Mazis, M.B. (1986). Measuring Emotional Responses to Advertising. In: Advances in Consumer Research. Vol. 13. 164-169.

Hirschman, E.C. and Holbrook, M.B. (1982). Hedonic Consumption: Emerging Concepts, Methods and Propositions. In: Journal of Marketing. Vol. 46 (Summer). 92-101.

Hirschman, E.C. and Thompson, C.J. (1997). Why Media Matter: Toward a Richer Understanding of Consumers' Relationships with Advertising and Mass Media. In: Journal of Advertising. Vol. 26 (Spring). 43-60.

Hite, R. and Fraser, C. (1990). Configuration and coordination of global advertising. In: Journal of Business Research. Vol. 21. 335-344.

Hochbaum, G.M. (1958). Public Participation in Medical Screening Programs: A Socio-psychological Study. (Public Health Service Publication No. 572). Washington, DC: Government Printing Office.

Hoeck, J. and Gendall, P. (2002). Direct-to-Consumer Advertising Down Under: An Alternative Perspective and Regulatory Framework. In: Journal of Public Policy and Marketing. Vol. 21. 202-212.

Hoek, J./Gendall, P./Feetham, P. (2001). Could less be more? An Analysis of Direct to Consumer Advertising of Prescription Medicines. In: Marketing Bulletin. Vol. 12. 1-15.

Hofstede, F.T./Steenkamp, J-B.E.M./Wedel, M. (1999). International Market Segmentation Based on Consumer Product Relations. In: Journal of Marketing Research. Vol. 36(1). 1-17.

Hofstede, G. (1980). Culture's Consequences: International Differences in Work-Related Values. Thousand Oaks, CA: Sage.

Hofstede, G. (1984). National cultures and corporate cultures. In: Samovar, L.A. and Porter, R.E. (eds.). Communication between Cultures. Belmont, CA: Wadsworth.

Hofstede, G. (1990). Expressions of culture at different levels. Working paper 90-006. University of Limburg, Netherlands.

Hofstede, G. (2001). Culture's consequences: Comparing values, behaviors, institutions, and organizations across nations. Thousand Oaks: Sage.

Hofstede, G. (2005). Cultures and Organizations. Software of the Mind. 2nd ed. New York: McGraw-Hill.

Hofstede, G. (2010). The GLOBE debate: Back to relevance. In: Journal of International Business Studies. Vol. 41 (November/December). 1339-1346.

Hofstede, G. and Bond, M.H. (1988). The Confucius Connection: From cultural roots to economic growth. In: Organizational Dynamics. Vol. 16 (Spring). 5-21.

Hofstede, G. and Hofstede, G.J. (2005). Cultures and Organizations. Software of the Mind. 2nd ed. New York: McGraw-Hill.

Hofstede, G. and Minkov, M. (2010). Cultures and Organizations - Software of the Mind: Intercultural Cooperation and Its Importance for Survival. New York: McGraw Hill.

Hofstede, G./Hofstede, G.J./Minkov, M. (2010). Cultures and Organizations - Software of the Mind: Intercultural Cooperation and Its Importance for Survival. New York: McGraw Hill.

Hohn, M. D. (1997). Empowerment health education in adult literacy: A guide for public health and adult literacy practitioners, policy makers, and founders. US National Institute for Literacy. Retrieved from http://www.eric.ed.gov/PDFS/ED425342.pdf (accessed 10.02.2013)

Holbrook, M.B. (1978). Beyond Attitude Structure: Toward the Information Determinants of Attitude. In: Journal of Marketing Research. Vol. 15. 545-556.

Holbrook, M.B. (1984). Emotion in the Consumption Experience: Mr. Blandings Builds a New Model of the Human Consumer. In: Peterson, R.A./Hoyer, W.D./Wilson, W.R. (eds.).The Role of Affect in Consumer Behavior: Emerging Theories and Applications. Austin, TX: University of Texas Press.

Holbrook, M.B. and Batra, R. (1987). Assessing the Role of Emotions as Mediators of Consumer Responses to Advertising. In: Journal of Consumer Research. Vol. 14. 404-420.

Holbrook, M.B. and Hirschman, E.C. (1982). The Experiential Aspects of Consumption: Consumer Fantasies, Feelings, and Fun. In: Journal of Consumer Research, Vol. 9 (September), 132-140.

Hollon, M.F. (1999). Direct-to-consumer Marketing of Prescription Drugs: Creating consumer demand. In: Journal of the American Medical Association. Vol. 281. 382-384.

Holt, D./Quelch, J.A./Taylor, E.L. (2004). How global brands compete. In: Harvard Business Review. Vol. 82(9). 68-75.

Holt, D.B. (2002). Why Do Brands Cause Trouble? A Dialectical Theory of Consumer Culture and Branding. In: Journal of Consumer Research. Vol. 29 (June). 70–90.

Holton, R.J. and Turner, B.S. (1986). Talcott Pearsons on Economy and Society. London: Routledge.

Homburg, C. and Baumgartner, H. (1998): Beurteilung von Kausalmodellen. Bestandsaufnahmen und Anwendungsempfehlungen. In: Homburg, C. and Hildebrandt, L. (eds.). Die Kausalanalyse – Instrument der empirischen betriebswirtschaftlichen Forschung. Stuttgart: Schäffer-Poeschel. 343–369.

Homer, P.M. (1990). The Mediating Role of Attitude toward the Ad: Some Additional Evidence. In: Journal of Marketing Research. Vol. 27. 78-86.

Homer, P.M. (2008). Perceived Quality and Image: When All Is Not 'Rosy'. In: Journal of Business Research. Vol. 61(7). 715-723.

Hong, J.W. and Zinkhan, G.M. (1995). Self-concept and advertising effectiveness; the influence of congruency, conspicuousness, and response mode. In: Psychology and Marketing. Vol. 12. 53-77.

Honneth, A./Knödler-Bunte, E./Widmann, A. (1981). The Dialectics of Rationalization: An Interview with Jürgen Habermas. In: Telos. Vol. 49. 4-31.

Hooper, D./Coughlan, J./Mullen, M.R. (2008). Structural Equation Modelling: Guidelines for Determining Model Fit. In: The Electronic Journal of Business Research Methods. Vol. 6(1). 53-60.

Horn, J.L. (1991). Comments on 'issues in factorial invariance'. In: Collins, L.M. and Horn, J.L. (eds.). Best methods for the analysis of change. Washington, DC: American Psychological Association. 114-125.

Horn, J.L. and McArdle, J.J. (1992). A practical guide to measurement invariance in aging research. In: Experimental Aging Research. Vol. 18(3). 117-144.

Horn, J.L./McArdle, J.J./Mason, R. (1983). When is invariance not invariant? A practical scientist's view of the ethereal concept of factorial invariance. In: The Southern Psychologist. Vol. 1. 179-188.

Hornik, R. (ed.) (2002). Public Health Communication: Evidence for Behavior Change. Hillsdale, NJ: Lawrence Erlbaum Associates.

Hornik, R.C. (2002). Public health communication: Making sense of contradictory evidence. In: Hornik, R.C. (ed.). Public Health Communication: Evidence for behavior change. Mahwah, NJ: Lawrence Erlbaum. 1-22.

House of Commons Health Committee. (2005). The influence of the pharmaceutical industry. Vol 1. London: The Stationery Office.

House, R. J./Hanges, P.J./Javidan, M./Dorfman, P.W./Gupta, V. (eds.) (2004). Culture, leadership, and organizations. The GLOBE study of 62 societies. Thousand Oaks, CA: Sage.

House, R.J./Quigley, N./de Luque, M.S. (2010). Insights from Project GLOBE: Extending global advertising research through a contremporary framework. In: International Journal of Advertising. Vol. 29(1). 111-139.

Houston, M.J. and Rothschild, M.L. (1977). A Paradigm for Research on Consumer Involvement. Working Paper. Graduate School of Business: University of Wisconsin-Madison.

Hovland, C.I./Janis, I.L./Kelley, J.J. (1953). Communication and Persuasion. New Haven: Yale University Press.

Howard, D.G. and Ryans, J.K. Jr. (1989). Advertising Executives' Perceptions of Satellite TV's Potential Impact on the European Market. In: European Journal of Marketing. Vol. 23(5). 22-30.

Howard, J.A. and Woodside, A.G. (1977). Personal Values affecting consumer psychology. In: Pitts, R.E. and Woodside, A.G. (eds.). Personal values and consumer psychology. Lexington, MA: D.C. Health and Company. 35-54.

Hu, L.T. and Bentler, P.M. (1999). Cutoff Criteria for Fit Indexes in Covariance Structure Analysis: Conventional Criteria versus New Alternatives. In: Structural Equation Modeling. Vol. 6 (1). 1-55.

Hudson, S./Hung, C.L./Padley, L. (2002). Cross-National Standardization of Advertisements: A Study of the Effectiveness of TV Advertisements targeted at Chinese Canadians in Canada. In: International Journal of Advertising. Vol. 21. 345-366.

Huh, J./DeLorme, D.E./Reid, L.N. (2004). Media Credibility and Informativeness of Direct-to-Consumer Prescription Drug Advertising. In: Health Marketing Quarterly. Vol. 21(3). 27-60.

Huh, J./DeLorme, D.E./Reid, L.N. (2012). Skepticism towards DTC advertising: A comparative study of Korean and Caucasian Americans. In: International Journal of Advertising. Vol. 31(1). 147-168.

Hunter, M.S./O'Dea, I./Britten, N. (1997). Decision-making and hormone replacement therapy: a qualitative analysis. In: Social Science and Medicine. Vol. 45(10). 1541–1548.

Hurd Clarke, L./Griffin, M., et al. (2008). Failing bodies: Body image and multiple chronic conditions in later life. In: Qualitative Health Research. Vol. 18. 1084-1095.

IGEPHA (2011). IGEPHA – OTC-Markt. Retrieved from http://igepha.at/de/der_markt/otc-markt (accessed 19.12.2014)

Illich I. (1975). Medical nemesis. New York: Pantheon.

Illich, I. (1975). The medicalization of life. In: Journal of Medical Ethics. Vol. 1(2). 73-77.

Illich, I. (1976). Medical Nemesis – The Expropriation of Health. New York, NY: Penguin.

Institute of Medicine. (2003). Health Literacy: A Prescription to End Confusion. Retrieved from http://www.nap.edu/openbook.php?record_id=10883 (accessed 11.04.2014)

Iriart, C./Franco, T./Merhy, E.E. (2011). The creation of the health consumer: challenges on health sector regulation after managed care era. In: Globalization and Health. Vol. 7(2). 1-12.

Irwin, H. (1989). Health communication: the research agenda. In: Media Information Australia. Vol. 54. 32-40.

Janis, I.L. (1954). Personality Correlates of Persuasion. In: Journal of Personality. Vol. 22(1). 504-518.

Jansson, C./Marlow, N./Bristow, M. (2004). The influence of colour on visual search times in cluttered environments. In: Journal of Marketing Communications. Vol. 10 (September). 183-193.

Jansson-Boyd, C.V. (2010). Consumer Psychology. New York: Open University Press.

Janz, N. K. and Becker, M. H. (1984). The health belief model: A decade later. In: Health Education Quarterly. Vol. 11(1). 1-47.

Jarvis, C.B./Mackenzie, S.B./Padsakoff, P.M. (2003). A Critical View of Construct Indicators and Measurement Model Misspecification in Marketing and Consumer Research. In: Journal of Consumer Research. Vol. 30 (September). 199-218.

Javidan, M. (2004). Performance Orientation. In: House, R.J./Hanges, P.J./Javidan, M. (eds.). Culture, Leadership, and Organizations: The GLOBE Study of 62 Societies. Thousand Oaks, CA: Sage. 239-281.

Jenkins, D.C. (2003). Building better health: a handbook for behavioral change. Washington, D.C.: PAHO.

Jensen, T.D./Carlson, L./Tripp, C. (1989). The Dimensionality of Involvement: An Empirical Test. In: Advances of Consumer Research. Vol. 16. 680-689.

Jewson, N. (1976). The Disappearance of the Sick Man from Medical Cosmology 1770-1870. In: Sociology. Vol. 10. 225-244.

Johansson, J.K. (1989). Determinants and Effects of the Use of 'Made in' Labels. In: International Marketing Review. Vol. 6(1). 47-58.

Johar, J.S. and Sirgy, J. (1991). Value-expressive versus utilitarian advertising appeals: When and why to use which appeal. In: Journal of Advertising. Vol. 20. 23-33.

Johnson, A. and Proctor, R.W. (2004). Attention: Theory and Practice. New York: SAGE Publications.

Jonas, S./Goldsteen, R./Goldsteen, K. (2007). An introduction to the U.S. health care system. New York: Springer Publishing.

Jones, S.C. and Owen, N. (2006). Using fear appeals to promote cancer screening—are we scaring the wrong people? In: International Journal of Nonprofit and Voluntary Sector Marketing. Vol. 11(2). Special Issue. 93-103.

Jöreskog, K. and Sörbom, D. (1996). LISREL 8: User's Reference Guide. Chicago, IL: Scientific Software International Inc.

Jöreskog, K.G. (1971). Simultaneous factor analysis in several populations. In: Psychometrika. Vol. 36. 409–426.

Kabasakal, H. and Badur, M. (2004). Humane Orientation in Societies, Organizations, and Leader Attributes. In: House, R.J./Hanges, P.J./Javidan, M. (eds.). Culture, Leadership, and Organizations: The GLOBE Study of 62 Societies. Thousand Oaks, CA: Sage. 564-601.

Kahle, L.R. (ed.). (1983). Social values and social change: Adaptions to life in America. New York: Praeger.

Kamins, M.A. (1989). Celebrity and Non-Celebrity Advertising in a Two-Sided Context. In: Journal of Advertising Research. Vol. 18. 34-42.

Kamins, M.A. (1990). An Investigation into the 'Match-Up' Hypothesis in Celebrity Advertising: When Beauty May be Only Skin Deep. In: Journal of Advertising. Vol. 19(1). 4-13.

Kamins, M.A./Brand, M.J./Hoeke, S.A./Moe, J.C. (1989). Two-sided versus one-sided celebrity endorsements in a two-sided context. In: Journal of Advertising Research. Vol. 18(2). 4-10.

Kanso, A. (1992). International Advertising Strategies: Global Commitment to Local Vision. In: Journal of Advertising Research. Vol. 32(1). 10-14.

Kantar Health. (2014). Healthcare Consumer OTC/DTC Study (MARS). Retrieved from http://kantarmedia.us/product/healthcare-consumer-otcdtc-study-mars (accessed 22.11.2014)

Kapferer, J.-N. and Laurent, G. (1985). Consumer Involvement Profiles: A new practical approach to consumer involvement. In: Journal of Advertising Research. Vol. 25(6). 48-56.

Kaplan, D. (1990). Evaluating and modifying covariance structure models: A review and recommendation. In: Multivariate Behavioral Research. Vol. 25. 137-155.

Kar, S.B./Alcalay, R./Alex, S. (eds.) (2001). Health Communication: A Multicultural Perspective. Thousand Oaks, CA: Sage.

Kar, S.B./Pascual, C.A./Chickering, K. L. (1999). Empowerment of women for health promotion: a meta-analysis. In: Social Science and Medicine. Vol. 49. 1431–1460.

Kasen, S./Vaughan, R.D./Walter, H.J. (1992). Self-efficacy for AIDS: preventive behaviors among tenth grade students. In: Health Education Quarterly. Vol. 19. 187-202.

Kashima, E.S. and Kashima, Y. (1998). Culture and Language: The Case of Cultural Dimensions and Personal Pronoun Use. In: Journal of Cross-Cultural Psychology. Vol. 29(3). 461-486.

Kasl, S.A. and Cobb, S. (1966). Health behavior, illness behavior, and sick role behavior: 1. Health and illness behavior. In: Archivess of Environmental Health. Vol. 12. 246-266.

Kassarjian, H.H. and Kassarjian, W.M. (1979). Attitudes under Low Commitment Conditions. In: Maloney, J.C. and Silverman, B. (eds.). Attitude Research Plays for High Stakes. Chicago: American Marketing Association. 3-15.

Kasser, T. and Kanner, A.D. (2003). Where is the psychology of consumer culture? In: Kasser, T. and Kanner, A.D. (eds). Psychology and consumer culture: The struggle for a good life in a materialistic world. Washington, DC: American Psychological Association.

Kasser, T. and Kanner, A.D. (eds) (2003). Psychology and consumer culture: The struggle for a good life in a materialistic world. Washington, DC: American Psychological Association.

Keillor, B. D./D'Amico, M./Horton, V. (2001). Global consumer tendencies. In: Psychology and Marketing. Vol. 18. 1-19.

Keller, K.L. (1991). Memory and Evaluation Effects in Competitive Advertising Environments. In: Journal of Consumer Research. Vol. 17 (March). 463-476.

Kelley, H.H. (1947). Two Functions of Reference Groups. In: Swanson, G.E./Newcomb, T.M./Hartley, E.L. (eds.). Readings in Social Psychology. New York: Holt, Rinehart and Winston. 410-414.

Kelman, H. (1953). Attitude Change as a Function of Response Restriction. In: Human Relations. Vol. 6. 185-214.

Kelman, H.C. (1961). Process of opinion change. In: Public Opinion Quarterly. Vol. 25(1). 57-78.

Kennedy, S.H. (1977). Nurturing Corporate Images: Total Communication or Ego Trip? In: European Journal of Marketing. Vol. 11 (3). 119-164.

Kickbusch, I. (1989). Self-care in health promotion. In: Social Science and Medicine. Vol. 29. 125-130.

Kim, H./Gwang, J.K./Park, H.W./Rice, R.E. (2007). Configurations of relationships in different media: FtF, email, instant messenger, mobile phone, and SMS. In: Journal of Computer-Mediated Communication. Vol. 12(4). 1183–1207.

Kim, K.H./Cramond, B./Bandalos, D. L. (2006). The latent structure and measurement invariance of scores on the Torrance tests of creative thinking-figural. In: Educational and Psychological Measurement. Vol. 66. 459–477.

Kinnear, T. C./Bernhadt, K. L./Krentler, K. A. (1995). Principles of marketing. 4th ed. New York: Longman.

Kirscht, J. P. (1988). The health belief model and predictions of health actions. In: Gochman, D. (ed.). Health Behavior. New York: Plenum Press. 27-41.

Kirscht, J.P. (1974). The Health Belief Model and Illness Behavior. In: Health Education Monographs. Vol. 2. 387-408.

Kitayama, S./Markus, H.R./Matsumoto, H./Norassakkunkit, V. (1997). Individual and Collectivistic processes in the construction of the self: Self-Enhancement in the United States and self-criticism in Japan. In: Journal of Personality and Social Psychology. Vol. 72. 1245-1276.

Kittinger, P. and Herrick, D (2005). Patient power: over-the-counter drugs. Retrieved from http://www.ncpa.org/pdfs/ba524.pdf (accessed 08.10.2013)

Kleppner, O. (1979). Advertising Procedure. 7th ed. New Jersey: Prentice Hall.

Kline, R.B. (2005). Principles and Practice of Structural Equation Modeling. 2nd ed. New York: The Guilford Press.

Kline. (2010). OTC Drugs: U.S. Competitor Cost Structures 2010. Retrieved from http://www.klinegroup.com/reports/brochures/y617b/factsheet.pdf (accessed 14.03.2013)

Klinger, E. (1975). Consequences of commitment to and disengagement from incentives. In: Psychological Review. Vol. 82. 1–25.

Kluckhohn, F. and Strodtbeck, R. (1961). Variations in Value Orientations. Evanston, IL: Row Peterson.

Koco, L. (2000). Service bar to rise in next decade. In: National Underwriter. Vol. 104(19). 27-28.

Koinig, I. (2012). Pharmaceutical advertising: A content analysis of over-the-counter drug promotions in Germany/Austria and the United States with focus on ad design, gender portrayal and ad appeal. Master's thesis submitted at the Alpen-Adria-Universität Klagenfurt (unpublished).

Koinig, I. and Diehl, S. (2013). Standaradized Pharmaceutical Advertising? An International Comparison of Non-Prescription Drug Advertising with Regard to Ad Appeal in General and CSR Appeal in Particular. Paper presented at the Conference on Corporate Communication 2013. New York. June 4-7.

Kotler, P. (1972). What Consumerism means for Marketers. In: Harvard Business Review. Vol. 50. 48-57.

Kotler, P. and Roberto, E.L. (1989). Social Marketing. Strategies for Changing Public Behavior. New York: Free Press.

Kotlikoff, L.J. and Burns, S. (2005). The coming generational storm: What you need to know about America's economic future. Cambridge, MA: MIT Press.

Kozinets, R. (2002), Can consumers escape the market? Emancipatory illuminations from burning man, In: Journal of Consumer Research. Vol. 29. 20-38.

Kozinets, R. and Handelmann, J. (2004), Adversaries of consumption: consumer movements, activism and ideology. In: Journal of Consumer Research. Vol. 28(1). 67-88.

Kracov, D. and Davar, M. (2010). The International Comparative Legal Guide to: Pharmaceutical Advertising 2010. A practical cross-border insight into pharmaceutical advertising – USA. 321-331. Retrieved from http://www.iclg.co.uk/khadmin/Publications/pdf/3789.pdf (accessed 10.05.2011)

Kreps, D. (1979). A Representation Theorem for Preference for Flexibility. In: Econometrica. Vol. 41. 565-577.

Krips, H. (2010). The Politics of the Gaze: Foucault, Lacan and Zizek. In: Culture Unbound. Vol. 2. 91-102.

Krisberg, K. (2004). Millions of Americans Suffer from Low Health Literacy. Retrieved from http://www.medscape.com/viewarticle/479968 (accessed 15.06.2014)

Kroeber-Riel, W. (1986). Nonverbal Measurement of Emotional Advertising Effects. In: Olsen, J.C. and Sentis, K. (eds.). Advertising and Consumer Psychology. Vol. 3. New York: Westport.

Kroeber-Riel, W. and Esch, F.-R. (2011). Strategie und Technik der Werbung. 7th ed. Stuttgart: Kohlhammer.

Kroeber-Riel, W./Weinberg, A./Gröppel-Klein. (2009). Konsumentenerhalten. 9th ed. Munich: Vahlen.

Krugman, H. (1975). What makes advertising effective? In: Harvard Business Review. Vol. 53. 96-103.

Krugman, H.E. (1965). The Impact of Television Advertising: Learning Without Involvement. In: Public Opinion Quarterly. Vol. 29. 349-356.

Kuhlmann, E. and Kolip, P. (2005). Gender und Public Health. Weinheim: Juventa.

Kurman, J. (2002). Measured cross-cultural differences in self-enhancement and the sensitivity of the self-enhancement measure to modesty response. In: Cross-Cultural Research. Vol. 36. 73-95.

La Ferle, C./Edwards, S./Lee, W. (2008). Culture, Attitudes, and Media Patterns in China, Taiwan, and the U.S.: Balancing Standardization and Localization Decisions. In: Journal of Global Marketing. Vol. 21. 191-205.

Lacan, J. (1981). The Four Fundamental Concepts of Psychoanalysis. New York: Norton.

Laczniak, R.N./Kempf, D.S./Muehling, D.D. (1999). Advertising Message Involvement: The Role of Enduring and Situational Factors. In: Journal of Current Issues and Research in Advertising. Vol. 21(1). 51-61.

Laczniak, R.N./Muehling, D.D./Grossbart, S. (1989). Manipulating Message Involvement in Advertising Research. In: Journal of Advertising. Vol. 18(2). 28-38.

Lafferty, B. A. and Goldsmith, R. E. (1999). Corporate credibility's role in consumers' attitudes and purchase intentions when a high versus a low credibility endorser is used in the Ad. In: Journal of Business Research. Vol. 44. 109-116.

Lambin, J.J. (1976). Advertising, Competition, and Market Conduct in Oligopoly over time. Amsterdam: North-Holland.

Lane, D.R./Harrington, N.G./Donohew, L./Zimmerman, R.S. (2006). Dimensions and validation of a perceived message cognition value scale. In: Communication Research Reports. Vol. 23. 149-161.

Langer, E. and Rodin, J. (1976). The Effects of Choice and Enhanced Personal Responsibility for the Aged: A Field Experiment in an Institutional Setting. In: Journal of Personality and Social Psychology. Vol. 34. 191-198.

Langer, E.J. (1983). The Psychology of Control. Beverly Hills, CA: SAGE.

Lappé, M. (1979). Holistic health: a valuable approach to medical care. In: Western Journal of Medicine. Vol. 131(6). 475-478.

Laurent, G. and Kapferer, J-N. (1985). Measuring Consumer Involvement Profiles. In: Journal of Marketing Research. Vol. 22 (February). 41-53.

Lau-Walker, M (2006) A conceptual care model for individualised care approach in cardiac rehabilitation – combining both illness representation and self-efficacy. In: British Journal of Health Psychology. Vol. 11. 103-117.

Lawton, J. (2003). Lay Experiences of Health and Illness: State of Knowledge and Perspectives for Research. In: Sociology of Health and Illness. Vol. 25. 23–40.

Lee, S.Y./Hwang, H./Hawkins, R./Pingree, S. (2008). Interplay of negative emotion and health self-efficacy on the use of health information and its outcomes. In: Communication Research. Vol. 35(2). 358-381.

Lefebre, R.C. (2013). Social Marketing and Social Change: Strategies and Tools for Improving Health, Well-Being, and the Environment. San Francisco, CA: Jossey-Bass.

Lefebvre, P. and Miller, G. (2006). Pharmaceutical giants and corporate social responsibility: A hard pill to swallow: Corporate Social Responsibility. Retrieved from http://www.rockhurst.edu/news/events/images/projecti/lefebvre.pdf (accessed 28.10.2013)

Leonidou, L.C. and Leonidou, C.N. (2009). Rational Versus Emotional Appeals in Newspaper Advertising: Copy, Art, and Layout Differences. In: Journal of Promotion Management. Vol. 15. 522-546.

Leventhal, H. and Deifenbach, M. (1991). The active side of illness cognition. In: Skelton, J. A. and Croyle, R. T. (eds.). Mental Representation in Health and Illness. New York: Springer. 247-272.

Leventhal, H./Benyamini, Y./Brownlee, S./Deifenbach, M./Leventhal, E.A./Patrick-Miller, L./Robitaille, C. (1997). Illness representations: theoretical foundations. In: Petrie, K. J. and Weinman, J. (eds.). Perceptions of health and illness. Amsterdam, Harwood Academic. 155-188.

Leventhal, H./Meyer, D./Nerenz, D. (1980). The common sense representation of illness danger. In: Rachman, S. (ed.). Contributions to medical psychology. New York: Pergamon Press. 7-30.

Leventhal, H./Nerenz, D. R./Steele, D. J. (1984). Illness representations and coping with health threats. In: Baum, A./Taylor, S. E./Singer, J. E. (eds.). Handbook of Psychology and health. Vol. IV: Psychological Aspects of Health. Hillsdale, NJ: Erlbaum. 219-252.

Levitt, G. (1996). Advertising Prescription Drugs Directly to the Consumer: Can FDA Stop Worrying and Learn to Love Direct-To-Consumer Advertising? Retrieved from http://www.venable.com/advertising-prescription-drugs-directly-to-the-consumer-can-fda-stop-worrying-and-learn-to-love-direct-to-consumer-advertising-04-01-1996/ (accessed 02.06.2014)

Levitt, T. (1983). The globalization of markets. In: Harvard Business Review. Vol. 61(3). 69-81.

Levy Simon, B. (1994). The Empowerment Tradition in American Social Work: A History, New York: Columbia University Press.

Levy, R. (1999). Give and Take. Cambridge, MA: Harvard Business School Press.

Lewis, E.S. (1903). Catch-Line and Argument. In: The Book-Keeper. Vol. 15 (February). 124.

Limbu, Y. and Torres, I.M. (2009). The Effects of Involvement and Ad Type on Attitude toward Direct-to-Consumer Advertising of prescription drugs. In: Journal of Health and Human Services Administration. Vol. 32(1). 107-138.

Lin, C. (2001). Defining and defending the "social": a Chinese tale. In: Hitotsubashi Journal of Social Studies. Vol. 33(1). 57-68.

Lindström, B. and Eriksson, M. (2005). Salutogenesis. In: Journal of Epidemiology and Community Health. Vol. 59. 440-442.

Lindström, B. and Eriksson, M. (2005). The salutogenic perspective and mental health. In: Herrman, H./Saxena, S./Moodie, R. (eds.) Promoting mental health. Concepts, emerging evidence, practice. Geneva. WHO. 50-51.

Link, G.L. (1988). Global advertising: an update. In: The Journal of Consumer Marketing. Vol. 5(2). 69-74.

Lippke, S. and Ziegelmann, J.P. (2006). Understanding and modeling health behavior change: The multi-stage model of health behavior change. In: Journal of Health Psychology. Vol. 11. 37-50.

Locander, W.B. and Hermann, P.W. (1980). The Effect of Self-Confidence and Anxiety on Information Seeking in Consumer Risk Reduction. In: Journal of Marketing Research. Vol. 16 (May). 268-274.

Lock, M. (1987). Models and practice in medicine: menopause as syndrome or life transition? In: Hahn, R. and Gaines, A. (eds.). Physicians of Western Medicine. Anthropological Approaches to Theory and Practice. Dodrecht: D. Reidel. 115-140.

Locker, D. (1981). Symptoms and Illness: the cognitive organization of disorder. London: Tavistock.

Loibl, C./Cho, S.H./Diekmann, F./Batte, M.T. (2009), Consumer Self-Confidence in Searching for Information. In: Journal of Consumer Affairs. Vol. 43(1). 26-55.

Lord, C.G. (1980). Schemas and Images as Memory Aids: Two Modes of Processing Social Information. In: Journal of Personality and Social Psychology. Vol. 38 (February). 257-269.

Lorig, K. R. and Holman, H. (2003). Self-management education: history, definition, outcomes and mechanisms. In: Annals of Behavioral Medicine. Vol. 26(1). 1-7.

Lucas, K. and Lloyd, B. (2005). Health Promotion: Evidence and Experience. London: Sage.

Lumme-Sandt, K./Hervonen, A./Jylhä, M. (2000). Interpretative repertoires of medication among the oldest-old. In: Social Science and Medicine. Vol. 50(12), 1843-1850.

Lupton, D. (1994). Medicine as Culture: Illness, Disease and the Body in Western Societies. London: Sage.

Lupton, D. (1995). The Imperative of Health: Public Health and the Regulated Body. London: Sage.

Lupton, D. (1997). Foucault and the Medicalization critique. In: Petersen, A. and Bunton, R. (eds.). Foucault, Health and Medicine. London: Routledge. 94-110.

Lupton, D. (2012). Medicine as Culture: Illness, Disease and the Body. 3rd ed. London: SAGE.

Lutz, R.J. (1975). Changing Brand Attitudes through Modifications of Cognitive Structure. In: Journal of Consumer Research. Vol. 1. 49-59.

Lutz, R.J. (1985) Affective and cognitive antecedents of attitude toward the ad: A conceptual framework. In: Alwitt, L.F. and Mitchell, A. A. (eds.).Psychological Processes and Advertising effects: Theory, Research and Application. Hillsdale, NJ: Lawrence Erlbaum Associates. 45-63.

Lutz, R.J. (1991). The Role of Attitude Theory in Marketing. In: Kassarjian, H.H., and Robertson, T.S. (eds.). Perspectives in Consumer Behavior. Englewood Cliffs, NJ: Prentice Hall. 317-339.

Lutz, R.J. and Swasy, J.L. (1977). Integrating Cognitive Structure and Cognitive Response Approaches to Monitoring Communications Effects. In: Advances in Consumer Research. Vol. 4. 363-371.

Lutz, R.J./MacKenzie, S.B./Belch, G.E. (1983). Attitude toward the Ad as a Mediator of Advertising Effectiveness. Determinants and Consequences. In: Advances in Consumer Research. Vol. 10. 532-539.

Lyles, A. (2002). Direct Marketing of Pharmaceuticals to consumers. In: Annual Review of Public Health. Vol. 23. 73-91.

Lynch, J.G. Jr. (1999). Theory and external validity. In: The Journal of Academy of Marketing Science. Vol. 27 (3). 367-376.

Lynch, M. (1984). Harvard's Levitt called global marketing guru. In: Advertising Age. 25 June 1984. 49.

Lynch, P.J. and Horton, S. (1999). Web Style Guide: Basic Design for Creating Websites. New Haven, CT: Yale University Press.

Lyons, A. and Chamberlain, K. (2006). Health psychology: A critical introduction. Cambridge: Cambridge University Press.

MacCallum, R./Rosnowski, M./Mar, C./Reith, J. (1994). Alternative Strategies for Cross-Validation of Covariance Structure Models. In: Multivariate Behavioral Research. Vol. 29. 1-32.

MacCallum, R.C. and Austin, J.T. (2000). Applications of structural equation modeling in psychological research. In: Annual Review of Psychology. Vol. 51. 201-226.

MacCallum, R.C. and Hong, S. (1997). Power analysis in covariance structure modeling using GFI and AGFI. In: Multivariate Behavioral Research. Vol. 32. 193-210.

MacCallum, R.C./Browne, M.W./Sugawara, H., M. (1996). Power Analysis and Determination of Sample Size for Covariance Structure Modeling. In: Psychological Methods. Vol. 1 (2). 130-149.

MacCallum, R.C./Roznowski, M./Necowitz, L.B. (1992). Model modification in covariance structure analysis: The problem of capitalization on chance. In: Psychological Bulletin. Vol. 111. 490-504.

MacInnes, A. and Milburn, K. (1994). Belief systems and social circumstances influencing the health choices of people in Lochaber. In: Health Education Journal. Vol. 53. 58-72.

MacIntyre, A. (1985). After Virtue. London: Duckworth.

MacKenzie, S.B. and Lutz, R.J. (1989). An Empirical Examination of the Structural Antecedents of Attitude toward the Ad in an Advertising Pretesting Context. In: Journal of Marketing. Vol. 53. 48-65.

MacKenzie, S.B./Lutz R.J./Belch, G.E. (1986). The role of attitude toward the ad as a mediator of advertising effectiveness: A test of competing explanations. In: Journal of Marketing Research. Vol. 23(2). 130-143.

Maddux, J. E. and Rogers, R. W. (1973). Protection motivation and self-efficacy: A revised theory of fear appeals and attitude change. In: Journal of Experimental Social Psychology. Vol. 19. 469-479.

Magazines Canada. (2011). Fast Facts: How Magazine Advertising Works. Retrieved from http://www.magazinescanada.ca/uploads/File/AdServices/FastFacts/2011ConsumerEN/FastFacts2011Final.pdf (accessed 19.03.2014)

Magazines.org. (2012). MagazineMedia: extraordinary content, premium audiences, immersive experiences. Factbook 2012/13. Retrieved from http://www.magazine.org/sites/default/files/factbook-2012.pdf (accessed 01.01.2014)

Magen, R.H. and Glajchen, M. (1999). Cancer support groups: Client outcome and the context of group process. In: Research on Social Group Practice. Vol. 9. 541-554.

Magnusson, P./Wilson, R.T./Zdravkovic, S./Zhou, J.X./Westjohn, S.A. (2008). Breaking through the cultural clutter: a comparative assessment of multiple cultural and institutional frameworks. In: International Marketing Review. Vol. 25(2). 183–201.

Maibach, E. and Murphy, D.A. (1995). Self-efficacy in Helath Promotion Research and Practice: Conceptualization and Measurement. In: Health Education Research: Theory and Practice. Vol. 10(1). 37-50.

Maibach, E.W./Flora, J.A./Nass, C. (1991). Changes in self-efficacy and health behavior in response to a minimal contact community health campaign. In: Health Communication. Vol. 3(1). 1–15.

Maibach, E.W./Weber, D./Massett, H./Hancock, G.R./Price, S. (2006). Understanding consumers' health information preferences: Development and validation of a brief screening instruments. In: Journal of Health Communication. Vol. 11. 717-736.

Maignan, I. and Ralston, D.A. (2002). Corporate Social Responsibility in Europe and the U.S.: Insights from Businesses' Self-presentations. In: Journal of International Business Studies. Vol. (33)3. 497-514.

Maiman, L. A. and Becker, M. H. (1974). The Health Belief Model: Origins and correlates in psychological theory. In: Health Education Monographs. Vol. 2. 336-353.

Main, K.J./Argo, J.J./Huhmann, B.A. (2004). Pharmaceutical Advertising in the USA: information or influence? In: International Journal of Advertising. Vol. 23. 119-112.

Makovsky. (2015). Fifth Annual "Pulse of Online Health" Survey Finds 66% of Americans Eager To Leverage Digital Tools To Manage Personal Health. Retrieved from http://www.makovsky.com/insights/articles/733 (01.03.2015)

Maletzke, G. (1976). Intercultural and international communication. In: Fischer, H.-D. and Merrill, J.C. (eds.). International and intercultural communication. New York: Hastings House.

Malinowski, B. (1944). A Scientific Theory of Culture and Other Essays. Chapel Hill, NC: University of North Carolina.

Malmelin, N. (2010). What Is Advertising Literacy? Exploring the Dimensions of Advertising Literacy. In: Journal of Visual Literacy. Vol. 29(2). 129-142.

Maloney, J.C. (1963). Is advertising believability really important? In: Journal of Marketing. Vol. 27(4). 1-8.

Mandel, N./Petrova, P.K./Cialdini, R.B. (2006). Images of Success and the Preference for Luxury Brands. In: Journal of Consumer Psychology. Vol. 16(1). 57–69.

Manoff, R.K. (1985). Social Marketing: a New Imperative for Public Health. New York: Praeger.

MarketLine. (2013). Europe – OTC Pharmaceuticals Industry Profile: Europe. Datamonitor Group.

MarketLine. (2013). Global – OTC Pharmaceuticals Industry Profile. Datamonitor Group.

MarketLine. (2014). OTC Pharmaceuticals Industry Profile: Brazil. Datamonitor Group.

MarketLine. (2014). OTC Pharmaceuticals Industry Profile: Europe. Datamonitor Group.

MarketLine. (2014). OTC Pharmaceuticals Industry Profile: Germany. Datamonitor Group.

MarketLine. (2014). OTC Pharmaceuticals: Global Industry Profile. Datamonitor Group.

MarketLine. (2014). United States – OTC Pharmaceuticals Industry Profile. Datamonitor Group.

Marks, R./Allegrante, J. P./Lorig, K. (2005). A review and synthesis of research evidence for self-efficacy-enhancing interventions for reducing chronic disability: implications for health education practice (part II). In: Health Promotion Practice. Vol. 6(2). 148-156.

Markus, H.R. and Kitayama, S. (1991). Culture and the self: implications for cognition, emotion and motivation. In: Psychological Review, Vol. 98(6), 224–253.

Marlatt, G. A. (2002). Harm reduction: Pragmatic strategies for managing high-risk behaviors. New York: Guilford.

Marlatt, G.A./Baer, J.S./Quigley, L.A. (1995). Self-efficacy and addictive behavior. In: Bandura, A. (ed.). Self-efficacy in changing societies. New York: Cambridge University Press. 289-315.

Marsh, H.W. and Hocevar, D. (1985). Application of confirmatory factor analysis to the study of self-concept: First- and higher order factor models and their invariance across groups. In: Psychological Bulletin. Vol. 97(3). 562-582.

Marshall, B.L. (2009). Sexual medicine, sexual bodies and the pharmaceutical imagination. In: Science as Culture. Vol. 18(2). 133-149.

Marshall, R. and Na, W. (2003). An experimental study of the role of brand strength in the relationship between the medium of communication and perceived credibility of the message. In: Journal of Interactive Marketing. Vol. 17(3). 75-79.

Martin, B.A.S./Wentzel, D./Romczak, T. (2008). Effects of susceptibility to normative influence and type of testimonial on attitudes toward print advertising. In: Journal of Advertising. Vol. 37(1). 29-43.

Martin, E. (2006) The pharmaceutical person. In: Bio Societies. Vol. 1. 273-287.

Martin, G.P. (2008) Ordinary People Only: Knowledge, reprensativeness, and the publics of public participation in healthcare. In: Sociology of Health and Illness. Vol. 30(1). 35-54.

Martin, L.H./Gutman, H./Hutton, P.D. (eds.) (1988). Technologies of the self. A Seminar with Michel Foucault. London: Tavistock.

Masuda, T./Wang, H./Ito, K./Senzaki, S. (2012). Culture and the mind: implications for art, design and advertising. In: Okazaki, S. (ed.). Handbook of Research on International Advertising. Northhampton, MA: Edgar Elgar.

Mattila, A.S. and Cranage, D. (2005), The impact of choice on fairness in the context of service recovery. In: Journal of Services Marketing. Vol. 19(5). 271-279.

Mattson, M. (1999). Toward a reconceptualization of communication cues to action in the Health Belief Model: HIV test counseling. In: Communication Monographs. Vol. 66(3). 240-265.

Mayfield, Z. (2006). Fear Appeal Messages and their Effectiveness in Advertising. Retrieved from /http://voices.yahoo.com/fear-appeal-messages-their-effectiveness-advertising-31626.html (accessed 22.03.2013)

Maynes, E. S. (1990). The Future of Consumerism. In: At Home with Consumers. Vol. 11(6/7). 10.

Mayo, E. (1933). The Human Problems of an Industrial Civilisation. New York: Macmillan.

McCarty, J.A. and Hattwick, P.M. (1992). Cultural Value Orientations: a Comparison of Magazine Advertisements From the United States and Mexico. In: Advances in Consumer Research. Vol. 19. 34-38.

McCormick-Brown, K. (1999). Health Belief Model. Retrieved from http://www.jblearning.com/samples/0763743836/chapter%204.pdf (accessed 01.09.2012)

McCracken, G. (1986). Culture and consumption: A theoretical account of the structure and movement in the cultural meaning of consumer goods. In: Journal of Consumer Research. Vol. 13(1). 71-84.

McCracken, G. (1988). Culture and Consumption: New approaches to the symbolic character of consumer good and activities. Bloomington: Indiana University Press.

McDivitt, J.A./Zimicki, S./Hornik, R.C. (1997). Explaining the Impact of Communication Campaigns to Change Vaccination Knowledge and Coverage in the Philippines. In: Health Communication. Vol. 9. 95-118.

McDonald, R.P. and Ho, M.-H.R. (2002). Principles and Practice in Reporting Statistical Equation Analyses. In: Psychological Methods. Vol. 7 (1). 64-82.

McGinnis, J. and Foege, W. (1993). Actual Causes of Death in the United States. In: Journal of the American Medical Association. Vol. 270(18). 2207-2211.

McGrath, J.M. and Mahood, C. (2004). The Impact of Arousing Programming and Product Involvement on Advertising Effectiveness. In: Journal of Current Issues and Research in Advertising. Vol. 26(2). 41-52.

McGuire, W.J. (1968). Personality and Susceptibility to Social Influence. In: Borgatta, E.F. and Lambert, W.W. (eds.). Handbook of Personality Theory and Research. Chicago: Rand McNally. 1130-1187.

McGuire, W.J. (1974). Psychological Motives and Communication Gratification. In: Blumler, J.G. and Katz, E. (eds.). The Uses of Mass Communications: Current Perspectives on Gratifications Research. Beverly Hills, CA: Sage.

McGuire, W.J. (1976). Some Internal Psychological Factors Influencing Brand Choice. In: Journal of Consumer Research. Vol. 2 (March). 302-319.

McIntire, C. (1849). The Importance of the Study of Medical Sociology. In: Bulletin of the American Academy of Medicine. Vol. 1. 425-434.

McIntosh, C. (2006). Rethinking fit assessment in structural equation modelling: A commentary and elaboration on Barrett (2007). In: Personality and Individual Differences. Vol. 42(5). 859-867.

McLaurin, P. (1995). An examination of the effect of culture on pro-social messages directed at African-American at-risk youth. In: Communication Monographs. Vol. 62. 301-326.

McNay, L. (1992). Foucault and Feminism: Power, Gender and the Self. Oxford: Polity.

McQuarrie, E.F. and Langmeyer, D. (1985). Using Values to Measure Attitudes Towards Discontinuous Innovation. In: Psychology and Marketing. Vol. 2(4). 239-253.

McQuarrie, E.F. and Phillips, B.J. (2005). Indirect Persuasion in Advertising. In: Journal of Advertising. Vol. 34(2). 7-20.

McQuarrie, E.F. and Phillips, B.J. (2008). It's not your father's magazine ad: magnitude and direction of recent changes in advertising style. In: Journal of Advertising, Vol. 37(3). 95–106.

Mead, G.H. (1934). Mind, Self, and Society. Chicago: Chicago University Press.

Meichenbaum, D. (1984). Teaching thinking: a cognitive-behavioral perspective. In: Glaser, R./Chipman, S./Segal, J. (eds.). Thinking and Learning Skills. Relating Instruction to research. Vol. 1. Hillsdale, NJ: Erlbaum.

Melewar, T.C. and Vemmervik, C. (2004). International advertising strategy: A review, reassessment and recommendation. In: Management Decision. Vol. 42(7). 863-881.

Meline, K.P. (1996). Truth in the Meaning of Advertisements. In: Advances in Consumer Research. Vol. 23. 237-241.

Menon, A.M./Deshpande, A.D./Perri, M. III/Zinkhan, G.M. (2003). Consumers' attention to the brief summary in print direct-to-consumer advertisements: perceived usefulness in patient-physician discussions. In: Journal of Public Policy and Marketing. Vol. 22(2). 181-191.

Menon, A.M./Deshpande, A.D./Perry, M./Zinkhan, G.M. (2002). Trust in on-line prescription drug information among Internet users: The impact on information search behavior after exposure to direct-to-consumer advertising. In: Health Marketing Quarterly. Vol. 20(1). 17-35.

Menon, A.M./Deshpande, A.D./Zinkhan, G.M./Perri, M. III. (2004). A model assessing the effectiveness of direct-to-consumer advertising: integration of concepts and measures from marketing and healthcare. In: International Journal of Advertising. Vol. 23. 91-118.

Meredith, W. (1993). Measurement invariance, factor analysis and factorial invariance. In: Psychometrika. Vol. 58(4). 525-543.

Merriam Webster. (2014). Biomedicine. Retrieved from http://www.merriam-webster.com/dictionary/biomedicine (accessed 13.05.2014)

Merton, R.K. and Rossi, A.K. (1949). Contributions to the Theory of Reference Group Behavior. In: Merton, R.K. (ed.). Social Theory and Social Structure. New York: The Free Press. 225-275.

Meyerowitz, B.W. and Chaiken, S. (1987). The effect of message framing on breast self-examination attitudes, intentions, and behaviors. In: Journal of Personality and Social Psychology. Vol. 52. 500-510.

Michie, S./Miles, J./Weinman, J. (2003). Patient-centredness in chronic illness: what is it and does it matter? In: Patient Education and Counseling. Vol. 51. 197-206.

Mikellides, B. (1990). Color and physiological arousal. In: The Journal of Architectural and Planning Research. Vol. 7. 13-20.

Miles, J. and Shevlin, M. (1998). Effects of sample size, model specification and factor loadings on the GFI in confirmatory factor analysis. In: Personality and Individual Differences. Vol. 25. 85-90.

Milfont, T.L. and Fischer, R. (2010). Testing measurement invariance across groups: Applications in cross-cultural research. In: International Journal of Psychological Research. Vol. 3(1). 111-121.

Miller, J.G. (1999). Cultural conceptions of duty: Implications for motivation and morality. In: Munroe, D./Schumaker, J.F./Carr, S.C. (eds.). Motivation and Culture. New York: Routledge. 178–192.

Milne, S./Orbell, S./Sheeran, P. (2002). Combining motivational and volitional interventions to promote exercise participation: Protection motivation theory and implementation intentions. In: British Journal of Health Psychology. Vol. 7. 163-184.

Milner, L. and Collins, J. (2000). Sex-role portrayals and the gender of nations. In: Journal of Advertising. Vol. 29(1). 67-79.

Minkov, M. (2007). What makes us different and similar: a new interpretation of the World Values Survey and other cross-cultural data? Sofia: Klasika i Stil.

Mintzes, B. (2006). Direct-to-Consumer Advertising of Prescription Drugs in Canada. What are the Public Health Implications? Health Council of Canada: Toronto.

Mirowsky, J. and Ross, C.E. (2003). Education, Social Status, and Health. New York: Aldine de Gruyter.

Mischel, W./Cantor, N./Feldman, S. (1996). Principles of Self-Regulation: The Nature of Willpower and Self-Control. In: Higgins, E.T. and Kruglanski, A.W. (eds.). Social Psychology. Handbook of Basic Principles. New York: Guilford. 329-360.

Mitchell, A.A. and Olson, J.C. (1977). Cognitive Effects of Advertising Repetition. In: Advances in Consumer Research. Vol. 4. 213-220.

Mitchell, A.A. and Olson, J.C. (1981). Are Product Attribute Beliefs the Only Mediator of Advertising Effects on Brand Attitude? In: Journal of Marketing Research. Vol. 18. 318-332.

Mittal, B.(1989). Measuring purchase-decision involvement. In: Psychology and Marketing. Vol. 2(6). 147-162.

Mittal, M. (1982). The Dimensions of Advertising Involvement. In: Advances in Consumer Research. Vol. 8. 25-30.

Monaghan, L.F. and Hardey, M. (2009). Body sensibility: Vocabularies of the discredited male body. In: Critical Public Health. Vol. 19(3). 341-362.

Monga, A.B. and John, D.R. (2007). Cultural Differences in Brand Extension Evaluation: The Influence of Analytic versus Holistic Thinking. In: Journal of Consumer Research. Vol. 33 (March). 529-536.

Monroe, K. B. and Krishnan, R. (1985). The effect of price on subjective product evaluations, perceived quality: How consumers view stores and merchandise. In: Advances in Consumer Research. Vol. 12. 85-90.

Monroe, K.B. and Krishnan, R. (1985). The Effect of Price on Subjective Product Evaluations. In: Jacoby, J. and Olsen, J. (eds.). Perceived Quality. Lexington, MA: Lexington Books. 209-232.

Moorman, C. and Matulich, E. (1993). A model of consumers' preventive health behaviors: the role of health motivation and health ability. In: Journal of Consumer Research. Vol. 20. 208-228.

Morgan, S.E./Palmgreen, P./Stephenson, M.T./Hoyle, R.H./Lorch, E.P. (2003). Associations between message features and subjective evaluations of the sensation value of antidrug public service announcements. In: Journal of Communication. Vol. 53(3). 512-526.

Moriarty, S.E. (1991). Creative Advertising: Theory and Practice. Englewood Cliffs, NJ: Prentice Hall.

Morris, L./Mazis, B./Brinberg, D. (1989). Risk disclosures in televised prescription drug advertising to consumers. In: Journal of Public Policy and Marketing. Vol. 8. 64-80.

Morrison, D.G. (1979). Purchase Intentions and Purchase Behaviour. In: Journal of Marketing. Vol. 43. 65-74.

Morse, R.L. (ed.) (1993). The Consumer Movement: Lectures by Colson E. Warne. Manhattan, KA: Family Economics Trust.

Moss, G.E. (1973). Illness, Immunity and Social Interaction. New York: John Wiley.

Mowen, J.C. (1980). On Product Endorsers Effectiveness: A Balance Model Approach. In: Leigh, J.A. and Martin, C.R. (eds.). Current Issues and Research in Advertising. Ann Arbor, MI: University of Michigan. 41-57.

Moynihan, R. and Cassels, A. (2005). Selling sickness: How the world's largest pharmaceutical companies are turning us all into patients. New York, NY: Nation Books.

Muehling, D.D./Laczniak, R.N./Andrews, J.C. (1993). Defining, Operationalizing, and Using Involvement in Advertising Research: A Review. In: Journal of Current Issues and Research in Advertising. Vol. 15(1). 21-57.

Mueller, B. (1987). Reflections of Culture: An Analysis of Japanese and American Advertising Appeals. In: Journal of Advertising Research. Vol. 27(3). 51-59.

Mueller, B. (2006). The role of Product involvement in advertising message perception and believability. In: Diehl, S. and Terlutter, R. (eds.). International Advertising and Communication: Current Insights and Empirical Findings. Wiesbaden: Gabler. 3-22.

Mueller, B. (2011). Dynamics of International Advertising: Theoretical and Practical Perspectives. 2nd ed. New York: Peter Lang.

Mueller, B./Diehl, S./Terlutter, R. (2015). GLOBE Cultural Dimensions: Providing Insights for Advertising Execution in the Global Marketplace. In: Banks, I.B./De Pelsmacker, P./Okazaki, S. (eds.). Advances in Advertising Research. Vol. V. Wiesbaden: Springer. 161-175.

Mukherjee, A. and Hoyer, W.D. (2001). The Effect of Novel Attributes on Product Evaluation. In: Journal of Consumer Research. Vol. 28(3). 462-472.

Mulaik, S.A./James, L.R./Van Alstine, J./Bennet, N./Lind, S./Stilwell, C.D. (1989). Evaluation of Goodness-of-Fit Indices for Structural Equation Models. In: Psychological Bulletin. Vol. 105(3). 430-445.

Murray, K. and Vogel, C.M. (1997). Using a hierarchy-of-effects approach to gauge the effectiveness of corporate social responsibility to generate goodwill toward the firm: financial versus nonfinancial impacts. In: Journal of Business Responsibility. Vol. 38(2). 141-160.

Murray-Johnson, L. and Witte, K. (2003). Looking toward the future: Health message design strategies. In: Thompson, T.L./Dorsey, A./Miller, K./Parrott, R. (eds.). Handbook of Health Communication. Mahwah, New Jersey: Lawrence Erlbaum. 473-495.

Murray-Johnson, L. and Witte, K. (2010). International health communication campaigns in developing countries. In: Thompson, T.L./Parrott, R./Nussbaum, J.F. (eds.). The Routledge handbook of health communication. 2nd ed. New York: Routledge. 220-234.

Muthukrishnan, A.V. and Weitz, B.A. (1991). Role of Product Knowledge in Evaluation of Brand Extension. In: Advances in Consumer Research. Vol. 18. 407-413.

Muturi, N. (2005). Communication for HIV/AIDS prevention in Kenya: social-cultural considerations. In: Journal of Health Communication. Vol. 10(1). 77-98.

Nan, X. and Heo, K. (2007). Consumer Responses to Corporate Social Responsibility (CSR) Initiatives: Examining the Role of Brand-Cause Fit in Cause-Related Marketing. In: Journal of Advertising. Vol. 36(2). 63-74.

Narayan, D. (ed.) (2002). Empowerment and Poverty Reduction: A Sourcebook. New York: World Bank.

National Cancer Institute and National Institutes of Health. (2002). Health Behavior Constructs: Theory, Measurment, and Research. Retrieved from http://cancercontrol.cancer.gov/brp/constructs/barriers/ba2.html (accessed 03.10.2013)

National Health Council. (2002). Direct-to-Consumer Prescription Drug Advertising: Overview and Recommendations. Retrieved from www.nationalhealthcouncil.org/advocacy/DTC_paper.pdf (accessed 01.10.2012)

NCCAM. (2013). Homeopathy: An Introduction. Retrieved from http://nccam.nih.gov/health/homeopathy (accessed 24.10.2014)

NDMA. (1992). Self-Medication in the '90s. Practices and Perceptions. Washington, D.C.

Nelkin, D. (2001). Beyond risk. Reporting about genetics in the post-Asilomar press. In: Perspectives of Biological Medicine. Vol. 44(2). 199-207.

Nelson, M. and Shavitt, S. (2002). Horizontal and vertical individualism and achievement values: A multi-method examination of Denmark and the U.S. In: Journal of Cross-Cultural Psychology. Vol. 33. 439-458.

Nelson, M. R. and Paek, H.-J. (2008). Nudity of female and male models in primetime TV advertising across seven countries. In: International Journal of Advertising. Vol. 27. 715-744.

Nelson, P. (1970). Information and Consumer Behavior. In: Journal of Political Economy. Vol. 78(2). 45-57.

Nenkov, G.Y./Inman, J.J./Hulland, J. (2007). Considering the Future: The Conceptualization and Measurement of Elaboration on Potential Outcomes. In: Journal of Consumer Research. Vol. 35 (June). 126-141.

Nettleton, S. (1989). Power and pain: the location of pain and fear in dentistry and the creation of the dental subject. In: Social Science and Medicine. Vol. 29(10). 1183-1190.

Nettleton, S. (1995). The Sociology of Health and Illness. Cambridge: Polity.

Nettleton, S. (1997). Governing the risky self: How to become healthy, wealthy and wise. In: Petersen, A. and Bunton, R. (eds.). Foucault, Health and Medicine. London: Routledge. 207-222.

Nettleton, S. and Watson, J. (1998). The Body in Everyday Life. London: Routledge.

Neuhauser, L. and Kreps, G.L. (2003). Rethinking communication on the e-health era. In: Journal of Health Psychology. Vol. 8. 7-23.

Newholm, T./Laing, A./Hogg, G. (2006). Assumed empowerment: consuming professional services in the knowledge economy. In: European Journal of Marketing. Vol. 40(9/10). 994-1012.

Niebel, K. and Davidson, E. (2012). Raising the Bar for HIV Awareness. In: Marketing Health Services. Vol. 32(4). 5-7.

Niederdeppe, J./Hornik, R./Kelly, B./Frosch, D./Romantan, A./Stevens, R./Barg, F./Weiner, J./Schwarz, S. (2007). Examining the dimensions of cancer-related information scanning and seeking behavior. In: Health Communication. Vol. 22. 153–167.

Nielsen and IMS. (2013). Understanding Trust in OTC Medicines: Consumer and Healthcare Provider Perspectives. Retrieved from http://www.yourhealthathand.org/images/uploads/CHPA_OTC_Trust_Survey_White_Paper.pdf (accessed 10.04.2014)

Nielsen. (2012). The Global, Socially Conscious Consumer. Retrieved from http://www.nielsen.com/content/dam/corporate/us/en/reports-downloads/2012-Reports/Nielsen-Global-Social-Responsibility-Report-March-2012.pdf (accessed 04.04.2014)

Nielsen. (2013). Consumers who care and say they'll reward companies with their wallets. Retrieved from http://hk.nielsen.com/site/documents/NielsenGlobalReportConsumersWhoCareAugust2013.pdf (accessed 04.04.2014)

Nielsen. (2014). Doing Well By Doing Good. Retrieved from http://www.nielsen.com/content/dam/nielsenglobal/apac/docs/reports/2014/Nielsen-Global-Corporate-Social-Responsibility-Report-June-2014.pdf (accessed 10.04.2014)

Nisbett, R. E./Choi, I./Peng, K./Norenzayan, A. (2001). Culture and systems of thought: Holistic versus analytic cognition. In: Psychological Review. Vol. 108(2). 291-310.

Norman, P. and Conner, M. (1996). The role of social cognition models in predicting health behaviors: Future directions. In: Conner, M. and Norman, P. (eds.). Predicting health behavior: Research and practice with social cognition models. Buckingham, UK: Open University Press. 197-225.

Norris, P./Herxheimer, A./Lexhin, J./Mansfield, P. (2004). Drug Promotion. What we know, what we have yet to learn. Reviews of Materials in the WHO/HAI Database on Drug Promotion. Retrieved from http://www.who.int/medicines/areas/rational_use/drugPromodhai.pdf (accessed 09.05.2013)

Nunnally, J.C. (1978). Psychometric Theory. New York: McGraw-Hill.

Nussbaum, A.K. (2009). Ethical corporate social responsibility (CSR) and the pharmaceutical industry: A happy couple? In: Journal of Medical Marketing. Vol. 9(1). 67-76.

Nutbeam, D. (1998). Health promotion glossary. In: Health Promotion International. Vol. 13. 349-364.

Nutbeam, D. (2000). Health literacy as a public health goal: a challenge for contemporary health education and communication strategies into the 21st century. In: Health Promotion International. Vol. 15(3). 259-267.

Nutbeam, D. (2008). The evolving concept of health literacy. In: Social Science and Medicine. Vol. 67. 2072-2078.

NYC Department of Health and Mental Hygiene. (2012). Health Department launches new smoking cessation campaign, suffering every minute, which depicts the health consequences of smoking. Retrieved from http://www.nyc.gov/html/doh/html/pr2012/pr023-12.shtml (accessed 22.03.2013)

O'Donnell, M. (1989). Definition of Health Promotion: Part III: Expanding the Definition. In: American Journal of Health Promotion. Vol. 3(3). 5-5.

O'Hair, D./Friedrich, G.W./Dixon, L.L. (2002). Strategic Communication in Business and the Professions. 4th ed. Boston: Houghton Mifflin.

O'Keefe, D. (2012). From Psychological Theory to Message Designs: Lessons from the Story of Gain-Framed and Loss-Framed Persuasive Messages. In: Cho, H. (ed.). Health Communication and Message Design: Theory and Practice. Los Angeles, CA: Sage. 3-20.

O'Reilly, K.B. (2010). FDA task force calls for more disclosure of drug, device information. Retrieved from http://www.amednews.com/article/20100607/profession/306079953/4/ (accessed 09.05.2013)

Obermiller, C. (1995). The Baby is Sick/The Baby is Well: A Test of Environmental Communication Appeals. In: Journal of Advertising. Vol. 24(2). 55- 70.

Obermiller, C. and Spanberg, E.R. (1998). Development of a scale to measure consumer skepticism toward advertising. In: Journal of Consumer Psychology. Vol. 7(2). 159-186.

Obermiller, C./ Spangenberg, E./MacLachlan, D.L. (2005). Ad skepticism: The consequences of disbelief. In: Journal of Advertising. Vol. 34 (3). 7-17.

Obermiller, C./Spanberg, E.R./MacLachlan, D.L. (2005). Ad skepticism: the consequences of disbelief. In: Journal of Advertising. Vol. 34(3). 7-17.

Ogden, J. (1995). Psychosocial theory and the creation of the risky self. In: Social Science and Medicine. Vol. 40(3). 409-415.

Ohanian, R. (1990). Construction and Validation of A Scale to Measure Celebrity Endorser's Perceived Expertise, Trustworthiness, and Attractiveness. In: Journal of Advertising. Vol. 19(3). 39-52.

Ohanian, R. (1991). The impact of celebrity spokesperson's perceived image on consumers intention to purchase. In: Journal of Advertising Research. Vol. 31(1). 46-55.

Okazaki, S. and Mueller, B. (2007). Cross-cultural advertising research: where we have been and where we need to go. In: International Marketing Review. Vol. 24(5). 499–518.

Okazaki, S. and Taylor, C.R. (2006). Towards an Understanding of Advertising standardization in the European Union: a theoretical framework and research propositions. In: Diehl, S. and Terlutter, R. (eds.). International Advertising and Communication: Current Insights and Empirical Findings. Wiesbaden: Gabler. 439-454.

Okazaki, S./Hirose, M./Li, H. (2011). QR Code Mobile Promotion: An initial Inquiry. In: Okazaki, S. (ed). Advances in Advertising Research. Vol. 2. Wiesbaden: Gabler. 405-420.

Okazaki, S./Mueller, B./Diehl, S. (2013). A Multi-Country Examination of Hard-Sell and Soft-Sell Advertising: Comparing Global Consumer Positioning in Holistic- and Analytic-Thinking Cultures. In: Journal of Advertising Research. Vol. 53(3). 1-24.

Okazaki, S./Mueller, B./Taylor, C.R. (2010). Global Consumer Culture Positioning: Testing Perceptions of Soft-Sell and Hard-Sell Advertising Appeals Between U.S. and Japanese Consumers. In: Journal of International Marketing. Vol. 18(2). 20-34.

Okazaki, S./Mueller, B./Taylor, C.R. (2010). Measuring Soft-Sell Versus Hard-Sell Advertising Appeals. In: Journal of Advertising. Vol. 39(2). 5-20.

Okazaki, S./Taylor, C. R./Zou, S. (2006). Advertising Standardization's Positive Impact on the Bottom Line. A Model of When and How Standardization Improves Financial and Strategic Performance. In: Journal of Advertising. Vol. 35(3). 17-33.

Oliver, R. (1981). Measurement and Evaluation of Satisfaction Process in Retail Settings. In: Journal of Retailing. Vol. 57 (Fall). 25-48.

Olson, J.C. and Jacoby, J. (1972). Cue Utilization in the Quality Perception Processes. In: Venkatesan, M. (ed.). Proceedings of the Third Annual Conference of the Association for Consumer Research. Iowa City, 1972. Association for Consumer Research. 167-179.

Olson, J.C. and Mitchell, A.A. (1975). The Process of Attitude Acquisition: The Value of a Developmental Approach to Consumer Attitude Research. In: Advances in Consumer Research. Vol. 2. 249-264.

Olson, J.C./Toy, D.R./Dover, P.A. (1978). Mediating Effects of Cognitive Responses to Advertising on Cognitive Structure. In: Advances in Consumer Research. Vol. 5. 72-78.

Onkvisit , S. and Shaw, J.J. (2003). International marketing – Analysis and strategy. 4th ed. European Editon. New York: Routledge.

Onkvisit, S. and Shaw, J. J. (1990). Global advertising: revolution or myopia. In: Journal of International Consumer Marketing. Vol. 2(3). 97-112.

Onkvisit, S. and Shaw, J.J. (1999). Standardized International Advertising: Some Research Issues and Implications. In: Journal of Advertising Research. November/December 1999. 19-24.

Orlie, M. (2002), The desire for freedom and the consumption of politics, In: Philosophy and Social Criticism. Vol. 28(4). 395-417.

Osborne, T. (1997). Of health and statecraft. In: Petersen, A. and Bunton, R. (eds.). Foucault, Health and Medicine. London: Routledge. 173-188.

Oskamp, S. (2000). A Sustainable Future for Humanity? How Can Psychology Help? In: American Psychologist. Vol. 55(5). 496-508.

Ozomer, A./Bodur, M./Cavusgil, S.T. (1991). Marketing standardization by multinationals in an emerging market. In: European Journal of Marketing. Vol. 25(12). 50-64.

Paasche-Orlow, M.K. and Wolf, M.S. (2007). The Causal Pathways Linking Health Literary to Health Outcomes. In: American Journal of Health Behavior. Vol. 31. Supplement 1. 19-26.

Pae, J. H./Samiee, S./ Tai, S. (2002). Global advertising strategy: The moderating role of brand familiarity and execution style. In: International Marketing Review. Vol. 19(2). 176-189.

Palmgreen, P./Stephenson, M.T./Everett, M.W./Basehart, J.R./Francies, R. (2002). Perceived message sensation value (PMSV) and the dimensions and validation of a PMSV scale. In: Health Communication. Vol. 14(4). 403-428.

Pappas, C. (2000). Ad nauseam. In: Advertising Age. 10 July 2000. 16-18.

Pardo del Val, M. and Lloyd, B. (2002). Measuring Empowerment. In: Leadership and Organizational Development Journal. Vol. 24(2). 102-108.

Park, C. W. and Young, S. Mark (1986). The Effect of TV Program Involvement on Involvement with Commercials. In: Advances in Consumer Research. Vol. 13. 544-548.

Park, C.W. and Lessing, P.W. (1977). Students and Housewives: Differences in Susceptibility to Reference Group Influence. In: Journal of Consumer Research. Vol. 4 (September). 102-110.

Park, C.W. and Mittal, B. (1985). A theory of involvement in consumer behavior. Problems and issues. In: Sheth, J.N. (ed.). Research in Consumer Behavior 1. Greenwich, CT: JAI Press.

Park, C.W. and Young, S.M. (1984). The Effects of Involvement and Executional Factors of a Television Commercial on Brand Attitude Formation. Cambridge, MA: Marketing Science Institute.

Parker, J and Thorson, E. (2008). Preface. In: Parker, J. and Thorson, E. (eds.). Health Communication in the new media landscape. New York: Springer. xxxi-xxxii.

Parker, J.C./Woelfel, R.L./Hart, E.S./Brown, G.. (2008). The Challenge of Health Care and Disability. In: Parker, J. and Thorson, E. (eds.). Health Communication in the new media landscape. New York: Springer. 3-21.

Parrott, R. (2003). Media Issues. In: Thompson, Teresa L./Dorsey, Alicia M./Miller, Katherine I./Parrott, Roxanne. (eds.). Handbook of Health Communication. London: Lawrence Erlbaum Associates. 445-448.

Parrott, R. (2004). Emphasizing 'Communication' in Health Communication. In: Journal of Communication. Vol. 54(4). 751-787.

Parrott, R.F./Hall, S.J.G./Lloyd, D.M. (1998). Heart rate and stress hormone responses of sheep to road transport following two different loading responses. In: Animal Welfare. Vol. 7. 257-267.

Parsons, T. (1951). The Social System. New York: Free Press.

Patterson, R.B. (1997). Religion or spirituality: a distinction. In: Self-Help and Psychology Magazine. Pioneer Development Resources.

Patti, C. and Freizer, C. F. (1988). Advertising. Chicago: The Dryden Press.

Patzer, G.L. (1985). Research Claims that Beauty is Wallet-Deep. In: Marketing News. August 30, 1985. 4.

Paunio, M./Virtanen, M./Poltola, H./Cantell, K./Paunio, P./Valle, M./Karanko, V./Heinonen, O.P. (1991). Increase of Vaccination Coverage by Mass Media and Individual Approach: Intensified Measles, Mumps and Rubella Prevention Program in Finland. In: American Journal of Epidemiology. Vol. 133(11). 1152-1160.

Pechmann, C. (1992). Predicting when two-sided ads will be more effective than one-sided ads: the role of correlational and correspondent inferences. In: Journal of Marketing Research. Vol. 29(4). 441-453.

Pechmann, C. (2001), A Comparison of Health Communication Models: Risk Learning Versus Stereotype Priming. In: Media Psychology. Vol. 3(2). 189-210.

Pechmann, C./Zhao, G./Goldberg, M. E./Reibling, E. T. (2003). What to Convey in Antismoking Advertisements for Adolescents: The use of Protection Motivation Theory to identify Effective Message Themes. In: Journal of Marketing. Vol. 67. 1-18.

Pelz, D.C. (1983). Use of information channels in urban innovations. In: Science Communication. Vol. 5. 3-25.

Peng, K. and Nisbett, R. E. (1999). Culture, dialectics and reasoning about contradiction. In: American Psychologist. Vol. 54. 741-754.

Pérez-Stable, E.J./Sabogal, F./Otero-Sabogal, R./Hiatt, R.A./McPhee, S.J. (1992). Misconceptions about Cancer among Latinos and Anglos. In: Journal of the American Marketing Association. Vol. 268(22). 3219-3223.

Perkins, D. and Zimmerman, M. (1995). Empowerment theory, research and application. In: American Journal of Community Psychology. Vol. 23(5). 569-579.

Pescosolido, B.A. and Boyer, C.A. (2006). The American Health Care System: Entering the Twenty-first Century with High Risk, Major Challenges, and Great Opportunities. In: Cockerham, W.C. (ed.). The Blackwell Companion to Medical Sociology. Oxford: Blackwell. 180-198.

Pescosolido, B.A. and Kronenfeld, J.J. (1995). Health, Illness, and Healing in an Uncertain Era: Challenges from and for Medical Sociology. In: Journal of Health and Social Behavior. Special Issue. 5-33.

Pescosolido, B.A./Martin, J.K./Link, B.G./Kikuzawa, S./Burgos, G./Swindle, R./Phelan, J. (2000). Americans' Views of Mental Health and Illness at Century's End: Continuity and Change. Bloomington, IN: Indiana Consortium for Mental Health Services Research.

Petersen, A. (1997). Risk, governance and the new public health. In: Petersen, A. and Bunton, R. (eds.). Foucault, Health and Medicine. London: Routledge. 189-206.

Petersen, A. and Lupton, D. (1997). The New Public Health: Health and Self in the Age of Risk. London: SAGE.

Petersen, A.R. (1994). Governing images: media constructions of the 'normal', 'healthy' subject. In: Media Information Australia. Vol. 72. 32-40.

Petrie, K.J./Jago, L.A./Devcich, D.A. (2007). The role of illness perceptions in patients with medical conditions. In: Current Opinion in Psychiatry. Vol. 20. 163-167.

Petty, R. A. and Cacioppo, J. T. (1981a). Issues Involvement as a Moderator of the Effects on Attitude of Advertising Content and Context. In: Advances in Consumer Research. Vol. 8. 20-24.

Petty, R. A. and Cacioppo, J. T. (1981b). Attitudes and Persuasion: Classic and Contemporary Approaches. Dubuque, IA: William C. Brown.

Petty, R.E. (1977). A cognitive response analysis of the temporal persistence of attitude changes induced by persuasive communication. Doctoral Disseration: Ohio State University.

Petty, R.E. (1981). The Role of Cognitive Response in Attitude Change Processes. In: Petty, R.E./Ostrom, T.M./Brook, T.C. (eds.). Cognitive Responses in Persuasion. Hillsdale, NJ: Lawrence Erlbaum and Associates.

Petty, R.E. and Cacioppo, J.T. (1978). Effects of forwarning of persuasive intent and involvement on cognitive responses and persuasion. In: Personality and Social Psychology Bulletin. Vol. 5. 173–176.

Petty, R.E. and Cacioppo, J.T. (1980). Effects of Issue Involvement Can Increase or Decrease Persuasion by Enhancing Message-Relevant Cognitive Responses. In: Gorn, G.G. and Goldberg, M.E. (eds.). Proceedings of the Division 23 Program. Montreal, Canada: American Psychological Association. 75-79.

Petty, R.E. and Cacioppo, J.T. (1983). Central and Peripheral Routes to Persuasion: Application to Advertising. In: Percy, L. and Woodside, A. (eds.). Advertising and Consumer Psychology. Lexington, MA: Lexington Books. 3-23.

Petty, R.E. and Cacioppo, J.T. (1986). Communication and Persuasion. New York: Springer.

Petty, R.E. and Cacioppo, J.T. (1986). The Elaboration Likelihood Model of Persuasion. In: Advances in Experimental Social Psychology. Vol. 19. 123-192.

Petty, R.E./Barta, P.E./Pearlson, G.D./McGilchrist, I.K./Lewis, R.W./Tien, A.Y./Pulver, A./Vaughn, D.D./Casanova, M.F./Powers, R.E. (1995). Reversal of Assymetry of the planum temporale in schizophrenia. In: American Journal of Psychiatry. Vol. 152. 715-721.

Petty, R.E./Briñol, P./DeMarree, K.G. (2007). The meta-cognitive model (MCM) of attitudes: Implications for attitude measurement, change, and strength. In: Social Cognition. Vol. 25. 657–686.

Petty, R.E./Cacioppo, J.T./Schumann, D. (1983). Central and peripheral routes to advertising effectiveness. The moderating role of involvement. In: Journal of Consumer Research. Vol. 10. 135-146.

PEW Internet and American Life Project. (2007). E-Patients with a Disability or Chronic Disease. Retrieved from http://www.pewinternet.org/files/old-media/Files/Reports/2007/EPatients_Chronic_Conditions_2007.pdf.pdf (accessed 22.03.2013)

Phelps, J. and Thorson, E. (1991). Brand Familiarity and Product Involvement Effects on the Attitude Toward and Ad-Brand Attitude Relationship. In: Advances in Consumer Research. Vol. 18(1). 202-209.

PhRMA. (2010). Pharmaceutical Industry Profile. Retrieved from http://www.phrma.org/sites/default/files/159/profile_2010_final.pdf (accessed 21.10.2012)

Pieters, R./Rosbergen, E./Wedel, M. (1999). Visual Attention to Repeated Print Advertising: A Test of Scanpath Theory. In: Journal of Marketing Research. Vol. 36(4). 424-438.

Pignone, M. P. and DeWalt, D. A. (2006). Literacy and health outcomes: is adherence the missing link? In: Journal of General Internal Medicine. Vol. 21(8). 896-897.

Piller, I. (2001). Identity Constructions in Multilingual Advertising. In: Language and Society. Vol. 30. 153-186.

Pinderhughes, E. (1983). Empowerment for our clients and for ourselves. In: Social Casework: The Journal of Contemporary Social Work. Vol. 64(6). 331-338.

Ping, R.A. Jr. (2004). On assuring valid measures for theoretical models using survey data. In: Journal of Business Research. Vol. 57. 125-141.

Pires, G.D./Stanton, J./Rita, P. (2006). COMMENTARY: The internet, consumer empowerment and marketing strategies. In: European Journal of Marketing. Vol. 40(9/10). 936-949.

Pollay, R.W. (1985). The Subsiding Sizzle: A Descriptive History of Print Advertising, 19OO-198O. In: Journal of Marketing. Vol. 49(3). 24-37.

Polly, R.W. and Mittal, B. (1993). Here are the beef factors, determinants, and segments in consumer criticism of Advertising. In: Journal of Advertising. Vol. 57(7). 99-114.

Pomering, A.A. (2011). Communicating corporate social responsibility through corporate image advertising. In: Ihlen, O./Bartlett, J.L./May, S. (eds.), The Handbook of Communication and Corporate Social Responsibility. Chichester, UK.: John Wiley and Sons. 379-398.

Pond, R./Stephens, C./Alpass, F. (2010). Virtuously watching one's health: Older adults' regulation of self in the pursuit of health. In: Journal of Health Psychology. Vol. 15(5). 734–743.

Popay, J./Bennett, S./Thomas, C./Williams, G./Gatrell, A./Bostock, L. (2003). Beyond 'beer, fags, egg and chips'? Exploring lay understandings of social inequalities in health. In: Sociology of Health and Illness. Vol. 25(1). 1-23.

Porter, R. (1985). Introduction. In: Porter, R. (ed.). Patients and Practitioners: Lay Perceptions of Medicine in Pre-Industrial Society. Cambridge: Cambridge University Press. 1-22.

Porter, R. (1992). The Patient in England, 1660-1800. In: Wear, A. (ed.). Medicine in Society: Historical Essays. Cambridge: Cambridge University Press. 91-118.

Porter, R. (1997). The Greatest Benefit to Mankind: A Medical History of Humanity. New York: Norton.

Porter, R.W./Steinglass, R./Kaiser, J./Olkhovsky, P./Rasmuson, M./Dzhatdoeva, F.A./Fishman, B./Bragina, V. (2000). Role of Health Communication in Russia's Diphtheria Immunization Program. In: Journal of Infectious Diseases. Vol. 181 (Supplement 1). 220-227.

Pound, P./Britten, N./Morgan, M./Yardley, L./Pope, C./Daker-White, G./Campbell, R. (2005). Resisting medicines: a synthesis of qualitative studies of medicine taking. In: Social Science and Medicine. Vol. 61(1). 133–155.

Prentice-Dunn, S. and Rogers, R. W. (1986). Protection motivation theory and preventive health: Beyond the health belief model. In: Health Education Research. Vol. 1. 153-161.

Press, I. (1980). Problems of Definition and Classification of Medical Systems. In: Social Science and Medicine. Vol. 14B. 45-57.

Priester, J.R./Nayakankuppam, D./Fleming, M.A. and Godek, J. (2004). The A2SC2 Model: The Influence of Attitudes and Attitude Strength on Consideration and Choice. In: Journal of Consumer Research. Vol. 30 (March). 574–587.

Prochaska, J.O. and DiClemente, C.C. (1984). Self change processes, self efficacy and decisional balance across five stages of smoking cessation. In: Advances in cancer control. New York, NY: Alan R. Liss.

Prochaska, J.O./Johnson, S.S./Lee, P. (2009). The Transtheoretical Model of Behavior Change. In: Schumaker, S./Schorn, E., Ockenes, J./Richert, K. (eds.). The handbook of health behavior change, 3rd ed. New York: Springer. 59-83.

Pusey, M. (1987). Jürgen Habermas. London: Ellis Horwood.

Puto, C.P and Wells, W.D. (1984). Informational and Transformational Advertising: The Differential Effects of Time. In: Advances in Consumer Research. Vol. 11. 638-643.

Quah, S. (1985). Self-Medication in Singapore. In: Singapore Medical Journal. Vol. 26. 123-129.

Quah, S. (2006). Health and Culture. In: Cockerham, W.C. (ed.). The Blackwell Companion to Medical Sociology. Oxford: Blackwell. 23-42.

Quelch, J. (2003). The return of the global brand. In: Harvard Business Review. Vol. 81. 22.

Quelch, J.A. and Hoff, E.J. (1986). Customizing global marketing. In: Harvard Business Review. Vol. 64. 59-68.

Rabinow, P. (1984). The Foucault Reader. New York: Pantheon Books.

Rabinow, P. (1984). The Foucault Reader: An Introduction to Foucault's Thought. London: Penguin.

Radley, A. (1994). Making sense of illness: the social psychology of health and disease. London: Sage.

Rains, S. and Turner, M.M. (2007). Psychological reactance and persuasive health communication: A test and extension of the interwinded model. In: Human Communication Research. Vol. 33. 241-269.

Raju, P.S. (1977). Product Familiarity, Brand Name, and Price Influences on Product Evaluation. In: Advances in Consumer Research. Vol. 4. 64-71.

Ramirez, A.G./Villarreal, R./McAlister, A./Gallion, K.J./Suarez, L./Gomez, P. (1999). Advancing the Role of Participatory Communication in the Diffusion of Cancer Screening Among Hispanics. In: Journal of Health Communication. Vol. 4(1). 31-36.

Rappaport, J. (1981). In praise of paradox: a social policy of empowerment over prevention. In: American Journal of Community Psychology. Vol. 9. 1-25.

Rappaport, J. (1987). Terms of Empowerment/Exemplars of Prevention. Toward a Theory for Community Psychology. In: American Journal of Community Psychology. Vol. 15(2). 121-148.

Rappaport, J./Swift, C./Hess, R. (1984). Studies in Empowerment: Steps toward Understanding and Action. New York: Haworth.

Ravald, A. and Grönroos, C. (1996). The Value Concept and Relationship Marketing. In: European Journal of Marketing. Vol. 30(2). 19-30.

Raykov, T. (2001). Estimation of congeneric scale reliability using covariance structure analysis with nonlinear constraints. In: British Journal of Mathematical and Statistical Psychology. Vol. 54. 315-323.

Reeder, L.G. (1972). The Patient-Client as a Consumer: Some Observations on the Changing Professional-Client Relationship. In: Journal of Health and Social Behavior. Vol. 13(4). 406-412.

Reid, M. (1999). Global corporate report: Advertising – Drug makers advertise illness, not cures; Firms push sales without touting the product. In: Wall Street Journal. 26 November 1999. 1.

Reise, S. P./Widaman, K. F./Pugh, R. H. (1993). Confirmatory factor analysis and item response theory: Two approaches for exploring measurement invariance. In: Psychological Bulletin. Vol. 114. 552-566.

Rha, J.Y. and Widdows, R. (2002), The internet and the consumer: countervailing power revisited. In: Prometheus: Critical Studies in Innovation. Vol. 20(2). 107-118.

Rice, R. (2004). Influences, usage, and outcomes of Internet health information searching: Multivariate results from selected Pew surveys. Retrieved from http://www.escholarship.org/uc/item/0m10f3x5 (accessed 19.05.2013)

Richards, J.I. (1990). Deceptive Advertising: Behavioral Study of a Legal Concept. Hillsdale, NJ: Lawrence Erlbaum and Associates.

Richards, J.I. and Curran, C.M. (2002). Oracles on "Advertising": Searching for a Definition. In: Journal of Advertising, Vol. 21(2). 63-77.

Richins, M.L./ Bloch, P.H./McQuarrie, E.F. (1992). How Enduring and Situational Involvement Combine to Create Involvement Responses. In: Journal of Consumer Psychology. Vol. 1(2). 143-153.

Rifon, N.J./Choi, S.M./Trimble, C.S./Li, H. (2004). Congruence Effects in Sponsorships: The Mediating role of Sponsor Credibility and Consumer Attributions of Sponsor Motive. In: Journal of Advertising. Vol. 33(1). 29-42.

Rimal, R. N./Lapinski, M. K./Cook, R. J./Real, K. (2005). Moving toward a theory of normative influences: How perceived benefits and similarity moderate the impact of descriptive norms on behaviors. In: Journal of Health Communication. Vol. 10(5). 433–450.

Rimal, R.N. (2001). Perceived risk and self-efficacy as motivators: understanding individuals' long-term use of health information. In: Journal of Communication. Vol. 51(4). 633-654.

Rimal, R.N. and Adkins, A.D. (2010). Using Computers to Narrowcast Health Messages: The Role of Audience Segmentation, Targeting, and Tailoring in Health Promotion. In: Thompson,

T.L./Dorsey, A.M./Miller, K.I./Parrott, R. (eds.). Handbook of Health Communication. London: Lawrence Erlbaum Associates. 497-514.

Risse, G. (1992). Medicine in the age of Enlightenment. In: Wear, A. (ed.). Medicine in Society: Historical Essays. Cambridge: Cambridge University Press. 149-196.

Rissel, C. (1994). Empowerment: the holy grail of health promotion? In: Health Promotion International. Vol. 9(1). 39-47.

Ritzer, G. (2007). The Globalization of Nothing 2. London: Pine Forge Press.

Robertson, T.S. (1976). Low-Commitment Consumer Behavior. In: Journal of Advertising Research. Vol. 16. 19-24.

Robinson, M.M. and Zhang, X. (2011). The World Medicines Situation Report. Retrieved from http://www.who.int/medicines/areas/policy/world_medicines_situation/en/ (accessed 19.11.2013)

Rock, D.A./Werts, C.E./Flaugher, R.L. (1978). The issue of analysis of covariance structures for comparing the psychometric properties of multiple variables across populations. In: Multivariate Behavioral Research. Vol. 13. 403-418.

Rod, M. and Saunders, S. (2004). The informative and persuasive components of pharmaceutical promotion: An argument for why the two can coexist. In: International Journal of Advertising. Vol. 28(2). 313-349.

Rodgers, W.C. and Schneider, K.C. (1993). An Empirical Evaluation of the Kapferer-Laurent Consumer Involvement Profile Scale. In: Psychology and Marketing. Vol. 10(4). 333-345.

Rogers, E.M. (1996). The field of health communication today: An up-to-date report. In: Journal of Health Communication. Vol. 1. 15-23.

Rogers, E.M. and Storey, D. (1988). Communication Campaigns. In: Berger, C.R. and Chaffee, S.H. (eds.). Handbook of Communication Science, Newbury Park, CA: SAGE.

Rogers, R. W. (1975). A protection motivation theory of fear appeals and attitude change. In: Journal of Psychology. Vol. 91. 93-114.

Rogers, R. W. (1983). Cognitive and psychological processes in fear appeals and attitude change: a revised theory of protection motivation. In: Cacioppo, B. L. and Petty, L. L. (eds.). Social psychophysiology: A source book. London: Guildford Press. 153-176.

Rokeach, M. (1973). The Nature of Human Values. New York, NY: The Free Press.

Ronis, D. L. (1992). Conditional health threats: Health beliefs, decisions, and behaviors among adults. In: Health Psychology. Vol. 11. 127-134.

Rosal, M. and Bodenlos, J. (2009). Culture and health-related behavior. In: Schumaker, S./Ockene, J./Riekert, K. A. (eds.). The Handbook of Health Behavior Change. 3rd ed. New York: Springer.

Rose, G. (1989). Governing the enterprising self. In: Heelas, P. and Morris, P. (eds.). The Values of the Enterprise Culture: the Moral Debate. London: Routledge. 141-164.

Rose, N. (1990). Governing the soul: The Shaping of the Private Self. London: Routledge.

Rose, N. (1992). Governing the enterprising self. In: Heelas, P., and Morris, P. (eds.). The Values of the Enterprise Culture. London: Routledge.

Rose, N. (1994). Medicine, history, and the present. In: Jones, C. and Porter, R. (eds.). Reassessing Foucault: Power, Medicine and the Body. London: Routledge.

Rose, N. (2000). Tod des Soziden? Eine Neubestimmung der Grenzen des Regierens. In: Bröckling, U./ Krasmann, S./Lemke, Th. (eds.), Gouvernementalität der Gegenwart. Studien zur Ökonomisierung des Sozialen. Frankfurt: Suhrkamp. 72-109.

Rose, N. (2001). The politics of life itself. In: Theory, Culture, Society. Vol. 18(6). 1-30.

Rosenstock, I. M. (1974). Historical origins of the health belief model. In: Health Education Monographs. Vol. 2. 328-335.

Rosenstock, I.M. (1966). Why people use health services. In: Milbank Memorial Fund Quarterly. Vol. 83(4). 1-32.

Rosenstock, I.M. (1974). The Health Belief Model and preventive health behavior. In: Health Education Monographs. Vol. 2. 354-386.

Rosenstock, I.M./Strecher, V.J./Becker, M.H. (1994). The health belief model and HIV risk behavior change. In: DiClemente, R.J. and Petersen, J.L. (eds.). Preventing AIDS: Theories and methods of behavioral interventions. New York: Springer. 5-24.

Rosenstock, I.M./Strecker, V.J./Becker, M.H. (1988). Social Learning Theory and the Health Belief Model. In: Health Education Quarterly. Vol. 15(2). 175-183.

Ross, J.K./Patterson, L.T./Stutts, M.A. (1992). Consumer Perceptions of Organizations that use Cause-Related Marketing. In: Journal of the Academy of Marketing Science. Vol. 20(1). 93-97.

Rossiter, J. R. and Percy, L. (1997). Advertising Communications and Promotion Management. 2nd ed. New York, NY: McGraw-Hill.

Rossiter, J.R. and Bellman, S. (2005). Marketing Communications: Theory and Applications. French Forest: Pearson Education Australia.

Rossiter, J.R. and Percy, L. (1980). Attitude change through visual imagery in advertising. In: Journal of Advertising. Vol. 9(2). 10-16.

Rossiter, J.R. and Percy, L. (1985). Advertising Communication Models. In: Advances in Consumer Research. Vol. 12. 510-524.

Roter, D.L. and Hall, J.A. (1992). Doctors talking with patients, patients talking with doctors: improving communication in medical visits. Westport: Auburn House.

Roter, D.L./Hall, J.A./Merisca, R./Nordstrom, B./Cretin, D./Svarstad, B. (1998). Effectiveness of interventions to improve patient compliance: a meta-analysis. In: Medical Care. Vol. 36(8). 1138–1161.

Rothschild, M.L. (1984). Perspectives on Involvement: Current Problems and Future Directions. In: Advances in Consumer Research. Vol. 11. 216-217.

Rotter, J.B. (1966). Generalized expectancies for internal versus external control of reinforcement. In: Psychological Monographs. Vol. 80(1) 1-28.

Rotter, J.B. (1990). Internal Versus External Control of Reinforcement: A Case History of a Variable. In: American Psychologist. Vol. 45. 490-493.

Rouse, J. (2003). Power/Knowledge. In: Gutting, G. (ed.). The Cambridge Companion to Foucault. Cambridge: Cambridge University Press. 95-122.

Rouse, S.V. and Haas, H.A. (2003). Exploring the accuracies and inaccuracies of personality perception following internet-mediated communication. In: Journal of Research in Personality. Vol. 37. 446-467.

Rowe, J.W. and Kahn, R.L. (1998). Successful aging. New York: Random House.

Royne, M.B. and Myers, S. (2008). Recognizing consumer issues in DTC pharmaceutical advertising. In: The Journal of Consumer Affairs. Vol. 42(1). 60-78.

Russell, J.A. (1994). Is there universal recognition of emotion from facial expression? A review of the cross-cultural studies. In: Psychological Bulletin. Vol. 115. 102–141.

Ryan, M. J. and Vaithianathan, R. (2009). Truth-In-Advertising Laws and Pharmaceutical Promotion. Retrieved from http://www.economics.unimelb.edu.au/seminars/app/UploadedDocs/Doc592.pdf (accessed 19.11.2011)

Sabel, C. (1990). Moebius strip organizations and open labor markets: some consequences of the reintegration of conception and execution in a volatile economy. In: Bourdieu, P. and Coleman, J.S. (eds.). Social Theory for a Changing Society. Boulder, CO: Westview Press. 23-54.

Salmon, C. and Atkin, C.K. (2003). Media campaigns for health promotion. In: Thompson, T.L./Dorsey, A.M./Miller, K.I./Parrott, R. (eds.). Handbook of Health Communication. Mahwah, NJ: Lawrene Erlbaum.

Salovey, P./Schneider, T.R./Apanovitch, A.M. (2002). Message framing in the prevention and early detection of illness. In: Dillard, J.P. and Pfau, M. (eds.). The Persuasion Handbook: Developments in theory and Practice. Thousand Oaks, CA: Sage. 391-406.

Samiee, S. and Jeong, I. (1994). Cross-cultural research in advertising: an assessment of methodologies. In: Journal of the Academy of Marketing Science. Vol. 22(3). 205–217.

Samovar, L. and Porter, R.E. (1994). Intercultural communication: A reader. Belmont, CA: Wadsworth.

Sawicki, J. (1994). Foucault, Feminism and Questions of Identity. In: Gutting, G. (ed.). The Cambridge Companion to Foucault. Cambridge: Cambridge University Press. 286-313.

Sawyer, A.G. and Howard, D.J. (1991). Effects of Omitting Conclusions in Advertisements to Involved and Uninvolved Audiences. In: Journal of Marketing Research. Vol. 28. 467-474.

Schank, R.C. and Abelson, R. (1977). Scripts, Plans, Goals, and Understanding. Hillsdale, NJ: Lawrence Erlbaum.

Scheier, M.F./Carver, C.C./Bridges, M.W. (1984). Distinguishing Optimism from Neuroticism (and Trait Anxiety, Self-Mastery, and Self-Esteem): A Reevaluation of the Life Orientation Test. In: Journal of Personality and Social Psychology. Vol. 67(6). 1063-1078.

Scheufele, D.A. (1999). Framing as a theory of media effects. In: Journal of Communication. Vol. 49(1). 103–122

Schiavo, R. (2007). Health Communication: From Theory to Practice. San Francisco: Wiley and Sons.

Schiavo, R. (2014). Health Communication: From Theory to Practice. 2nd ed. San Francisco, CA: Jossey-Bass.

Schiffman, L. G. and Kanuk, L.L. (2004). Consumer behavior. 8th ed. Upper Saddle River, NJ: Pearson Prentice Hall.

Schillinger, D./Grumach, K./Piette, J./Osmond, D./Daher, C./Palacios, J. et al. (2002). Association of health literacy with diabetes outcomes. In: Journal of the American Medical Association. Vol. 288. 475-482.

Schulz, P.J. and Nakamoto, K. (2013). Health literacy and patient empowerment in health communication: The importance of separating conjoined twins. In: Patient Education and Counseling. Vol. 90. 4-11.

Schumacker R.E. and Lomax R.G. (2004). A beginner's guide to structural equation modeling. 2nd ed. Mahwah, NJ: Lawrence Erlbaum Associates.

Schwartz, B. (2004), The Paradox of Choice: Why more is less. New York, NY: Harper Collins.

Schwartz, S.H. (1992). Universals in the content and structure of values: Theory and empirical tests in 20 countries. In: Advances in experimental social psychology. Vol. 15. 1-65.

Schwarzer, R. (1992). Self-efficacy in the adoption and maintenance of health behaviors: Theoretical approaches and a new model. In: Schwarzer, R. (ed.). Self-efficacyy: Thought control of action. Washington, DC: Hemisphere. 217-243.

Schwarzer, R. (1994). Critical variables in the adoption, initiation and maintenance of health behaviours. In: Health Psychology Update. Vol. 15. 12-15.

Schwarzer, R. (1994). Optimism, vulnerability, and self-beliefs as health-related cognitions: A systematic overview. In: Psychology and Health. Vol. 9. 161-180.

Schwarzer, R. (ed.) (1992). Self-efficacy: Thought control of action. Washington, DC: Hemisphere.

Schwarzer, R. and Fuchs, R. (1996). Self-efficacy and health behaviors. In: Conner, M. and Norman, P. (eds.). Predicting health behavior: Research and practice with social cognition models. Buckingham, UK: Open University Press. 163-196.

Schwarzer, R. and Jerusalem, M. (1995). Generalized Self-Efficacy scale. In: Weinman, J./Wright, S./Johnston, M. (eds.). Measures in health psychology: A user's portfolio. Causal and control beliefs. Windsor, UK: NFER-NELSON. 35-37.

Schwarzer, R. and Luszczynska, A. (2008). How to overcome Health-Comprising Behaviors: The Health Action Process Approach. In: European Psychologist. Vol. 13(2). 141-151.

Schwarzer, R./Schüz, B./Ziegelmann, J.P./Lippke, S./Luszczynska, A./Scholz, U. (2007). Adoption and maintenance of four health behaviors: Theory-guided longitudinal studies on dental flossing, seat belt use, dietary behavior, and physical activity. In: Annals of Behavioral Medicine. Vol. 33(2). 156-166.

Schwarzer, Ralf. (2011). The Health Action Process Approach (HAPA). Retrieved from http://userpage.fu-berlin.de/health/hapa.htm (accessed 05.02.2013)

Science Daily. (2008). Big Pharma Spends more on Advertising than Research and Development. Study Finds. Retrieved from http://www.sciencedaily.com/releases/2008/01/080105140107.htm (accessed 01.03.2015)

Scott, L. (1994). Images in Advertising: The need for a theory of visual rhetoric. In: Journal of Consumer Research. Vol. 21. 252-273.

Scott, S. and Williams, G. (1991). Introduction. In: Scott, S./Williams, G./Platt, S./Thomas, H. (eds.). Private Risks and Public Dangers. Aldershot: Avebury.

Scott, S./Williams, G./Platt, S./Thomas, H. (eds.) (1991). Private Risks and Public Dangers. Aldershot: Avebury.

Sears, D.O./Peplau, L.A./Taylor, S.E. (1991). Social Psychology. 7th ed. Englewood Cliffs, NJ: Prentice-Hall.

Seedhouse, D. (1986). Health – The Foundations of Achievement. Chichester, UK: John Wiley and Sons.

Seedhouse, D. (2001). Health – The Foundations of Achievement. 2nd ed. Chichester, UK: John Wiley and Sons.

Segars, A. (1997). Assessing the unidimensionality of measurement: A paradigm and illustration within the context of information systems research. In: Omega. Vol. 25(1). 107-121.

Segen's Medical Dictionary. (2012). Mainstream Medicine. Retrieved from http://medical-dictionary.thefreedictionary.com/mainstream+medicine (accessed 20.03.2014)

Selden, C.R./Zorn, M./Ratzan, S.C./Parker, R.M. (2000). Health Literacy. Retrieved from http://www.nih.gov/clearcommunication/healthliteracy.htm (accessed 20.03.2014)

Sen, S. and Bhattacharya, C.B. (2001). Does going good always lead to doing better? Consumer reactions to corporate social responsibility. In: Journal of Marketing Research. Vol. 38(2). 225-243.

Sentis, K. and Markus, H. (1986). Brand personality and self. In: Olson, J. and Sentis, K. (eds.). Advertising and Consumer Psychology. New York: Praeger.

Shavitt, S./Lee, A.Y./Johnson, T.P. (2008). Cross-cultural consumer psychology. In: Haugtvedt, C./Herr, P./Kardes, F. (eds.). Handbook of Consumer Psychology. Mahwah, NJ: Lawrence Erlbaum. 1103-1131.

Shaw, I. (2002). How lay are lay health beliefs? In: Health. Vol. 6(3). 287-299.

Shearer, N.B. (2007). Toward a nursing theory of health empowerment in homebound older women. In: Journal of Gerontological Nursing. Vol. 33. 38-45.

Shearer, N.B.C. (2009). Health Empowerment Theory as a Guide for Practice. In: Geriatric Nursing. Vol. 30 (Supplement 2). 4-10.

Shearer, N.B.C. and Reed, P.G. (2004). Empowerment: Reformulation of a non-Rogerian concept. In: Nursing Science Quarterly. Vol. 17. 253-259.

Sheeran, P and Abraham, S.C.S. (1996). The health belief model. In: Conner, M. and Norman, P. (eds.). Predicting Health Behaviour. Buckingham, UK: Open University Press. 23–61.

Sheppard, A. (2009). Opportunities and Challenges in an Ever Generic World. In: Journal of Generic Medicines – the Business Journal for the Generic Medicine Sector. Vol. 6. 303-313.

Sherif, C.W./Sherif, M./Nebergall, R.E. (1965). Attitude and Attitude Change. Philadelphia: Saunders.

Sherif, M. and Cantrill, H. (1947). The Psychology of Ego Involvement. New York: Wiley.

Sheth, J.N./Newman, B.I./Gross, B.L. (1991). Why We Buy What We Buy: A Theory of Consumption Values. In: Journal of Business Research. Vol. 22. 159-170.

Shim, M./Kelly, B./Hornik, R. (2006). Cancer information scanning and seeking behavior is associated with knowledge, lifestyle choices, and screening. In: Journal of Health Communication. Vol. 11(1). 157-172.

Shimp, T.A. (1981). Attitude Toward the Ad as a Mediator of Consumer Brand Choice. In: Journal of Advertising. Vol. 10(2). 9-15.

Shiv, B. and Fedorikhin, A. (1999). Heart and mind in conflict: the interplay of affect and cognition in consumer decision making. In: Journal of Consumer Research. Vol. 26. 278-292.

Shoemaker, S.J. and de Oliveira, D.R. (2007). Understanding the meaning of medications for patients: The medication experience. In: International Journal of Clinical Pharmacy and Pharmaceutical Care. Vol. 30(1). 86-91.

Shoham, A. (1999). Bounded rationality, planning, standardization of international strategy, and export performance: a structural model examination. In: Journal of International Marketing. Vol. 7(2). 24-50.

Sillup, G.P. and Porth, G.P. (2008). Ethical issues in the pharmaceutical industry: an analysis of US newspapers. In: International Journal of Pharmaceutical and Healthcare Marketing. Vol. 2(3). 163-180.

Simmons, C. and Becker-Olsen, K. (2004). When do Social Sponsorships enhance or dilute equity: Fit, message source and the persistence of effect. In: Advances in Consumer Research. Vol. 29. 287-289.

Sirgy, M.J. (1982). Self-concept in consumer behavior: A critical review. In: Journal of Consumer Research. Vol. 9. 287-299.

Slama, M.E. and Tashchian, A. (1985). Selected Socioeconomic and Demographic characteristics Associated with Purchasing Involvement. In: Journal of Marketing. Vol. 49(1). 72-82.

Smart, B. (1985). Michel Foucault. London: Ellis Horwood.

Smith, G. (1985). Prescribing the rules of health: self-help and advice in the late eighteenth century. In: Porter, R. (ed.). Patients and Practitioners: Lay Perceptions of Medicine in Pre-Industrial Society. Cambridge: Cambridge University Press. 249-282.

Smith, M.S./Wallston, K.A./Smith, C.A. (1995). The development and validation of the Perceived Health Competence Scale. In: Health Communication Research: Theory and Practice. Vol. 10. 54-61.

Smith, S.S. and Alcorn, D.S. (1991). Cause Marketing: A New Direction in the Marketing of Social Responsibility. In: Journal of Consumer Marketing. Vol. 8(3). 19-34.

Snyder, L. B. and M. A. Hamilton (2002). A Meta-Analysis of U.S. Health Campaign Effects on Behavior: Emphasize Enforcement, Exposure, and New Information, and Beware the Secular

Trend. In: Hornik, R.C. (ed.). Public Health Communication. Evidence for Behavior Change. London: Lawrence Erlbaum Associates: 357-383.

Snyder, L.B. (2001). Development of Communication Campaigns. In: Gudykunst, W.B. and Mody, B. (eds.). Handbook of International and Intercultural Communication. 2nd ed. Thousand Oaks, CA: SAGE. 457-478.

Snyder, M. (1974). Self-monitoring of expressive behavior. In: Journal of Personality and Social Psychology. Vol 30(4). 526-537.

Soh, H./Reid, L.N./King, K.W. (2009). Measuring trust in advertising. Development and validation of the ADTRUST scale. In: Journal of Advertising. Vol. 38(2). 83-102.

Sonnenberg, F.A. (1997) Health information on the Internet: opportunities and pitfalls. In: Archives of Internal Medicine. Vol. 157. 151–152.

Soong, R. (2004). Environmentalism in Latin America. Retrieved from http://www.zonalatina.com/zldata39.htm (accessed 12.10.2013)

Spain, J.W./Siegel, C.F./Ramsey, R.P. (2001). Selling drugs online: Distribution-related legal/regulatory issues. In: International Marketing Review. Vol. 18(4). 432-449.

Spies, K./Hesse, F/Loesch K. (1997). Store atmosphere, mood and purchasing behavior. In: International Journal of Research in Marketing. Vol. 14. 1-17.

Spitzack, C. (1987). Confessions and signification: the systematic inscription of body consciousness. In: The Journal of Medicine and Philosophy. Vol. 12(4). 357-369.

Springston, J.K. and Weaver Lariscy, R.A. (2010). Health as Profit: Public Relations in Health Communications. In: Thompson, T.L./Dorsey, A.M./Miller, K.I./Parrott, R. (eds.). Handbook of Health Communication. London: Lawrence Erlbaum Associates. 537-556.

Stacey, M. (1998) The Sociology of Health and Healing. London: Unwin Hyman.

Stafford, J.E. and Cocanaugher, B.A. (1977). Reference Group Theory. In: Selected Aspects of Consumer Behavior. Washington, DC: U.S. Government Printing Office.

Statista. (2014). DAX 30 Unternehmen: Bayer AG. Retrieved from http://de.statista.com/themen/179/bayer/ (accessed 25.08.2014)

Steenkamp, J. and Baumgartner, H. (1998). Assessing Measurement Invariance in Cross-Cultural Research. In: Journal of Consumer Research. Vol. 25(June). 78-79.

Steenkamp, J.B.E.M. and de Jong, M.G. (2010). A Global Investigation Into the Constellation of Consumer Attitudes Toward Global and Local Products. In: Journal of Marketing. Vol. 74 (November). 18-40.

Steiger, J.H. (1989). EZPATH. A supplementary module for SYSTAT and SYGRAPH. Evanston, IL: SYSTAT.

Stephens, C./Budge, R.C./Carryer, J. (2002). What is this thing called hormone replacement therapy? Discursive construction of medication in situated practice. In: Qualitative Health Research. Vol. 12(3). 347–359.

Stephens, K.K./Rimal, R.N./Flora, J.A. (2004). Expanding the reach of health campaigns: Community organizations as meta-channels of the dissemination of health information. In: Journal of Health Communication. Vol. 9(1). 97-111.

Sternthal, B. and Craig, C.S. (1982). Consumer Behavior: An Information Processing Perspective. Englewood Cliffs, NJ: Prentice Hall.

Sternthal, B./Dholakia, R./Leavitt, C. (1978). The Persuasive Effect of Source Credibility: Tests of Cognitive Response. In: Journal of Consumer Research. Vol. 4. 252-260.

Steward, E. (1972). American cultural patterns: A cross cultural perspective. Pittsburgh, PA: Intercultural Communications Network.

Stewart, R.A./Kearney, P./Plax, T.G. (1985). Locus of control as a mediator: A study of college students' reactions to teachers attempts to gain compliance. In: McLaughlin, M.L. (ed.). Communication Yearbook. Vol. 9. Beverly Hills, CA: Sage. 691-704.

Stewart-Allen, L.A. (1998). Europe ready for cause related campaigns. In: Marketing News. Vol. 32(1). 9-10.

Steyer, R. (1999). Do drug ads educate or mislead consumers? In: St. Louis Post-Dispatch. 20 June 1999. A9.

Street, R. (2003). Communication in medical encounters. An ecological perspective. In: Thompson, T.L./Dorsey, A.M./Miller, K.I./Parrott, R. (eds.). Handbook of Health Communication. Mahwah, NJ: Erlbaum. 63-93.

Stretcher, V. and Rosenstock, I.M. (1997). The Health Belief Model. In: Glanz, K./Lewis, F.M./Rimer, B.K. (eds.). Health Behavior and Health Education: Theory, Research and Practice. 2nd ed. San Francisco, CA: Jossey-Bass.

Sturges, J.W. and Rogers, R.W. (1996). Preventive health psychology from a developmental perspective: An extension of protection motivation theory. In: Health Psychology. Vol. 15(3). 158-166.

Sujan, M. (1985). Consumer Knowledge: Effects on Evaluation Strategies Mediating Consumer Judgments. In: Journal of Consumer Research. Vol. 12(June). 31-46.

Sullivan, D.I./Schomer, J.C./Birdwell, S.W. (1999). Consumer retention of risk information from direct-to consumer advertising. In: Drug Information Journal. Vol. 37(1). 281-289.

Sutton, S. (2005). Stage theories of health behavior. In: Conner, M. and Norman P. (eds.). Predicting Health Behavior: research and practice with social cognition models. Buckingham, UK: Open University Press. 223-275.

Sutton, S. R. (1982). Fear arousing communications: A critical examination of theory and research. In: Eiser, J. R. (ed.). Social psychology and behavioral medicine. New York: Wiley. 303-338.

Sutton, Stephen. (2008). How does the Health Action Process Approach (HAPA) Bridge the Intention-Behavior Gap? An Examination of the Model's Causal Structure. In: Applied Psychology: An International Review. Vol. 57(1). 66-74.

Swagler, R. (1994). Evolution and applications of the term consumerism: Theme and Variations. In: The Journal of Consumer Affairs. Vol. 28(2). 347-360.

Swann, W.B. and Miller, L.C. (1982). Why never forgetting a face matters: Visual imagery and social memory. In: Journal of Personality and Social Psychology. Vol. 43. 475-480.

Tabachnick, B.G. and Fidell, L.S. (2007). Using Multivariate Statistics. 5th ed. New York: Allyn and Bacon.

Tanaka, J.S. (1993). Multifaceted conceptions of fit in structural equation models. In: Bollen, K.A. and Long, J.S. (eds.). Testing Structural Equation Models. Beverly Hills, CA: Sage.

Tatzel, M. (2003). The art of buying: Coming to terms with money and materialism. In: Journal of Happiness Studies. Vol. 4. 405-435.

Taylor, C.R. (2005). Moving International Advertising Research Forward: A New Research Agenda. In: Journal of Advertising. Vol. 34 (Winter). 7-16.

Taylor, C.R. (2007). Recent Trends in International Advertising Research: Current State of Knowledge and Where We Need to Go. Proceedings of the 2007 Conference of the American Academy of Advertising.

Taylor, C.R. (2010). Editorial: Measuring return on investment from advertising: 'holy grail'or necessary tool? In: International Journal of Advertising. Vol. 29(3). 345-348.

Taylor, C.R. and C. Johnson (2002). Standardized vs. Specialized International Advertising Campaigns: What We Have Leaned from Academic Research in the 1990s. In: Advances in International Marketing. Vol. 12. 45-66.

Taylor, E.B. (1871). Primitive culture. London: John Murray.

Taylor, M./Hoyes, L./Lart, R./Means, R. (1992). User Empowerment in Community Care: Unravelling the Issues. Bristol: School for Advanced Urban Studies.

Tench, R./Bowd, R./Jones, B. (2007). Perceptions and perspectives: corporate social responsibility and the media. In: Journal of Communication Management. Vol. 11(4). 348-369.

Teng, L. L. M. and Huihuang, Z. (2007). The effects of multiple-ads and multiple-brands on consumer attitude and purchase behavior. In: Journal of Consumer Marketing. Vol. 24(1). 27-35.

Terlutter, R./Diehl, S./Mueller, B. (2006). The GLOBE study - applicability of a new typology of cultural dimensions for cross-cultural marketing and advertising research. In: Diehl, S. and Terlutter, R. (eds.) International Advertising and Communication: Current Insights and Empirical Findings. Wiesbaden: Gabler. 420-438.

Thaler, R.H. (1985). Mental accounting and consumer choice. In: Marketing Science. Vol. 4. 199-214.

The Wirthlin Report. (1999). Hablamos Juntos: We Speak Together. Retrieved from http://www.hablamosjuntos.org/pdf_files/wirthlin_report.pdf (accessed 15.02.2013)

Thomas, K.W. and Velthouse, B.A. (1990). Cognitive elements of empowerment: an 'interpretive' model of intrinsic task motivation. In: Academy of Management Review. Vol. 15(4). 666-681.

Thompson, T./Parrott, R./Nussbaum, J. (2011). The Routledge Handbook of Health Communication. 2nd ed., New York: Routledge.

Thompson, T.L. (2000). The nature and language of illness explanations. In: Whaley, B.B. (ed.). Explaining illness: Research, Theory and Strategies. Mahwah, NJ: Erlbaum. 3-40.

Thomsen, C.J./Borgida, E./Lavine, H. (1995). The causes and consequences of personal involvement. In: Petty, R.E. and Krosnick, J.A. (eds.). Attitude strength: Antecedents and consequences. Hillsdale, NJ: Lawrence Erlbaum Associates. 191-214.

Tones, B.K. (1979). Past Achievement, Future Success. In: Sutherland, I. (ed.). Health Education Perspectives and Choices. London: Allen and Unwin.

Tones, B.K. (1981). Affective education and health. In: Cowley, J./David, K./Williams, T. (eds.). Health Education in Schools. London: Harper and Row.

Tones, B.K. (1987). Devising Strategies for preventing drug misuse: the role of the health action model. In: Health Education Research. Vol. 2. 305-318.

Tones, K. (1984). Education and health promotion: new direction. In: Journal of the Institute of Health Education. Vol. 21. 121-129.

Tones, K. (1984). Health education and the ideology of health promotion: a review of alternative approaches. In: Health Education Research. Vol. 1. 3-12.

Tones, K. (1992). Measuring success in health promotion – selecting indicators of performance. In: Hygie. Vol. 11. 10-14.

Tones, K. and Tilford, S. (2001). Health Promotion: effectiveness, efficiency and equity. 3rd ed. Cheltenham, UK: Nelson Thornes.

Torres, I.M./Sierra, J.J./Heiser, R.S. (2007). The effects of warning-label placement in print ads: a social contract perspective. In: Journal of Advertising. Vol. 36(2). 49-62.

Townsend, P./Davidson, N./Whitehead, M. (1988). Inequalities in Health (The Black Report and the Health Divide). London: Pelican.

Traulsen, J. and Noerreslet, M. (2004). The new consumer of medicine - the pharmacy technicians' perspective. In: Pharmacy World and Science. Vol. 26(4). 203.

Treacy, M. and Wiersema, F. (1993). Customer Intimacy and other value disciplines. In: Harvard Business Review. January. 84-93.

Triandis, H.C. (1995). Individualism and collectivism. Boulder, Co: Westview Press.

Triandis, H.C. (2004). Foreword. In: House, R. J./Hanges, P.J./Javidan, M./Dorfman, P.W./Gupta, V. (eds.) (2004). Culture, leadership, and organizations. The GLOBE study of 62 societies. Thousand Oaks, CA: Sage. xv-xix.

Trommsdorf, V. and Teichert, T. (2011). Konsumentenverhalten. 8th ed. Stuttgart: Kohlhammer.

Tsao, J.C. (1997). Informational and symbolic content of over-the-counter drug advertising on television. In: Journal of Drug Education. Vol. 27(2).173-197.

Tseng, W. T./Dornyei, Z./Schmitt, N. (2006). A new approach to assessing strategic learning: The case of self-regulation in vocabulary acquisition. In: Applied Linguistics. Vol. 27. 78-102.

Tu, H. T. and Hargraves, J. L. (2003). Seeking health care information: Most consumers still on the sidelines. In: Issue Briefs, Center for the Study of Health Systems Change. Vol. 61. 1–4.

Turner, B. (1996). The Body and Society: Explorations in Social Theory. 2nd ed. London: SAGE.

Turner, B.S. (1984). The Body and Society. Explorations in Social Theory. Oxford: Blackwell.

Turner, B.S. (1992). Regulating Bodies: Essays in Medical Sociology. London: Routledge.

Turner, B.S. (1997). From governmentality to risk: Some reflections on Foucault's contribution to medical sociology. In: Petersen, A. and Bunton, R. (eds.). Foucault, Health and Medicine. London: Routledge. ix-xxi.

Turner, B.S. (2004). The New Medical Sociology: Social Forms of Health and Illness. London: Norton.

Turner, L.W./Hunt, S.B/DiBrezzo, R./Jones, C. (2004). Design and Implementation of an osteoporosis prevention program using the health belief model. In: American Journal of Health Studies. Vol. 19(2). 115-121.

Turner, M.M. (2012). Using Emotional Appeals in Health Messages. In: Cho, H. (ed.). Health Communication Message Design: Theory and Practice. Los Angeles, CA: Sage. 59-71.

Turner, M.M./Rimal, R.N./Morrison, D./Kim, H. (2006). The role of anxiety in seeking and retaining risk information: Testing the risk perception attitude framework in two studies. In: Human Communication Research. Vol. 32(2). 130-156.

Turnquist, C. (2004). VP value chain services, Syntegra and Stan Elbaum, VP. Aberdeen: Strategic Solutions.

Twenge, J.M. and Crocker, J. (2000). Race and self-esteem: Meta-analyses comparing Whites, Blacks, Hispanics, Asians, and American Indians and comment on Gray-Little and Hafdahl (2000). In: Psychological Bulletin. Vol. 128. 371-408.

Twibell, D. and Anzalone, M. (2001). DTC on the Web: Fad or Fundamental? In: DTC PERSPECTIVES. May/June 2001. 28-29.

Tyebjee, T.T. (1979). Refinement of the Involvement Concept: An Advertising Planning Point of View. In: Maloney, J.C. and Silverman, B. (eds.). Attitude Research Plays for High Stakes. Chicago: American Advertising Association. 94-111.

U.S. Department of Health and Human Services. (2005). Making Health Communication Programs Work. Retrieved from http://www.cancer.gov/publications/health-communication/pink-book.pdf (accessed 10.02.2013)

U.S. Department of Health and Human Services. (2014). What is health literacy. Retrieved from http://www.health.gov/communication/literacy/ (accessed 10.02.2013)

Umphrey, L.R. (2004). Message defensiveness, efficacy, and health-related behavioral intentions. In: Communication Research Reports. Vol. 21(4). 329-337.

UNICEF. (2013). Communication for Development (C4D). Retrieved from http://www.unicef.org/cbsc/index_42148.html (accessed 22.03.2013)

US Department of Health and Human Services. (2000). Healthy People 2010: Understanding and improving health and objectives for improving health. US Department of Health and Human Services. Washington, DC. Retrieved from http://www.cdc.gov/nchs/data/hpdata2010/hp2010_final_review.pdf (accessed 10.02.2013)

UTexas. (2011). Lost in translation: Health communication researchers devise strategies to empower people to make informed decisions about their health. Retrieved from http://www.utexas.edu/features/2011/09/26/health_literacy/ (accessed 26.01.2014)

Vakratsas, D. and Ambler, T. (1999). How advertising works: what do we really know. In: Journal of Marketing. Vol. 63. 26-43.

Vallacher, R.R. and Wegner, D.M. (1985). A theory of action identification. Hillsdale, NJ: Erlbaum.

Vallacher, R.R. and Wegner, D.M. (1987). What do people think they're doing? Action identification and human behavior. In: Psychological Review. Vol. 94. 3-15.

Vallacher, R.R. and Wegner, D.M. (1989). Levels of Personal Agency: Individual Variation in Action Identification. In: Journal of Personality and Social Psychology. Vol. 57(4). 660-671.

van de Schoot, R./Lugtig, P./Hox, J. (2012). A checklist for testing measurement invariance. In: European Journal of Developmental Psychology. Vol. 9(4). 486-492.

van der Molen, B. (1999). Relating information needs to the cancer experience: Information as a key coping strategy. In: European Journal of Cancer Care. Vol. 8(4). 238-244.

van Ittersum, K., and Wong, N. (2010). The Lexus or the olive tree? Trading off between global convergence and local divergence. In: International Journal of Research in Marketing. Vol. 27. 107-118.

van Mulken, M. and Hornikx, J. (2011). The influence of scientese on ad credibility and ad liking: A cross-cultural investigation of ads for beauty products. In: Information Design Journal. Vol. 19(2). 92-102.

van Raaij, W.F. (1993). Postmodern Consumption: Architecture, Art, and Consumer Behavior. In: Advances in Consumer Research. Vol. 1. 550-558.

Vandenberg, R.J. and Lance, C.E. (2000). A review and synthesis of the measurement invariance literature: Suggestions, practices, and recommendations for organizational research. In: Organizational Research Methods. Vol. 3. 4–70.

Varnum, M.E.W./Grossmann, I./Kitayama, S./Nisbett, R.E. (2010). The origin of cultural differences in cognition: The social orientation hypothesis. In: Current Directions in Psychological Science. Vol. 19. 9-13.

Vaughn, R. (1980). How advertising works: a planning model. In: Journal of Advertising Research. Vol. 20(5). 27-33.

Vaughn, R. (1986). How Advertising Works: A Planning Model Revisited. In: Journal of Advertising Research. Vol. 26(1). 57-66.

Veblen, T. (1899). The Theory of the Leisure Class: An Economic Study of Institutions. New York: MacMillan.

Verbraucheranalyse (2008). Kleine Viren, Großer Markt. Retrieved from www.verbraucheranalyse.de/downloads/3/VA-aktuell_Nr_4_OTC.pdf (accessed 19.11.2013)

Verdurme, A. and Viaene, J. (2003). Consumer beliefs and attitude towards genetically modified food: Basis for segmentation and implications for communication. In: Agribusiness. Vol. 19(1). 91-113.

Viera, A.L. (2011). Interactive LISREL in Practice. Springer Briefs in Statistics. New York: Springer.

Viswanath, K. (2005). Science and society: The communications revolution and cancer control. In: National Review of Cancer. Vol. 5(10). 828–835.

Viswanath, K./Blake, K.D./Meissner, H.I./Saiontz, N.G./Mull, C./Freeman, C.S./Hesse, B./Croyle, R.T. (2008). Occupational practices and the making of health news: a national survey of US Health and medical science journalists. In: Journal of Health Communication. Vol. 13(8). 759-777.

Vogel, D. (2006) The Market for Virtue – The Potential and Limits of Corporate Social Responsibility. Washington, DC: Brookings Institution Press.

Voight, J. (2000). The Consumer Rebellion. In: Adweek (Eastern ed.). Vol. 41(2). 46-50.

VOX. (2015). 9 of top 10 drug marketers spend more on marketing than research. Retrieved from http://www.vox.com/2015/2/11/8018691/big-pharma-research-advertising (accessed 01.03.2015)

Vuckovic, N. and Nichter, N. (1997). Changing patterns of pharmaceutical practice in the United States. In: Social Science and Medicine. Vol. 44. 1285-1302.

Waite, R.L. (2006). Variations in the experiences and expressions of depression among ethnic minorities. In: Journal of National Black Nurses' Association. Vol. 17(1). 29-35.

Wakefield, M.A./Loken, B./Hornik, R.C. (2010). Use of mass media campaigns to change health behaviour. In: Lancet. Vol. 376. 1261-1271.

Walker, R.H./Craig-Lees, M./Hecker, R./Francis, H. (2002). Technology-Enabled Service Delivery: An Investigation of Reasons Affecting Customer Adoption and Rejection. In: International Journal of Service Industry Management. Vol. 13(1). 91-106.

Wallerstein, N. (1992). Powerlessness, empowerment, and health: implications for health promotion programs. In: American Journal for Health Promotion. Vol. 6. 197-205.

Wallston, K.A. (1982). Health Locus of Control. In: Patient Education Newsletter. Vol. 5. 56-57.

Wallston, K.A. and Wallston, B.S. (1981). Health locus of control scales. In: Lefcourt, H. (ed.) Research with the locus of control construct. Volume 1. New York: Academic Press

Walsh, C.F. (2012). Country report: The healthcare market in Germany. Retrieved from http://www.pmlive.com/pharma_intelligence/country_report_the_healthcare_market_in_germany_395666 (accessed 09.04.2014)

Wang, Q./Dacko, S./Gad, M. (2008). Factors Influencing Consumers' Evaluation and Adoption Intention of Really-New Products or Services: Prior Knowledge, Innovativeness and Timing of Product Evaluation. In: Advances in Consumer Research. Vol. 35. 416-422.

Ward, E.C. (2007). Examining different treatment effects of depression among ethnic minority women: A qualitative systematic review. In: Journal of the National Medical Association. Vol. 99(3). 265-274.

Warwick-Booth, L./Cross, L./Lowcock, D. (2012). Contemporary Health Studies: An Introduction. Cambridge: Polity.

Washington Post. (2008). BLUMENTHAL, KO, and MUTTER: The first wealth is health. Retrieved from http://www.washingtontimes.com/news/2008/nov/02/the-first-wealth-is-health/?page=all (accessed 09.03.2012)

Waters, M. (1995). Globalisation. London: Routledge.

Wathieu, L./Benner, L./Carmon, Z., Chattopadhyay, A./Wertenbroch, K./Drolet, A.,/Gourville,J./Muthukrishnan, A.V./Novemsky, N./Ratner, R.K./Wu, G. (2002), Consumer control and empowerment: a primer. In: Marketing Letters. Vol. 13(3). 297-305.

Wegner, D.M. and Vallacher, R.R. (1986). Action identification. In: Sorrentino, R.M. and Higgins, E.T. (eds). Handbook of motivation and cognition: foundations of social behavior. New York: Guildford. 550-582.

Weiber, R. and Mühlhaus, D. (2014). Strukturgleichungsmodellierung: Eine anwendungsorientierte Einführung in die Kausalanalyse mit Hilfe von AMOS, Smart PLS and SPSS. 2nd ed. Berlin: Springer.

Weilbacher, W.M. (2001). Point of View: Does Advertising Cause a "Hierarchy of Effects"? In: Journal of Advertising Research. Vol. 41(6). 19-26.

Weinman, J. and Petrie, K. J. (1997). Illness perceptions: a new paradigm for psychosomatics? In: Journal of Psychosomatic Research. Vol. 42. 113-116.

Weinman, J./Petrie, K. J./Moss-Morris, R./Horne, R. (1996). The Illness Perception Questionnaire: a new method for assessing illness perceptions. In: Psychology and Health. Vol. 11. 431-446.

Weinstein, N.D. (1993). Testing Four Competing Theories of Health-Protective Behavior. In: Health Psychology. Vol. 12(4). 324-33.

Weinstein, N.D. (2007). Misleading tests of health behavior theories. In: Annals of Behavioral Medicine. Vol. 33. 1-10.

Weinstein, N.D. and Rothman, A.J. (2005). Revitalizing Research on health behavior theories. In: Health Education Research. Vol. 20. 294-297.

Welch Cline, R.J. (2003). At the intersection of micro and macro: opportunities and challenges for physician-patient communication research. In: Patient Education and Counceling. Vol. 50. 13-16.

Wells, W./Burnett, J./Moriarty, S.E. (2003). Advertising: Principles and practice. 6th ed. Upper Saddle River, NJ: Prentice Hall.

Wells, W./Moriarty, S./Burnett, J. (2006). Advertising – Principles and Practice. 7th ed. Upper Saddle River, NJ: Pearson Prentice Hall.

Wells, W.D. (1993). Discovery-oriented consumer research. In: Journal of Consumer Research. Vol. 19(4). 489-504

Wenben Lai, A. (1995). Consumer Values, Product Benefits and Customer Value: a Consumption Behavior Approach. In: Advances in Consumer Research. Vol. 22. 381-388.

Wheaton, B./Muthen, B./Alwin, D.F./Summers, G. (1977). Assessing Reliability and Stability in Panel Models. In: Sociological Methodology. Vol. 8 (1). 84-136.

Wheaton, W. (1987). Assessment of fit in overidentified models with latent variables. In: Sociological Methods and Research. Vol. 16. 118-154

Whitlark, D.B./Geurts, M.D./Swenson, M.J. (1993). New product forecasting with a purchase intention survey. In: The Journal of Business Forecasting Methods and Systems. Vol. 12(3). 18-21.

Whittingham, J./Ruiter, R.A.C./Zimbile, F./Kok, G. (2008). Experimental pretesting of public health campaigns: a case study. In: Journal of Health Communication: International Perspectives. Vol. 13. 216-229

Whittler, T.E. and Spira, J.S. (2002). Model's Race: A Peripheral Cue in Advertising Messages? In: Journal of Consumer Psychology. Vol. 12(4). 291-301.

WHO. (1946). Preamble to the Constitution of the World Health Organization as adopted by the International Health Conference, New York, 19 June - 22 July 1946. Retrieved from http://www.who.int/suggestions/faq/en/index.html (accessed 01.03.2014)

WHO. (1978). Report on the International Conference on Primary Health Care. Alma Ata. 6-12 September 1978. Geneva, Switzerland.

WHO. (1986). Ottawa Charter for Health Promotion. First International Conference on Health Promotion. Retrieved from http://www.who.int/healthpromotion/conferences/previous/ottawa/en/ (accessed 15.02.2013)

WHO. (2001). Climate and Health. Factsheet 266. Geneva: WHO.

WHO. (2001). Evaluation in Health Promotion: Principles and Perspectives. Retrieved from http://www.euro.who.int/__data/assets/pdf_file/0007/108934/E73455.pdf (accessed 07.04.2013)

WHO. (2002). The WORLD HEALTH REPORT 2002: Reducing Risks, Promoting Healthy Life. Retrieved from http://www.who.int/whr/2002/en/whr02_en.pdf?ua=1 (accessed 01.03.2014)

WHO. (2006). Constitution of the World Health Organization. Basic Documents. 45th ed. Geneva, Switzerland. Retrieved from http://www.who.int/governance/eb/who_constitution_en.pdf (accessed 11.06.2014)

WHO. (2007). Achieving health equity: From root causes to fair outcomes. Geneva. WHO Commission on the Social Determinants of Health. Retrieved from http://whqlibdoc.who.int/publications/2007/interim_statement_eng.pdf (accessed 06.02.2013)

WHO. (2013). The right to health. Retrieved from http://www.who.int/mediacentre/factsheets/fs323/en/ (accessed 01.03.2014)

Wickerham, G. (1986). Power and power analysis: beyond Foucault? In: Gane, M. (ed.). Toward a Critique of Foucault. London: Routledge.

Widder, J. (2004). The origins of medical evidence: Communication and experimentation. In: Medicine, Health Care and Philosophy. Vol. 7. 99–104.

Wiles, C. R./Wiles, J. A./Tiernlund, A. (1996). The Ideology of Advertising: The United States and Sweden. In: Journal of Advertising Research. Vol. 36(3).57-66.

Wilkinson, A. (1998). Empowerment theory and practice. In: Personnel Review. Vol. 27(1). 40.

Williams, L.J. and Holahan, P.J. (1994). Parsimony-based fit indices for multiple-indicator models: Do they work? In: Structural Equation Modeling. Vol. 1. 161–189.

Williams, S.J. and Calnan, M. (eds.) (1996). Modern Medicine: Lay Perspectives and Experiences. London: UCL Press.

Williams, S.J./Gabe, J./Davis, P. (2008). The sociology of pharmaceuticals: progress and Prospects. In: Sociology of Health and Illness. Vol. 30(6). 813-824.

Williams, S.J./Seale, C./Boden, S./Lowe, P./Steinberg, D.L. (2008). Waking up to sleepiness: modafinil, the media and the pharmaceuticalisation of everyday/ night life. In: Sociology of Health and Illness. Vol. 30. 839-855.

Williamson, G.S. and Pearse, I.H. (1966). Science, Synthesis, and Sanity: An Inquiry into the Nature of Living. Chicago: Regency Press.

Williamson, J. (1978). Decoding advertisements – Ideology and Meaning in Advertising. London: Marion Boyars.

Willis, P. (1990). Common Culture: Symbolic Work at Play in the Everyday Cultures of the Young. Milton Keynes: Open University Press.

Wilson, P. (2001). A Policy Analysis of the Expert Patient in the United Kingdom: Self-Care as an Expression of Pastoral Power? In: Health and Social Care in the Community. Vol. 9(3). 134-142.

Wind, J. and Mahajan, V. (2001), The challenge of digital marketing. In: Wind, J. and Mahajan, V. (eds.). Digital Marketing: Global Strategies from the World's Leading Experts. New York, NY: Wiley. 3-25.

Wind, Y. and Rangaswamy, A. (2001). Customerization: the next revolution in mass customization. In: Journal of Interactive Marketing. Vol. 15(1). 13-32.

Wind, Y.J. (1994). Pharmaceutical Advertising – A Business School Perspective. In: Archives of Family Medicine. Vol. 3(4). 321-323.

Winer, R.S. (1999): Experimentation in the 21st Century: The Importance of External Validity. In: Journal of the Academy of Marketing Science. Vol. 27(3). 349-358.

Witte, K. (1992). Preventing AIDS through persuasive communications: A framework for constructing effective, culturally-specific, preventive health messages. In: International and Intercultural Annual. Vol. 16. 67-86.

Witte, K. (1992). Putting the fear back into fear appeals: the extended parallel process model. In: Communication Monographs. Vol. 59. 329-349.

Witte, K. (1993). Message and conceptual confounds in fear appeals: The role of judgment methods. In: Southern Communication Journal. Vol. 58. 147-155.

Witte, K. (1995). Generating effective risk messages. How scary should your risk communication be? In: Communication Yearbook. Vol. 18. 229-254.

Witte, K. and Allen, A. (2000). A Meta-Analysis of Fear Appeals: Implications for Public Health Campaigns. In: Health Education and Behavior. Vol. 27(5). 591-615.

Witte, K./Stokols, D./Iturate, P./Scheander, M. (1993). Testing the health belief model in a field study to promote bicycle safety helmets. In: Communication Research. Vol. 20. 564-586.

Wolfe, S.M. (2002) Direct-to-consumer advertising – education or emotion promotion? In: New England Journal of Medicine. Vol. 346(18). 524-526.

Woodside, A. and Taylor, J. (1978). Consumer Purchase Intentions of Product Quality and National Advertising. In: Journal of Advertising. Vol. 7(1). 48-51.

Worcester, N. and Whately, M. (1992). The Selling of HRT: playing on the fear factor. In: Feminist Review. Vol. 41. 1-26.

World Bank. (2002). Social Capital and development. World Bank's Social Capital Team-Social Development Department. Retrieved from http://web.worldbank.org/WBSITE/EXTERNAL/TOPICS/EXTSOCIALDEVELOPMENT/EXTTSOCIALCAPITAL/0,,contentMDK:20194767~menuPK:401035~pagePK:148956~piPK:216618~theSitePK:401015~isCURL:Y,00.html (accessed 10.02.2013)

World Health Organization. (2003). Mediterranean Centre for Vulnerability Reduction. Mobilizing for Action, Communication-for-Behavioural-Impact (COMBI). The Communication Initiative. Retrieved from https://www.k4health.org/sites/default/files/COMBI.pdf (accessed 11.06.2014)

Wright, K.B./Sparks, L./O'Hair, H.D. (2008). Health Communication in the 21st century. Oxford: Blackwell.

Wright, L.T./Newman, A./Dennis, C. (2006). Enhancing consumer empowerment. In: Emerald Journal of Marketing. Vol. 40(9/10). 925-935.

Wright, P.L. (1974). On the Direct Monitoring of Cognitive Responses to Advertising. In: Hughes, G. and Ray, M. (eds.). Buyer/Consumer Information Processing. Chapel Hill: University of North Carolina Press.

Wright, R.A./Junious, T.R./Neal, C./Avello, A./Graham, C./Herrmann, L./Junious, S./Walton, N. (2007). Mental fatigue influence on effort-related cardiovascular response. In: International Journal of Psychophysiology. Vol. 69(2). 127-133.

Wurtele, S. K. and Maddux, J. E. (1987). Relative contributions of protection motivation theory components in predicting exercise intentions and behavior. In: Health Psychology. Vol. 6. 435-466.

Yanovitzky, I. and Stryker, J. (2001). Mass media, social norms, and health promotion efforts: An longitudinal study of media effects on youth binge drinking. In: Communication Research. Vol. 28. 208-239.

Yin, J. (1999). International Advertising Strategies in China: A Worldwide Survey of Foreign Advertisers. In: Journal of Advertising Research. Vol. 39. 25-35.

Young, J.R. (2003). Prozac campus: more students seek counseling and take psychiatric medication. Retrieved from http://business.highbeam.com/434953/article-1G1-147122694/prozac-campus-more-students-seek-counseling-and-take (accessed 24.05.2013)

Yuan, K.H. (2005). Fit Indices Versus Test Statistics. In: Multivariate Behavioral Research. Vol. 40(1). 115-48.

Yzer, M. (2012). The Integrative Model of Behavioral Prediction as a Tool for Designinig Health Messages. In: Cho, H. (ed.). Health Communication Message Design: Theory and Practice. Los Angeles, CA: Sage. 21-40.

Zagaria, M.A.E. (2004). Low Health Literacy: Raising Awareness for Optimal Health Communication. In: U.S. Pharmacist. Vol. 10. 41–48.

Zaichkowsky, J.L. (1985). Measuring the Involvement Construct. In: Journal of Consumer Research. Vol. 12 (3). 341-352.

Zaichkowsky, J.L. (1994). The personal involvement inventory: reduction, revision, and application to advertising. In: Journal of Advertising. Vol. 23(4). 59-70.

Zandpour, F. and Campos, V. (1994). Global reach and local touch: Achieving cultural fitness in TV advertising. In: Journal of Advertising Research. Vol. 34(5). 35.

Zarcadoolas, C./Pleasant, A./Greer, D.S. (2005). Understanding Health Literacy: an expanded model. In: Health Promotion International. Vol. 20(2). 195-203.

Zeithaml, V.A. (1988). Consumer perceptions of price, quality, and value: a means-end and synthesis of evidence. In: Journal of Marketing, Vol. 52(3). 2-22.

Zinkhan, G.M. (1994). International Advertising: A Research Agenda. In: Journal of Advertising. Vol. 23(1). 11-15.

Zola, I. (1972). Medicine as an institution of social control. In: Sociological Review. Vol. 20. 487-503.

Zou, S. and Cavusgil, S. T. (2002). The GMS: A Broad Conceptualization of Global Marketing Strategy and Its Effects on Firm Performance. In: Journal of Marketing. Vol. 66(4). 40-56.

Zuckerman, M. (1988). Behavior and biology: Research on sensation seeking and reactions to the media. In: Donohew, L./Sypher, H.E./Higgins, E.T. (eds.). Communication, social cognition, and affect. Hillsdale, NJ: Erlbaum. 173–194.

Zuckerman, M. (1991). Psychobiology of personality. Cambridge: Cambridge University Press.

9 Appendix

Appendix A: Advertisements

Informative Ad

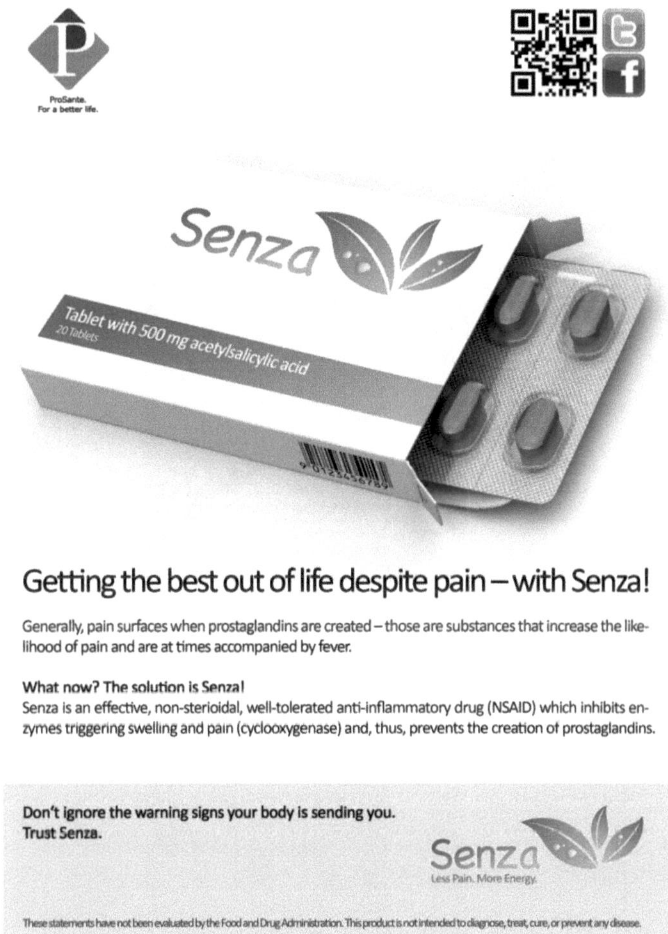

Emotional Ad

Mixed Ad

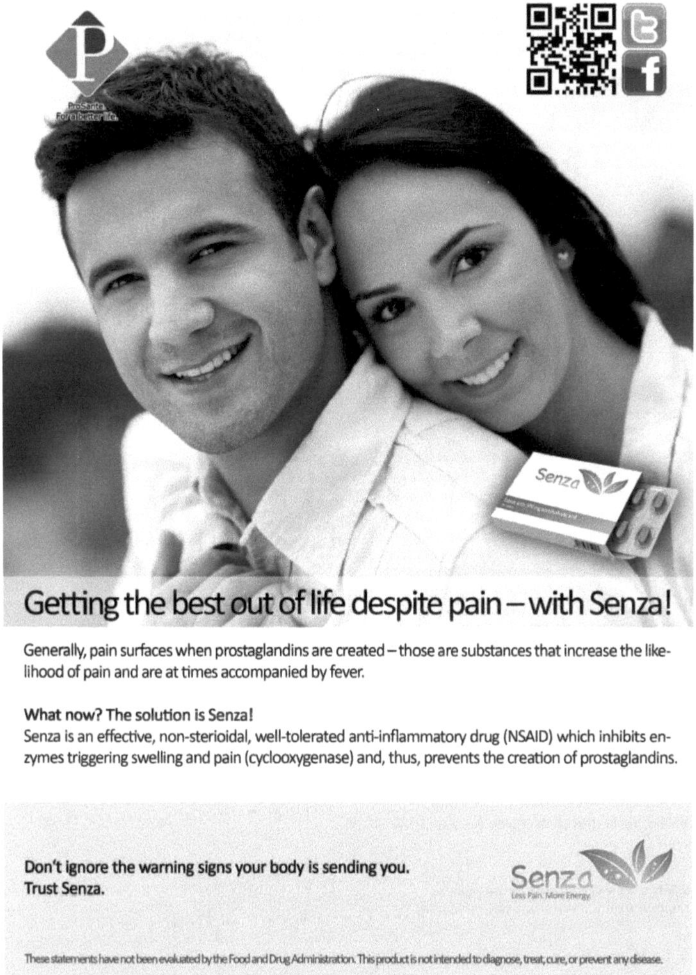
ProSante.
For a better life.
Senza
Getting the best out of life despite pain – with Senza!
Generally, pain surfaces when prostaglandins are created – those are substances that increase the likelihood of pain and are at times accompanied by fever.
What now? The solution is Senza!
Senza is an effective, non-sterioidal, well-tolerated anti-inflammatory drug (NSAID) which inhibits enzymes triggering swelling and pain (cyclooxygenase) and, thus, prevents the creation of prostaglandins.
Don't ignore the warning signs your body is sending you.
Trust Senza.
Senza
Less Pain. More Energy.
These statements have not been evaluated by the Food and Drug Administration. This product is not intended to diagnose, treat, cure, or prevent any disease.

CSR Ad

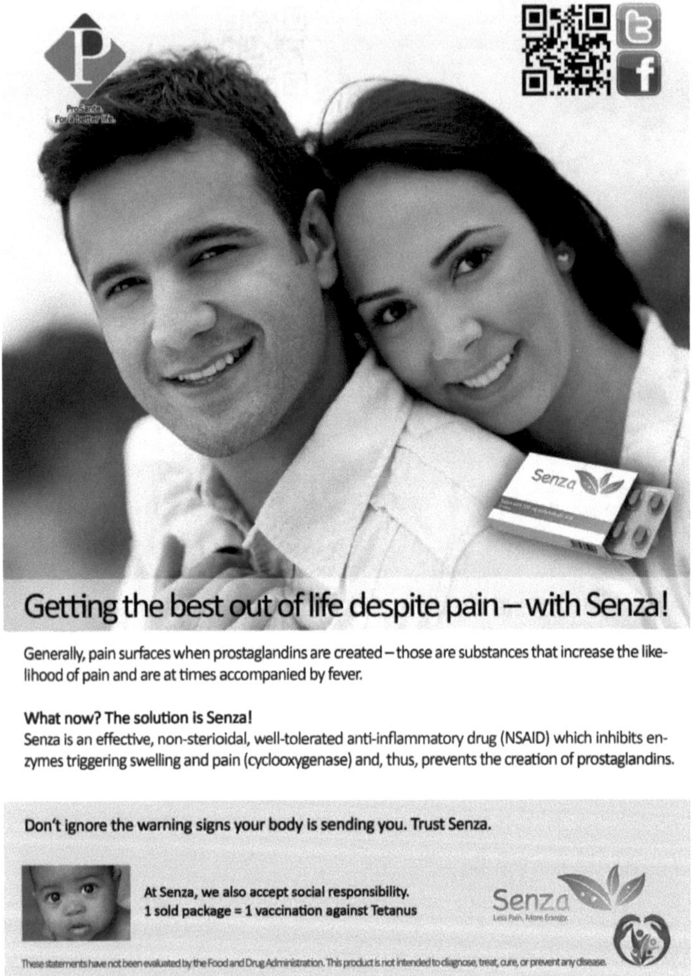
ProSante
For a better life.
Senza
Getting the best out of life despite pain – with Senza!
Generally, pain surfaces when prostaglandins are created – those are substances that increase the likelihood of pain and are at times accompanied by fever.
What now? The solution is Senza!
Senza is an effective, non-sterioidal, well-tolerated anti-inflammatory drug (NSAID) which inhibits enzymes triggering swelling and pain (cyclooxygenase) and, thus, prevents the creation of prostaglandins.
Don't ignore the warning signs your body is sending you. Trust Senza.
At Senza, we also accept social responsibility.
1 sold package = 1 vaccination against Tetanus
Senza
Less Pain, More Energy.
These statements have not been evaluated by the Food and Drug Administration. This product is not intended to diagnose, treat, cure, or prevent any disease.

Appendix B: Questionnaire

Questionnaire on health, communication and the effectiveness of OTC drug advertisements

General Information on filling in the questionnaire

Good day,
I would kindly ask you to briefly answer some questions on the topics of health, communication and advertising.
Please bear in mind that answers are neither correct nor incorrect but solely reflect your personal opinion. If you are unsure which answer to pick, trust your instinct.
Of course, all answers are anonymous. Please indicate your estimation by checking a box ❑. By use of the different boxes you can level your degree of approval.
In total, the questionnaire will take approximately 10 minutes to complete.
Thank you for your participation!

Part 1: Health Behavior and Attitude towards (the topic of) health

A	**To which degree do you agree with the following statements?**	
		I do not agree at all … I fully agree
A1	My health depends on how well I take care of myself.	❑ --- ❑ ---❑ ---❑ ---❑ ---❑ ---❑
A2	I actively try to prevent disease and illness.	❑ --- ❑ ---❑ ---❑ ---❑ ---❑ ---❑
A3	I am in good physical health.	❑ --- ❑ ---❑ ---❑ ---❑ ---❑ ---❑
A4	I reflect about my health a lot.	❑ --- ❑ ---❑ ---❑ ---❑ ---❑ ---❑
A5	I am very self-conscious about my health.	❑ --- ❑ ---❑ ---❑ ---❑ ---❑ ---❑
A6	I am constantly examining my health.	❑ --- ❑ ---❑ ---❑ ---❑ ---❑ ---❑
A7	In general, I know my health status very well.	❑ --- ❑ ---❑ ---❑ ---❑ ---❑ ---❑
A8	I am very involved with my health.	❑ --- ❑ ---❑ ---❑ ---❑ ---❑ ---❑
A9	Please indicate your weight.	_____ lbs
A10	Please indicate your height.	_____ ft

B	**To which degree do you agree with the following statements?**	
		I do not agree at all … I fully agree
B1	The amount of health information available today makes it easier for me to take care of my health.	❑ --- ❑ ---❑ ---❑ ---❑ ---❑ ---❑
B2	To be and stay healthy it's critical to be informed about health issues.	❑ --- ❑ ---❑ ---❑ ---❑ ---❑ ---❑
B3	When sick, I try to get information about my disease.	❑ --- ❑ ---❑ ---❑ ---❑ ---❑ ---❑
B4	Before making a decision about my health, I find out everything I can about this issue.	❑ --- ❑ ---❑ ---❑ ---❑ ---❑ ---❑
B5	I like to get health information from a variety of sources.	❑ --- ❑ ---❑ ---❑ ---❑ ---❑ ---❑
B6	I know where to look to find the pharmaceutical product information I need.	❑ --- ❑ ---❑ ---❑ ---❑ ---❑ ---❑
B7	I feel overwhelmed with the variety of drugs available on the market.	❑ --- ❑ ---❑ ---❑ ---❑ ---❑ ---❑
B8	Choosing a pharmaceutical product takes a lot of careful thought.	❑ --- ❑ ---❑ ---❑ ---❑ ---❑ ---❑
B9	I trust my own judgment when deciding which pharmaceutical product to consider.	❑ --- ❑ ---❑ ---❑ ---❑ ---❑ ---❑

C	How important are the following sources when searching for health-related information?	
		not important at all … very important
C1	family (partner, parents, children, etc.)	❑ --- ❑ ---❑ ---❑ ---❑ ---❑ ---❑
C2	friends, acquaintances/colleagues	❑ --- ❑ ---❑ ---❑ ---❑ ---❑ ---❑
C3	doctors, pharmacists or alternative practitioners	❑ --- ❑ ---❑ ---❑ ---❑ ---❑ ---❑
C4	advertising in newspapers and magazines	❑ --- ❑ ---❑ ---❑ ---❑ ---❑ ---❑
C5	advertising on TV and the radio	❑ --- ❑ ---❑ ---❑ ---❑ ---❑ ---❑
C6	advertising on social media sites (e.g., facebook)	❑ --- ❑ ---❑ ---❑ ---❑ ---❑ ---❑
C7	advertising on the Internet	❑ --- ❑ ---❑ ---❑ ---❑ ---❑ ---❑
C8	editorial content in print media	❑ --- ❑ ---❑ ---❑ ---❑ ---❑ ---❑
C9	editorial content in broadcasting	❑ --- ❑ ---❑ ---❑ ---❑ ---❑ ---❑
C10	editorial content on the Internet	❑ --- ❑ ---❑ ---❑ ---❑ ---❑ ---❑
C11	specialist literature (e.g., medical books or magazines)	❑ --- ❑ ---❑ ---❑ ---❑ ---❑ ---❑
C12	Other: ____________________	❑ --- ❑ ---❑ ---❑ ---❑ ---❑ ---❑

D	To which degree do you agree with the following statements?	
		I do not agree at all … I fully agree
D1	I consider myself capable of taking care of my body.	❑ --- ❑ ---❑ ---❑ ---❑ ---❑ ---❑
D2	I consider myself capable of finding the right information to make qualified health decisions.	❑ --- ❑ ---❑ ---❑ ---❑ ---❑ ---❑
D3	Usually, I can make sense of the health information I am presented with.	❑ --- ❑ ---❑ ---❑ ---❑ ---❑ ---❑
D4	I can use my knowledge to improve my health.	❑ --- ❑ ---❑ ---❑ ---❑ ---❑ ---❑
D5	I rely more on doctors and/or pharmacists than on self-medication.	❑ --- ❑ ---❑ ---❑ ---❑ ---❑ ---❑
D6	I am interested in self-medication.	❑ --- ❑ ---❑ ---❑ ---❑ ---❑ ---❑
D7	I consider myself capable of self-medication.	❑ --- ❑ ---❑ ---❑ ---❑ ---❑ ---❑
D8	I already practice self-medication.	❑ --- ❑ ---❑ ---❑ ---❑ ---❑ ---❑
		very often … never
D9	How often do you practice self-medication?	❑ --- ❑ ---❑ ---❑ ---❑ ---❑ ---❑

Part 2: Advertising and Health

E	To which degree do you agree with the following statements?	
		I do not agree at all … I fully agree
E1	Advertisers know how to provide the information that is needed to make a qualified decision.	❑ --- ❑ ---❑ ---❑ ---❑ ---❑ ---❑
E2	Overall, I consider advertising a good thing.	❑ --- ❑ ---❑ ---❑ ---❑ ---❑ ---❑
E3	My general opinion about advertising is unfavorable.	❑ --- ❑ ---❑ ---❑ ---❑ ---❑ ---❑
E4	Overall, I do like advertising.	❑ --- ❑ ---❑ ---❑ ---❑ ---❑ ---❑
E5	I can depend on getting the truth in most advertising.	❑ --- ❑ ---❑ ---❑ ---❑ ---❑ ---❑
E6	Advertising's aim is to inform the consumer.	❑ --- ❑ ---❑ ---❑ ---❑ ---❑ ---❑
E7	I feel I have been accurately informed after viewing most advertisements.	❑ --- ❑ ---❑ ---❑ ---❑ ---❑ ---❑

F	To which degree do you agree with the following statements?	
		I do not agree at all … I fully agree
F1	Advertisers for pharmaceuticals know how to provide the information that is needed to make a qualified decision.	❑ --- ❑ ---❑ ---❑ ---❑ ---❑ ---❑
F2	Overall, I consider advertising for pharmaceuticals a good thing.	❑ --- ❑ ---❑ ---❑ ---❑ ---❑ ---❑
F3	My general opinion about advertising for pharmaceuticals is unfavorable.	❑ --- ❑ ---❑ ---❑ ---❑ ---❑ ---❑

F4	Overall, I do like advertising for pharmaceuticals.	❑ --- ❑ ---❑ ---❑ ---❑ ---❑ ---❑
F5	I can depend on getting the truth in most advertising for pharmaceuticals.	❑ --- ❑ ---❑ ---❑ ---❑ ---❑ ---❑
F6	Advertising for pharmaceuticals' aim is to inform the consumer.	❑ --- ❑ ---❑ ---❑ ---❑ ---❑ ---❑
F7	I feel I have been accurately informed after viewing most advertisements for pharmaceuticals.	❑ --- ❑ ---❑ ---❑ ---❑ ---❑ ---❑
G	**The ad you are about to evaluate is for non-prescription, over-the counter (OTC) medication. So in advance, I would like to know to which degree you do agree with the following statements.**	
		I do not agree at all — I fully agree
G1	I think advertising for OTC medications is strictly regulated by the government.	❑ --- ❑ ---❑ ---❑ ---❑ ---❑ ---❑ ❑ I don't know
G2	Most OTC drug ads provide balanced information (risks and benefits).	❑ --- ❑ ---❑ ---❑ ---❑ ---❑ ---❑
G3	My previous experiences with OTC drugs were positive.	❑ --- ❑ ---❑ ---❑ ---❑ ---❑ ---❑
G4	I consider OTC drugs as effective as prescription drugs.	❑ --- ❑ ---❑ ---❑ ---❑ ---❑ ---❑
H	**How do you evaluate the following types of medicine?**	
		not good at all — very good
H1	conventional/mainstream medicine	❑ --- ❑ ---❑ ---❑ ---❑ ---❑ ---❑
H2	homeopathic substances/homeopathy	❑ --- ❑ ---❑ ---❑ ---❑ ---❑ ---❑
H3	herbal substances	❑ --- ❑ ---❑ ---❑ ---❑ ---❑ ---❑
H4	Other______________________________	❑ --- ❑ ---❑ ---❑ ---❑ ---❑ ---❑
I	**How often do you usually take the following substances within a year?**	
		never — very often
I1	non-prescription/OTC medicines	❑ --- ❑ ---❑ ---❑ ---❑ ---❑ ---❑
I2	prescription medicines	❑ --- ❑ ---❑ ---❑ ---❑ ---❑ ---❑
J	**To which degree do you agree with the following statements?**	
		I do not agree at all — I fully agree
J1	I am interested in non-prescription (OTC) drugs.	❑ --- ❑ ---❑ ---❑ ---❑ ---❑ ---❑
J2	Non-prescription (OTC) drugs are important to me.	❑ --- ❑ ---❑ ---❑ ---❑ ---❑ ---❑
J3	I attach (great) importance to non-prescription (OTC) drugs.	❑ --- ❑ ---❑ ---❑ ---❑ ---❑ ---❑

If you are here, please inform the interviewer, so that he/she can provide you with the ad to be examined.

Part 3: OTC Print Ad Analysis

		not good at all — very good
K	**In general, I find the ad ...**	❑ --- ❑ ---❑ ---❑ ---❑ ---❑ ---❑

L	To which degree do you agree with the following statements?	
	The advertisement is…	I do not agree at all … I fully agree
L1	interesting	❑ --- ❑ ---❑ ---❑ ---❑ ---❑ ---❑
L2	emotional	❑ --- ❑ ---❑ ---❑ ---❑ ---❑ ---❑
L3	pleasant	❑ --- ❑ ---❑ ---❑ ---❑ ---❑ ---❑
L4	good	❑ --- ❑ ---❑ ---❑ ---❑ ---❑ ---❑
L5	favorable	❑ --- ❑ ---❑ ---❑ ---❑ ---❑ ---❑
L6	positive	❑ --- ❑ ---❑ ---❑ ---❑ ---❑ ---❑
L7	informative	❑ --- ❑ ---❑ ---❑ ---❑ ---❑ ---❑
L8	convincing	❑ --- ❑ ---❑ ---❑ ---❑ ---❑ ---❑
L9	credible	❑ --- ❑ ---❑ ---❑ ---❑ ---❑ ---❑
L10	truthful	❑ --- ❑ ---❑ ---❑ ---❑ ---❑ ---❑
L11	believable	❑ --- ❑ ---❑ ---❑ ---❑ ---❑ ---❑
L12	comprehensible	❑ --- ❑ ---❑ ---❑ ---❑ ---❑ ---❑
L13	well structured	❑ --- ❑ ---❑ ---❑ ---❑ ---❑ ---❑
L14	clear	❑ --- ❑ ---❑ ---❑ ---❑ ---❑ ---❑

M	To which degree do you agree with the following statements?	
		I do not agree at all … I fully agree
M1	The ad makes valid claims.	❑ --- ❑ ---❑ ---❑ ---❑ ---❑ ---❑
M2	The ad presents accurate information.	❑ --- ❑ ---❑ ---❑ ---❑ ---❑ ---❑
M3	The message was easy to follow.	❑ --- ❑ ---❑ ---❑ ---❑ ---❑ ---❑
M4	I think the ad addresses relevant product features.	❑ --- ❑ ---❑ ---❑ ---❑ ---❑ ---❑
M5	I understand the features well enough to evaluate the product.	❑ --- ❑ ---❑ ---❑ ---❑ ---❑ ---❑
M6	The ad improves my level of information regarding pharmaceuticals.	❑ --- ❑ ---❑ ---❑ ---❑ ---❑ ---❑

N	The ad you have seen was promoting a pain killer. To which degree do you agree with the following statements?	
		I do not agree at all … I fully agree
N1	I have a positive attitude towards pain medications.	❑ --- ❑ ---❑ ---❑ ---❑ ---❑ ---❑
N2	I am confident that pain medications can improve my current health status.	❑ --- ❑ ---❑ ---❑ ---❑ ---❑ ---❑
		never … very often
N3	How often do you take pain medications?	❑ --- ❑ ---❑ ---❑ ---❑ ---❑ ---❑

O	To which degree do you agree with the following statements?	
		I do not agree at all … I fully agree
O1	The ad allows me to objectively evaluate SENZA.	❑ --- ❑ ---❑ ---❑ ---❑ ---❑ ---❑
O2	I learned something from this advertisement that I did not know before about pain medications.	❑ --- ❑ ---❑ ---❑ ---❑ ---❑ ---❑
O3	I can now accurately compare SENZA with other competing brands on matters that are important to me.	❑ --- ❑ ---❑ ---❑ ---❑ ---❑ ---❑
O4	I would have more confidence in using SENZA now than before I saw this commercial.	❑ --- ❑ ---❑ ---❑ ---❑ ---❑ ---❑
O5	The advertisement was useful and provided me with new insights regarding pain and pain medication.	❑ --- ❑ ---❑ ---❑ ---❑ ---❑ ---❑
O6	I feel more confident in my self-medication skills/practices after having studied this ad.	❑ --- ❑ ---❑ ---❑ ---❑ ---❑ ---❑

O7	I am more interested in self-medication now than before seeing the ad.	❑ --- ❑ ---❑ ---❑ ---❑ ---❑ ---❑
O8	After seeing the ad I feel more autonomous with regard to my health.	❑ --- ❑ ---❑ ---❑ ---❑ ---❑ ---❑
O9	After seeing the ad I feel more capable with regard to my health.	❑ --- ❑ ---❑ ---❑ ---❑ ---❑ ---❑
O10	I feel like I have a greater say in my health after seeing the ad.	❑ --- ❑ ---❑ ---❑ ---❑ ---❑ ---❑
O11	The advertising message gives me stronger control over my health.	❑ --- ❑ ---❑ ---❑ ---❑ ---❑ ---❑
O12	The advertising message enables me to improve my health.	❑ --- ❑ ---❑ ---❑ ---❑ ---❑ ---❑
O13	The advertising message empowers me to make better health-related decisions.	❑ --- ❑ ---❑ ---❑ ---❑ ---❑ ---❑
P	**To which degree do you agree with the following statements?**	
		I do not agree at all ... I fully agree
P1	The advertised product (SENZA) makes a good impression.	❑ --- ❑ ---❑ ---❑ ---❑ ---❑ ---❑
P2	SENZA is of high-quality.	❑ --- ❑ ---❑ ---❑ ---❑ ---❑ ---❑
P3	SENZA is attractive.	❑ --- ❑ ---❑ ---❑ ---❑ ---❑ ---❑
P4	SENZA is appealing.	❑ --- ❑ ---❑ ---❑ ---❑ ---❑ ---❑
Q	**To which degree do you agree with the following statements?**	
		I do not agree at all ... I fully agree
Q1	I could imagine trying SENZA.	❑ --- ❑ ---❑ ---❑ ---❑ ---❑ ---❑
Q2	I could imagine buying SENZA.	❑ --- ❑ ---❑ ---❑ ---❑ ---❑ ---❑
Q3	I could imagine SENZA being one of my most likely choices for my next purchases.	❑ --- ❑ ---❑ ---❑ ---❑ ---❑ ---❑
Q4	I am interested in more information on SENZA and will look it up online (on facebook, twitter, google+).	❑ --- ❑ ---❑ ---❑ ---❑ ---❑ ---❑
R	**To which degree do you agree with the following statements?**	
		I do not agree at all ... I fully agree
R1	I think positively about enterprises which act socially responsible.	❑ --- ❑ ---❑ ---❑ ---❑ ---❑ ---❑
R2	It is important to me that enterprises increasingly consider social issues.	❑ --- ❑ ---❑ ---❑ ---❑ ---❑ ---❑
R3	I would increasingly purchase products from enterprises which act socially responsible.	❑ --- ❑ ---❑ ---❑ ---❑ ---❑ ---❑
R4	I have the impression ProSante (producer of SENZA) is a socially responsible company.	❑ --- ❑ ---❑ ---❑ ---❑ ---❑ ---❑
R5	I think that ProSante donating vaccines to reduce infant death caused by Tetanus represents a good match between the product and the cause.	❑ --- ❑ ---❑ ---❑ ---❑ ---❑ ---❑

Part 4: Demographic Information		
S1	Are you a student?	❑ yes ❑ no
S2	Are you employed?	❑ yes ❑ no
S3	Do you work full time or part time?	❑ full time ❑ part time
S4	Please indicate your profession.	___________________________
T	**To which degree do you agree with the following statements?**	
	My daily activities are…	I do not agree at all … I fully agree
T1	physically demanding.	❑ --- ❑ --- ❑ --- ❑ --- ❑ --- ❑ --- ❑
T2	hectic.	❑ --- ❑ --- ❑ --- ❑ --- ❑ --- ❑ --- ❑
U1	Please indicate your sex.	❑ female ❑ male
U2	Please indicate your nationality.	____________________
U3	How old are you?	______ years
V	Please indicate your (highest) level of education.	❑ no graduation ❑ primary school graduation ❑ graduation from secondary modern school ❑ graduation from high school ❑ graduation from university/college
W1	Do you live in a domestic partnership?	❑ yes ❑ no
W2	Do you have children?	❑ yes ❑ no
W3	If yes, how many children do you have?	_______ child/ren
Thank you for your participation! For further questions, please send an email to senza@aau.at or visit www.aau.at/senza.		

Appendix C: Mean values

General Questions

Part 1: Health Behavior and Attitude towards (the topic of) health (Countries)

A	**To which degree do you agree with the following statements?**					
		Total	**AUT**	**GER**	**USA**	**BRA**
A1	My health depends on how well I take care of myself.	5.961	5.854	5.721	6.132	6.137
A2	I actively try to prevent disease and illness.	5.358	5.150	5.131	5.789	5.361
A3	I am in good physical health.	5.666	5.917	5.807	5.694	5.245
A4	I reflect about my health a lot.	5.015	5.088	4.627	5.211	5.137
A5	I am very self-conscious about my health.	5.165	5.462	5.160	4.861	5.180
A6	I am constantly examining my health.	4.221	4.063	3.765	4.545	4.515
A7	In general, I know my health status very well.	5.245	5.483	5.144	5.352	5.001
A8	I am very involved with my health.	5.308	5.621	5.610	5.201	4.796
A9	Please indicate your weight.	72.55	69.87	74.19	75.58	70.50
A10	Please indicate your height.	171.94	172.15	173.69	172.16	169.76

B	**To which degree do you agree with the following statements?**					
		Total	**AUT**	**GER**	**USA**	**BRA**
B1	The amount of health information available today makes it easier for me to take care of my health.	5.280	4.879	4.770	5.798	5.676
B2	To be and stay healthy it's critical to be informed about health issues.	5.428	5.006	4.879	5.898	5.934
B3	When sick, I try to get information about my disease.	5.689	5.596	5.414	5.926	5.822
B4	Before making a decision about my health, I find out everything I can about this issue.	5.223	5.050	4.952	5.756	5.133
B5	I like to get health information from a variety of sources.	5.458	5.462	5.371	5.762	5.237
B6	I know where to look to find the pharmaceutical product information I need.	5.239	5.638	5.176	5.294	4.847
B7	I feel overwhelmed with the variety of drugs available on the market.	4.579	4.717	4.603	4.635	4.363
B8	Choosing a pharmaceutical product takes a lot of careful thought.	5.302	5.225	5.166	5.453	5.365
B9	I trust my own judgment when deciding which pharmaceutical product to consider.	4.364	4.678	4.439	4.828	3.510

C	**How important are the following sources when searching for health-related information?**					
		Total	**AUT**	**GER**	**USA**	**BRA**
C1	family (partner, parents, children, etc.)	5.621	5.837	5.765	5.512	5.369
C2	friends, acquaintances/colleagues	4.780	4.958	4.955	4.620	4.587
C3	doctors, pharmacists or alternative practitioners	6.367	6.232	6.221	6.512	6.502
C4	advertising in newspapers and magazines	3.061	2.863	2.680	3.227	3.477
C5	advertising on TV and the radio	2.961	2.708	2.520	3.145	3.473
C6	advertising on social media sites (e.g., facebook)	2.488	2.231	2.045	2.818	2.861
C7	advertising on the Internet	2.601	2.390	2.078	3.015	2.926
C8	editorial content in print media	3.385	3.349	3.250	3.698	3.242
C9	editorial content in broadcasting	3.179	3.000	2.881	3.574	3.261
C10	editorial content on the Internet	3.336	3.025	3.178	3.753	3.387
C11	specialist literature (e.g., medical books or magazines)	4.676	4.643	4.340	4.977	4.746

D	To which degree do you agree with the following statements?					
		Total	AUT	GER	USA	BRA
D1	I consider myself capable of taking care of my body.	5.901	6.154	5.967	6.095	5.386
D2	I consider myself capable of finding the right information to make qualified health decisions.	5.466	5.712	5.492	5.839	4.822
D3	Usually, I can make sense of the health information I am presented with.	5.615	5.775	5.519	5.825	5.341
D4	I can use my knowledge to improve my health.	5.752	5.658	5.565	6.085	5.701
D5	I rely more on doctors and/or pharmacists than on self-medication.	5.498	5.381	5.180	5.163	6.274
D6	I am interested in self-medication.	4.129	4.175	4.258	4.446	3.635
D7	I consider myself capable of self-medication.	4.268	4.408	4.627	4.616	3.415
D8	I already practice self-medication.	3.911	3.837	4.019	3.884	3.903

Part 2: Advertising and Health

E	To which degree do you agree with the following statements?					
		Total	AUT	GER	USA	BRA
E1	Advertisers know how to provide the information that is needed to make a qualified decision.	3.697	4.021	4.081	3.227	3.456
E2	Overall, I consider advertising a good thing.	3.974	3.967	3.652	3.744	4.539
E3	My general opinion about advertising is unfavorable.	3.941	3.858	3.525	3.896	4.489
E4	Overall, I do like advertising.	3.684	3.609	3.243	3.883	4.004
E5	I can depend on getting the truth in most advertising.	2.750	2.541	2.353	2.693	3.416
E6	Advertising's aim is to inform the consumer.	3.290	3.214	2.985	3.026	3.942
E7	I feel I have been accurately informed after viewing most advertisements.	2.874	2.891	2.627	2.781	3.199

F	To which degree do you agree with the following statements?					
		Total	AUT	GER	USA	BRA
F1	Advertisers for pharmaceuticals know how to provide the information that is needed to make a qualified decision.	3.758	3.966	3.881	3.409	3.775
F2	Overall, I consider advertising for pharmaceuticals a good thing.	3.494	3.525	3.207	3.360	3.890
F3	My general opinion about advertising for pharmaceuticals is unfavorable.	3.697	3.608	3.660	3.508	4.001
F4	Overall, I do like advertising for pharmaceuticals.	3.112	3.168	2.734	3.322	3.228
F5	I can depend on getting the truth in most advertising for pharmaceuticals.	3.007	3.038	2.758	2.855	3.382
F6	Advertising for pharmaceuticals' aim is to inform the consumer.	3.361	3.408	3.088	3.273	3.680
F7	I feel I have been accurately informed after viewing most advertisements for pharmaceuticals.	2.985	3.171	2.906	2.979	2.888

G	The ad you are about to evaluate is for non-prescription, over-the counter (OTC) medication. So in advance, I would like to know to which degree you do agree with the following statements.					
		Total	AUT	GER	USA	BRA
G1	I think advertising for OTC medications is strictly regulated by the government.	3.055	3.331	2.935	2.969	2.988
G2	Most OTC drug ads provide balanced information (risks and benefits).	3.378	3.275	2.977	3.730	3.531
G3	My previous experiences with OTC drugs were positive.	4.797	4.828	4.741	4.973	4.680

G4	I consider OTC drugs as effective as prescription drugs.	4.101	4.376	4.321	4.084	3.622
H	**How do you evaluate the following types of medicine?**					
		Total	**AUT**	**GER**	**USA**	**BRA**
H1	conventional/mainstream medicine	5.567	5.542	5.586	5.236	5.905
H2	homeopathic substances/homeopathy	4.698	4.733	4.443	4.532	5.087
H3	herbal substances	4.927	5.066	4.777	4.491	5.377
H4	Other____________________					
I	**How often do you usually take the following substances within a year?**					
		Total	**AUT**	**GER**	**USA**	**BRA**
I1	non-prescription/OTC medicines	4.248	4.078	4.096	4.207	4.614
I2	prescription medicines	3.994	3.846	3.582	4.198	4.353
J	**To which degree do you agree with the following statements?**					
		Total	**AUT**	**GER**	**USA**	**BRA**
J1	I am interested in non-prescription (OTC) drugs.	4.195	4.079	4.102	4.335	4.266
J2	Non-prescription (OTC) drugs are important to me.	4.024	3.817	3.885	4.223	4.170
J3	I attach (great) importance to non-prescription (OTC) drugs.	3.828	3.712	3.749	3.698	4.154
N	**The ad you have seen was promoting a pain killer. To which degree do you agree with the following statements?**					
		Total	**AUT**	**GER**	**USA**	**BRA**
N1	I have a positive attitude towards pain medications.	4.384	3.929	3.973	4.649	4.988
N2	I am confident that pain medications can improve my current health status.	3.803	3.475	3.434	3.781	4.527
N3	How often do you take pain medications?	3.385	2.942	3.018	3.398	5.187
R	**To which degree do you agree with the following statements?**					
		Total	**AUT**	**GER**	**USA**	**BRA**
R1	I think positively about enterprises which act socially responsible.	5.535	5.404	5.246	5.645	5.846
R2	It is important to me that enterprises increasingly consider social issues.	5.588	5.319	5.351	5.587	6.095
R3	I would increasingly purchase products from enterprises which act socially responsible.	5.168	4.829	4.750	5.343	5.826
	Part 4: Demographic Information					
T	**To which degree do you agree with the following statements?**					
	My daily activities are…	**Total**	**AUT**	**GER**	**USA**	**BRA**
T1	physically demanding.	4.792	4.824	4.852	4.491	5.004
T2	hectic.	4.795	4.782	4.444	4.961	4.996

Factorized General Scores

Factor	Total	Austria	Germany	USA	Brazil
Health Consciousness	4.9907	5.1435	4.8613	5.0341	4.9259
Self-Medication Ability	5.6465	5.7362	5.5446	5.8013	5.5048
Attitude towards Self-Medication	4.1027	4.1402	4.3014	4.3152	3.6510
Attitude towards Advertising	3.7824	3.8715	3.6487	3.6120	4.0000
Attitude towards Pharmaceutical Advertising	3.4520	3.5527	3.2702	3.3636	3.6262
Skepticism towards Advertising	5.0307	5.1336	5.3514	5.1736	4.4583
Skepticism towards pharmaceutical Advertising	4.8799	4.8037	5.0944	4.9542	4.6624
Attitude towards OTC drugs	4.0157	3.8692	3.9121	4.0854	4.1964
Attitude towards CSR	5.4361	5.1841	5.1156	5.5248	5.9225

Ad scores (informative)

Part 3: OTC Print Ad Analysis (informative – countries)						
		Total	**AUT**	**GER**	**USA**	**BRA**
K	**In general, I find the ad ...**	4.344	4.212	4.311	4.036	4.817
L	**To which degree do you agree with the following statements?**					
	The advertisement is...	**Total**	**AUT**	**GER**	**USA**	**BRA**
L1	interesting	4.261	4.150	4.361	3.600	4.933
L2	emotional	2.797	3.033	3.180	2.517	2.450
L3	pleasant	4.121	4.050	4.197	3.987	4.250
L4	good	4.195	4.233	3.984	3.867	4.700
L5	favorable	4.091	3.767	3.934	3.917	4.750
L6	positive	4.556	4.267	4.607	4.350	5.000
L7	informative	4.332	4.300	4.393	3.883	4.750
L8	convincing	3.639	3.717	3.508	3.200	4.133
L9	credible	3.632	3.757	3.836	3.000	3.933
L10	truthful	3.726	3.608	3.631	3.350	4.317
L11	believable	3.909	3.817	3.885	3.517	4.417
L12	comprehensible	4.328	4.717	3.852	3.983	4.767
L13	well structured	4.498	4.567	4.361	4.400	4.667
L14	clear	4.578	4.733	4.164	4.569	4.853
M	**To which degree do you agree with the following statements?**					
		Total	**AUT**	**GER**	**USA**	**BRA**
M1	The ad makes valid claims.	4.186	4.166	4.115	3.517	4.950
M2	The ad presents accurate information.	4.000	4.067	3.836	3.750	4.350
M3	The message was easy to follow.	4.830	5.017	4.607	4.800	4.900
M4	I think the ad addresses relevant product features.	4.241	4.183	4.246	4.083	4.450
M5	I understand the features well enough to evaluate the product.	4.000	4.300	3.623	3.450	4.633
M6	The ad improves my level of information regarding pharmaceuticals.	3.490	3.383	3.098	3.283	4.200

O	To which degree do you agree with the following statements?					
		Total	**AUT**	**GER**	**USA**	**BRA**
O1	The ad allows me to objectively evaluate SENZA.	3.705	3.717	3.623	3.333	4.150
O2	I learned something from this advertisement that I did not know before about pain medications.	3.593	3.200	3.393	3.667	4.117
O3	I can now accurately compare SENZA with other competing brands on matters that are important to me.	3.170	3.083	2.639	3.200	3.767
O4	I would have more confidence in using SENZA now than before I saw this commercial.	3.216	2.817	2.902	3.167	3.983
O5	The advertisement was useful and provided me with new insights regarding pain and pain medication.	3.386	2.967	2.967	3.433	4.183
O6	I feel more confident in my self-medication skills/practices after having studied this ad.	2.850	2.750	2.607	2.996	3.050
O7	I am more interested in self-medication now than before seeing the ad.	2.577	2.433	2.279	2.633	2.967
O8	After seeing the ad I feel more autonomous with regard to my health.	2.656	2.550	2.279	2.833	2.967
O9	After seeing the ad I feel more capable with regard to my health.	2.726	2.600	2.361	2.867	3.083
O10	I feel like I have a greater say in my health after seeing the ad.	2.598	2.217	2.262	2.767	3.150
O11	The advertising message gives me stronger control over my health.	2.619	2.353	2.311	2.867	2.950
O12	The advertising message enables me to improve my health.	2.756	2.700	2.547	2.745	3.033
O13	The advertising message empowers me to make better health-related decisions.	2.736	2.600	2.372	2.850	3.128

P	To which degree do you agree with the following statements?					
		Total	**AUT**	**GER**	**USA**	**BRA**
P1	The advertised product (SENZA) makes a good impression.	4.295	4.167	4.180	4.018	4.817
P2	SENZA is of high-quality.	3.697	3.500	3.918	3.450	3.917
P3	SENZA is attractive.	3.924	3.633	3.787	3.978	4.300
P4	SENZA is appealing.	3.932	3.533	4.066	3.828	4.300

Q	To which degree do you agree with the following statements?					
		Total	**AUT**	**GER**	**USA**	**BRA**
Q1	I could imagine trying SENZA.	3.524	3.067	3.645	3.533	3.850
Q2	I could imagine buying SENZA.	3.283	2.917	3.264	3.202	3.750
Q3	I could imagine SENZA being one of my most likely choices for my next purchases.	2.954	2.817	3.230	2.433	3.333
Q4	I am interested in more information on SENZA and will look it up online (on facebook, twitter, google+).	2.945	2.429	2.705	3.350	3.300

R	To which degree do you agree with the following statements?					
		Total	**AUT**	**GER**	**USA**	**BRA**
R4	I have the impression ProSante (producer of SENZA) is a socially responsible company.	3.496	3.376	3.164	3.350	4.100

Factorized Ad Scores (informative)

Factor	Total	Austria	Germany	USA	Brazil
Emotional Involvement with Ad or Ad Evaluation	4.2575	4.0583	4.2746	3.9635	4.7333
Cognitive Involvement with Ad – Credibility	3.7265	3.7245	3.7150	3.2667	4.2000
Message Involvement	3.3638	3.2056	3.0546	3.2333	4.8192
Message Empowerment	3.4141	3.1567	3.1049	3.3600	4.0400
Health Empowerment	2.6816	2.5032	2.3553	2.8214	3.0519
Product Evaluation	3.9621	3.7083	3.9877	3.8186	4.3333
Purchase Intention	3.2540	2.9333	3.3798	3.0563	3.6444

Ad scores (emotional)

Part 3: OTC Print Ad Analysis (emotional – countries)						
		Total	**AUT**	**GER**	**USA**	**BRA**
K	**In general, I find the ad …**	3.884	3.831	3.970	3.229	4.506
L	**To which degree do you agree with the following statements?**					
	The advertisement is…	**Total**	**AUT**	**GER**	**USA**	**BRA**
L1	interesting	3.633	3.633	3.639	3.000	4.258
L2	emotional	3.600	4.283	3.623	3.419	3.097
L3	pleasant	4.352	4.567	4.213	4.504	4.129
L4	good	3.763	3.933	3.639	3.403	4.080
L5	favorable	3.763	3.800	3.475	3.435	4.338
L6	positive	4.349	4.523	4.213	4.258	4.403
L7	informative	3.106	2.967	2.754	2.065	4.629
L8	convincing	3.065	3.133	2.967	2.177	3.984
L9	credible	3.000	3.150	3.148	2.226	3.484
L10	truthful	3.183	3.124	3.246	2.491	3.871
L11	believable	3.310	3.417	3.459	2.435	3.935
L12	comprehensible	3.850	4.283	4.049	3.097	3.986
L13	well structured	3.870	4.283	4.016	3.052	4.145
L14	clear	3.699	3.883	3.822	3.019	4.081
M	**To which degree do you agree with the following statements?**					
		Total	**AUT**	**GER**	**USA**	**BRA**
M1	The ad makes valid claims.	3.339	3.300	2.819	2.484	4.742
M2	The ad presents accurate information.	3.309	3.333	3.045	2.452	4.403
M3	The message was easy to follow.	4.460	4.917	4.984	3.703	4.258
M4	I think the ad addresses relevant product features.	3.420	3.717	3.623	2.468	3.887
M5	I understand the features well enough to evaluate the product.	3.200	3.400	3.213	2.113	4.081
M6	The ad improves my level of information regarding pharmaceuticals.	2.976	2.717	2.967	1.871	4.339
O	**To which degree do you agree with the following statements?**					
		Total	**AUT**	**GER**	**USA**	**BRA**
O1	The ad allows me to objectively evaluate SENZA.	2.984	2.833	2.934	2.387	3.774
O2	I learned something from this advertisement that I did not know before about pain medications.	2.555	2.267	2.246	1.823	3.871

O3	I can now accurately compare SENZA with other competing brands on matters that are important to me.	2.527	2.417	2.148	2.145	3.387
O4	I would have more confidence in using SENZA now than before I saw this commercial.	2.543	2.401	2.361	2.081	3.323
O5	The advertisement was useful and provided me with new insights regarding pain and pain medication.	2.580	2.383	2.148	2.032	3.742
O6	I feel more confident in my self-medication skills/practices after having studied this ad.	2.437	2.500	2.164	2.032	3.048
O7	I am more interested in self-medication now than before seeing the ad.	2.370	2.300	2.197	1.871	3.106
O8	After seeing the ad I feel more autonomous with regard to my health.	2.457	2.433	2.115	2.129	3.145
O9	After seeing the ad I feel more capable with regard to my health.	2.478	2.367	2.230	2.097	3.210
O10	I feel like I have a greater say in my health after seeing the ad.	2.382	2.276	2.049	2.161	3.032
O11	The advertising message gives me stronger control over my health.	2.420	2.200	2.213	2.129	3.129
O12	The advertising message enables me to improve my health.	2.444	2.383	2.295	2.097	2.995
O13	The advertising message empowers me to make better health-related decisions.	2.429	2.333	2.115	2.129	3.129
P	**To which degree do you agree with the following statements?**					
		Total	**AUT**	**GER**	**USA**	**BRA**
P1	The advertised product (SENZA) makes a good impression.	3.694	3.815	3.590	3.113	4.226
P2	SENZA is of high-quality.	3.172	3.175	3.435	2.581	3.500
P3	SENZA is attractive.	3.497	3.495	3.459	2.952	4.081
P4	SENZA is appealing.	3.438	3.412	3.651	2.806	3.887
Q	**To which degree do you agree with the following statements?**					
		Total	**AUT**	**GER**	**USA**	**BRA**
Q1	I could imagine trying SENZA.	3.127	3.200	3.311	2.629	3.371
Q2	I could imagine buying SENZA.	2.833	2.867	3.002	2.258	3.210
Q3	I could imagine SENZA being one of my most likely choices for my next purchases.	2.730	3.017	3.000	1.823	3.095
Q4	I am interested in more information on SENZA and will look it up online (on facebook, twitter, google+).	2.652	2.433	2.508	2.097	3.560
R	**To which degree do you agree with the following statements?**					
		Total	**AUT**	**GER**	**USA**	**BRA**
R4	I have the impression ProSante (producer of SENZA) is a socially responsible company.	3.260	3.133	3.033	2.745	4.211

Factorized Ad Scores (emotional)

Factor	Total	Austria	Germany	USA	Brazil
Emotional Involvement with Ad or Ad Evaluation	4.0241	4.1308	3.8852	3.7994	4.2820
Cognitive Involvement with Ad – Credibility	3.1397	3.2061	3.2049	2.3325	3.8185
Message Involvement	3.1986	3.2778	3.2678	2.1505	4.1021
Message Empowerment	2.6845	2.5504	2.4809	2.2043	3.4946
Health Empowerment	2.4349	2.3322	2.1694	2.1237	3.1067
Product Evaluation	3.4502	3.4833	3.5337	2.8629	3.9234
Purchase Intention	2.8966	3.0278	3.1045	2.2366	3.2252

Ad scores (mixed)

Part 3: OTC Print Ad Analysis (mixed – countries)						
		Total	**AUT**	**GER**	**USA**	**BRA**
K	**In general, I find the ad ...**	4.534	4.371	4.303	4.167	5.308
L	**To which degree do you agree with the following statements?**					
	The advertisement is…	**Total**	**AUT**	**GER**	**USA**	**BRA**
L1	interesting	4.410	3.817	4.100	4.267	5.475
L2	emotional	4.004	3.841	4.417	3.567	4.194
L3	pleasant	4.642	4.237	4.650	4.471	5.220
L4	good	4.305	3.849	4.233	4.017	5.136
L5	favorable	4.184	3.614	4.067	4.100	4.966
L6	positive	4.621	4.433	4.400	4.700	4.956
L7	informative	4.296	4.331	3.850	4.033	4.980
L8	convincing	3.713	3.240	3.667	3.283	4.678
L9	credible	3.773	3.381	3.674	3.083	4.973
L10	truthful	3.698	3.208	3.358	3.300	4.949
L11	believable	3.997	3.705	3.717	3.667	4.915
L12	comprehensible	4.482	4.569	4.102	4.333	4.932
L13	well structured	4.553	4.620	4.383	4.350	4.864
L14	clear	4.415	4.588	3.967	4.117	5.000
M	**To which degree do you agree with the following statements?**					
		Total	**AUT**	**GER**	**USA**	**BRA**
M1	The ad makes valid claims.	4.540	3.983	4.117	4.050	6.034
M2	The ad presents accurate information.	4.192	3.717	3.800	4.083	5.186
M3	The message was easy to follow.	4.707	4.433	4.217	4.817	5.373
M4	I think the ad addresses relevant product features.	4.498	4.150	4.300	4.467	5.085
M5	I understand the features well enough to evaluate the product.	4.121	3.783	3.850	3.550	5.322
M6	The ad improves my level of information regarding pharmaceuticals.	3.763	3.283	3.200	3.539	5.051

O	To which degree do you agree with the following statements?					
		Total	**AUT**	**GER**	**USA**	**BRA**
O1	The ad allows me to objectively evaluate SENZA.	3.753	3.217	3.333	3.417	5.068
O2	I learned something from this advertisement that I did not know before about pain medications.	3.854	3.167	3.383	4.050	4.831
O3	I can now accurately compare SENZA with other competing brands on matters that are important to me.	3.364	2.867	3.150	3.133	4.322
O4	I would have more confidence in using SENZA now than before I saw this commercial.	3.582	2.667	3.500	3.117	5.068
O5	The advertisement was useful and provided me with new insights regarding pain and pain medication.	3.780	2.853	3.320	4.000	4.966
O6	I feel more confident in my self-medication skills/practices after having studied this ad.	3.007	2.730	2.850	3.167	3.288
O7	I am more interested in self-medication now than before seeing the ad.	2.724	2.417	2.583	2.750	3.153
O8	After seeing the ad I feel more autonomous with regard to my health.	2.835	2.550	2.417	2.667	3.722
O9	After seeing the ad I feel more capable with regard to my health.	2.828	2.515	2.500	2.767	3.542
O10	I feel like I have a greater say in my health after seeing the ad.	2.848	2.683	2.376	2.700	3.644
O11	The advertising message gives me stronger control over my health.	2.827	2.810	2.503	2.583	3.424
O12	The advertising message enables me to improve my health.	3.011	2.833	2.912	2.717	3.593
O13	The advertising message empowers me to make better health-related decisions.	3.011	2.800	2.644	3.117	3.492

P	To which degree do you agree with the following statements?					
		Total	**AUT**	**GER**	**USA**	**BRA**
P1	The advertised product (SENZA) makes a good impression.	4.381	3.817	4.083	4.167	5.475
P2	SENZA is of high-quality.	3.849	3.333	3.967	3.350	4.763
P3	SENZA is attractive.	3.965	3.562	3.883	3.600	4.831
P4	SENZA is appealing.	3.946	3.467	3.917	3.700	4.712

Q	To which degree do you agree with the following statements?					
		Total	**AUT**	**GER**	**USA**	**BRA**
Q1	I could imagine trying SENZA.	3.791	2.867	3.567	3.617	5.136
Q2	I could imagine buying SENZA.	3.506	2.683	3.167	3.467	4.729
Q3	I could imagine SENZA being one of my most likely choices for my next purchases.	3.163	2.533	3.367	2.733	4.034
Q4	I am interested in more information on SENZA and will look it up online (on facebook, twitter, google+).	2.812	2.517	2.783	3.233	2.712

R	To which degree do you agree with the following statements?					
		Total	**AUT**	**GER**	**USA**	**BRA**
R4	I have the impression ProSante (producer of SENZA) is a socially responsible company.	3.633	3.376	3.660	3.233	4.271

Factorized Ad Scores (mixed)

Factor	Total	Austria	Germany	USA	Brazil
Emotional Involvement with Ad or Ad Evaluation	4.4642	4.0254	4.3042	4.3843	5.1542
Cognitive Involvement with Ad – Credibility	3.7953	3.3832	3.6037	3.3333	4.8789
Message Involvement	4.1274	3.7389	3.7833	3.8520	5.1525
Message Empowerment	3.5662	2.9167	3.3278	3.2222	4.8192
Health Empowerment	2.8934	2.6985	2.5586	2.7583	3.5696
Product Evaluation	4.0353	3.5446	3.9625	3.7042	4.9449
Purchase Intention	3.4868	2.6944	3.3667	3.2722	4.6328

Ad scores (CSR)

Part 3: OTC Print Ad Analysis (CSR – countries)						
		Total	**AUT**	**GER**	**USA**	**BRA**
K	**In general, I find the ad ...**	3.954	4.207	3.583	4.056	3.983
L	**To which degree do you agree with the following statements?**					
	The advertisement is...	**Total**	**AUT**	**GER**	**USA**	**BRA**
L1	interesting	3.690	3.783	3.226	3.567	4.200
L2	emotional	3.388	4.583	3.452	3.350	2.167
L3	pleasant	3.847	4.550	3.403	3.800	3.650
L4	good	3.616	3.950	3.065	3.533	3.933
L5	favorable	3.685	3.964	3.113	3.699	3.983
L6	positive	4.080	4.557	3.532	4.267	3.983
L7	informative	3.645	4.017	3.097	3.633	3.850
L8	convincing	3.121	3.433	2.774	3.050	3.240
L9	credible	3.273	3.733	3.000	3.267	3.100
L10	truthful	3.277	3.467	3.047	3.417	3.183
L11	believable	3.348	3.611	3.081	3.500	3.211
L12	comprehensible	3.910	4.283	3.210	3.838	4.333
L13	well structured	3.989	4.683	3.468	3.604	4.217
L14	clear	3.922	4.200	3.486	3.750	4.267
M	**To which degree do you agree with the following statements?**					
		Total	**AUT**	**GER**	**USA**	**BRA**
M1	The ad makes valid claims.	3.731	4.133	3.596	3.250	3.950
M2	The ad presents accurate information.	3.588	4.096	3.589	3.317	3.350
M3	The message was easy to follow.	4.343	4.917	4.161	3.700	4.600
M4	I think the ad addresses relevant product features.	3.822	4.517	3.565	3.517	3.700
M5	I understand the features well enough to evaluate the product.	3.661	4.217	3.597	3.083	3.750
M6	The ad improves my level of information regarding pharmaceuticals.	3.201	3.612	2.903	2.850	3.450
O	**To which degree do you agree with the following statements?**					
		Total	**AUT**	**GER**	**USA**	**BRA**
O1	The ad allows me to objectively evaluate SENZA.	3.289	3.733	3.113	3.100	3.217
O2	I learned something from this advertisement that I did not know before about pain medications.	3.208	3.317	2.871	3.038	3.617

O3	I can now accurately compare SENZA with other competing brands on matters that are important to me.	2.959	3.317	2.645	2.917	2.967
O4	I would have more confidence in using SENZA now than before I saw this commercial.	2.992	3.235	2.403	2.801	3.550
O5	The advertisement was useful and provided me with new insights regarding pain and pain medication.	3.107	3.150	2.661	2.850	3.783
O6	I feel more confident in my self-medication skills/practices after having studied this ad.	2.830	2.717	2.710	3.213	2.683
O7	I am more interested in self-medication now than before seeing the ad.	2.665	2.800	2.129	3.150	2.600
O8	After seeing the ad I feel more autonomous with regard to my health.	2.545	2.600	2.419	2.833	2.333
O9	After seeing the ad I feel more capable with regard to my health.	2.498	2.550	2.333	2.767	2.350
O10	I feel like I have a greater say in my health after seeing the ad.	2.486	2.500	2.445	2.650	2.350
O11	The advertising message gives me stronger control over my health.	2.453	2.393	2.323	2.900	2.200
O12	The advertising message enables me to improve my health.	2.572	2.628	2.500	2.795	2.367
O13	The advertising message empowers me to make better health-related decisions.	2.501	2.600	2.409	2.883	2.117
P	**To which degree do you agree with the following statements?**					
		Total	**AUT**	**GER**	**USA**	**BRA**
P1	The advertised product (SENZA) makes a good impression.	3.917	4.200	3.129	3.850	4.517
P2	SENZA is of high-quality.	3.380	3.517	3.154	3.275	3.583
P3	SENZA is attractive.	3.449	3.500	3.048	3.478	3.783
P4	SENZA is appealing.	3.485	3.678	3.016	3.528	3.733
Q	**To which degree do you agree with the following statements?**					
		Total	**AUT**	**GER**	**USA**	**BRA**
Q1	I could imagine trying SENZA.	3.041	3.033	2.629	2.717	3.800
Q2	I could imagine buying SENZA.	2.893	2.850	2.290	2.767	3.683
Q3	I could imagine SENZA being one of my most likely choices for my next purchases.	2.736	3.000	2.274	2.450	3.233
Q4	I am interested in more information on SENZA and will look it up online (on facebook, twitter, google+).	2.507	2.617	2.113	2.933	2.379
R	**To which degree do you agree with the following statements?**					
		Total	**AUT**	**GER**	**USA**	**BRA**
R4	I have the impression ProSante (producer of SENZA) is a socially responsible company.	3.951	4.060	3.413	3.450	4.900
R5	I think that ProSante donating vaccines to reduce infant death caused by Tetanus represents a good match between the product and the cause.	4.180	4.280	3.160	4.020	5.250

Factorized Ad Scores (CSR)

Factor	Total	Austria	Germany	USA	Brazil
Emotional Involvement with Ad or Ad Evaluation	3.8256	4.2136	3.3185	3.8330	3.9541
Cognitive Involvement with Ad – Credibility	3.2548	3.5610	2.9756	3.3083	3.1834
Message Involvement	3.5616	4.1151	3.3548	3.1500	3.6333
Message Empowerment	3.0801	3.4282	2.7204	2.9393	3.2444
Health Empowerment	2.5093	2.5452	2.4047	2.8047	2.2861
Product Evaluation	3.5580	3.7237	3.0868	3.5330	3.9042
Purchase Intention	2.8898	2.9611	2.3978	2.6444	3.5722

Appendix D: T-Tests/Contrast Tests

General Questions

	[A1] My health depends on how well I take care of myself	**[A2] I actively try to prevent disease and illness.**	**[D1] I consider myself capable of taking care of my body.**	**[D2] I consider myself capable of finding the right information to make qualified health decisions.**	**[A8] I am very involved with my health.**
Austria	5.85	5.15	6.15	5.71	5.62
Germany	5.72	5.13	5.97	5.49	5.61
p	.172	.887	.031	.039	.932
Austria	5.85	5.15	6.15	5.71	5.62
United States	6.13	5.79	6.01	5.84	5.20
p	.007	**.000**	.510	.231	**.001**
Austria	5.85	5.15	6.15	5.71	5.62
Brazil	6.13	5.36	5.39	4.82	4.80
p	.007	.121	**.000**	**.000**	**.000**
Germany	5.72	5.13	5.97	5.49	5.61
United States	6.13	5.79	6.01	5.84	5.20
p	**.000**	**.000**	.165	**.001**	**.001**
Germany	5.72	5.13	5.97	5.49	5.61
Brazil	6.13	5.36	5.39	4.82	4.80
p	**.000**	.082	**.000**	**.000**	**.000**
United States	6.13	5.79	6.01	5.84	5.20
Brazil	6.13	5.36	5.39	4.82	4.80
p	.965	**.001**	**.000**	**.000**	**.003**

Health Consciousness | Self-Medication Ability | Attitude towards Self-Medication

Health Consciousness	Loading
I reflect about my health a lot.	.761
I am very self-conscious about my health.	.771
I am constantly examining my health.	.793
In general, I know my health status very well.	.803
I am very involved with my health.	.792
KMO	.798
Significance	.000
Cronbach α	.841

Self-Medication Ability	Loading
I consider myself capable of taking care of my body.	.757
I consider myself capable of finding the right information to make qualified health decisions.	.845
Usually, I can make sense of the health information I am presented with.	.828
I can use my knowledge to improve my health.	.784
KMO	.781
Significance	.000
Cronbach α	.817

Attitude towards Self-Medication	Loading
I am interested in self-medication.	.913
I consider myself capable of self-medication.	.910
I already practice self-medication.	.886
KMO	.742
Significance	.000
Cronbach α	.885

	Health Consciousness	Self-Medication Ability	Attitude towards Self-Medication	[D8] I already practice self-medication
Austria	5.14	5.74	4.14	3.84
Germany	4.86	5.54	4.30	4.02
p	.006	.006	.300	.303
Austria	5.14	5.74	4.14	3.84
United States	5.03	5.80	4.32	3.88
p	.308	.316	.252	.798
Austria	5.14	5.74	4.14	3.84
Brazil	4.93	5.50	3.65	3.90
p	.055	**.005**	**.002**	.721
Germany	4.86	5.54	4.30	4.02
United States	5.03	5.80	4.32	3.88
p	.099	**.000**	.925	.444
Germany	4.86	5.54	4.30	4.02
Brazil	4.93	5.50	3.65	3.90
p	.559	.631	**.000**	.519
United States	5.03	5.80	4.32	3.88
Brazil	4.93	5.50	3.65	3.90
p	.344	**.000**	**.000**	.916

Evaluation of Different Medication Types

	[H1] Mainstream/ Conventional medicine	[H2] Homeopathy	[H3] Herbal Sub-stances	[I1] Non-prescription drugs	[I2] Prescription drugs
Austria	5.54	4.73	5.01	4.08	3.85
Germany	5.59	4.44	4.77	4.10	3.58
p	.672	.075	.049	.895	.081
Austria	5.54	4.73	5.01	4.08	3.85
United States	5.24	4.53	4.49	4.21	4.20
p	.007	.182	**.000**	.405	.047
Austria	5.54	4.73	5.01	4.08	3.85
Brazil	5.91	5.09	5.38	4.61	4.35
p	**.001**	.022	.035	**.000**	**.002**
Germany	5.59	4.44	4.77	4.10	3.58
United States	5.24	4.53	4.49	4.21	4.20
p	**.002**	.536	.048	.464	**.000**
Germany	5.59	4.44	4.77	4.10	3.58
Brazil	5.91	5.09	5.38	4.61	4.35
p	**.003**	**.000**	**.000**	**.000**	**.000**
United States	5.24	4.53	4.49	4.21	4.20
Brazil	5.91	5.09	5.38	4.61	4.35
p	**.000**	**.000**	**.000**	.010	.385

Attitude towards OTC Drugs and Pain Medications

Attitude towards OTC drugs	Loading
I am interested in non-prescription (OTC) drugs.	.893
Non-prescription (OTC) drugs are important to me.	.928
I attach (great) importance to non-prescription (OTC) drugs.	.877
KMO	.721
Significance	.000
Cronbach α	.882

	[N1] I have a positive attitude towards pain medications.	[N2] I am confident that pain medications can improve my current health status.	Attitude towards OTC drugs	[N3] Pain Medication Usage Rates
Austria	3.93	3.48	3.87	2.94
Germany	3.97	3.43	3.91	3.02
p	.787	.808	.744	.575
Austria	3.93	3.48	3.87	2.94
United States	4.65	3.78	4.09	3.40
p	**.000**	.066	.121	**.002**
Austria	3.93	3.48	3.87	2.94
Brazil	4.99	4.53	4.20	4.19
p	**.000**	**.000**	.023	**.000**
Germany	3.97	3.43	3.91	3.02
United States	4.65	3.78	4.09	3.40
p	**.000**	.039	.199	.008
Germany	3.97	3.43	3.91	3.02
Brazil	4.99	4.53	4.20	4.19
p	**.000**	**.000**	.042	**.000**
United States	4.65	3.78	4.09	3.40
Brazil	4.99	4.53	4.20	4.19
p	.021	**.000**	.450	**.000**

Sources of Health Information I

	[C1] Family	[C2] Friends and Colleagues	[C3] Doctors and Pharmacists	[C11] Specialist Literature	[C4] Advertising in Newspa-pers and Magazines	[C5] Advertising on TV and the Radio
Austria	5.84	4.96	6.23	4.64	2.86	2.71
Germany	5.77	4.96	6.22	4.34	2.68	2.52
p	.543	.981	.906	.081	.215	.193
Austria	5.84	4.96	6.23	4.64	2.86	2.71
United States	5.52	4.62	6.51	4.98	3.23	3.15
p	.017	.017	**.002**	.049	.022	**.005**
Austria	5.84	4.96	6.23	4.64	2.86	2.71
Brazil	5.37	4.59	6.50	4.75	3.48	3.47
p	**.001**	.015	**.005**	.582	**.000**	**.000**
Germany	5.77	4.96	6.22	4.34	2.68	2.52
United States	5.52	4.62	6.51	4.98	3.23	3.15
p	.060	.018	**.001**	**.000**	**.000**	**.000**
Germany	5.77	4.96	6.22	4.34	2.68	2.52
Brazil	5.37	4.59	6.50	4.75	3.48	3.47
p	**.004**	.015	**.004**	.029	**.000**	**.000**
United States	5.52	4.62	6.51	4.98	3.23	3.15
Brazil	5.37	4.59	6.50	4.75	3.48	3.47
p	.343	.832	.912	.203	.137	.050

Sources of Health Information II

	[C6] Advertising on Social Media Sites	[C7] Advertising on the Internet	[C8] Editorial Content in print media	[C9] Editorial Content in Broadcasting	[C5] Editorial Content on the Internet
Austria	2.32	2.39	3.35	3.00	3.03
Germany	2.05	2.08	3.25	2.88	3.18
p	.181	.027	.538	.452	.341
Austria	2.32	2.39	3.35	3.00	3.03
United States	2.82	3.02	3.70	3.58	3.75
p	**.000**	**.000**	.033	**.000**	**.000**
Austria	2.32	2.39	3.35	3.00	3.03
Brazil	2.86	2.92	3.24	3.26	3.39
p	**.000**	**.001**	.531	.120	.036
Germany	2.05	2.08	3.25	2.88	3.18
United States	2.82	3.02	3.70	3.58	3.75
p	**.000**	**.000**	**.004**	**.000**	**.000**
Germany	2.05	2.08	3.25	2.88	3.18
Brazil	2.86	2.92	3.24	3.26	3.39
p	**.000**	**.000**	.962	.020	.217
United States	2.82	3.02	3.70	3.58	3.75
Brazil	2.86	2.92	3.24	3.26	3.39
p	.800	.601	.006	.058	.035

Attitude/Skepticism towards (Pharmaceutical) Advertising

Attitude towards Advertising	Loading
Advertisers know how to provide the information that is needed to make a qualified decision.	.736
Overall, I consider advertising a good thing.	.894
Overall, I do like advertising.	.820
KMO	.616
Significance	.000
Cronbach α	.750

Attitude towards Pharmaceutical Advertising	Loading
Advertisers for pharmaceuticals know how to provide the information that is needed to make a qualified decision.	.811
Overall, I consider advertising for pharmaceuticals a good thing.	.910
Overall, I do like advertising for pharmaceuticals.	.851
KMO	.670
Significance	.000
Cronbach α	.750

Skepticism towards Advertising	Loading
I can depend on getting the truth in most advertising. (R)	.876
Advertising's aim is to inform the consumer. (R)	.875
I feel I have been accurately informed after viewing most advertisements. (R)	.924
KMO	.782
Significance	.000
Cronbach α	.867

Skepticism towards Pharmaceutical Advertising	Loading
I can depend on getting the truth in most advertising for pharmaceuticals. (R)	.785
Advertising for pharmaceuticals' aim is to inform the consumer. (R)	.767
I feel I have been accurately informed after viewing most advertisements for pharmaceuticals. (R)	.848
KMO	.816
Significance	.000
Cronbach α	.872

	Attitude towards Advertising	Attitude towards Pharmaceutical Advertising	Skepticism towards Advertising	Skepticism towards Pharmaceutical Advertising
Austria	3.8715	3.5527	5.1336	4.8037
Germany	3.6487	3.2702	5.3514	5.0944
p	.074	.019	.098	.029
Austria	3.8715	3.5527	5.1336	4.8037
United States	3.6120	3.3636	5.1736	4.9542
p	.041	.144	.763	.265
Austria	3.8715	3.5527	5.1336	4.8037
Brazil	4.0000	3.6262	4.4583	4.6624
p	.325	.590	**.000**	.323
Germany	3.6487	3.2702	5.3514	5.0944
United States	3.6120	3.3636	5.1736	4.9542
p	.770	.451	.161	.275
Germany	3.6487	3.2702	5.3514	5.0944
Brazil	4.0000	3.6262	4.4583	4.6624
p	**.007**	**.007**	**.000**	**.002**
United States	3.6120	3.3636	5.1736	4.9542
Brazil	4.0000	3.6262	4.4583	4.6624
p	**.003**	.058	**.008**	**.036**

Ad Evaluation

Ad Evaluation (single item)					
	Total	**Austria**	**Germany**	**United States**	**Brazil**
informative	4.34	4.21	4.31	4.04	4.82
mixed	4.53	4.37	4.30	4.17	5.31
p	.148	.504	.973	.613	.076
informative	4.34	4.21	4.31	4.04	4.82
CSR	3.95	4.21	3.58	4.06	3.98
p	**.005**	.985	**.008**	.940	**.007**
informative	4.34	4.21	4.31	4.04	4.82
emotional	3.88	3.83	3.97	3.23	4.51
p	**.001**	.151	.169	**.002**	.314
mixed	4.53	4.37	4.30	4.17	5.31
emotional	3.88	3.83	3.97	3.23	4.51
p	**.000**	.034	.165	**.001**	**.003**
CSR	3.95	4.21	3.58	4.06	3.98
emotional	3.88	3.83	3.97	3.23	4.51
p	.617	.170	.141	**.003**	.073

Ad Evaluation (multi-item Model Variable)	Loading
favorable	.887
interesting	.835
positive	.833
pleasant	.822
KMO	.813
Significance	.000
Cronbach α	.889

Ad Evaluation (multi-item Model Variable)					
	Total	**Austria**	**Germany**	**United States**	**Brazil**
informative	4.26	4.06	4.27	3.96	4.73
mixed	4.46	4.03	4.30	4.38	5.15
p	.111	.895	.913	.081	.091
informative	4.26	4.06	4.27	3.96	4.73
CSR	3.83	4.21	3.32	3.83	3.95
p	**.002**	.550	**.000**	.644	**.004**
informative	4.26	4.06	4.27	3.96	4.73
emotional	4.02	4.13	3.89	3.80	4.28
p	.071	.770	.107	.496	.125
mixed	4.46	4.03	4.30	4.38	5.15
emotional	4.02	4.13	3.89	3.80	4.28
p	**.001**	.663	.112	.011	**.002**
CSR	3.83	4.21	3.32	3.83	3.95
emotional	4.02	4.13	3.89	3.80	4.28
p	.143	.742	.026	.901	.270

Credibility (Model Variable)

Credibility (Model Variable)	Loading
believable	.891
convincing	.900
truthful	.908
credible	.915
KMO	.831
Significance	.000
Cronbach α	.924

Credibility (Model Variable)					
	Total	**Austria**	**Germany**	**United States**	**Brazil**
informative	3.73	3.72	3.72	3.27	4.20
mixed	3.80	3.38	3.60	3.33	4.88
p	.622	.211	.670	.783	.018
informative	3.73	3.72	3.72	3.27	4.20
CSR	3.25	3.56	2.98	3.31	3.18
p	**.001**	.553	**.004**	.886	**.000**
informative	3.73	3.72	3.72	3.27	4.20
emotional	3.14	3.21	3.20	2.33	3.82
p	**.000**	.074	.033	**.000**	.210
mixed	3.80	3.38	3.60	3.33	4.88
emotional	3.14	3.21	3.20	2.33	3.82
p	**.000**	.508	.112	**.000**	**.001**
CSR	3.25	3.56	2.98	3.31	3.18
emotional	3.14	3.21	3.20	2.33	3.82
p	.410	.191	.344	**.001**	.029

Comprehensibility (Model Variable)

Comprehensibility (Model Variable)					
	Total	**Austria**	**Germany**	**United States**	**Brazil**
informative	4.33	4.72	3.85	3.98	4.77
mixed	4.48	4.57	4.10	4.33	4.93
p	.337	.651	.452	.247	.591
informative	4.33	4.72	3.85	3.98	4.77
CSR	3.91	4.28	3.21	3.84	4.33
p	.013	.179	.043	.668	.204
informative	4.33	4.72	3.85	3.98	4.77
emotional	3.85	4.28	4.05	3.10	3.99
p	**.005**	.207	.546	.007	.027
mixed	4.48	4.57	4.10	4.33	4.93
emotional	3.85	4.28	4.05	3.10	3.99
p	**.000**	.389	.871	**.000**	**.004**
CSR	3.91	4.28	3.21	3.84	4.33
emotional	3.85	4.28	4.05	3.10	3.99
p	.721	1.000	.008	.030	.321

Product Evaluation (Model Variable)

Product Evaluation (Model Variable)	Loading
The advertised product (Senza) makes a good impression.	.901
Senza is of high quality.	.905
Senza is attractive.	.949
Senza is appealing.	.943
KMO	.835
Significance	.000
Cronbach α	.943

Product Evaluation (Model Variable)					
	Total	Austria	Germany	United States	Brazil
informative	3.96	3.71	3.99	3.82	4.33
mixed	4.04	3.54	3.96	3.70	4.94
p	.614	.558	.925	.699	.034
informative	3.96	3.71	3.99	3.82	4.33
CSR	3.56	3.72	3.09	3.53	3.90
p	**.005**	.955	**.001**	.353	.146
informative	3.96	3.71	3.99	3.82	4.33
emotional	3.45	3.48	3.53	2.86	3.92
p	**.000**	.410	.061	**.001**	.211
mixed	4.04	3.54	3.96	3.70	4.94
emotional	3.45	3.48	3.53	2.86	3.92
p	**.000**	.825	.099	**.004**	**.001**
CSR	3.56	3.72	3.09	3.53	3.90
emotional	3.45	3.48	3.53	2.86	3.92
p	.455	.373	.069	.027	.952

Purchase Intention (Model Variable)

Purchase Intention (Model Variable)	**Loading**
I could imagine trying Senza.	.960
I could imagine buying Senza.	.970
I could imagine Senza being one of my most likely choices for my next purchases.	.936
KMO	.749
Significance	.000
Cronbach α	.952

Purchase Intention (Model Variable)					
	Total	**Austria**	**Germany**	**United States**	**Brazil**
informative	3.25	2.93	3.38	3.06	3.64
mixed	3.49	2.69	3.37	3.27	4.63
p	.157	.446	.968	.492	**.002**
informative	3.25	2.93	3.38	3.06	3.64
CSR	2.89	2.96	2.40	2.64	3.57
p	.026	.933	**.001**	.159	.843
informative	3.25	2.93	3.38	3.06	3.64
emotional	2.90	3.03	3.10	2.24	3.23
p	.028	.774	.369	**.004**	.249
mixed	3.49	2.69	3.37	3.27	4.63
emotional	2.90	3.03	3.10	2.24	3.23
p	**.000**	.308	.414	**.001**	**.000**
CSR	2.89	2.96	2.40	2.64	3.57
emotional	2.90	3.03	3.10	2.24	3.23
p	.967	.845	.018	.131	.368

Need for Additional Information

Need for additional information					
	Total	**Austria**	**Germany**	**United States**	**Brazil**
informative	2.95	2.43	2.71	3.35	3.30
mixed	2.81	2.52	2.78	3.23	2.71
p	.439	.778	.813	.749	.100
informative	2.95	2.43	2.71	3.35	3.30
CSR	2.51	2.62	2.11	2.93	2.38
p	.011	.565	.065	.236	.011
informative	2.95	2.43	2.71	3.35	3.30
emotional	2.65	2.43	2.51	2.10	3.56
p	.090	.989	.528	**.000**	.524
mixed	2.81	2.52	2.78	3.23	2.71
emotional	2.65	2.43	2.51	2.10	3.56
p	.352	.794	.384	**.001**	.030
CSR	2.51	2.62	2.11	2.93	2.38
emotional	2.65	2.43	2.51	2.10	3.56
p	.396	.581	.194	**.007**	**.003**

Message-Empowerment (Model Variable)

Message-Empowerment (Model Variable)	Loading
The ad allows me to objectively evaluate Senza.	.877
I can now accurately compare Senza with other comparable brands on matters that are important to me.	.927
I would have more confidence in using Senza now than before I saw this commercial.	.903
KMO	.729
Significance	.000
Cronbach α	.886

Message-Empowerment (Model Variable)					
	Total	**Austria**	**Germany**	**United States**	**Brazil**
informative	3.36	3.21	3.05	3.23	3.97
mixed	3.57	2.92	3.32	3.22	4.82
p	.170	.286	.315	.970	**.002**
informative	3.36	3.21	3.05	3.23	3.97
CSR	3.08	3.43	2.72	2.94	3.24
p	.052	.427	.178	.355	.018
informative	3.36	3.21	3.05	3.23	3.97
emotional	2.68	2.55	2.48	2.20	3.49
p	**.000**	.026	.015	**.000**	.147
mixed	3.57	2.92	3.32	3.22	4.82
emotional	2.68	2.55	2.48	2.20	3.49
p	**.000**	.182	**.002**	**.000**	**.000**
CSR	3.08	3.43	2.72	2.94	3.24
emotional	2.68	2.55	2.48	2.20	3.49
p	.007	**.002**	.325	.012	.439

Self-Medication Empowerment

Self-Medication Empowerment (Confidence)					
	Total	Austria	Germany	United States	Brazil
informative	2.85	2.75	2.61	3.00	3.05
mixed	3.00	2.73	2.85	3.17	3.29
p	.312	.948	.386	.601	.470
informative	2.85	2.75	2.61	3.00	3.05
CSR	2.83	2.72	2.71	3.21	2.68
p	.908	.918	.725	.540	.291
informative	2.85	2.75	2.61	3.00	3.05
emotional	2.44	2.50	2.16	2.03	3.05
p	.008	.427	.083	**.001**	.996
mixed	3.00	2.73	2.85	3.17	3.29
emotional	2.44	2.50	2.16	2.03	3.05
p	**.000**	.444	.011	**.000**	.494
CSR	2.83	2.72	2.71	3.21	2.68
emotional	2.44	2.50	2.16	2.03	3.05
p	.014	.492	.053	**.000**	.319

Self-Medication Empowerment (Interest)					
	Total	Austria	Germany	United States	Brazil
informative	2.58	2.43	2.28	2.63	2.97
mixed	2.72	2.42	2.58	2.75	3.15
p	.329	.055	.284	.687	.565
informative	2.58	2.43	2.28	2.63	2.97
CSR	2.67	2.80	2.13	3.15	2.60
p	.580	.255	.578	.114	.293
informative	2.58	2.43	2.28	2.63	2.97
emotional	2.37	2.30	2.20	1.87	3.11
p	.178	.664	.746	.006	.701
mixed	2.72	2.42	2.58	2.75	3.15
emotional	2.37	2.30	2.20	1.87	3.11
p	.019	.694	.170	**.001**	.890
CSR	2.67	2.80	2.13	3.15	2.60
emotional	2.37	2.30	2.20	1.87	3.11
p	.064	.117	.799	**.000**	.158

Health Empowerment

Health Empowerment	Loading
After seeing the ad I feel more autonomous with regard to my health.	.913
After seeing the ad I feel more capable with regard to my health.	.938
I feel like I have a greater say in my health after seeing the ad.	.938
The advertising message gives me stronger control over my health.	.944
The advertising message enables me to improve my health.	.903
The advertising message empowers me to make better health-related decisions.	.912
KMO	.913
Significance	.000
Cronbach α	.966

Health Empowerment					
	Total	**Austria**	**Germany**	**United States**	**Brazil**
informative	2.68	2.50	2.36	2.82	3.05
mixed	2.89	2.70	2.56	2.76	3.57
p	.128	.485	.440	.812	.071
informative	2.68	2.50	2.36	2.82	3.05
CSR	2.51	2.55	2.40	2.80	2.29
p	.213	.880	.848	.955	.006
informative	2.68	2.50	2.36	2.82	3.05
emotional	2.43	2.33	2.17	2.12	3.11
p	.085	.562	.432	.011	.863
mixed	2.89	2.70	2.56	2.76	3.57
emotional	2.43	2.33	2.17	2.12	3.11
p	**.001**	.229	.120	.010	.144
CSR	2.51	2.55	2.40	2.80	2.29
emotional	2.43	2.33	2.17	2.12	3.11
p	.602	.481	.334	.014	.008

Appendix E: Discriminant Validity and Path Estimates

Individualistic – Discriminant Validity

	Comprehen-sibility	Ad Evaluation	Credibility	Self Empowerment	Product Evaluation	Purchase Intention
Comprehensibility	---	506.500	530.361	547.354	552.091	589.357
Ad Evaluation		---	516.157	533.158	537.761	575.017
Credibility			---	509.252	513.580	551.099
Self-Empowerment				---	496.814	534.144
Product Evaluation					---	529.470
Purchase Intention						---
Original Chi^2 Value: 492.167 Requirement: Chi^2 Difference Value ≥ 3.841						

	Comprehen-sibility	Ad Evaluation	Credibility	Self Empow-er-ment	Product Evaluation	Purchase Intention
AVE	**1.000**	**.649**	**.746**	**.706**	**.797**	**.784**
Comprehensibility	---	.444	.498	.340	.411	.414
Ad Evaluation		---	.717	.637	.587	.475
Credibility			---	**.721**	.740	.771
Self-Empowerment				---	.754	.686
Product Evaluation					---	.763
Purchase Intention						---
Requirement: AVE ≥ Squared Correlations						

Collectivistic/Brazil – Discriminant Validity

	Comprehen-sibility	Ad Evaluation	Credibility	Self Empowerment	Product Evaluation	Purchase Intention
Comprehen-sibility	---	373.313	344.071	349.216	353.731	360.973
Ad Evaluation		---	339.485	345.235	351.739	358.980
Credibility			---	340.456	347.693	356.205
Self-Empowerment				---	339.853	349.070
Product Evaluation					---	345.618
Purchase Intention						---
Original Chi² Value: 335.360 Requirement: Chi² Difference Value ≥ 3.841						

	Comprehen-sibility	Ad Evaluation	Credibility	Self Empowerment	Product Evaluation	Purchase Intention
AVE	**1.000**	**.727**	**.744**	**.733**	**.819**	**.805**
Comprehen-sibility	---	.636	.684	.539	.497	.443
Ad Evaluation		---	.739	.648	.650	.573
Credibility			---	**.749**	.686	.612
Self-Empowerment				---	.805	.730
Product Evaluation					---	.762
Purchase Intention						---
Requirement: AVE ≥ Squared Correlations						

Austria – Discriminant Validity

	Comprehen-sibility	Ad Evaluation	Credibility	Self Empowerment	Product Evaluation	Purchase Intention
Comprehen-sibility	---	284.190	294.887	298.858	302.305	315.749
Ad Evaluation		---	281.490	285.374	291.073	302.477
Credibility			---	273.714	279.674	292.081
Self-Empowerment				---	275.831	288.179
Product Evaluation					---	284.218
Purchase Intention						---
Original Chi² Value: 271.438 Requirement: Chi² Difference Value ≥ 3.841						

	Comprehensibility	Ad Evaluation	Credibility	Self-Empowerment	Product Evaluation	Purchase Intention
AVE	**1.000**	**.593**	**.735**	**.786**	**.799**	**.877**
Comprehensibility	---	.491	.543	.378	.397	.324
Ad Evaluation		---	**.737**	.639	.771	.711
Credibility			---	.729	.725	.600
Self-Empowerment				---	.665	.616
Product Evaluation					---	.700
Purchase Intention						---
Requirement: AVE ≥ Squared Correlations						

Germany – Discriminant Validity

	Comprehensibility	Ad Evaluation	Credibility	Self-Empowerment	Product Evaluation	Purchase Intention
Comprehensibility	---	408.034	428.688	439.585	444.487	448.133
Ad Evaluation		---	422.769	434.695	440.559	444.206
Credibility			---	413.070	418.952	415.099
Self-Empowerment				---	414.744	410.005
Product Evaluation					---	406.124
Purchase Intention						---
Original Chi^2 Value: 402.288 **Requirement: Chi^2 Difference Value ≥ 3.841**						

	Comprehensibility	Ad Evaluation	Credibility	Self Empowerment	Product Evaluation	Purchase Intention
AVE	1.000	.699	.805	.693	.797	.874
Comprehensibility	---	.660	.642	.424	.571	.444
Ad Evaluation		---	.800	.614	.620	.660
Credibility			---	.695	.769	.655
Self-Empowerment				---	.750	.692
Product Evaluation					---	.782
Purchase Intention						---
Requirement: AVE ≥ Squared Correlations						

United States – Discriminant Validity

	Comprehen-sibility	Ad Evaluation	Credibility	Self Empowerment	Product Evaluation	Purchase Intention
Comprehen-sibility	---	279.634	291.480	301.799	310.287	362.193
Ad Evaluation		---	282.207	290.038	300.888	352.842
Credibility			---	280.788	289.177	341.140
Self-Empowerment				---	278.603	330.794
Product Evaluation					---	323.000
Purchase Intention						---
Original Chi^2 Value: 270.427						
Requirement: Chi^2 Difference Value ≥ 3.841						

	Comprehen-sibility	Ad Evaluation	Credibility	Self Empowerment	Product Evaluation	Purchase Intention
AVE	1.000	.634	.801	.748	.804	.706
Comprehen-sibility	---	.631	.612	.521	.527	.473
Ad Evaluation		---	.798	.649	.726	.645
Credibility			---	**.762**	.759	.687
Self-Empowerment				---	.599	.765
Product Evaluation					---	**.721**
Purchase Intention						---
Requirement: AVE ≥ Squared Correlations						

Individualistic – Path Estimates

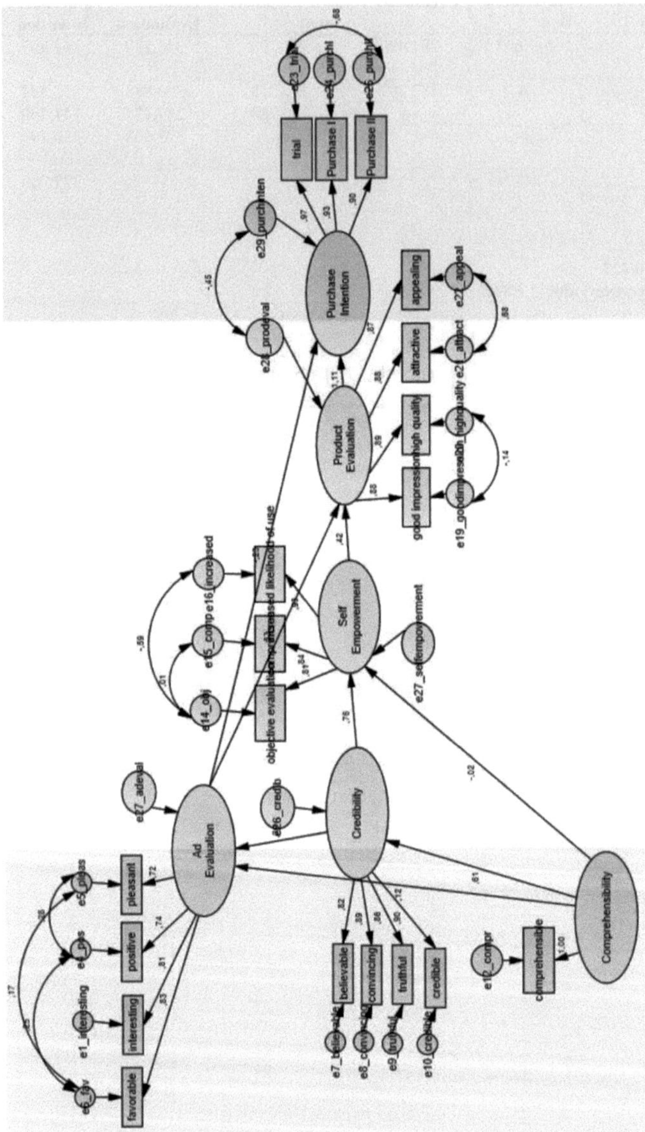

Austria – Path Estimates

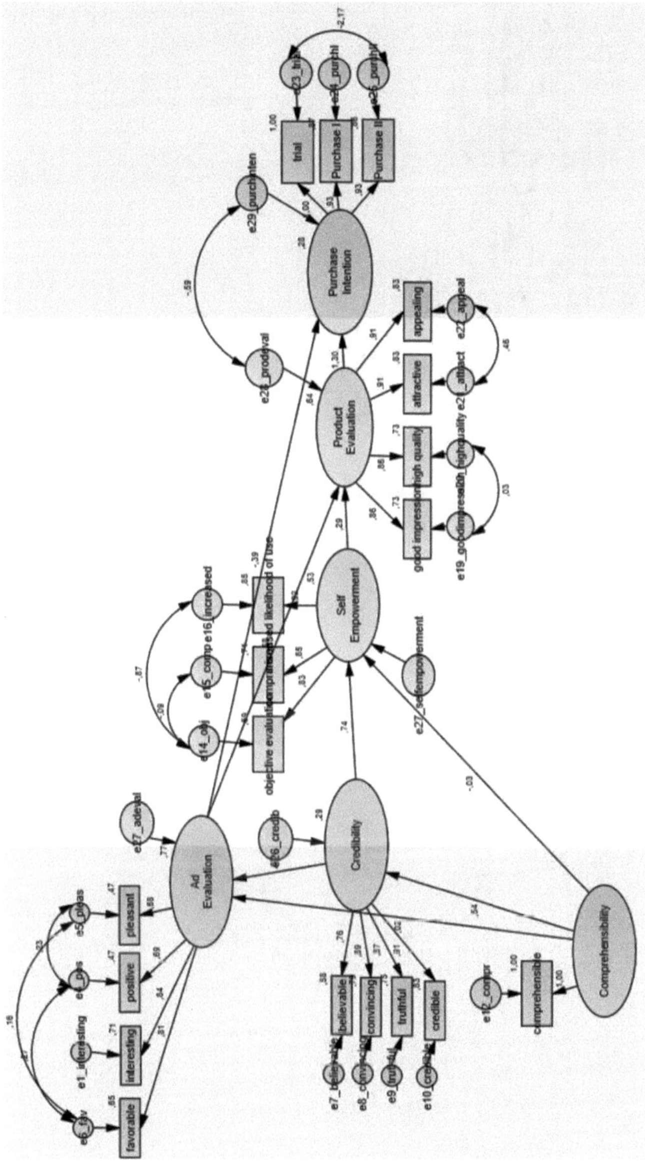

Germany – Path Estimates

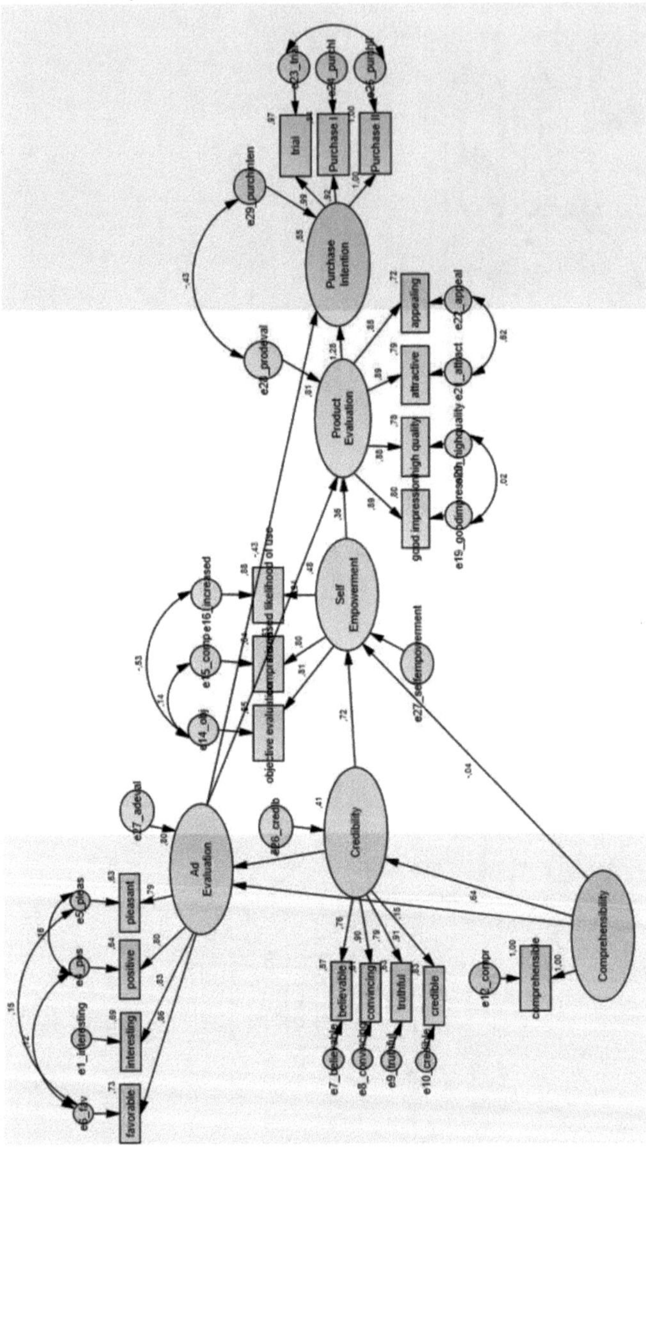

United States – Path Estimates

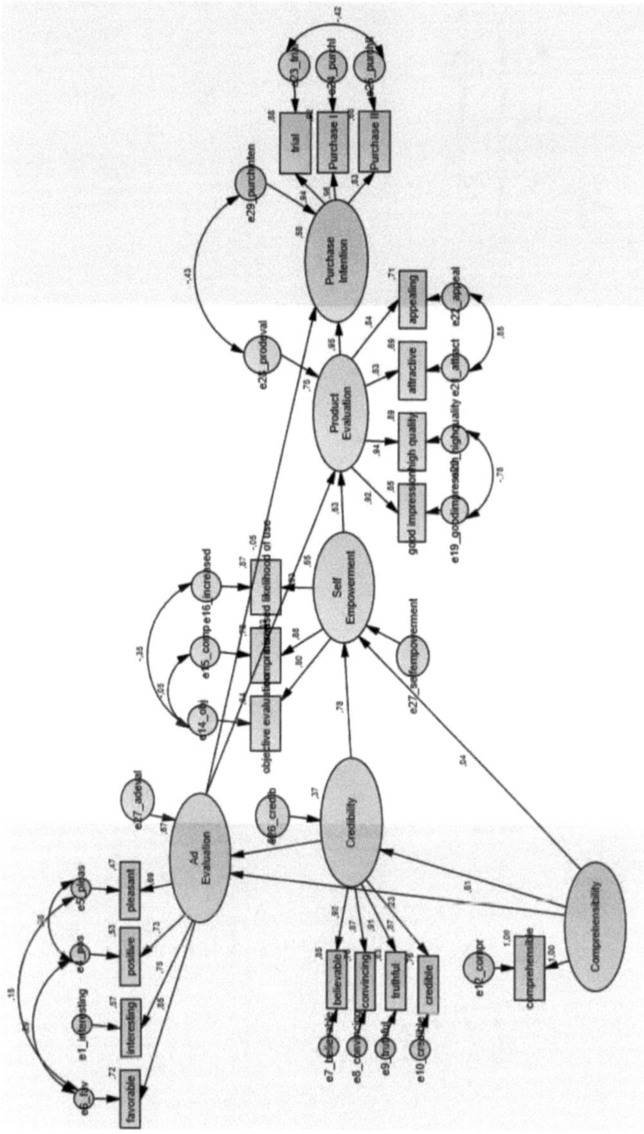

Collectivistic/Brazil – Path Estimates

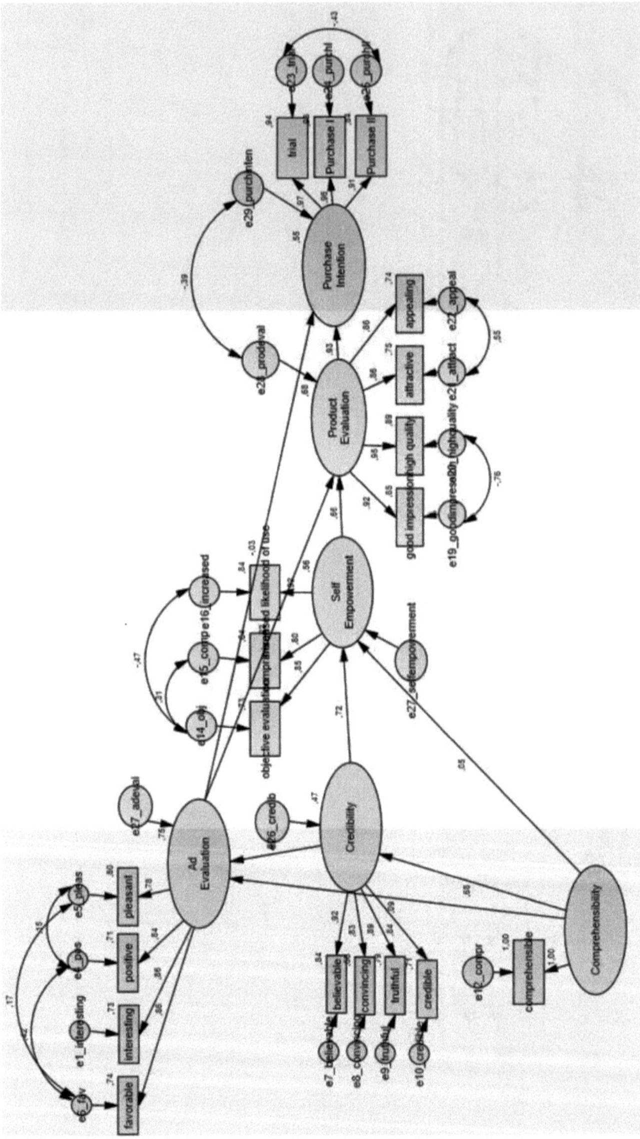

MIX
Papier aus verantwortungsvollen Quellen
Paper from responsible sources
FSC® C105338

If you have any concerns about our products,
you can contact us on
ProductSafety@springernature.com

In case Publisher is established outside the EU,
the EU authorized representative is:
Springer Nature Customer Service Center GmbH
Europaplatz 3, 69115 Heidelberg, Germany

Printed by Libri Plureos GmbH
in Hamburg, Germany